ROUTLEDGE LIBRARY EDITIONS:
COLONIALISM AND IMPERIALISM

Volume 41

PRELUDE TO IMPERIALISM

PRELUDE TO IMPERIALISM

British Reactions to Central African Society, 1840–1890

H. ALAN C. CAIRNS

LONDON AND NEW YORK

First published in 1965 by Routledge and Kegan Paul Ltd

This edition first published in 2023
by Routledge
4 Park Square, Milton Park, Abingdon, Oxon OX14 4RN

and by Routledge
605 Third Avenue, New York, NY 10158

Routledge is an imprint of the Taylor & Francis Group, an informa business

© 1965 H.A.C. Cairns

All rights reserved. No part of this book may be reprinted or reproduced or utilised in any form or by any electronic, mechanical, or other means, now known or hereafter invented, including photocopying and recording, or in any information storage or retrieval system, without permission in writing from the publishers.

Trademark notice: Product or corporate names may be trademarks or registered trademarks, and are used only for identification and explanation without intent to infringe.

British Library Cataloguing in Publication Data
A catalogue record for this book is available from the British Library

ISBN: 978-1-032-41054-8 (Set)
ISBN: 978-1-032-45591-4 (Volume 41) (hbk)
ISBN: 978-1-032-45592-1 (Volume 41) (pbk)
ISBN: 978-1-003-37770-2 (Volume 41) (ebk)

DOI: 10.4324/9781003377702

Publisher's Note
The publisher has gone to great lengths to ensure the quality of this reprint but points out that some imperfections in the original copies may be apparent.

Disclaimer
The publisher has made every effort to trace copyright holders and would welcome correspondence from those they have been unable to trace.

PRELUDE TO IMPERIALISM

British Reactions

to Central African Society

1840–1890

by

H. Alan C. Cairns

ROUTLEDGE & KEGAN PAUL
LONDON

*First published 1965
by Routledge and Kegan Paul Ltd
Broadway House, 68–74 Carter Lane
London, E.C.4*

*Printed in Great Britain
by Butler and Tanner Ltd*

© *H. A. C. Cairns 1965*

*No part of this book may be reproduced
in any form without permission from
the publisher, except for the quotation
of brief passages in criticism*

To Pat
for her help and love

CONTENTS

		page
	ABBREVIATIONS	ix
	PREFACE	xi
I.	THE CENTRAL AFRICAN FRONTIER	1
II.	WHITE MEETS BLACK	35
III.	CONTEMPORARY ANCESTORS	73
IV.	THE NOBLE SAVAGE	102
V.	THE IMPOSSIBILITY OF CULTURAL RELATIVISM	120
VI.	BRITISH, CHRISTIAN, AND WHITE	147
VII.	REVOLUTIONARIES BEFORE THE REVOLUTION	168
VIII.	HOW CAN SAVAGES BE CIVILIZED?	189
IX.	THE BEGINNING OF A NEW ERA	231
	NOTES	251
	BIBLIOGRAPHY	303
	INDEX	325

ABBREVIATIONS

The Church Missionary Intelligencer	*C.M.I.*
Church Missionary Society	C.M.S.
The Journal of the (Royal) Anthropological Institute	*J.R.A.I.*
The Journal of the Royal Geographical Society	*J.R.G.S.*
London Missionary Society	L.M.S.
London Missionary Society (Matabeleland mission)	L.M.S.M.
London Missionary Society (Lake Tanganyika mission)	L.M.S.T.
The Missionary Magazine and Chronicle: Chiefly Relating to the Missions of the London Missionary Society	*L.M.S. Chronicle*
Proceedings of the Royal Colonial Institute	*Proc. R.C.I.*
Proceedings of the Royal Geographical Society	*Proc. R.G.S.*
The Scottish Geographical Magazine	*S.G.M.*
Universities Mission to Central Africa	U.M.C.A.
Zanzibar Secretariat Archives	Z.A.
Zanzibar Museum	Z.M.

PREFACE

1

IN the half century preceding imperial control of Central Africa some hundreds of Europeans—missionaries, explorers, hunters, traders, concession seekers, and other less classifiable wanderers of the earth's surface—experienced contact with tribalism. This study is concerned with the British element in these early pioneers, special attention being paid to their intellectual and emotional reactions to the situations they encountered. The singling out of the British for study is based on the fact that throughout most of this period they were the largest new intruding element in Central Africa, and, secondly, on the fact that the entire area, with the temporary exception of German East Africa and the consolidation of Portuguese rule inland and on the coast, subsequently fell under British control. For the purposes of this study Central Africa is defined as the area stretching from the East coast inland to Matabeleland in the south and Buganda in the north. It is not, however, a geographically precise area. Accordingly a certain latitude has been taken in the selection of material. In addition, material which seems particularly relevant has been selected, on occasion, from the early imperial era.

In a social history of this nature, race[1] relations constitute the unifying thread with respect to which various themes are investigated. The natural unity of this period springs from the special context in which race relations took place. In the imperial era the cultural and racial hierarchy natural to whites in contact with tribal peoples was sanctioned and enforced by the technological and military superiority possessed by white-administered colonial governments. In the pre-imperial period, by contrast, the British lived and travelled in societies they did not control. These microcosmic multi-racial societies were African dominated. Pioneer conditions and the paucity of whites evoked a greater degree of intimacy with, and dependence on, Africans than was the case with a later generation of colonists. On the one hand, the absence of European power allowed a certain indulgence in conduct regarded as status degrading; the early pioneer

PREFACE

with an African wife or mistress did not have to concern himself with the prospects of ostracism by a race-conscious white community. On the other hand, the limitations imposed by African power more than counterbalanced this partial expansion of permissible actions. It is this political factor—negatively, the absence of imperialism, positively, the ubiquitous fact of non-white power—which gives race relations in this period a special and distinguishing interest.

This study examines in some detail the reactions of these early pioneers to a diversity of contact situations within the general context of a racial distribution of power untypical of British or western experience. While the physical hardships of pioneer life in Africa receive some attention, more space is devoted to the psychological problems facing the British. The hardships associated with heat, disease, and hunger were insignificant compared to the difficult adjustment to an almost total absence of success in some mission fields, the emotional problems of living in isolation punctuated by recurrent illness and death in the midst of alien societies, and the challenge which Africa offered to the preservation of cultural standards acquired in London or rural Wales.

While some attention is perforce directed to developments in Britain, it is essentially the British in Africa, men varying from the genius of Livingstone to the obscure and humble trader, who form the basic human material for this study. The large missionary element among these pioneers, and the intrinsic importance of missionaries as transmitters of western civilization, have led to the placing of heavy emphasis on these agents of Christian expansion.

By and large these pioneers saw little of virtue in African cultures. Their observations, usually biased, frequently contradictory, and often simply wrong, are replete with danger to the uncritical research worker. In almost all the nineteenth-century books on Africa the figure of the white man is writ large on the African landscape. In the middle of the dark continent he assumes novel and grandiose proportions. In moral, spiritual, and technological matters he appears as a giant among pygmies, dwarfing the Africans among whom his activities are carried out. Missionary publications, torn between the demands of truth, the propaganda necessities of the cause, and sentiments of fidelity to the martyrs who have passed on to their reward, distort culture contact into a one-way flow of benevolence. In travel books the only constant amidst ever changing scenes is the dauntless explorer, surmounting hardship and overcoming human and climatic obstacles by the force of his iron will. Evidences of a glorious past do not bid the traveller to tarry and reflect on his own insignificance while admiring the achievements of an alien culture. On the contrary, the picture of African life presented to the reader is Hobbesian in its

PREFACE

harshness and primeval in the dominance of nature over man. In these European accounts individual Africans emerge but rarely from the mass as distinct personalities. As objects of salvation, obstacles to rapid travel, or as faithful followers, they are relegated to a secondary position.

An uncritical assessment of such one-sided ethnocentric source material can easily lead to the acceptance of views of African cultures more prejudicial than factual, a danger especially pronounced when contact takes place between a literate and a pre-literate culture. If analysis is not to slide easily and comfortably into the mould of patriotism and racial pride, the value judgements which accompanied and sanctioned western expansion must be handled with discretion. There is a contrary tendency of equal danger. The noble Nordic pioneer introducing the benefits of civilization to the degraded backward savage has been replaced by the derogatory concept of the 'settler' who, by his mere presence, acts as a barrier to the self-determination of oppressed peoples. The untutored barbarian is out of favour and a mystique of the African folk soul, the African personality, and a long exploited race emerging into dignity and manhood has become fashionable. The pull of contemporary liberal opinion, opposed to policies of imperialism and racial hegemony, may incline the researcher to select his material in favour of the non-white races. A statement by Dean Inge is apposite. 'If you marry the Spirit of your generation you will be a widow in the next.'[2]

The very subject of race relations is imbued with humanitarian fervour. It is assumed that there are good race relations and bad race relations, that the latter should be exposed, and the path to a more just society made clear by social engineering. This too presents a subtle danger to the researcher.[3] The general point is that race relations have historically been characterized by a high degree of conflict and brutality, factors inimical to academic impartiality. Finally, the researcher, with his own passions and political viewpoints, is quickly faced with the realization that the 'correct' analysis of what happened over seventy years ago in Central Africa is not irrelevant to the claims and counterclaims for the retention or abolition of racial hierarchies in some parts of Central Africa today. The interpretation of history, if not a guide for understanding the present, often provides a justification for changing it. In the midst of such a complex of emotional and ideological cross-currents, humility should prevent premature claims of success by those who seek impartiality.[4]

A minimum requirement which this study attempts to meet is to give some indication of the bias and preconceptions of these early pioneers which so markedly influenced their attitudes to the indigenous African peoples. This is the more important because it is to their

PREFACE

writings that historians still turn for an understanding of pre-imperial Africa.

Since World War II the dissolution of empire and the political emergence of hitherto subject races have reflected the weakening of ideas capable of sustaining racial hierarchies. Ideas of the biological inferiority of any racial group have been academically undermined by the inability of eliciting scientific proof of important racial differences, or even of satisfactorily delineating racial boundaries. The Scottish verdict 'Not proven' has been given, and the equation of culture with race has become untenable. The eradication of such beliefs has gone even further. The sense of mission which characterized late nineteenth-century British expansion has been eroded by two world wars and the inability of the West to master the technology which was the ultimate proof of her superiority. Cultural relativism, no longer confined to anthropologists, has evoked an unwillingness to judge different cultures by a universal standard. The mid-twentieth-century European is less convinced of his racial and cultural superiority than were his supremely self-confident predecessors.

No such inner doubts troubled the humanitarian element among these early pioneers. To attempt to improve the social, religious, and economic condition of the African was a self-evident obligation requiring no elaborate justification. Few Britons favoured leaving the African in his tribal condition. There was, however, much diversity and confusion of ideas as to whether or not he was capable of being raised to a higher rung on the ladder of human existence, and if so, by what methods. Considerable attention is devoted to this problem.

The period ends with the arrival of European administrations. The policies of European governments which painted the map of Africa in a variety of colours, and the complex of factors which brought about this changed attitude in Europe to the annexation of large areas of a defenceless continent, are peripheral to the approach adopted here. Imperialism is discussed almost entirely from the viewpoints of those Britons already in Africa, and with respect to its role in creating the conditions without which the future of the African would have been bleak.

2

It is necessary to mention one unavoidable weakness of this study. Professor Gluckman has suggested that 'unless the historian knows something of tribal politics and organization he cannot even evaluate the records left by travellers, missionaries and others. . . .' He adds that the historian dealing with such 'one-sided records' must analyse the relations between each white writer and particular African groups.[5] While the wisdom of this assertion is readily admitted, the

PREFACE

number of African tribes in the area covered by this study is far too large for a single student to assimilate and digest the requisite amount of knowledge which such an ideal handling of the topic would involve. The non-anthropological student, surveying such a vast field, inevitably leaves himself open to the possibility of serious mistakes in his interpretation of African conduct. At the same time, there does remain some utility in the study of one side of the contact situation. British attitudes and responses had a logic of their own. They derived from a fairly consistent climate of opinion which conditioned and moulded their perceptions and reactions. The study of these aspects does have, therefore, a legitimate place in the broader study of culture contact of which they form a part. If an analogy may be permitted, it can be suggested that while marriage is perhaps best studied as a partnership, a separate study of husbands and wives does shed light on the marriage relationship.

3

This study has employed a variety of materials. Important background information has been found in the two classics of the late Professor R. Coupland[6] which still provide the most comprehensive account of the history of Zanzibar, the East African coast, and the penetration of the interior. His works can now be supplemented by scholarly works on the beginnings of European activity in Nyasaland[7] and Northern Rhodesia,[8] and by an excellent analysis of the missionary factor in East Africa.[9] Recent biographies of Lord Lugard[10] and Sir Harry Johnston[11] examine two of the key figures in the imperialist camp and illustrate the light that can be thrown on culture contact by comprehensive biographies of the more significant participants. In addition to these and other modern sources, the profusion of nineteenth-century books and articles by, and about, some of the more significant of these early pioneers has been extensively used. The journals and proceedings of various geographical societies, missionary societies, anthropological societies, and the Royal Colonial Institute have proven exceptionally useful.

The limitations of time and money have rendered archival work less extensive than perfection might dictate. I have used the L.M.S. archives for the Tanganyika and Matabele missions of that society; the Public Record Office for consular despatches from 1883 from Nyasaland, and for the Frere Mission to Zanzibar; the Zanzibar archives, a massive unwieldy collection, for official British interest in the mainland, and for numerous valuable letters from Britons in the interior; the special collection of important documents placed in the Zanzibar museum, and the exceptionally valuable collection of

PREFACE

diaries, correspondence, and unpublished articles and reminiscences in the National Archives of Southern Rhodesia. I have also examined collections of documents and papers in the U.M.C.A. archives in London and Zanzibar, and Free Church of Scotland material at Livingstonia.

Had time allowed I would have done research in archives of the C.M.S., the Church of Scotland and the Free Church of Scotland. On the other hand, in a study such as this, which is not concerned with the clarification of particular historical facts, or the tracing of a series of chronological events, 'one quickly reaches the point where the testimony of great numbers of additional informants provides no further validation'.[12] The claims to originality of this study are not based on the presentation of new material dealing with a particular historical situation, but with its contribution to providing general insights into the process of culture contact. It is an attempt to indicate the importance of a range of cultural and psychological phenomena which has hitherto been largely ignored by students of this period of Central African history. Indirectly it is hoped that this work will act as a restraint on scholars who assess African societies on the basis of uncritical acceptance of the writings of those who were by no means objective in their approach.

4

This study was originally prepared as a thesis for the degree of Doctor of Philosophy at the University of Oxford. It is published in substantially unchanged form with the exception of some minor stylistic alterations, and a significant reduction in the number of footnotes.

The pleasant duty remains of thanking those individuals who have helped to clarify my thoughts. My first thanks go to my supervisor, Professor Kenneth Kirkwood, who has cajoled, encouraged, and scolded at appropriate times to bring this work to completion. Dr. Per Hassing and the Rev. A. Sandilands provided valuable comments on an earlier draft. My main intellectual debt is to Mr. Lewis Gann who also read an earlier version of this study, and who gave me many stimulating ideas while I was doing research in Salisbury.

The librarians, whose patience I was unable to exhaust, are too numerous to mention. Their assistance is deeply appreciated. My thanks are also due to the Imperial Order Daughters of the Empire and the Canada Council for giving me financial assistance while studying at Oxford. My mother, who typed the final copy, and my wife Pat, who helped throughout the study, deserve the warmest thanks of all.

H. A. C. C.

I

THE CENTRAL AFRICAN FRONTIER

1

IN the middle of the nineteenth century the civilized world knew little and cared less about Central Africa. The geography of the interior was unknown, the numbers and customs of its human inhabitants outside the boundaries of existing knowledge, and official interest by the governments of Europe almost non-existent. Unlike the west coast, an extension of Europe which had received a steady stream of white contact for centuries, the east coast was an extension of Asia. Asia was represented by the Arabs, well-armed adaptable frontiersmen who opened up the mainland, and also by the ubiquitous Indian trader who helped channel the beads, the cloth, the guns and powder of Europe throughout the interior in exchange for ivory and slaves. There was on this coast nothing comparable to Liberia or Sierra Leone as a monument to humanitarian interest. The only significant indication of the European presence was found in the stagnant, corrupt, and demoralized Portuguese colonies south of the Rovuma River and on the banks of the Zambesi.

In 1841 Captain Atkins Hamerton arrived in Zanzibar, the focal point for the aggressive Arab penetration of the mainland, to take up the joint appointment of British Consul under the Foreign Office and Political Agent of the Government of India. Hamerton and his successors pursued policies designed to safeguard the western route to India by retaining British control of the Indian Ocean, restrict the slave trade by the application of pressure on the Arab Sultanate, and protect and extend the commercial interests of resident British Indian traders. Hamerton was not the first foreign consul in Zanzibar and other European nations soon established diplomatic representation at this headquarters of Arab power, but the influence of Britain was predominant throughout most of the pre-imperial period.

After the death of Sultan Seyyid Said in 1856 the Sultanate existed more or less on sufferance with the British Consul at Zanzibar, backed by the British navy, assuming an ever greater influence and power. Britain, unwilling to assume direct imperial control in Central Africa, attempted with moderate success to extend the authority of Zanzibar on the mainland and simultaneously to make such extension consonant with British objectives. It was a policy limited by the incompatibility of British and Arab attitudes to the slave trade, and by the absence of a governmental basis to the Arab penetration of the interior. It did represent, however, an attempt at a working alliance between Christian and Moslem, Briton and Arab, West and East.

Hamerton had not been long at his new post when Johann Ludwig Krapf, a German Lutheran in the employ of the Church Missionary Society, arrived at Mombasa in 1844. His missionary labours in Abyssinia (1836–43) ended by the hostility of its rulers, he selected Mombasa as a point of departure for the country of the Galla, a tribe which he held in singularly high esteem. While official British policy was predicated on the employment of Arab influence, Krapf had no illusions as to the threat which the Arabs and Islam posed to his missionary prospects. Secular Britons might idly debate the suitability of Islam for the African—an inferior religion for an inferior race—and might grant the Arab the respect accorded to martial peoples, but Krapf and later missionaries correctly viewed the religion of the prophet as their major antagonist for the spiritual control of Central Africa. He soon found, however, a more elemental enemy in the health hazards of tropical life. A few months after settling at Mombasa his wife and infant daughter were dead. Yet Krapf, like many another missionary, had a 'wonderful capacity for seeing a right purpose in every trial'. He informed the London headquarters of his mission that the 'lonely missionary grave' of his wife was a 'sign' of a commencing

> struggle with this part of the world; and as the victories of the Church are gained by stepping over the graves of her members, you may be the more convinced that the hour is at hand when you are summoned to the conversion of Africa from its eastern shore.[1]

Krapf's fortuitous arrival initiated the modern missionary penetration of the mainland. Although he had visions of a great missionary expansion, he and his colleague Rebmann, who joined him in 1846, are remembered less for their conversions, which were minimal, than for their contributions to geography and linguistics. Rebmann sighted Kilimanjaro on May 11, 1848, while Krapf discovered Mount Kenya in the autumn of 1849. Ill health forced Krapf's retirement in 1853, but Rebmann was still at Rabai Mpia, the Mission station inland from Mombasa, when a C.M.S. party arrived in 1874 to found a settlement for freed slaves. Totally blind, living in a miserable hut, and surrounded by a little community of about a dozen African Christians, Rebmann, who had not been home for twenty-nine years, retired with reluctance to Germany in 1875 where, a year later, he died.

In 1856 James Erhardt, another German member of the C.M.S., published a provisional map of the interior based on African information which indicated the fragmentary and contradictory nature of existing geographical knowledge. His map and those of two reputable British geographers, Cooley and Macqueen, were as 'utterly dissimilar and discordant in all their physical features as it was well possible to imagine'. There was, as Francis Galton informed a meeting of the Royal Geographical Society, a 'state of exceeding ignorance' concerning the geography of the mainland.[2]

This ignorance was rapidly overcome. Within a decade of Galton's speech a small band of intrepid Britons—Livingstone, Burton, Speke, Grant, and Baker—had delineated the lake system of the interior, the major sources of the Nile, and other basic geographical features. In bulky volumes they presented the British public with an idea of the tribal complexity of Central Africa and some of the main problems which would face the seekers of profits and the seekers of souls. The continued wanderings of Livingstone, the travels of Stanley, Cameron, Thomson, and a growing number of explorers from continental Europe, filled in many of the geographical details and stimulated and helped to satisfy that 'phenomenal interest in all things African' which Joseph Thomson rightly regarded as one of the most remarkable features of the nineteenth century.[3]

2

The picture which emerged from explorers' accounts deterred all but the brave and the foolhardy from directing their footsteps to Central Africa. In the first place there were the inescapable hazards to life and health posed by tropical conditions. Burton's appearance after his return from the discovery of Lake Tanganyika left an indelible impression on his future wife.

> I shall never forget Richard as he was then; he had had twenty-one attacks of fever, and had been partially paralyzed and partially blind; he was a mere skeleton, with brown yellow skin hanging in bags, his eyes protruding, and his lips drawn away from his teeth.[4]

THE CENTRAL AFRICAN FRONTIER

V. L. Cameron was on the verge of scurvy when he arrived at Benguella after his epic east–west crossing of the continent. H. M. Stanley, powerful, rugged, and tenacious, lost seventy-six pounds in his search for Livingstone. At journey's end his black hair was streaked with grey, and his round boyish face was gaunt and bony. Yet Burton, Cameron, and Stanley were fortunate. They survived. Two of Cameron's three white colleagues died. On his first two trips Stanley's five white companions all perished. This factor alone sufficed to ensure that the tales of travellers, sportsmen, and missionaries which flooded the British market in the last half of the nineteenth century would evoke widespread admiration and little emulation.

These early pioneers, whether they sought souls, elephant tusks, or the fame of a major geographical discovery, not only risked their lives in their heroic ventures, but they were also compelled to adapt to the uncomfortable fact that their activities took place within a framework of non-western political authority. A good-humoured description of the power of Moselekatse, the Matabele chief, is revealing.

> Moselekatse is a powerful chief, and must be treated with respect. About two days' journey from his 'kraal' or kingly enclosure, the etiquette is to send a messenger on to announce your coming, and to ask permission to draw nearer the august Black. Your name, height, and weight, and 'how many horses your father's got', etc., should be stated, or particulars quite as ridiculous. The answer may be '*no*' and may be '*yes*', if yes, you may approach entirely as a dependent before his lord, though he is jolly enough on a nearer acquaintance. You ask permission to hunt, and he gives it sometimes after several days' delay, and then you go in the direction he pleases, and his people see that you go in no other.[5]

Military superiority, although important to individual travellers— H. M. Stanley killed five Africans and sank two canoes with four explosive bullets from his elephant gun—was more than counterbalanced by the paucity of white contact. No one marched recklessly through the territories of the Matabele or the Baganda. Almost a quarter of a century elapsed between Speke's first visit to Lake Victoria and the successful expedition of Joseph Thomson in 1883 through the territory of the warlike Masai, the shortest way to the east side of the lake.[6] Indeed, as Thomson pointed out, even a minor chief could raise the surrounding countryside against an expedition.[7] African chiefs frequently used their power to block the progress of a caravan to exact by 'maddening extortions'[8] as much cloth, beads, guns, and powder as possible from the supplies of the passing traveller. African travel was an exhausting, nerve-racking business. Mrs. Annie Hore, the wife of a missionary, was distressed to find that her 'brief and ofttimes most vexatious acquaintance with the Africans [on a trip to Lake Tanganyika], failed sadly to encourage those feelings' she thought she possessed, and which her missionary calling required. 'Too often I could regard the natives only as savages opposing our passage, and seeking to hinder and rob, if not to molest us to a still more serious extent.'[9]

In addition to the general difficulties of travel in a politically fragmented area, there was a widespread breakdown of law and order as African societies reeled under the impact of the trade in slaves and ivory and a growing diffusion of guns and powder which rendered tribal wars more bloody and destructive. Conditions of almost endemic war, to which intruding elements of 'Turks' from the north, Arabs and Swahili from the east coast, and Portuguese from both coasts contributed, substantiated beliefs in the savagery of the African, seriously limited white contact, and caused grave difficulties to those Europeans who discarded prudence for adventure. Travellers were frequently involved in or delayed by intertribal wars. The great trade route between Bagomoyo and Lake Tanganyika was often disrupted by almost chronic if frequently desultory warfare between the Arab community at Taborah and the Wanyamwesi. On the Zambesi intermittent war between dissident tribesmen, half-caste warlords, and the Portuguese, made it difficult to keep open the only usable water communications system which Central Africa possessed. There were constant thefts from the little European community which grew up south of Lake Nyasa, and the African Lakes Corporation, established in 1878, was compelled to subsidize chiefs to prevent thieving of their goods when in transit to or from the coast.[10] To the south, an attempt was made to establish postal communications between Cape Town and the Zambesi when the London Missionary Society began work among the Matabele and the Makololo. The experiment foundered when five postmen were murdered due to civil war between rival claimants to a Bechuana chieftainship.[11]

The insecurity of conditions in the interior as a barrier to white contact was reinforced by the inadequacy of existing methods of transportation and communication. North of the Zambesi, access to the interior from the east coast followed the Arab caravan trails which spread a rough network of trade routes across the heart of Central Africa. These routes depended almost exclusively on Zanzibar and Wanyamwesi porters, men of remarkable endurance capable of carrying loads of sixty or seventy pounds day after day, and, in times of necessity, able to exist on very little food. While porters belonged to one of the few categories of Africans which received consistently high praise, they were capable of infuriating their European masters. Accustomed to the more leisurely pace of Arab caravans, they had to be bullied and cajoled. The problem of controlling these men, stated Guy Dawnay, a wealthy sportsman, was 'maddening', a 'recipe for dementia in the most aggravated form'. Continual worry was involved in dealing with '100 or more childish, quarrelsome, lying natives', hearing their complaints, adjusting their rows, and doctoring their ailments.[12] Not only was the porter prone to desert, especially in the early stages of a journey after he had received part of his pay, but he stole from the luggage in his care and from the villages through which the caravan passed—actions which endeared him neither to the villagers nor to his leader who might find his progress delayed by the resultant tribal hostility.

In addition to these recurrent and often infuriating difficulties with porters and African chiefs, there was the almost certain prospect of shortages of food and water at some stage on the journey. The provision of meat often entailed dangerous and tiring combats with wild animals. Finally, there were the constant bouts of fever which weakened the constitution and kept tempers on edge. African travel, as Burton truly remarked, was a small campaign, and the traveller an 'animal overworked'.[13]

The inadequacy of human porterage to open up Central Africa was apparent to all observers. Numerous attempts to find substitutes for this 'wretched and barbarous carrier mode of transit'[14] were tried and found wanting. The Indian elephant, other beasts of burden, and the South African ox-waggon all proved unsatisfactory. No more successful were the dogged efforts to find easy and rapid river communication with the interior. The Zambesi, with its shifting sandbanks at the mouth, its lack of depth, and the barrier of the Kebrabasa Rapids above Tete, was the best waterway which Central Africa had to offer. In conjunction with the Shire River it provided a water route to Lake Nyasa, although even here the Murchison Cataracts necessitated a forty-mile detour. It was far from ideal, but it helped to make the Lake Nyasa area a centre of British missionary and commercial interest in the pre-imperial period.

The most efficient form of transport in Central Africa, the sturdy ox-waggon, was confined to Matabeleland and Mashonaland. The disadvantages of ox-waggon travel—the difficulty of obtaining water for the oxen in the dry season, the frequent repairs necessitated by the rough jolting, and the desirability of not working the oxen under a hot sun—were more than counter-balanced by other factors. The plodding oxen, covering slightly over two miles an hour, gave the traveller considerable independence, and, when all went well, it seems to have been a pleasant carefree life. More important, it was a comparatively inexpensive form of travel.[15] It was possible to manage with a crew of three, and the larger waggons could transport from four to seven thousand pounds of goods—an amount which would have required upwards of one hundred porters—a marked improvement over conditions prevailing elsewhere in Central Africa.[16] Yet, although the ox-waggon contributed significantly to the opening up of the future colony of Southern Rhodesia by missionaries, hunters and traders, it was incapable of providing a stimulus to more than marginal European contact.

The absence of a reliable, cheap, and rapid form of transport, the perils of a tropical climate, and the insecurity of a Balkanized area in a state of incipient social disorganization made Central Africa an adventurers' frontier with no attraction to European commerce, investment, and colonization. It is doubtful if more than eight hundred Britons experienced contact with tribalism in the pre-imperial period.[17] In terms of age, sex, and occupation these pioneers were necessarily untypical of the diversity of British culture. Youth was almost a physical necessity to combat the arduous conditions of pioneer life. While harsh frontier conditions did not entirely exclude Victorian wives, it was not a family frontier. Children were usually sent outside to the civilized world for their schooling, and in order to escape contamination from proximity to the evils of paganism to which it was believed their youthful minds were especially susceptible. In terms of vocation these pioneers were composed of explorers, traders, hunters, prospectors, and missionaries. These, however, were over-lapping categories. A man such as Livingstone who advocated commerce, made basic geographical discoveries, and regarded himself as a missionary is ultimately unclassifiable in terms of vocational criteria. To a lesser extent this is true of all these early pioneers for frontier life imposed a diversity of roles as a price of survival. For our purposes a less precise but more useful division is between those who conceived their function in terms of ameliorating African life by introducing Christianity or other facets of western culture, and those who sought predominantly personal ends and were unconcerned about the impact of their activities on African society. With some significant exceptions this implies a rough division between missionaries and the remainder whose motives were based on secular considerations.

3

The expansion of the missionary movement into Central Africa was part of a broad change in the conception of Christian responsibility evidenced by the creation of large and powerful British missionary societies towards the end of the eighteenth century. Although many of the widespread changes which accompanied the demise of feudalism, such as the increasing emphasis on materialism and the growth of evolutionary theories, were antipathetic to the missionary movement, the emerging urban and industrial society of Britain, in spite of the deep-seated and complex problems which that society posed for Christianity, was fundamentally favourable to its growth. There was a phenomenal increase in man's knowledge of and interest in the physical universe. Increased contact with the non-western world stimulated European self-confidence by indicating the contrast between the progressive[18] west and the static societies of Africa and Asia, and thus rendered easy of acceptance the idea of a civilizing mission and eventually of imperial control.[19] It was an expansionist era in terms of trade, investment, and emigration to newly opened lands in order to relieve over-population at home. These factors created an outward-looking society and thereby aided movements desirous of diffusing the Gospel message throughout the globe. In the same way as capitalism sought justification in growth and an ever-increasing output, missionaries disseminated the thesis that Christian expansion was a proof of religious vitality, and that a non-missionary religion was a contradiction in terms. Advances in technology not only made communication less costly in time and money for those who sought to convert the populations of Fiji, Buganda or Bombay, but also created the wealth which mission societies could tap to finance their costly endeavours. Finally, the prevailing optimism of an expanding society stimulated movements requiring enthusiasm and self-confidence for their inception and continuation.

The growth of missionary interest in Central Africa reflected these factors in microcosm. Exploration of the interior made Britons aware of hitherto unknown concentrations of heathen and attracted funds and men to the newly discovered area. The life and writings of Livingstone were of special importance in directing British interest to Central Africa. His idealism, his dogged tenacity, his tendency to see Africa in essentially moral terms, and his own life—an epic success story from piecer in a cotton factory to world renown as a missionary explorer—help to account for his remarkable impact on the British public. Traders such as John Moir and H. B. Cotterill directed their steps to African shores in response to his pleas for legitimate commerce. Explorers as different in character as Joseph Thomson and Henry Morton Stanley spoke of themselves as Livingstone's followers. Finally, he had a direct influence on the decision of many individual missionaries to spend their life among the heathen of Central Africa. The dominating part played by this humble Christian in opening up the interior was entirely beneficial. He helped to create an image of the African as an improvable member of the human species, and he emphasized in his writings and in his conduct that European influences on tribal peoples should be ameliorating in their broad effects.

His chief influence naturally was among missionaries. When he arrived at Quilimane in 1856 the only British missionary society between the Limpopo River and Abyssinia was the small German staffed mission of the C.M.S. inland from Mombasa. A quarter of a century later there was a significant scattering of missionary centres throughout the length and breadth of Central Africa. The chronology of this growth in mission contact, readily available elsewhere, merits only brief attention here.

Livingstone's historic crossing of the continent transformed him from an obscure agent of the London Missionary Society to a national hero. Three missions were undertaken in direct response to his initial impact on the British conscience. His lectures at Cambridge led to the founding of the high Anglican Universities' Mission to Central Africa which placed itself under his guidance and established a mission south of Lake Nyasa in the early sixties. His own society, the L.M.S., which had laboured in Bechuanaland for three decades, sent missions to the Makololo and the Matabele in an attempt to take advantage of Livingstone's influence with the former, and the influence of his father-in-law, the venerable Robert Moffat, with Moselekatse, the chief of the latter. The mission to the Makololo ended disastrously. Six of the nine whites, including women and children, died, and the survivors retreated to the south in less than a year. The U.M.C.A. venture was only slightly less unfortunate and by 1864 the mission had withdrawn to Zanzibar to commence afresh and with more prudence the onslaught on heathenism. The fourth mission in this period was commenced by the Methodists who established themselves at Ribe in 1861 where, with their C.M.S. German neighbours, they struggled against heathen indifference, Arab hostility and climatic peril.

This first wave of mission penetration resulted in two failures and the creation of two Christian footholds, the Methodists in the Mombasa vicinity and the L.M.S. in Matabeleland. In conjunction with the C.M.S., which had maintained a tenuous existence since the arrival of Krapf in 1844, this comprised the extent of Protestant influence for the next decade.

The second wave of mission activity occurred in the seventies in the midst of a growing diversification of European interest in Central Africa. In 1873 a more decisive official British approach was forecast when, under duress, Sultan Seyyid Barghash of Zanzibar signed an anti-slave trade treaty which officially closed all slave markets in his dominions and completely prohibited the export of slaves from the east coast regardless of their destination. In Equatoria the attempts of Samuel Baker and General Gordon to extend Egyptian authority and eradicate the slave trade commenced the British identification with the Sudan which was to reach its climax in the death of Gordon at Khartoum in 1885. Reports of gold in Mashonaland and at Tati, following the investigations of the German Karl Mauch in 1867, stimulated mining interests in South Africa and in Britain and attracted prospectors and concession seekers to the Matabele kingdom and the areas subject to it. In 1876 the formation of the African International Association under the auspices of Leopold II of Belgium indicated a growing political interest which was to culminate in the Berlin Conference of 1885 and the imperial take-over of tropical Africa by the powers of Europe.

In the midst of this growing awareness of Sub-Saharan Africa missionary interest was specifically fostered by the drama of Livingstone's lonely death at Chitambo, the bringing of his embalmed body to the coast by his heroic porters, and his subsequent impressive burial in Westminster Abbey.[20] Missionary expeditions were organized and sent out to each of the three great lakes of the interior. The Church of Scotland and the Free Church of Scotland entered the Lake Nyasa region and initiated the proprietary interest of the Scottish people in that area, which has continued to this day. The Church Missionary Society also participated in the new outburst of missionary enthusiasm by establishing a settlement for freed slaves at Frere Town near Mombasa in 1874. Shortly after this, H. M Stanley's letter in the *Daily Telegraph* on November 15, 1875, eulogized the country and people of Buganda as a most hopeful field for missionary endeavour. Fortified by an anonymous offer of £5,000 the C.M.S. responded to the challenge. The first party of missionaries arrived at the court of Mtesa in July, 1877. The L.M.S., which received a similar grant from a wealthy ascetic Quaker, Mr. Robert Arthington of Leeds, turned away from its policy of expansion from the south and sent missionaries to Lake Tanganyika, the first members arriving in Ujiji in August, 1878. As a result of these ventures British Protestantism had established a scattered network of mission stations from Buganda to Matabeleland by 1880.[21]

4

It is important to understand the main factors which encouraged individual missionaries and the societies they represented to persevere in a struggle in which, the case of the Baganda apart, white martyrs out-numbered black converts. The purveyors of the Christian message were not received as long-awaited deliverers freeing man from the thraldom of sin. Initially their message made little impact. They were coveted for their goods and their technical abilities. The missionary attempt to enrol the African in the kingdom of believers was paralleled by the African attempt to enmesh the missionary in the web of tribal politics.

The death-rate was appallingly high. The understanding of tropical diseases was limited. The frequent absence of skilled medical men, medical supplies, and nourishing food slowed down recovery from debilitating sicknesses. There was also much carelessness among a youthful group; drinking water was seldom boiled; and the death-rate was no doubt higher than necessary. Out of eighty missionaries of the Free Church of Scotland, including wives, 'as many' as twenty-four died and twenty-seven were invalided between 1875 and 1900.[22] Of 197 members who joined the U.M.C.A. between 1860 and 1890, thirty-seven died and forty-five withdrew or were invalided home in five years or less.[23]

This toll in human life and suffering exacted by tropical conditions led even friends of the missionary movement to wonder whether discretion was not the better part of valour.[24] While such questions could not be completely disregarded, missionary actions were set in the context of a pattern of belief which, as the following illustrations reveal, constituted an important psychological buttress in the excessively trying days which accompanied the initial fumbling attempts to plant focal points for the diffusion of Christianity in Africa.

The L.M.S. mission to the Makololo (1859-60) included two missionaries, Price and Helmore, their wives, five children (one was born on the way), and the usual African attendants. Within a year six whites had died. Only Roger Price and two of the Helmore children survived the ravages of malaria to return to the safety of the Kuruman mission station. From a secular viewpoint a mission party which travelled without a doctor and included pregnant wives and infant children indicated 'a nearly criminal ignorance or a rare stupidity on the part of everyone concerned'.[25] Admittedly the wives were adamant on accompanying the party, a fact which exonerates the husbands from leading unwilling women to a lonely death; but this provides merely a further indication that missionary zeal and assumptions of divine protection overran the boundaries of ordinary prudence. The leader of the party, Holloway Helmore, was without the requisite ability for such a complex task, while the Directors of the society, 'enthusiastic without being thoughtful' in Tabler's succinct phrase,[26] were ignorant of the conditions involved. Yet missionaries saw the resultant disaster and similar events in the context of God's plan for man. To Robert Moffat, the veteran Bechuana missionary, the disaster revealed

> How mysterious are the dispensations of Providence to *us*, who know only in part, and see through a glass darkly! The large amount of expense

incurred, the labour and toil involved, the valuable instruments cut off, and the bright prospects enveloped in darkness, are depths of Divine Providence which we cannot now fathom, and which we must place to the 'all things' which work together for good. Like numberless similar events, they will remain mysteries to us till the light of eternity shall be thrown around them, when all shall appear harmony and love. What we know not now we shall know hereafter.[27]

Bishop Mackenzie, speaking in Cape Town before his departure for the Zambesi, was undaunted when he heard of the outcome of the Makololo venture. As missionaries, he felt they could not fail, for the

> prospect... does not depend upon our life or death... does not depend upon our successes during our lifetime, but depends entirely upon the grace of God; a prospect which will undoubtedly be realized in God's good time, for we know that 'the knowledge of the Lord shall cover the earth as the waters cover the sea;' and therefore it is a prospect to which we may confidently look forward, trusting and believing that God's work will prosper, and that His Name and saving grace will be known among all nations.[28]

Slightly over a year later Mackenzie himself died of fever after losing his quinine when his canoe overturned on the river Shire. The Bishop of Oxford vehemently denied that Mackenzie had thrown away his life.

> Mankind is raised, humanity is exalted, the church is purified by the examples of great heroic self-devotion, when God accepts the offering, and takes the man at once to his breast. Is his life thrown away?... It is nothing else but a miserable, wretched utilitarian philosophy which can hold such things as these. Great examples are great gifts.[29]

This approach not only sanctified death; it fostered it with the implicit assumption that caution and cowardice were synonymous. The trials of Bishop Tozer, Mackenzie's replacement, who set himself the task of reorganizing the mission, illustrated the pressures for rash actions which turned so many missionaries into dead martyrs.

Tozer was a practical man with the administrator's passion for tidiness and order, and the rationalist's distrust of the emotions. He did not subscribe to the adage that the heart had reasons which reason did not know. He arrived to take charge of a venture which had been inspired by humanitarian and missionary fervour fed by the overly optimistic reports of Livingstone, who tended to see difficulties in the light of his own insurmountable courage. The U.M.C.A. mission was meant to be an embodiment of Livingstone's thesis that

Christianity, Commerce and Civilization should work hand in hand for the rejuvenation of Africa. To that end the first party contained a shoemaker, a carpenter, a printer, and an agriculturist. It was hoped that the mission would be self-supporting within a few years of its arrival. The mission party possessed a second-hand cotton gin which, it was assumed, would be in constant operation. By the time Tozer arrived the mission had produced five martyrs, ginned no cotton, made no converts, been unable to commence the task of religious instruction, engaged in inter-tribal warfare, and wastefully squandered vast amounts of goods. Tozer critically surveyed the results of his predecessor's efforts—a struggling village of a hundred or so waifs and strays, the depredations of the Makololo who were bringing disrepute on the English name, a pestilent climate, an area in the throes of anarchy, and, with the imminent departure of Livingstone who had been recalled by the British Government, no regular communication with the coast—and, after a short attempt to resurrect the mission on Mount Morambala in Portuguese territory, he set sail for the Cape with Dr. Steere, his trusted friend and eventual successor. He correctly saw that, aside from the element of nobility which inspired it, and the heroism of its members, this ill-conceived mission had been an unmitigated disaster. Then, acting on an explicit authority to withdraw which he had received in England, he moved the mission to Zanzibar which he correctly viewed as the gateway to the interior.

His act of courage and wisdom was ill-rewarded. At the time 'every friend of the early Mission was dead against it'.[30] Livingstone testily informed Tozer that his action constituted the first modern instance in which Protestant missionaries had 'lost heart and bolted', adding correctly that Tozer would rue his retreat till his dying day.[31] He rebuked Tozer publicly,[32] and privately he unfairly remarked that he could not see what results could be hoped for in Central Africa 'by sitting at an island in the ocean and as it were stirring up the mass of heathenism or only poking at it I should say with a long pole'.[33] Tozer was not long in Zanzibar before he was a broken man. The mission itself sank into comparative obscurity (to be revived by Steere in the seventies) and home support fell off as Tozer's caution proved to have little appeal to the donors of funds in Britain. Tozer resigned in 1873, although he lived on until 1899. Professor Owen Chadwick is undoubtedly right when he states that Tozer does not make a moral appeal to the reader of his letters in contrast to the warm-hearted Mackenzie. Although admitting that Tozer's decision was correct, Chadwick writes that 'there are some matters upon which men will only be persuaded if there is more to persuade them than sound judgement'.[34] Surveying some of the follies which afflicted early mission plans one can only add, true—but unfortunate. While the subsequent history of the U.M.C.A. constitutes sufficient vindication of Tozer's action, it was typical of missionary psychology that his cold tactical courage evoked severe castigation at the time. There is a sense in which the real human tragedy of the U.M.C.A. was not Bishop Mackenzie, a recognized martyr in death, but Bishop Tozer, an unrecognized martyr in life, who did the right thing and paid heavily for his actions.

From one viewpoint missionaries were provided with a divinely inspired capacity to ignore obstacles which would have deterred individuals possessed of a more calculating mentality. From another viewpoint, missionary intrepidity resulted in the throwing away of valuable lives due to the simple absence of rational planning. The L.M.S. expedition to Lake Tanganyika provides an additional revealing example of missionary heroes rushing needlessly into a martyr's grave and encountering bitter criticism if they questioned the strategic wisdom of specific plans to implement the divine mandate to teach all nations.

On the crest of the wave of missionary zeal arising from Livingstone's death the society accepted an offer of £5,000 from Mr. Robert Arthington of Leeds on the express condition that a mission be established on Lake Tanganyika. With the recent failure of the Makololo mission to illustrate the insufficiency of faith, the undertaking of this daring venture provides a singular example of enthusiasm overcoming caution. With hundreds of thousands of untouched heathen residing in areas much easier of access, the L.M.S. sent its emissaries eight hundred miles into the heart of Africa to take up residence at an Arab centre, Ujiji, with no assured means of communication with the outside world.

With commendable caution the Directors dispatched Roger Price, an experienced missionary, to make a preliminary investigation of about one-third of the route and to experiment with ox-waggon travel. Price strongly advocated intermediate stations both before and after his exploratory trip. His protestations, like those of J. S. Moffat and Robert Moffat, were ignored. Mullens, the Foreign Secretary of the Society, was immune to criticism, arguing that 'nothing short of right through to Ujiji at once would be tolerated by the country'.[35] He claimed that 'God in his Providence' was producing a wonderful interest in the welfare of the people of Central Africa. Merchants were moving in, and King Leopold of Belgium was displaying a personal interest in the civilization of the African.

> And surely missionary societies ought not to be the last in the field. . . . How easy it is to reach Lake Tanganyika from Zanzibar . . . things are many years ahead of Stanley's meeting with Livingstone. We shall go

THE CENTRAL AFRICAN FRONTIER

thither with wheeled carriages, and in five years it will be easier to reach that place from Zanzibar than it used to be to get to Kuruman from Cape Town. The Directors know thoroughly well what they are about.³⁶

On July 21, 1877, the first L.M.S. mission party left Zanzibar for the mainland. There were four missionaries, Price, E. S. Clarke, J. B. Thomson, and A. W. Dodgshun; W. Hutley, an artisan; and E. C. Hore, Master Mariner. Three months later, the ox-waggon experiment having failed due to the tsetse fly, the expedition was stranded with its goods scattered from the coast to Mpwapwa. Price was deputed to return to England, lay the position before the Directors and advocate intermediate stations.³⁷ He was given a chilly reception as 'the parties whose grand scheme has failed . . . are simply savage with disappointment'.³⁸ Price, the only man with actual experience of East African conditions, was almost completely ignored in the formation of plans for the stranded expedition. On February 19, 1878, he was notified that his services were no longer required for the Central Africa mission.³⁹

For introducing sanity and caution into the mission plans Price, in effect, was dismissed from the expedition. Clarke left because of disagreement with the Directors' proposals. They were the victims of a practically ubiquitous passion for undertaking well-nigh impossible ventures deep in the heart of Africa with inadequate forethought, preparation, and understanding. Of the remaining four members of the mission, three reached Ujiji on August 23, 1878, thirteen months after their departure from Zanzibar. The fourth, Dodgshun, arrived on March 27, 1879, after a heroic journey of just under two years in which he had been engaged in bringing mission supplies to Ujiji with the trader Broyon. Thomson was dead in a month. Dodgshun lived only seven days at Ujiji. The mission was represented by an artisan and a Master Mariner in the heart of Africa.

The remainder of the story—the successive expeditions, the deaths, the retirements, the rededications to the missionary cause, and the disputes over the desirability of continuing the mission—is too complex to be told here. It represented a continuous attempt to repair the folly evoked by zeal without discretion. In his decennial report one missionary correctly pointed out that the mission was still founding itself.⁴⁰ It was a costly failure. Thirty-six missionaries, ordained, artisan, and medical, were appointed from 1877 to 1893. Eleven died, including the Foreign Secretary Mullens, who accompanied one party into the interior. Fourteen retired, usually after brief spells of service. On the lowest calculation the cost of the work was £40,000. The first convert was made in 1891. The historian of the L.M.S. appositely stated that the mission 'stands on the page of history rather as a striking example of how great missionary enterprises ought not to be attempted'. He added that there was 'no doubt the Directors sanctioned the mission without any true conception of the magnitude of the task they were undertaking'.[41]

The conventional approach to the type of instance cited above is dominated by admiration for the courage and heroism of individual missionaries. Related to this is an attitude suffused with admiration for a religion capable of inspiring such self-sacrifice in a selfish world. These approaches are not without their merit. It is, however, salutary to indicate that the missionary penetration of Central Africa was vitiated by an enthusiasm heedless of danger and comparatively devoid of forethought. This is not merely hindsight. In 1870 Thomas Leask gave a truly savage denunciation of mission mismanagement after seeing the conditions which faced the Rev. J. B. Thomson and his wife when they arrived at the L.M.S. station of Inyati in Matabeleland—no place to live 'but a pestilential room, rotten, damp and slimy, in which six men caught the fever last year, four of whom were buried within two or three hundred yards . . .' 'Is common sense too worldly a thing for mission societies? . . . A lesson or two taken from the calculating conduct of *worldly minded* men would in some cases save money and life—I place them in the order with which *they* seem to be regarded by missionary societies.'[42]

This lack of prudence was inherent in the very nature of the missionary movement. It reflected both the imperatives of religious bureaucracies dependent on public support for their funds and the psychology of individual missionaries. An admittedly extreme case illustrates the latter aspect. In 1881 Kirk informed the Foreign Office of a missionary who had just left for the interior 'under circumstances so peculiar as to call for passing notice'. Mr. Wm. Cruickshank, he wrote,

> came here [Zanzibar] from England to go to Manyuema and establish himself apart and independent of any other Mission. He . . knows no African language and has I think read very little of what has been lately written by persons practically acquainted with the country. . . . It was useless to tell him that the country is unhealthy to Europeans. . . .
>
> He goes off without an attendant, without the means of cooking the food that may be given him in charity and even without medicines. He leaves behind clothes and money as unnecessary, taking only a few dollars in his pockets and a bundle that he himself can carry and in this way he has set out for the country west of Tanganyika.[43]

'Argument and advice had no effect,' he wrote, in reporting Cruickshank's death a month later.[44]

The tendency for mission societies to establish stations deep in the interior was related to a variety of factors. In some cases the renown of certain tribes such as the Baganda, Matabele, and Makololo was an important consideration. There was also the belief noted by Hore that the 'real healthy active savage' lived in the interior while the coastal tribes were 'socially and physically degraded. . . .'[45] Finally, as J. S. Moffat cynically observed in 1878, promoters of missions were too apt to regard a tribe or chief as interesting 'only in proportion as the region is difficult of access and as the conditions are unpromising under which the missionary must accomplish his task'.[46] An important reason for this was that the first essential to open up a new mission area was funds, the collection of which was related to the amount of enthusiasm that could be generated among home constituencies. This enthusiasm, in turn, was often the product of a special event which stirred up interest in a new, obscure, and excitingly dangerous field. Once this had happened, as Moffat stated of the L.M.S. Tanganyika mission, 'nothing will . . . satisfy that unreasonable and impulsive power, Christian public, but a campaign, which may be wise and successful, God knows'.[47] This conflict between caution and public support underlay the recurring missionary tendency to undertake sensational ventures to stimulate and retain public interest.

Given the prevailing conditions of an African existence, a certain amount of enthusiasm was undoubtedly necessary to elicit any response, either from individuals or societies. An excess of enthusiasm, however, often catapulted missionaries into untenable situations which wiser plans could have avoided. The practice of plunging deep into the heart of Africa was, as Mackay of Uganda believed, 'a serious mistake in judgement, [which] would entail enormous expense and unnecessary loss of life'.[48] Yet, events which to the secular understanding simply indicate an almost suicidal waste of human life were but rarely seen in this fashion by the missionary movement.

The capacity of the missionary to persevere was closely related to a mentality which sanctified death by equating it with martyrdom. 'Is not a death for the faith', wrote Bishop Steere, 'the greatest blessing a man can meet with? Next to this to suffer wrong and be evil entreated was to the Apostles a subject of thankfulness.'[49] When the first reports of the losses of life in the Tanganyika mission reached their L.M.S. mission brethren in Matabeleland, one missionary wrote:

> The Society and the Mission and indeed the whole church have suffered severely. Surely if the future success of a mission in any way depends on loss and suffering attending its foundation, our new attempt for the evangelization of Africa ought to triumph gloriously. What a happy fate was theirs to be permitted thus to lay down their lives while yet in their prime, in the Master's Cause! Surely the whole church at home will be stirred up in the cause of Africa after hearing of these new martyrs. I

sometimes wish that I were at home again, that I might have a chance of filling one of the gaps.⁵⁰

Some years later when this same Tanganyika mission was going through one of its periodic crises D. P. Jones informed the Directors that if the high death-rate discouraged them,

> it is far more so to the Missionaries out here. We are as it were constantly brought face to face with death. It were only feigned courage to say that these sad visitations do not somewhat damp our spirit, and in consideration of these calamities it seems questionable whether it is not our duty to urge the Directors to withdraw from Central Africa.⁵¹

Two of his fellow missionaries disagreed with the project of abandonment, and when Jones and a colleague Rees returned home on medical grounds the L.M.S. missionary at Urambo characterized Jones' return as 'selfishness' and that of Rees as 'cowardice'.⁵²

The castigations heaped on men such as Tozer, Price, Jones, and Rees reveal the integral relationship between missionary beliefs and a pattern of conduct almost immune from critical appraisal as to its wisdom. The fundamental point was that the missionary movement contained a set of explanations which muted the impact of failure, disaster and death, and indeed, often transformed them into divine portents of future success—or as indications of the vitality of the Christian faith. Livingstone claimed that the 'sacrifice [of] so much valuable life' in West Africa might indicate missionary folly to some, 'but others . . . [it is] . . . telling evidence that our religion has lost none of its pristine power'.⁵³ Missionary deaths were explicable by the 'martyr' thesis,⁵⁴ or were accepted on the assumption that to question God's workings indicated a lack of faith. The veteran missionary William Sykes, for example, was greatly distressed at the death of a colleague, Cockin, who 'seemed to us to be just the man, and we had thanked the Lord, as well as the Directors, for guiding him hither'. Yet, he reflected, this merely showed the imperfection of human thought, for 'the *Master* himself knows all the whys and wherefores. It is ours to labour on *trust*.' ⁵⁵ On their journey to Lake Tanganyika the first party of White Fathers suffered severe hardship. The death of one of their most beloved missionaries was regarded as a blessing, for they would then have a more powerful advocate before God. Sickness was also a boon, for it helped them to pray, and took their minds away from the ephemeral things of this world.⁵⁶

This aspect of the missionary mentality, an important psychological asset in the difficult days of hardship and trial which attended the commencement of missionary work in Central Africa, represented a selective capacity to interpret events in a fashion congenial to the missionary. Thus, when 'evil' men died, the same pattern of belief produced an entirely different explanation. In such cases God assumed an Old Testament character and struck men dead who attempted to frustrate his plans. In a speech to the Conference on Foreign Missions held in London in 1886 John Moir, joint manager of the African Lakes Corporation, which refused to sell liquor to Africans, noted that God too was against the liquor traffic. He backed up his case by detailing the violent deaths of six liquor sellers. 'God in His Providence has protected these people [Africans] from the blight which evil men would bring upon them.' Horace Waller, in discussing some of the same incidents mentioned by Moir, argued that these were not the only instances in a 'series of the most marvellous tragedies . . . tragedies startling enough to make the most sceptical admit that God's hand is very plainly visible in the history of these efforts to raise the natives above that level to which the slave trader has depressed them'.[57] Evil men died by the wrath of God; good men were called to God, acted as a noble example, and became the seed of the new church.

Even with this pattern of belief as a stimulus, extreme difficulty was often experienced in attracting men to the mission fields of Central Africa.[58] Those who did volunteer often faced the prospect of work and travel on the mainland with considerable trepidation. The missionary, as numerous cases indicate, tended to see his acceptance of an African career as 'practical proof' that his Christianity was more than a veneer, and that it implied something more than a comfortable house and a quiet pleasant existence in a British parish. When William Waddell, a devout Scottish Christian, made known his intentions of joining a projected French Protestant mission to Barotseland, his friends bluntly informed him that he was going to 'commit suicide by going to such an unhealthy country'.[59] Although Waddell was not deterred, and did yeoman service for the mission in an artisan capacity, the biblical text which convinced him was highly indicative of prevalent attitudes to a Central African existence: 'I beseech you therefore brethren, by the mercies of God that ye present your bodies a living sacrifice wholly acceptable unto God, which is your reasonable service.'[60] W. P. Johnson, informed by friends that he was 'mad' to sacrifice a proferred career in the Indian Civil Service for mission work in Africa, was thankful for the opportunity of proving his belief 'practically' in the prevailing air of scepticism about Christianity among his university friends.[61]

The desire to undertake especially strenuous and dangerous tasks in Africa for Christ was the missionary counterpart of the lure of adventure which exercised the imaginations of the hunter and explorer. John Mackenzie of the L.M.S., after indicating that his first reason for wishing to pursue a missionary calling was to carry out the biblical imperative to 'Go ye and teach all nations', added that the second was to be found in the fact that the missionary, 'for Christ's sake', was faced with special privations and hardships which called for *more self-denial* than faced by the minister at home. Luxury, refinement, and ease, he indicated elsewhere, could stifle the spirit which would expand in the midst of the hardships and sufferings of an African existence.[62]

As Mackenzie's attitude indicates there was a certain exhilaration in the fulfilment of duty and the prospect of an individual assumption of responsibility among trying conditions. This was also true of Livingstone. As Schapera convincingly shows, he was markedly influenced by a desire to pioneer for Christ alone in the hinterland, 'to preach the gospel beyond every other man's line of things'.[63] It was always the unknown and the regions untouched by mission effort which attracted him. It was doubtless this almost obsessive desire to be individually in the very forefront of the mission conquest of Africa which accounts for his elation as he departed from Mikindani on his third great African trip. He was once again heading into the unknown in charge of a small caravan, this time untroubled by the complicating presence of other white men which had made his life such a torment on the recent Zambesi expedition. In oft-quoted words he wrote in his diary:

> Now that I am on the point of starting on another trip into Africa I feel quite exhilarated: when one travels with the specific object in view of ameliorating the condition of the natives every act becomes ennobled. ... No doubt much toil is involved, and fatigue of which travellers in the more temperate climes can form but a faint conception; but the sweat of one's brow is no longer a curse when one works for God: it proves a tonic to the system and is actually a blessing.[64]

To Livingstone there was a certain excitement in the elemental prospects of adventure and danger facing the expedition. There was, however, a more subtle form of psychological well-being than the sheer physical pleasure of wielding power or overcoming difficulties by strenuous effort. To Livingstone the inferiority of the African called not for brutality or exploitation but for the exercise of moral trusteeship. African backwardness elicited a feeling of responsibility owed by a moral aristocrat to the weak, the suffering, and the needy among whom he laboured. Superiority was a trust and its usage had conditions attached. The fact of superiority was not in question, but rather its obligations. Contentment sprang from well-doing, the consciousness of superiority justly utilized.

This aspect of humanitarian psychology was clearly illustrated in a series of letters written by Horace Waller to James Stewart after his return to Britain from the disastrous U.M.C.A. expedition to the

Shire Highlands in the sixties. Waller, eager to go back to Africa, was restrained by a lack of means and family opposition coupled with his father's invalidism. Like so many others who went to Africa he was dissatisfied with what he regarded as the complexity and artificiality of life in Britain—'this whirl of civilized life all so unreal, so strained, and false'—which he compared unfavourably to life in Africa, 'the doing or striving to do good so purely and simply'.[65] He felt no longer adapted to British life and longed to return to Africa where man lives

> nearer the simple state [he] is best fitted for, if he would only know it —not that we ever need go beyond that wholesome line enlightenment draws for us—not that we need become savages. But there's a great charm in the absence of hurry, the *pur et simple* resorting to nature to supply so many of your wants, the nearer approach to what I suppose was one of the happiest of lives, the patriarchal form. . . . I suppose after all it is the longing to do good to the poor things. . . . I also think there is a special charm in the being left so much to your own devices.[66]

Later he intimated to Stewart his desire to go abroad to manage a tea plantation in India, a coffee plantation in Borneo, or a sugar plantation at Johanna—somewhere where he could have a 'large number of natives under my care or rather management'.[67] Waller's motives symbolized the humanitarian quest for authority, a quest which sought an intermixture of romance, adventure, and the pleasure derived from wielding power over subject races in a responsible fashion. Waller, points out Chadwick, regarded Africans somewhat as a selfless and benevolent prince looked upon the subjects in his charge.[68]

Africa, in short, was a cause which provided an opportunity for humanitarians to do unquestioned good from positions of leadership. Missionary propaganda constantly informed the missionary of the importance of his work. Africans were 'waiting' for the gospel. Dead missionaries were martyrs, and live missionaries were heroes. Livingstone's Horatio Alger rise to prominence was doubtless not lost on his contemporaries.[69] At a minimum the missionary became a person of some importance on his furlough. If denied the audiences of the mighty, he was at least a leading attraction to the pious who came to hear about the carrying of the Gospel into the 'habitations of cruelty'. The aura which surrounded their work evoked what Wordsworth Poole called 'a peculiar self-satisfaction about the missionaries'. He attributed this to the missionary's idea of his own self-devotion, courage under difficulties and hardships willingly experienced for the 'good of black mankind'. Each, he claimed, 'takes a leaf out of Livingstone, Mackay, Hannington and pins it onto himself'.[70] This factor should not be underestimated. Missionaries clearly derived pleasure from a satisfying contemplation of the nobility of their actions. The desire to ameliorate the lot of the Africans was undoubtedly intermingled with a personal quest for the self-satisfaction of undertaking altruistic work.[71]

5

Central Africa offered Europeans few opportunities for profitable commercial ventures. African undertakings, it must be remembered, were very expensive. Where porters provided the only means of carriage, trade was confined to articles which could be arranged in convenient sizes and weights, and much of their loads was made up of their own food or cloth and beads to buy food. In 1890 George Mackenzie estimated that it cost £130 per ton to transport goods from the coast to Lake Victoria.[72] More than £11,000 was expended on Cameron's great expedition across Africa.[73]

Outside financial support was obviously necessary for such activities. Explorers usually received aid from the Royal Geographical Society or the British government, or like Stanley from the popular press, or, finally, like Samuel Baker, Montagu Kerr, A. J. Mounteney Jephson and J. S. Jameson, had sufficient funds to finance their own activities. Missionaries, with insignificant exceptions, were agents of British religious societies which recruited personnel, collected and disbursed the funds which their African activities necessitated, and selected the vineyards where their agents were to labour. The existence of the mission society facilitated continuity of effort by the replacement of personnel when sickness or death took its heavy toll, and, of especial importance, provided financial backing for activities which by their very nature were incapable of duration over time without outside support. Mission societies were not unconcerned with costs, but they were able to justify the high overhead costs of interior stations because their financial arrangements were not conducted on ordinary business principles. Critics were rebuffed with the unanswerable argument that the salvation of souls could not be measured in pounds, shillings and pence. Harry Johnston, who was much impressed with missionaries as pioneers of civilization, observed:

> These pioneers do not stop to ask whether it will pay to adventure their lives and their funds in these remote countries. They start on their self-imposed mission without *arrière-pensée*; here they fail, there they succeed: if they die nobody takes much notice and two men are always ready to supply one man's place. They make all the experiments and others reap the profit.[74]

THE CENTRAL AFRICAN FRONTIER

This factor of expense, and the special missionary attitude to it, largely explains the fact that for the British the area north of Lake Nyasa was predominantly a missionary frontier. In this area self-supporting activities could not be undertaken. There were few exploitable resources, and there was no naturally expansive white community in the background to eject its adventurers into the hinterland as in Southern Africa. The commercial exploitation of this area was undertaken by Arabs and Swahili, men who were culturally adapted to a frontier existence, and who, in an economic sense, possessed the advantage of being able to combine the trade in slaves with that in ivory—commodities for which the caravan was ideally suited.

Commerce was also seriously limited by the fact that most of the productions of nineteenth-century British civilization were not applicable to tribal conditions, either because of African poverty or the irrelevance of the articles to African desires. On the whole the products of civilization and the consumption demands of tribalism made only peripheral contact, and the reverse was equally true. Slaves, articles of commerce to Arab and African, met with no demand from British consumers, a factor which placed British traders at a disadvantage. The slaver, with his cloth, brass rings and beads, was often a popular arrival, especially among the principal men of a village. Commerce was also hampered by the absence of a readily divisible, widely accepted medium of exchange. Even where the African was habituated to the presence of strangers and had acquired a taste for foreign goods, barter was a tedious and often unprofitable affair sorely trying to the temper. There was also the problem of barter material for a succession of tribes with different preferences which often changed with Parisian rapidity. Beads good at Taveta were worthless at nearby Chagga.[75] It was, in fact, often difficult to get the African to understand commercial transactions at all.

In spite of these drawbacks, in areas where neither personal wealth nor outside financial support was a prerequisite to white contact, there was a significant entry of adventurous British traders and hunters. In the area subject to Matabele control, in Barotseland, and to a lesser extent south of Lake Nyasa, communications with the civilized world by the ox-waggon and the Zambesi gave the trader or hunter an outside chance of a profitable undertaking. Ivory, in growing use for such luxury products as billiard balls, piano keys, and ornaments, was the main article, but hippo teeth, ostrich feathers, rhino horns, hides, and, in the 1880's, museum specimens and live animals for zoos were marketable. Especially in Matabeleland and Mashonaland there was a sizeable entry of British adventurers. After Moselekatse, the Matabele chief, allowed hunters into Mashonaland in 1865 an annual stream of Britons and Afrikaners hunted for profit and excitement. Traders were equally active. By 1873 about twenty trading waggons were coming into Matabeleland yearly compared to two or three in the early sixties.[76] Trade, however, was seriously restrained by the rapacity of powerful chiefs such as Moselekatse, Lobengula, and Sepopo, who, on occasion, fleeced traders mercilessly as a part of their royal prerogative. When a powerful chief died, the resultant succession might bring a profitable trade to a sudden halt until political stability was restored. Further, markets were slow to develop due to the tendencies of chiefs to dominate commercial contacts with the outside world in the interests of their own power. Hunters had no less serious problems. Not only did they require courage, riding ability, and good marksmanship, but their expenses were heavy, often caused by serious losses of cattle and horses, and large returns were necessary to show a profit. In Matabeleland and Barotseland they had to pay a substantial fee to the chief for permission to hunt in a particular area. They had to compete with the frequent endeavours of chiefs to give their own tribesmen the preferred areas as guns increasingly found their way into African hands. In addition, ivory was a non-renewable resource. The diffusion of guns, the spread of knowledge of the value of ivory which formerly had been allowed to rot, and aggressive white hunters, often with armed bands of African assistants, resulted in a ruthless slaughter of elephants, and numberless other animals for that matter.[77] Each year the great beast receded further into the interior. No slow-breeding animal could withstand such indiscriminate destruction.

By 1870 the first period of the ivory hunter in Matabeleland was ended as elephants were henceforth found in 'fly' country which made hunting on horseback impossible. In 1878, so rapid and thorough had been the virtual annihilation, that Selous wrote despairingly that the Matabele country was 'utterly played out as far as trading and hunting are concerned, for elephants are almost a thing of the past'.[78]

The life of Selous provides a good illustration of the shifting economic possibilities of the African frontier. He arrived in the middle of the ivory hunting period, transferred to the role of a collector of museum species, and ended up as a scout and guide to the Pioneer Column of 1890. Throughout his career he supplemented his income by the sale of well-written accounts of his travel and adventures. The economic attractions were not great, but the frontier way of life had compensating advantages of freedom and adventure capable of attracting a small group of adaptable pioneers who sought fulfilment and escape in South Central Africa.

Scientific travellers, adventurous tourists, and, especially in the eighties, a growing number of concession seekers added their quotas to the number of whites who travelled and resided in Matabeleland, Mashonaland, and Barotseland before European control was imposed. While exact figures are unobtainable, over three hundred whites were probably active in these areas at various times.[79]

Further north, the Zambesi, in spite of all its shortcomings, was an important factor in opening up the Lake Nyasa area. The actions of independent traders and ivory hunters in this area were aided by the African Lakes Corporation which was founded in 1878 to relieve the supply problems of the Scottish missions. The company was ridiculously undercapitalized; its staff was never large; and it was not until its eighth year that the company paid its first dividend, a modest two and a half per cent. The company was at times unpopular because of its high prices, widespread allegations of managerial inefficiency, and the low calibre of the personnel it was compelled to recruit. Nevertheless it constituted a continuing element of British commercial interest which remains in Nyasaland to this day. Also, it provided employment for shifting groups of white ivory hunters as well as relieving the missions of some of the secular duties which were inevitable accompaniments of a frontier environment of exceptional difficulty. By the late eighties it was estimated that there were seventy-two missionaries, traders, planters, and hunters in the area.[80] Along with the territory subject to Matabele rule and the empire of the Barotse it was an area of far more diversified British contact than the regions north of Lake Nyasa where Britons and missionaries were almost synonymous terms.

6

The motivations of the secular whites among these early pioneers were fairly simple and straightforward. They sought in Africa an opportunity for a diversity of forms of self-expression inhibited by civilization. In many cases they were driven by a lure for the unknown and a desire for novelty and strangeness of experience.

Burton was impelled by an almost insatiable quest for new lands and strange customs. Prior to his Tanganyika trip he had already acquired fame for his trip to Mecca disguised as a Moslem, and for his penetration of the walled city of Harar in Somaliland. He felt the departure 'upon a distant journey into unknown lands' to be one of 'the gladdest moments in human life'. Man, he continued, feels once more happy when he has shaken off the 'fetters of Habit, the leaden weight of Routine, the cloak of many Cares and the slavery of Home'.

> Excitement lends unwonted vigour to the muscles, and the sudden sense of freedom adds a cubit to the mental stature. Afresh dawns the morn of

life; again the bright world is beautiful to the eye, and the glorious face of nature gladdens the soul. A journey, in fact, appeals to Imagination, to Memory, to Hope—the three sister Graces of our moral being.[81]

Such buoyant descriptions of frontier life constituted a major influence in attracting the early pioneers to Africa. The writings of the explorers and hunters in particular emphasized freedom, absence of convention, and a simple, hard, rough, challenging way of life offering scope for manliness and individuality. A major aspect of the lure of Africa was summed up by A. J. Swann, an L.M.S. missionary and later a member of the Nyasaland administration.

> The silence of the forest is a welcome change from the noisy city, and one's manhood seems to assert itself much more when entirely cut off from European associations.
> Perhaps the sense of individuality is the main attraction. In the constant whirl of civilization the personal element is somewhat lost in the mass. Out in the forests of Africa you are *the* man amongst your surroundings.[82]

One expression of this individuality was the assertion of power and leadership. On his journey to find Livingstone, Stanley described his departure from Bagomoyo with zest. He was riding a 'splendid bay horse', and was called 'Bana Mkuba', the 'big master', by his men. He was the 'vanguard, the reporter, the thinker, and the leader of the Expedition'.[83] Unexplored and uncivilized Africa was a heaven-sent blessing to Stanley. His workhouse background, the hardships of his youth, and his unsatisfied search for affection could all be forgotten. At the head of a caravan he sought the achievements which would serve 'to obliterate the stigma of pauperism which had been so deeply branded into his very soul by the Poor-Law methods'.[84] In Africa he was alone, an unquestioned leader with almost unlimited resources at his disposal. He enforced discipline with an iron hand as he determinedly strode over obstacles to succour Livingstone. In his treatment of his porters there was a callousness reminiscent of the brutality he had himself experienced in childhood and youth. His attitude to nature was equally masterful. In revealing language he compared himself at one point to a feudal lord ruling over vast areas:

> I felt momentarily proud that I owned such a vast domain, inhabited with such noble beasts. Here I possessed, within reach of a leaden ball, any one I chose of the beautiful animals, the pride of the African forests![85]

Stanley's lust for achievement, for power, and for dominance over man and beast was part of a dramatic journalistic approach to life which emphasized action at the expense of reflection. The style of his writing, pungent, and lacking in restraint or qualification, mirrored the man himself. The titles of his books—*How I Found Livingstone, In Darkest Africa, Through the Dark Continent*—clearly reveal his heroic, epic approach to African exploration. He agreed with a friend who pointed out that one of his addresses to his tired carriers was reminiscent of Tennyson's Ulysses.[86] While many were repelled by the hard ruthless vein in Stanley, he was nevertheless besieged with applications for the two major expeditions which followed his successful search for Livingstone. For his trans-Africa trip sponsored by the *Daily Telegraph* and the *New York Herald* he received over twelve hundred applications ranging from generals to mechanics and cooks, while on the Emin Pasha expedition he was flooded with requests.[87] There was, as Surgeon Parke, one of the successful applicants, noted, 'a halo of romance' forming around the prospect of a thrilling journey for the lost hero of Equatoria.[88]

Africa was an area where men could still perform noble and romantic deeds. Exploration could be a springboard to fame and occasionally power. Stanley, Baker, and Harry Johnston all moved up the ladder from exploration to governorships. Alfred Sharpe moved from hunting to exploration to the position of Governor of Nyasaland, as did Frederick Jackson in Uganda. John Kirk moved from exploration to the Consulate's chair at Zanzibar. Even Charles Livingstone, after his inglorious performance on the Zambesi expedition, was 'rewarded' with the position of Consul at Fernando Po. From a young elephant hunter who would shed his trousers when on the spoor of a wild animal, F. C. Selous became an acknowledged expert on big game and an intimate of President Theodore Roosevelt. Lugard, attempting to resolve a frustrated love affair, thought of suicide, adventure, or noble death in the performance of some great work, and finally went to Africa with the hope of joining the Italian army in its invasion of Ethiopia.[89] His choice of Africa was perhaps natural. In his schooldays he had written an essay 'On the various kinds of Courage' which concluded that Livingstone was the 'greatest' of England's heroes.[90] Arriving in Africa at an opportune time and almost penniless, Lugard found himself in the vanguard of imperial struggles in the Lake Nyasa district, published an important book,[91] and ended up as a great pro-consul.

The search for romance and masterful activity was also characteristic of the hunter who satisfied his desire for achievement and adventure by killing wild game in the midst of the chase. It was put bluntly by Karamoja Bell, a skilful elephant hunter of the early imperial period. 'Of all the thrills in the world,' he wrote, 'give me the standing within twenty yards of good elephant, waiting for a head to turn to send a tiny nickel bullet straight to the brain.'[92] Cornwallis Harris, an early hunter in the Transvaal, described the same feeling in less prosaic fashion. He wrote of his preference for a life of adventure, the privations and thrill of the chase 'constituting an excitement peculiarly adapted to my humour'. To wander among wild animals, 'these free-born denizens of the desert', he felt was 'truly soul-stirring and romantic'. To be perhaps the first white in such areas he compared to 'realizing . . . a new creation'.[93] To kill one of these 'free-born denizens of the desert' was the culminating ecstatic experience. Harris and his shooting friend performed 'prodigies of slaughter'.[94] The hunter, whatever else he represented, symbolized clearly the brutal exploitation and domination by man of his environment. An admittedly exceptional case illustrates the point with clarity. In 1860 at a hunt for Prince Alfred in the Orange Free State some 25,000 head of game were enclosed by Africans and some estimates of the number killed reach six thousand.[95] The same point can be made in microcosm by presenting the description by Harris of his first giraffe:

> I applied the muzzle of my rifle behind his dappled shoulder, with the right hand, and drew both triggers; but he still continued to shuffle along, and being afraid of losing him, should I dismount, among the extensive mimosa groves, with which the landscape was now obscured, I sat in my saddle, loading and firing behind the elbow, and then placing myself across his path, until, the tears trickling from his full brilliant eye, his lofty frame began to totter, and at the seventeenth discharge from the deadly grooved bore, like a falling minaret bowing his graceful head from the skies, his proud form was prostrate in the dust. Never shall I forget the tingling excitement of that moment. At last then the summit of hunting ambition was actually attained, and the towering giraffe laid low. Tossing my turbanless cap into the air, alone, in the wild wood, I hurraed with bursting exultation, and unsaddling my steed, sank exhausted beside the noble prize I had won.[96]

The more obscure traders and hunters did not have the opportunity for the public self-dramatization frequently indulged in by the writers of the hunting and travel books of the period. It seems, however, that, like their more celebrated compatriots, they took to frontier life for its freedom and adventure. The free and easy life of the interior, asserted Matabele Wilson, who arrived in Bulawayo in 1888, was irresistible to those who had partaken of its joys away from all the troubles and worries of civilization. His description, although long, is so candid and revealing that it deserves extensive quotation.

> Here a man lives a life, mixed with a dash of adventure, seeing new countries, new faces, and new peoples, never knowing what a day nor an hour may bring forth. He can live on a cookie and pumpkin, or mealie meal when he has nothing else, and on account of the healthy atmosphere, and the healthy exercises he takes, he never fares anything

but well, unless . . . staying . . . in sickly unhealthy malarial countries . . . one cannot blame he who has once tasted the veldt ever wishing he was back on it again. . . . 'One trip and the longing is always there.' I have often wondered why people who get sick and out of health in those large towns and cities do not try the veldt, they go to some watering place and after staying there a week or two they become acquainted with all the people around them, the said people, ten chances to one, are invalids, or people with an incurable disease, and one must guess that by talking with those people, the condition of the man staying there for health cannot be improved, and wherever he turns, he sees *nothing* but people on crutches or people being wheeled about, even those who are not sick now, have been sick, and can do nothing but talk about it. Look at the contrast going into the veldt. You have your comfortable ox waggon, and a couple of horses and a dog or two, and a gun and a rifle, some fishing gear, and a few good provisions, also your driver, and your voerlooper, and perhaps another boy you use as a cook, and then as a rule you can always pick up an extra hand if wanted for the time being. Every day takes you further and further away from towns and places of that description where certain kinds of sickness are always being contracted, here every day gives you a change of scenery and sometimes a change of game. . . . As you go along, you meet different people, with different habits, customs, and languages. . . . The things on the veldt which it is possible for one to occupy oneself in are too innumerable to mention. There is no old woman here to tell you 'You are looking pale' or 'Oh, I am sorry to see you looking so bad,' or having people fooling around you with a cup of tea or soup and other things you don't want. In fact, if a man is not altogether broken down, there is nothing in the world that will put him together quicker or better than a six months' trip on the veldt.[97]

As Wilson's diary entry makes clear, one of the most significant aspects of early pioneer motivations was the recurring and deeply felt antipathy for what Ward called the 'jostling and hurrying of civilization'.[98] Urban life in particular was regarded with contempt. Before his first Nile trip, Baker wrote to his sister of his secret determination to make a trip 'into the Unknown. . . . A wandering spirit . . . in my marrow . . . forbids rest. The time may come when I shall delight in cities; but at present I abhor them.'[99]

To these pioneers urban life implied not only an impersonality and anonymity destructive of individuality, but civilization in general meant interdependence, the opposite of independence which sprang from a 'farewell to civilization, and . . . the knowledge that henceforward one had to rely solely on one's own resources, and that success or failure depend on one's self'.[100] Civilization was equated with restriction and boredom, while freedom was simply felt to be an absence of externally imposed restraint. Men such as Joseph Thomson soon became 'thoroughly tired and disgusted with life in

England' after they had been to Africa.[101] Further, civilization represented the known, whereas Central Africa represented 'virgin soil',[102] 'unknown regions',[103] and the opportunity to see and travel 'where no one else has been'.[104] The desire to be first, to do and see something which no other white man had done or seen before—these were regarded as obvious and satisfying confirmations of one's own individuality.

Here the interesting point emerges that Africa was often discussed as if it lacked any human inhabitants. Implicit in many of the statements was the assumption that to be the first white man was equivalent to being the first man. The African was part of the background in which Europeans carried out their activities. His co-operation might be essential to the accomplishment of European objectives, but the overwhelming emphasis was a European centred approach. The recurring praise for the faithful porter indicates the supplemental rather than independent role assigned to Africans. It is indicative that the reader of early travel and other African literature has to make a deliberate effort not to see Central Africa as an area where all the important activities were carried on by a growing handful of Europeans in the midst of an environment in which Africans, elephants, and natural obstacles are lumped together as background landscape. This bias reveals the pervasive assumption of the non-missionary element that Africa was a colossal playground where the European personality could express itself in a fashion impossible in civilized lands.

7

The remaining chapters of this analysis will be devoted to a discussion of British attitudes to varying aspects of culture contact. In concluding this first chapter it only remains to place their response in the context of the incredibly difficult and arduous frontier problems with which they had to grapple.

The inhibitions evoked by membership in an advanced culture, no less than health requirements, rendered impossible any complete adaptation to the material standards of tribalism. In Central Africa the concerns of life were reduced to the basic essentials of food, health, shelter, and survival itself. As Thomas Baines pointed out, there was nothing 'intensely clerical' in the appearance of Sykes and Thomas, two L.M.S. missionaries in Matabeleland. They were not the 'sleek white-chokered, black-coated' stereotypes imagined by the British reader. The missionary, indeed, spent little time in direct teaching or spiritual work. His energies of necessity were directed to the provision of shelter, food, and comfort for his family; while his wife, often of 'delicate frame', performed 'tasks unsuited in our idea to her sex and station . . . not infrequently wearing herself too greatly by her exertions'.[105]

Initially there was the time-consuming necessity of erecting some permanent accommodation. In some cases, no sooner were habitable dwellings completed than the missionaries were compelled to move for health reasons, tribal hostility, or the migration of their potential flock, and to commence again in a new area.

Food raised further problems. The traveller could supplement his limited stock of dried fruits, vegetables, and tinned foods with game. Such delicacies as giraffe and eland meat were eagerly sought but not always obtainable. Spurred on by hunger men ate sweet and rancid zebra flesh, and even the remains of a lion's kill, covered with saliva, blood and dirt. Donkey, rat, monkey, insects, locusts, and snake flesh formed part of the diet of the European members of the Emin Pasha expedition.[106]

The resident missionary had no time to scour the country in order to maintain a well-stocked larder. Transportation expenses made provision of basic foods from Europe out of the question. Vegetables and grain crops were planted by most missionaries almost immediately on arrival, but crops often failed in the early years, and actual hunger was an ever-present threat. The wheat crop of the L.M.S. missionaries to the Matabele failed three years in succession, necessitating the sending of J. S. Moffat five hundred miles to the south so that the missionaries could have bread, 'the Englishman's staff of life and certainly an indispensable staff to European females in this climate'.

> It may be said [Sykes informed the Foreign Secretary of the L.M.S.] that all this has reference to our material comforts. And seeing that the Allwise God has given us a material side of our constitution—the healthy preservation of which is a *sine qua non* to our active usefulness—we do not regard it as immaterial to care for it.[107]

These problems were exacerbated by the frequent difficulty of securing willing African co-operation for their solution. African chiefs often made the sale or gift of food to whites an instrument of coercion. The Matabele also threatened to remove servants from whites who would not sell them ammunition.[108] The virtual impossibility of securing satisfactory African labour for the innumerable menial tasks of a frontier existence illustrated the difficulty of cross-cultural co-operation. In the case of the Matabele and the Baganda, tribal pride was a barrier to undertaking manual work for Europeans. Further the Matabele could not understand the practice of hiring servants. 'They must own them.' Those who did understand were fearful that staying with the white might reflect on their tribal loyalty.[109] They did not consider an oral contract to be binding. When they tired of their engagement with traders and hunters they demanded their full pay whether or not their time was up.[110] In Buganda Mackay found himself unable to procure African servants and unwilling to purchase slaves, the only option he had.[111] Where labour was available African wants were quickly satiated, which led to rapid labour turnover with resultant inefficiency and high cost. A unique and intriguing situation developed on the L.M.S. stations in the vicinity of Lake Tanganyika. Unable to procure local labour, the missionaries employed Moslem Wangwana from the coast, who busied themselves with spreading Islam while in the employ of their Christian masters. The humour of the situation was not apparent to the missionaries who eventually dismissed all the Wangwana and made fruitless attempts to utilize only untrained tribal workmen.

It must be remembered that the men who faced these frontier difficulties were devoid of any special training for their rugged existence, frequently weakened by fever, and enervated by heat. They experienced high death rates, suffered from loneliness, and, in many cases, were fearful that their isolation might jeopardize their retention of civilized values and standards. The missionary also had to adapt to the fact that, by and large, Africans displayed a monolithic indifference to the gospel message for the spread of which he had given up comfort, security, and friends. In this respect the hunter, the trader, and the explorer were more fortunate. They performed concrete tasks in which success was reasonably closely related to performance. Compared to the transformation in African life sought by the missionary there was an almost casual simplicity about shooting an elephant or discovering a new geographical feature.

The missionary not only attempted a more difficult task, but the fact that he was a resident, that he was often accompanied by wife and family, and that he required reasonably civilized surroundings, meant that he spent remarkably little time in direct attempts to spread the Christian message. Missionary complaints about the domination of their time by the manifold chores of a frontier existence were natural and legitimate. One missionary wife spoke bitterly of her '*so-called* missionary life', and compared herself to a '*farmer's wife*!!'[112] These were real and valid grievances which were not inherent in a Central African existence. The Roman Catholic method,[113] by which lay auxiliaries performed most of the temporal work and left the priests free to pursue the *raison d'être* of their African career, the conversion of the African, was eminently sensible compared to the more individualistic Protestant approach.

Yet, underlying the not infrequent expression of discontent and frustration by missionaries, there was a basic tenacity of purpose.

THE CENTRAL AFRICAN FRONTIER

Fortified by religious faith, racial pride, and identification with a global movement, missionaries were deterred neither by an environment hostile to the maintenance of health, the even more deadly indifference of Africans to the gospel, nor by their inevitable absorption in menial tasks. In establishing mission stations they created little outposts of European civilization in the midst of tribalism. Theologians such as Bishop Steere and W. A. Scott planned and superintended the building of imposing churches at Zanzibar and Blantyre which, confounding the sceptics, stand to this day. Churches, however, were secondary to converts. Unwritten languages had to be learned and written down before the difficult but vital task of Bible translation could be attempted. Initially the study of African languages implied no special respect for tribalism. It was simply a functional necessity for effective communication. Bishop Steere became a great Swahili scholar for, as his predecessor Tozer had discovered, it was no use being given boys to train by the Sultan of Zanzibar, boys who were to be the nucleus of a school for Christian prophets, if no one could speak to them. As the truths of the gospel were sacred, the job could not be undertaken lightly. Without effective and accurate communication it was impossible to wield the type of influence which the mission calling necessitated. Krapf and Rebmann, the German missionaries of the C.M.S., spent the major part of their careers in translating African languages. Throughout Central Africa missionaries and Africans painfully wrestled with the subtle shadings of word meanings and the complexities of grammar. The field of language exploration, more interesting and important than the exploration of rivers, lakes, or even snow-capped mountains, was perhaps the most fundamental activity of the early missionaries. It facilitated, without necessarily producing, an increased knowledge of and sympathy with Africans and their cultures. Edwin W. Smith has argued: 'I defy anyone to study a Bantu language thoroughly and retain an opinion that Africans are innately inferior to Europeans in intellect.' [114] It is clear that missionaries, from the beginnings of contact to the present day, have found in African languages not only vehicles of communication but media for human expression of beauty and flexibility. Finally, the diligence with which missionaries pursued their linguistic studies illustrated the fact that they aspired to a different type of influence over the African than later generations of administrators or settlers. They desired not only external conformity, but an inner change of ethical values and spiritual outlook. The magnitude of the change they sought was indeed the basic reason for their comparative lack of success in the pre-imperial period.

8

Compared to the flood of settlers who left Britain for North America and other temperate areas, only a trickle of adventurers directed their footsteps to the new world of Central Africa in the half century preceding the assumption of European imperial power. Yet, in view of the hardships they willingly encountered, and the insignificant economic attractions of the area, their numbers were relatively large.

These early pioneers, to resort to somewhat of an oversimplification, were composed of two groups: those who came to Central Africa to introduce civilization, and those who came to escape civilization. To the one group Africa was a cause. To the other, it was an area of freedom and self-expression. To both groups, it offered an opportunity for an escape from anonymity, and an emergence into individuality. Mannoni's theory that the attraction of areas of 'primitive' culture to Europeans is to be found in a Prospero complex, the desire to live in a world where individuality is enhanced by the possibility of ignoring the personalities of others, has been criticized for leaving out the 'economic realities of emigration'.[115] Yet it is the distinguishing feature of the pre-imperial period that economic motivations were virtually non-existent among these early pioneers. One does not have to be a psychologist to see the influence of a desire for a type of personal autonomy and freedom from social ties impossible in the complicated network of relationships which constitutes civilized society. This factor is written on page after page of the narratives of missionary, traveller, trader, and hunter which poured from the printing presses and were devoured by millions of avid readers. The very individualism of contemporary writing is indicative. Biography and autobiography were published in profusion, while travel was inevitably a record of the actions of a single individual. Yet the reality was not so simple. The early British pioneer lived and moved and had his being in the midst of peoples dominated by tribal values. He was inevitably compelled to respond to their presence, to enter into relationships with them, and somehow to reconcile his own assumptions of racial superiority with a contact situation in which no imperial power preserved social distance and his physical safety by the prestige and coercive power of a white-controlled colonial government.

II

WHITE MEETS BLACK

1

THE basic superiority of civilization over tribalism was found in the complex of factors which gave the west an exceptional degree of environmental control. The growth of bureaucracies, the quantification of time and space, an ideology of work and production which unleashed tremendous economic energies, objectively sound ideas of causal relationships, and technology working in a context of rationality gave to western man a qualitatively different capacity to manipulate his surroundings from that enjoyed by his predecessors. Armed with these techniques he was irresistible in any form of aggressive contact with either the developed cultures of Asia or the primitive tribal cultures which still existed throughout much of the habitable world. This objectively verifiable power not only gave him the capacity to subjugate the non-white peoples of Africa and Asia but, by proving superiority, tended to provide a justification for its use.

With respect to Africa, however, which the anti-slavery movement had conditioned the British to view in moral terms, the use of power was subject to the restraints of a collective national conscience. Indeed, one of the saving graces of twentieth-century British imperial control was the comparatively high content of moral responsibility with which it was suffused. The nineteenth-century humanitarianism and evangelicalism which evoked the missionary movement and the anti-slavery societies subjected later imperial power to significant internal restraints in the consciences of its possessors, and to external checks from the presence of watchful groups in Britain ever ready to dramatize imperial shortcomings by petitions, mass meetings, and the placing of pressure on the British government. The idea of trusteeship was implicit in the aristocratic racial assumptions which permeated British thought with the concept of responsibility long before it was publicized by the League of Nations.

WHITE MEETS BLACK

In this early period of culture contact a recurrent emphasis was placed on the necessity for a high moral content in the conduct of those who aspired to influence backward people. Livingstone's instructions to John Kirk on the Zambesi Expedition contain references to 'moral influence'—'an example of consistent moral conduct'—'treating the people with kindness'—'saying a few kind words in a natural respectful manner' to the sick—'the best security from attack consists in upright conduct'—and 'strictest justice in dealing with the people'. In summation he stated:

> In this enterprize in which we have the honour to be engaged, sympathy, consideration and kindness, which when viewed in detail may seem thrown away, if steadily persisted in, are sure ultimately to exercise a commanding influence. Depend upon it, a kind word or deed is never lost.[1]

There was, in brief, a typically British emphasis on character as a fundamental attribute of leadership which, by sheer force of moral example, would have an important educational and civilizing effect. While this emphasis was naturally most pronounced among the missionary element, it was far from being confined to them. Men such as Thomas Baines, Thomas Leask, and E. D. Young prided themselves on their reputation for fair treatment.[2] The dissolute sexual life of many of the white pioneers in Matabeleland aroused missionary ire, but Tabler reminds us that these men were known among the tribesmen for their just dealings.[3]

The significance of character was incorporated in the concept of the gentleman, a widely used descriptive term for the bundle of traits most appropriate for leadership positions, and most likely to command African respect.[4] The concept contained standards of probity and integrity, and implied a capacity for inspiring trust and responding to loyalty. It possessed elements of feudalism, chivalry, and aristocracy.[5] Its chief component was the definition of relations with inferiors and subordinates in terms of responsibility. With its hierarchical implications it indicated an obvious code of conduct in contact with 'primitive', 'inferior', or 'child' races.[6]

While the ideal gentlemanly pattern of behaviour must be distinguished from actual behaviour, it remains true that the image of the gentleman and the general emphasis on a moral basis for race contact were powerful conditioning factors in dictating norms of conduct towards Africans. It is particularly noteworthy that a high standard of conduct was felt to be an aspect of British national character. Englishmen, as Rowley informed a suspicious African chief, 'do not lie'.[7]

The second bundle of character traits in the possession of which

WHITE MEETS BLACK

Britons took especial pride laid particular emphasis on energy and courage. These early pioneers, men who relied on their own abilities to overcome danger, difficulty and hardship in the midst of an environment hostile to their efforts, were disturbed and felt it to be effeminate when carried in a hammock due to malaria, or more generally when their physical endurance was reduced by sickness. As Joseph Thomson phrased it, the rule for the traveller 'was simply to keep marching on as long as my legs would sustain me, and never to be carried by my men'.[8] Significantly, the qualities necessary to meet these rugged frontier conditions were at times regarded as indicative of the vitality and greatness of Britain.[9] When James Stewart arrived at the mouth of the Zambesi, he recorded proudly in his diary:

> I don't wonder, though, we as a people are the envy and astonishment of most other nations. Here in this particular case we come leaping ashore in sight of these miserable wretches of Portuguese with as much energy and activity as would almost eat them up. We walk about on the shore as if they [?it] were all our own, bring ship on ship laden with goods, and the means and appliances of civilization as well: while they, poor dogs, are dragging on an existence scarcely better than that of the miserable Africans they have made tenfold more wretched than they were before.[10]

Incident after incident reveals that displays of energy and courage became obligatory for Englishmen in contact with backward races. The famous hunter, F. C. Selous, doubted the validity of the widespread British belief that Africans despised the Portuguese and admired the superior strength and energy of Northern Europeans. In a thoughtful passage he argued that when Africans

> see an Englishman, Scotsman, German, or Swede—for all North Europeans I have observed have the same pride of a dominant race, that forbids them to show any sign of effeminacy before an inferior people—walking in the hot sun, bare-armed, and often bare-legged, carrying his own rifle and running after game, they think he only does so because he is poor and cannot afford to pay men to hunt for him, and porters to carry him in a palanquin, sheltered from the heat of the sun by an awning or an umbrella; and they despise him accordingly and contrast him unfavourably with the more effeminate and luxurious Portuguese, whom they respect more than the Englishman, because they think he is rich enough to afford comforts which the latter cannot command.[11]

Shortly after penning these reflections Selous recorded how he swam into a river to get out two dead hippos which his porters had refused to retrieve. As the river was full of crocodiles he admitted his folly, 'but one cannot help it, if only to show the natives that a white man will do what they dare not attempt'.[12]

It immediately becomes apparent that, psychologically, much of the white man's burden was found in a demanding, self-imposed standard of conduct. Superiority had to be constantly proved to oneself and to the watchful African. To the individual, superiority was not a permanent gift, but a possession contingent on justification in action. This meant that the ordinary human failings of indecision and lack of self-control had to be stifled.

This is revealed in striking fashion in Stanley's writings. His famous meeting with Livingstone at Ujiji provides one example. When he came in sight of the renowned missionary traveller, though he was greatly excited, Stanley restrained himself, for 'I must not let my face display my emotions, lest it shall detract from the dignity of a white man appearing under such extraordinary circumstances.'[13] The historic greeting with outstretched hand, and the formal 'Dr. Livingstone I presume', reflected the psychology of racial superiority. Before an inferior race it was necessary to present a façade of authority, power, and coolness in order to prevent the African from seeing those aspects of human nature which, by indicating emotionalism or indecision, might derogate from the assumed attributes of leadership and the aloofness of superior racial status.

Another incident in Stanely's candid writings revealed the impact of a self-image of superiority on conduct. Unwilling to admit that he was tired and ill, he left Unyanyembe for Lake Tanganyika while still weak from fever. It was a most 'injudicious act', but he was compelled to carry on for he had 'boasted ... that a white man never breaks his word, and my reputation as a white man would have been ruined had I stayed behind, or postponed the march, in consequence of feebleness'.[14] The precarious edifice of Stanley's white prestige was felt to be integrally related to the unfailing performance of one rashly promised act. A rational response to the fever which afflicted him was rendered impossible by his feeling of racial membership.

This pride of a dominant race with its associated fear of effeminacy produced a revulsion against weakness in oneself and in others. It placed a disproportionate emphasis on the masculine virtues of courage and vigour; it emphasized leadership at the expense of equality, and authority and obedience at the expense of intimacy and casual and easy association between the races. In Livingstone these traits were balanced and offset by gentler virtues and restrained by Christianity. Stanley's comment is appropriate:

> In him, religion exhibits its loveliest features; it governs his conduct not only towards his servants, but towards the natives, the bigoted Mohamedans, and all who come in contact with him. Without it, Livingstone, with his ardent temperament, his enthusiasm, his high spirit

and courage, must have become uncompanionable, and a hard master. Religion has tamed him, and made him a Christian gentleman: the crude and wilful have been refined and subdued; religion has made him the most companionable of men and indulgent of masters—a man whose society is pleasurable.[15]

In other Britons, such as Samuel Baker, an idealization of energy and vigour unaccompanied by compassion, humility, or feelings of humanity, degenerated into an amoral use of brute force and power. To a lesser extent, this was also true of Stanley, who was distinguished by an excess of drive and energy and a comparative deficiency of human sympathy.

2

Ideally, at a time when the gap between tribalism and civilization was becoming yearly more pronounced, relations between the civilized Briton and the tribal African should have been racially ordered within a hierarchical framework. The British viewed tribalism as the least developed form of social organization, and Africans as racially the least advanced members of the human species. African tribal systems, even those dignified as states, such as Buganda, or such powerful warrior tribes as the Matabele, did not fall within the orbit of the international community of states. The usual conventions, therefore, governing respect for rulers, regard for alien customs, and a willingness to accept existing authority and prevailing social values, applied only to a very limited extent to Britons in Africa.

The closest approximation to British assumptions of a legitimate racial order was found in the master-servant relationship of caravan travel. The description of Pilkington, C.M.S., is revealing:

> The first thing on arriving in camp is, for us, who have carried nothing heavier than an umbrella and a monstrous hat, to rest—for the men, who have carried a load of 50 lb. to 60 lb. (sometimes more), generally on their heads, to fetch firewood and water.... The contrast will have struck you already. The people, to whom we have come to preach, lie on the ground or in a reed or grass hut, eat rice and a bit of dried fish ... carry a load under a burning sun for ten or twelve miles which I should be sorry to carry for a mile in England, walk barefoot on the scorching ground, while we live in grand houses or tents (palaces to these people), sleep on beds as comfortable as any at home, eat chickens (carried in a box alive), preserved meat, green peas (preserved), tea, cocoa, biscuits, bread, butter, jam.[16]

Pilkington was doubtful about the contribution of such distinctions to the missionary cause. Few Britons, however, bothered to question such a natural distribution of privilege and authority. As Stanley indicated there was considerable exhilaration in the lonely exercise of power which was the lot of the caravan leader. Especially revealing was the evolution of the stereotype of the faithful porter. The quality of faithfulness was one of the most significant virtues of Livingstone's Makololo. His 'faithfuls' acquired a renown and popularity in Britain shared by few other Africans. Livingstone reciprocated the fidelity of his men by a sterling feeling of responsibility. This was especially evident on his arrival on the west coast at Luanda after months of arduous travel. Sick and weary, he refused a proffered return to Britain. Instead he plunged back into the interior to return his 'faithfuls' to their wives and families in Makolololand. This, equally if not more than his achievements as an explorer, moved the heart of the British public.[17] Here was an ideal relationship—that of a Christian gentleman and his heathen followers participating in a mutual relationship of responsibility and trust in which leadership rested squarely on the shoulders of the British Christian.

In part the concept of the faithful porter implied a division of function between the leadership qualities of intelligence and organization and the secondary qualities of muscle and brawn, the possessors of which obeyed orders and implemented the plans of others. Cotterill, who wrote of the 'courage and devotion of his "faithfuls" ', significantly noted that some of the Zanzibar and Wanyamwesi porters

> are magnificent developments of the human animal, with herculean frames.... Endurance rather than *élan* is the distinctive quality of the African—and it is the quality which the white man in Central Africa finds, by experience, to be the most useful.[18]

In more general terms, the 'faithful' was the good servant. Faithfulness is a quality for subordinates. The recurring praise for the porter for his qualities of cheerful endurance, physical strength and faithful obedience was not only a tribute to hardy men without whom the opening up of Central Africa would have been impossible, but a revelation of the naturalness of white leadership. Praise for faithful followers was implicitly praise of whites who had elicited such fidelity.

In any case, the concept of the faithful porter was somewhat mythical. It nearly always appeared in the closing pages of travel books. The preceding pages clearly indicated that the relation between the European leader of a caravan and his African 'faithfuls' was, in part, one of threatened strikes and revolts on the one hand, and the frequent applications of physical force on the other.

3

A typical incident was related by Harry Johnston. On the first day's march inland from Mombasa to Kilimanjaro his men refused to go the thirty miles he had planned.

> Now was the crisis in which my authority was to be asserted or for ever to be subordinated to the men's caprices. The Zanzibaris were waiting to see how I should act, and would gauge my disposition by the way in which I met my first difficulties. . . . I called on one man to pick up his burden and take the road. He promptly and curtly refused, and as quickly my Indian servant had him by the heels, whilst I soundly trounced him with his own walking stick. . . . Whilst the recalcitrant porter was still screaming abjectly for pardon, and I was still gravely counting the strokes of the wand—eight!—nine!—ten!—eleven!—the other men had hoisted their loads on their bullet-heads, and were falling into file along the narrow path, leaving my servant and myself alone with the victim of our wrath.[19]

This type of flogging was standard procedure on caravan travel. Missionary expeditions differed, if at all, only in degree.[20] One independent critic, active in missionary circles, noted a series of beatings administered by Bishop Hannington, C.M.S., and vigorously declared:

> if it is agreed, that an expedition cannot be carried on, unless the leader of it commits day by day acts of brute violence, the reply is, that *Missionary expeditions had better not be undertaken*. If Missions can only be worked by methods, which no supporter of the Mission would dare to state in detail on a Mission-platform, then Missions had better not be undertaken.[21]

Although Cust's criticisms were undoubtedly salutary, it is essential to place the use of force in its historical and social context. In the first place Africans were undoubtedly accustomed to a fair amount of physical brutality. The absence of prisons meant that physical chastisement and, among some tribes, mutilation were standard forms of punishment. Secondly, within Britain, in the armed services, in the workhouses, and in the schools, physical maltreatment was far from being infrequent. The sensitivity of the mid-twentieth-century observer to racial questions does not provide a wholly satisfactory basis for judgement of the actions of nineteenth-century Britons. In a sense it may seem almost perverse to deal with the minor harshness attending early race contact in Central Africa in comparison with the cruelties of the slave trade and tribal war, or the treatment then being meted out to other 'primitive' races in North America, Australia, or the Islands of the Pacific. The use of force is examined here not in any attempt to exaggerate the inhumanity of these early pioneers, but for the sound reason that physical brutality indicates a breakdown in human relations deserving of consideration. Admittedly, kicks and blows are qualitatively different from the genocide of the Tasmanian aborigines. They do not become, for that reason, desirable or praiseworthy.

The use of force was a response to various inciting factors.[22] It was used to overcome squabbles among porters for the lightest load, to stop plundering from the villages through which the caravan passed, to punish captured deserters, to stop stealing from the caravan supplies, to force the men to go on when they wished to halt and rest, and generally for the innumerable types of disobedience which seemed to challenge the authority of the white leader or imperil the achievement of his objectives. When these recurrent problems are placed in the context of fear, loneliness, and frequent bouts of fever, it is not surprising that there was more than an occasional application of a whip across the bare shoulders of porters.

Imperfect communication, either due to language difficulties or cultural misunderstandings between Briton and African, often led to a resort to force. More important was the basic difficulty of getting African co-operation in types of conduct based on European values. Force, as a universal, simple, rapid, and easily understood method of communication, inevitably occurs when differing cultural values make voluntary co-operation difficult to achieve. Cultural differences not only made the use of force helpful to the accomplishment of European objectives, but also made it easy for its employers to assume that the usual conventions of human relationships could be partially abrogated in contact with members of alien and inferior cultures. Feelings of sympathy and identification suffer a marked diminution in intensity as they are applied beyond the accepted boundaries of cultural, racial, or national membership.

The essential argument for flogging on caravans was that it worked. Surgeon Parke stated categorically that whatever might be suggested 'by members of philanthropic African societies' in England, eager to extend the 'rights of humanity', there was no possibility of getting a body of Zanzibar carriers across Africa 'without the use of a fair amount of physical persuasion'. In its absence the men became 'utterly reckless' and forgot 'all discipline'.[23] This was not merely special pleading. Joseph Thomson, in a burst of youthful idealism, resolved to establish an almost egalitarian relationship with his men, to take the porters into his confidence, and to replace flogging with fines levied on the disobedient. He was met with a strike and a demand for the restoration of the whip, as his men preferred the ephemeral pain of flogging to the device of fines which could result in a penniless return to Zanzibar. Thomson thenceforth flogged with vigour. On his next journey through Masailand he inflicted disciplinary measures rigorously from the outset, asserting that this reduced the necessity for later harshness.[24]

The use of force was also justified by a variety of beliefs which implied its special suitability for Africans. There was the assumption that since African society was ruled by a despotic application of force, Britons were justified in conforming their practice to local custom.[25] E. D. Young, for example, admitted that the Makololo were despots, but he added:

> I care not who the man is that has to govern in Africa, his rule in this respect must be the same; that is, he *must* assert his own authority and require obedience. He will be called 'Tatu' [father]; then let him behave like a father to his children, and when the rod is necessary let him not spoil the child because he happens to be the head of a Missionary settlement or the leader of . . . [a missionary] . . . expedition. . . .[26]

The parent-child analogy, indeed the whole set of hierarchical concepts through which relations between the races were viewed, gave the right of authority and punishment to the white man. Conciliation, with its implication of a measure of equality between the two parties to the relationship, was regarded as a sign of weakness and as racially degrading. This attitude was put succinctly by Lugard in his discussion of the best British policy in the small-scale war with half-caste Arabs and their African allies at the north end of Lake Nyasa in the late eighties. He was convinced that British experience had proven that no argument prevails with 'Natives' in arms as well as superior force. The best policy, therefore, was to 'thrash them first, conciliate afterwards; and by this method our prestige with the native tribes would be certainly greatly increased, and subsequent troubles with them would be less likely'.[27]

Lugard's argument fitted in with the pervasive belief that Africans were ungrateful for favours or kindnesses bestowed on them. Missionaries chronically complained of the absence of gratitude for the medical care they lavished on Africans. The implication was clear. 'I have invariably remarked,' observed Henry Faulkner, 'that the more you bestow upon a black man, either in specie or kindness, the less he does for you, and the more dissatisfied he will be, and *vice versa*.' The proper policy, therefore, was one of firmness, so that Africans would clearly understand who was the master. They could then be led 'easily, as natives are when made to feel the power and authority of their employers'.[28] The same argument was used by Burton who asserted that to the East African, gratitude 'is not even a sense of prospective favours; he looks upon a benefit as the weakness of his benefactor and his own strength'. He felt that 'leniency and forbearance are the vulnerable points of civilized policy, as they encourage attack by a suspicion of fear and weakness'.[29] It is significant that even gentle, kindly men such as Bishop Knight-Bruce reluctantly reached similar conclusions.[30]

Given this set of beliefs, it is somewhat surprising that brutality was not more widespread. In the employer-employee relationship of the caravan leader and his porters the use of physical force was a standard supplement to the arts of persuasion, camaraderie, and equitable treatment, which helped to elicit voluntary allegiance to the white leader. In general, however, British travellers were reluctant to use force to bulldoze their way past obstructive chiefs, and often they prided themselves on their self-restraint and on the absence of bloodshed which accompanied their explorations.[31]

The most striking exception to this was Henry Morton Stanley. When he fought with the Taborah Arabs against the Wanyamwesi chief Mirambo, he hoped the chief would attack so that if he came within the range of an American rifle he could discover 'what virtue lies in American lead'.[32] On his second trip, Stanley engaged in the notorious Bumbireh Island episode in which his elephant gun proved more than a match for the hapless Africans, who were cut down by the dauntless journalist turned explorer. He finished his trip in a blaze of gunfire, graphically described in his dramatic florid style, as he travelled down the Congo River to unlock yet another of Africa's secrets. It was not without justice that the British socialist H. M. Hyndman and Colonel Henry Yule characterized his efforts as a 'system of exploration by private war'.[33] Stanley was unique not only in his willingness to employ force, but in the lustful pleasure he seemed to derive from so doing. After lashing and chaining a runaway thief he reflected:

> I was becoming wise by experience, and I was compelled to observe that when mud and wet sapped the physical energy of the lazily inclined, a dog-whip became their backs, restoring them to a sound—sometimes to an extravagant activity.[34]

There were, as Pruen of the C.M.S. stated, only two ways of travel in Africa—the Livingstone way and the Stanley way.[35] The distinction was clearly revealed in Stanley's own writings when, on his trip with Livingstone to the north end of Lake Tanganyika, he was restrained by the missionary traveller from an unnecessary use of force on several occasions.[36] It is to their credit that most Britons preferred the slow and conciliatory way of Livingstone.

In part this was a reflection of necessity. Many caravans, missionary in particular, were so meagrely equipped with porters and supplies that they lacked the capacity to enforce their will on recalcitrant chiefs. In some cases, tribes such as the Matabele and the Baganda were simply too powerful for any caravan to attempt to gain its ends by a lavish use of force. On the other hand, practical considerations constitute only a partial explanation for the relative unwillingness to elevate brutality to the status of a policy. A sadistic delight in physical brutality seems to have been rare. On the contrary, an attitude of mind which regarded superiority as a trust had, as its corollary, the belief that power should only be used in a context of moral purpose.

In concluding this section on force, it is necessary to note that some of the most serious instances of brutality and blatant abuses of power occurred on mission stations, especially where a form of civil jurisdiction had been established.[37] Missionaries in the interior, unless they were prepared to live a life of ascetic simplicity after the manner of W. P. Johnson, frequently found themselves in the position of chiefs. In areas where social cohesion was weak, where, in Waller's words, the people were 'pulverized and triturated by the slave trade',[38] the African desire for security blended well with the missionaries' definition of their own role as protectors and deliverers. The result was a form of miniature state in which the missionaries, with no experience to guide them, became rulers of communities composed of Africans drawn from diverse tribal groups and possessed of little in common beyond a desire for freedom from the assaults of stronger tribes bent on conquest or slave raiding. The governing of such motley groups would have been a complex enough task at the best of times. In the prevailing conditions of Central Africa, and it must be remembered that such settlements tended to grow up in the areas of greatest insecurity, the task was often beyond the capacities of the missionaries. The early Church of Scotland mission at Blantyre, designed as the first instalment in reparation for the evils of British participation in the slave trade, was involved in macabre episodes resulting from the assumption of civil administration. Inexperienced missionaries, attempting to maintain law and order, found themselves passing sentences of death on Africans convicted of serious crimes and inflicting remarkably severe floggings for lesser misdemeanours.[39] Some of the artisan missionaries 'believed that the native despised leniency, and formed the opinion that the more they kicked him the more they were respected . . . an unfortunate interpretation of the servility of the African'.[40] At Frere Town, the C.M.S. settlement was the scene of brutal floggings of both men and women which shocked observers. The floggings were resorted to in order to extract confessions, and Streeter, the lay superintendent, argued that if they were forbidden, the mission might as well close down as it was the only way 'to make the native speak' of his offences. The results of one flogging prompted a visitor to assert that 'anything approaching this in the way of severity I had never before witnessed'. A second witness called the floggings of men and women

> simply brutal.... I saw two men whom I consider had their constitutions quite shattered by the flogging ... one poor wretched man bore two deep whales of the stick half round his stomach from a flogging more than two years since.... It would scarcely be believed in England that at the present date there would exist a mission station within one hundred and fifty miles, or twelve hours sail of Zanzibar, where these young Christian women could be tied hands and body to a tree and so brutally flogged, or that there could be found Englishmen who would countenance such a thing.[41]

This type of treatment was often lightly passed over in missionary publications, and it is a reasonable conjecture that it was much more widespread than is apparent from published material.

4

In addition to using force to obtain African cooperation or to protect racial prestige, these pioneers indulged in a variety of actions with the common objective of increasing their status and surrounding their persons with a protective aura of awe. A remarkably frequent device which 'never failed to produce a decided impression on the natives' [42] was to ostentatiously display rifle or revolver accuracy on some distant object. Petherick's account of his adventure among the hostile Azande reveals this technique:

> I seized a fowling piece ... and pointing to a vulture hovering over us, I fired; but before the bird touched the ground, the crowd was prostrate and grovelling in the dust, as if every man of them had been shot. The old man's head, with his hands on his ears, was at my feet; and when I raised him, his appearance was ghastly, and his eyes were fixed on me with a meaningless expression.[43]

The superior death-dealing capacity of the individual white which such incidents illustrated, and the awe with which it was surrounded, made an important contribution to the physical safety of these early pioneers.

Awe was also fostered by deliberately playing on African ignorance with respect to much of the gadgetry of western civilization such as mirrors, watches, and umbrellas. The fright of an African who attempted to catch the second hand of a watch 'was unmistakable—his limbs actually trembled', according to Duff Macdonald.[44] It was this type of fear which led Samuel Baker to assert that 'savages' could be ruled by either 'force' or 'humbug'.[45] Although not averse to force, humbug played a prominent part in Baker's African experiences. His supplies for the post of Governor of Equatoria included musical boxes, a magic lantern, a magnetic battery, wheels of life, fireworks, and silver balls that mirrored surrounding scenes. The magnetic battery was put to good use, and *Ismailia* is replete with accounts of chiefs and elders reeling over backwards after experiencing the wonders of the white man's civilization. Well satisfied with the results, Baker recommended such devices to anyone wishing to secure the attention and admiration of Africans.[46] Versions of this gimmick approach became almost standard in the repertoire of many travellers. There was the pipe bowl which could be filled with gunpowder and ceremoniously handed to a hostile chief who, after the inevitable explosion, looked upon the white 'as something almost superhuman, and respected accordingly'[47]—the giving of sniffs of concentrated ammonia to chiefs and councillors which evoked the satisfying retort, 'Oh, these white men know everything, the Arabs are dirt compared to them!'[48]—and the firing of rockets at night to shed an aura of magic protection over the camp of the traveller.

An analogous practice, the adoption of extreme forms of behaviour and attire, was often resorted to by Britons to indicate their importance and the consequent respect with which they should be treated. Before arriving at the court of one of the most highly organized and powerful tribes in Central Africa, Chaille-Long wrote ahead to Mtesa of Buganda that 'a great Prince would visit him, the great M'Tse, the greatest king of all Africa'. Attired in gold lace and red pantaloons and riding his horse he made a triumphant entrance before the chief. The stratagem was successful. Mtesa, who, according to Long, had never forgiven Captain Speke for insisting on sitting in his presence, was so flattered by this impressive entry that he granted the visitor a seat near his own while the ordinary people prostrated themselves before the new arrival.[49]

The occasional Briton who either did not try or failed in the attempt to be treated with the dignity becoming to a white man was frequently referred to in scathing terms by less compliant countrymen. The docile conduct of Swan and Faulkner, two Plymouth Brethren missionaries at the court of the Garenganze chief, Msidi, evoked the following critical comment from Alfred Sharpe:

> The missionaries treat Msidi as a great king; do *nothing* without first asking his permission, are at his beck and call, almost his slaves; he sends for them continually for trivial things; and they meekly submit. They dare not come to me on my arrival for two days, because Msidi told them not to come! They live like natives, on corn porridge and occasionally stinking meat. It seemed to me a humiliating thing to see white people taking up such a position with natives; and a great mistake also.[50]

WHITE MEETS BLACK

The basic point was simply that for many Britons a position of subordination to black 'savages' was practically intolerable, a violation of the natural order. In 1887, when several parties of white hunters and prospectors in Mashonaland experienced infuriating difficulties with their Matabele guides, Frank Johnson, the leader of one prospecting party, became almost choleric with rage at the hindrances being placed in his way. His regret that the 'polite laws of civilization' prevented him from elaborating on his real opinion of his 'black brothers', seems superfluous in view of his diary entry.

> Oh ye spirits of departed negrophilists and followers of 'Exeter Hall' if only you could feel what is felt by us today, at the knowledge that we white men and *Englishmen* too, are under the thumb and utterly in the power of a lot of black scoundrels there is little doubt that your '*brotherly love*' for niggars would receive a serious check!! Brothers indeed! d . . . scoundrels!! . . . To feel oneself under the power of a niggar is worse than being in prison and quite enough to bring on fever.[51]

Johnson noted that 'everyone talking "war" and estimating number of men required to wipe out the Matabele and the best way to come into the country to accomplish this very desirable end'. Some of the whites were in such a 'great rage' at Matabele obstructiveness that, but for the intervention of Selous, they would have killed Johnson's Matabele guides and then headed for Tete and Quilimane before an impi could be sent after them.[52]

The almost apoplectic rage which at times gripped Britons who found their plans and status aspirations thwarted by the African was more than a reflection of simple frustration. When the tribal African refused to grant the Briton the status which his racial membership demanded, or refused to fall in willingly with British goals, he denied the racial superiority which the Briton carried so proudly when among backward peoples. It was this denial of white superiority, so wounding to self-respect, that evoked the indignant fury of these pioneers.

The use of gimmicks to create awe, the attempts to be treated as equals by African chiefs, and the frequent contempt for those whites who acted in a subservient fashion before Africans reflected not only strong feelings as to the proper order of race relations, but also security considerations. It was widely believed that the numerical inferiority of these early pioneers had to be counter-balanced by a prestige and respect on which, according to Lugard, depended not only the influence of the white man, but 'often his very existence'. It was, he claimed, 'the greatest possible mistake' to suppose that influence could be acquired by adopting an African mode of existence; such would lower the European and would be totally unappreciated

WHITE MEETS BLACK

by the African who would assume it to be due to poverty and lack of social status.

> The whole influence of the European in Africa is gained by this assertion of a superiority which commands the respect and excites the emulation of the savage. To forego this vantage-ground is to lose influence for good.... [The European] must at all times assert himself, and repel an insolent familiarity, which is a thing entirely apart from friendship born of respect and affection. His dwelling-house should be as superior to those of the natives as he is himself superior to them.[53]

This anti-egalitarian approach strongly emphasized the necessity of a hierarchical framework to racial contact. By implication, deviations from this ideal were racially degrading. To men such as Lugard the redress of racial indignities was an affair of honour. While awaiting the departure of his ship from Mozambique, Lugard observed an Indian Mohammedan trader, impatient at the delay in handling his goods for shipment, behaving in an 'insolent manner', and making 'gross remarks' to the English officer in charge of the ship's cargo. 'Extremely indignant at such an affront,' Lugard took matters into his own hands when the officer 'tamely submit[ted] to be thus insulted by a native'.

> I ... told the Buniah ... that had he used one-half the insolence to me that I had heard him use towards the ships officer, he would have had cause to regret it. Thereupon he included me. Not liking to strike a native with my fist, I gave him a heavy box on the ear. He seemed inclined to show fight, for he was a strong-built man, but received another similar cuff, which effectually silenced him, but unfortunately broke a bone in my hand, spraining also my thumb and wrist against his cast-iron head. This caused me very great pain subsequently, and my hand became perfectly useless, nor did I regain the full use of it for a month or more.[54]

To most Britons any inroads into the racial prestige which Lugard so vigorously defended were both insulting and dangerous to the preservation of white security. The murder of a white man, the ultimate indication of a breakdown of prestige, was thus an event of great symbolic importance. On the coast, where the anti-slave squadron of the British navy could be employed, decisive retaliatory action was possible in such cases. In 1874 the murder of Lieut. McCausland was followed by the destruction of the village in which the incident occurred, without even the courtesy of informing the Sultan.[55] In another case, when villagers between Tanga and Mtangata attacked and fired on British sailors trying to arrest the crew of an alleged slaving vessel, their village, this time with the Sultan's consent, was destroyed when the local chiefs refused to surrender.[56]

WHITE MEETS BLACK

No such punitive action was possible in the interior. Admittedly the British Consul did have some influence among the inland tribes and among those Arabs who regularly returned to Zanzibar. It was standard practice for any party leaving for the interior to obtain, with Consular help, letters of introduction from the Sultan to the principal Arabs in the interior. Missionaries consistently attempted to use Consular pressure to ensure that their plans were not thwarted by the intransigence of Arabs or leading chiefs. Yet the coercive capacity of Consular directives was basically limited by the extent of Arab influence, and also by the willingness of Arabs, voluntarily or under pressure, to aid in the fulfilment of British objectives. This was made clear when Carter and Cadenhead were killed after becoming accidentally involved in a tribal war with Mirambo. This aroused the ire of the British Consul, John Kirk, but plans to send a punitive expedition into the interior had to be shelved due to the distance involved.[57] Murder, robbery, or serious maltreatment of a white in the interior were beyond the scope of the predominantly coastal British influence.

This meant that any indication that the sanction of awe had been dissipated to a point of ineffectiveness was felt to be extremely serious for isolated and practically defenceless whites whose security depended on African toleration. This can be seen by the events which surrounded the killing of Bishop Hannington by Mwanga of Buganda. Prior to the murder, Ashe, C.M.S. missionary, had been stopped by Mwanga's soldiers when trying to get to the south end of Lake Victoria.

> The Rubicon had at length been passed by Mwanga's insolent soldiers, and the terror with which we, as Bazungu (white men), had hitherto been regarded, seemed to have disappeared. Now the Baganda could see that we were merely helpless mortals, and that it would be an easy matter to make an end of us. Truly this was a serious crisis for us.[58]

His worst fears were realized when the Baganda Grand Council discussed what course to adopt with respect to the unwelcome approach of Bishop Hannington towards the east side of Lake Victoria. A key consideration was the fact that two original members of the C.M.S., Smith and O'Neill, had been killed in Ukerewe, and, although it had been said if whites were killed 'the country would be ruined', no such results had followed. LuKongo, the chief, was still there.[59] Hannington himself had great self-confidence and believed that Africans would not try to kill a European. It was a false hope as Mwanga, the Baganda chief, ordered his death. He was killed in Busoga. The Baganda, observed Ashe with considerable trepidation, now imagined that Britons might be killed with impunity.[60]

This type of situation was both intolerable and insoluble in the pre-imperial period. A prestige which was insufficiently backed by force could only survive if freely granted by Africans on grounds which had some durability over time. An ephemeral attitude of awe in the face of the strange and incomprehensible was inadequate to fulfil this function.

The L.M.S. missionaries at Fwambo on the Nyasa-Tanganyika plateau were faced with this unpalatable fact when the killing of Weissenberger, a traveller in the area, indicated the disappearance of that mystery with which whites had been surrounded and which constituted a 'great protection to all early pioneers'. No longer, apparently, did the Africans feel that some 'serious unknown calamity' might befall their tribe should they harm these whites.[61] The missionary dilemma was underlined by Jones. To do nothing would lead the Africans to believe that the murder of one white man did not concern other whites—a dangerous precedent—while if the missionaries did use force they might provoke an attack which they would be unable to repel. Either course would be disastrous to white safety.[62] It was one of those perplexing situations which frequently disturbed these isolated outposts of white civilization. There was no solution short of European political control.

Security considerations, by emphasizing the protective function of awe, stressed aloofness at the expense of intimacy. It is, however, important to note that contradictory tendencies were often simultaneously operative. In the same letter which noted with concern the growth of disrespect accompanied by thieving which had occurred when the Baguha ceased to regard the missionaries as 'supernatural beings and powerful wizards', D. P. Jones discussed the remarkable influence which the coastal Swahili had over the local Africans. 'I can only account for this by the fact that the Wangwana live amongst them, in a simple manner like themselves, intermarry with them, and to some extent partake of their notions.' In contrast, the life of the white missionaries was 'far above them', and, despairing of 'ever becoming like' the white man, they held his religion to be 'altogether unsuitable' to them. The solution? 'I feel sure in my own mind, if we were to bring ourselves nearer their own level—as near it as our health and character as Christians would allow—we would gradually raise them up to a higher standard, and to a more civilized life.'[63]

The prestige necessity dictated by the desire for personal security was contradicted by the vocational necessity for the missionary to make his religion relevant to the African. As Jones clearly saw, this meant making an attempt to minimize distinctions between the missionary and his potential converts so that the example of Christian living placed before the African did not appear completely irrelevant and incompatible with the material basis of a tribal existence. The argument that the missionary should mingle with the Africans, become intimate with them as individuals, understand their modes of thoughts and customs, and minimize irrelevant external distinctions, was a recurrent strand in missionary thought. The European missionary, asserted Chauncy Maples of the U.M.C.A., '*must* become an African to win Africans'. Some of the 'most ignorant of the natives', he held, even after several years of acquaintance still looked on whites as 'uncanny' beings, 'somewhat other than human, and certainly not possessing passions and feelings like their own'. Hence the missionary should do nothing to encourage the idea of white supremacy, and he should eat African food and, where possible, wear African clothes.[64]

Yet, theorists of the missionary cause usually admitted the virtual impossibility of white assimilation to African life.[65] In matters of clothing, for example, the White Fathers, whose 'distinguishing feature' was to be the sharing of the exterior life of the 'natives . . . as regards language, food and clothing', did not give up the Arab attire they had adopted in Algeria when they established themselves in Central Africa.[66] The acceptance of African moral standards was obviously never advocated, and the acceptance of African material standards conflicted with modesty, decency, health, and deeply ingrained civilized habits. Yet valiant attempts were made by some missionaries to deliberately minimize the civilized content of their material existence. The U.M.C.A. in particular exerted itself to that end.

Bishop Smythies, the fourth U.M.C.A. Bishop, ate with his fingers when dining with Africans, but was forced to admit that he was unable to manage sleeping in an African hut 'with its perpetual fire and, to say the least, not without terrors of unpleasant occupants'.[67] His predecessor, Bishop Steere, told a member of the mission who was complaining of isolation that 'the company of Europeans keeps a man separate from the natives, and no one will ever be a good missionary who cannot be happy among the natives'.[68] Maples was reported reluctant to have tables at Likoma, for had not Bishop Steere always been happy to do his writing on an upturned box?[69] The supreme U.M.C.A. exponent of simplicity, however, was the Oxford-educated ascetic and iconoclast Wm. Percival Johnson who spent half a century, mainly on the east side of Lake Nyasa, eating African food, living in African huts, and generally accommodating himself to the spartan simplicity of an African existence. 'There was no use in presenting Johnson with anything,' stated Robert Laws, 'for he would give it away to the natives.'[70] He scorned ostentatious church buildings mushrooming up in the midst of African poverty, cogently asking who was to provide for their eventual maintenance.[71] An admirer of African culture, he saw a purified and revivified tribalism moving forward as a more desirable goal than the westernization of Africa and the Africans.[72]

While the U.M.C.A. was partially unique in this respect, there was a general difference in attitude to the African displayed by missionaries. The implantation of new beliefs and values necessitated long and detailed relationships with individuals which could not be satisfactorily undertaken on a basis of authority or force. Especially in the early years when conversions were few and administrative problems insignificant, there was a high degree of intimate and personal missionary contact with Africans.

5

For a predominantly youthful male group the question of sexual relations with African women was of obvious interest. Yet, except for veiled missionary allusions to the immoralities of traders and hunters, Victorian reticence dictated silence on the subject. In his private journals Livingstone remarked that he could not imagine any European being so captivated with an African woman 'as to covet criminal intercourse'. He had never met 'a beautiful woman among the black people'. A few were 'passable', but 'none at all to be compared to what one may meet with among English servant girls'.[73] Livingstone's patriotic views were somewhat untypical. Differences of skin colour were quickly forgotten, and seem to have played little part in attitudes to African appearance.[74] It is also worth noting that British stereotypes of African facial features were almost exclusively derived from the centuries' long association with the west coast, in particular the Gulf of Guinea. The physical features of the Central African, especially the Nilotic and Hamitic people, were often favourably compared with the negroid characteristics of everted lips and wide nostrils.[75] To many Britons the African maiden was not without her physical charms. The artist Thomas Baines commented that the young Matabele women 'moved or stood with unembarrassed ease and freedom, in attitudes which a sculptor might long to witness, while their forms were in many instances sufficiently perfect to serve him as models of beauty'.[76] Frank Mandy, writing of the same tribe, asserted that the women were 'as a rule pleasant looking and beautifully formed. Grown up maidens expose the "human form divine" in all its naked loveliness.'[77] While such rhapsodic comments were not common, there was fairly widespread agreement that African women, if not disfigured by the lip-ring or worn out from frequent child-bearing, were physically attractive. They were also, in some areas at least, readily available.[78] No missionary faithful to his calling could ever consider accepting the offer of an African wife.[79] Among other whites less concerned with questions of status, there was a much greater willingness to submit to the importuning of African maidens, and to accept chiefly offers to provide sexual gratification on a permanent or temporary basis.

The readiness to accept such offers was doubtless conditioned by a fairly widespread view of an abandoned sensuality as typical of African women. Burton, an expert on erotica, claimed that as usual

> in damp-hot climates ... the sexual requirements of the passive exceed those of the active sex; and the result is a dissolute social state, contrasting with mountain countries, dry-cold or damp-cold, where the conditions are either equally balanced or are reversed.[80]

Not only was a hot and humid climate regarded as conducive to sexual excess,[81] but the comparative nudity of African women was in itself productive of sexual excitement among white men.[82]

For obvious reasons it is difficult to obtain reliable information on the sexual aspect of race relations, especially when travel was in isolated areas and only the writer's own account exists.[83] Yet sufficient data are available to indicate that abstinence was not widespread among unmarried traders and hunters. In the absence of white women and removed from the social pressures of their own culture, a temporary or permanent alliance with an African woman was a natural, almost inevitable response. Among some whites there was a partial equation of frontier life, up to and including the early years of white administration, with sexual freedom and indulgence.[84]

The British response to the opportunities for sexual gratification across the racial line depended on several variables. The main determinants seem to have been the closely related factors of vocation and status feeling. The missionary was prohibited by his ethical code and his racial pride from sexual intercourse with African women whether within or without the marriage bond. His negative response was also determined by the requirements of the home society financing his endeavours. Head Office control was maintained by regular correspondence and by the fact that moral dereliction could result in disgrace and dismissal for the errant missionary. In positive terms the link with a base in Britain enhanced the missionary's feeling that he was an emissary with a specific task, a representative of a religious society whose moral and spiritual values it was his function to spread. Secular whites were more prone to regard Africa as a no-man's land in terms of moral conduct. Their existence was not predicated on adherence to any special system of ethics, the violation of which could result in personal disgrace and dismissal by distant directors sitting in London board rooms. The explorer, admittedly, often saw himself as one whose actions would redound to the credit or discredit of his nation; but the ordinary traders and hunters were under no vocational obligation to regard themselves as religious or cultural representatives of the west. From one viewpoint they had less to sustain them in adherence to a European moral code. From another there was less to restrain them from a partial 'lowering of standards' if they felt so inclined. Intimate contact, ranging from ephemeral sex encounters to a reasonably stable relationship with an African woman, was not only permissible, but to the resident trader might well be a commercial asset.[85]

The non-missionary attitude to sex can best be illustrated by the way of life of the bachelor element among the small semi-resident body of gregarious adventurers who traded, hunted, and performed odd jobs in Matabeleland. Their entire way of life—a convivial, carefree, uninhibited existence characterized by indifference to African backwardness and a comparative absence of concern with status problems—deserves mention due to its marked contrast with that of the missionary. Their life in the midst of tribalism beyond the bounds of white power facilitated the dropping of loosely held cultural conventions. There was little of that fear of 'going native' which was the gnawing worry of the missionary. These adventurers did not see Africa as a testing ground for the preservation of their own moral standards, nor as an area to be saved for the forces of Christendom and western civilization. A plentiful supply of beer and a willing coterie of Matabele maidens were part of the good life. They took life as they found it, and while they felt superior to Africans, they did not let their feelings inhibit the pleasures and consolations which casual sex and bouts of drinking could bring. They were pragmatic rather than idealistic and their morals were adaptable. Although their personal relations with missionaries seem to have been cordial, they were, on the whole, probably antagonistic to missionary principles and tended to be cynical about attempts to convert the Matabele.[86] Significantly, they circulated a considerable number of anti-missionary jokes, in many of which Lobengula was shown as discomfiting the missionaries.[87]

Among these whites, especially those living at the chief's kraal, Matabele beer flowed freely. As one of them reminisced:

> When I was living [in Matabeleland] I used to have a cup of coffee in the morning only. After that it was Kaffir beer all day long. We all drank it freely. It was good beer. The best beer was made of Kaffir corn. Made of mealies it was too sweet.[88]

It was a free and easy and, at times, a dissolute life.[89] In 1891

J. S. Moffat claimed that drunkenness was regarded 'as a rather commendable frolic, so long as a man does not get the horrors'. He stated that outside of the government camp and the mission stations there was barely a man 'who had not one native concubine at least'.[90] Westbeech, the famous ivory trader, periodically went down south to Hopetown or Potchefstroom with his colleague 'Elephant' Phillips. As long as the proceeds of their ivory lasted, they would 'paint the town red', occasionally ending up in prison. One of their acquaintances claimed they could have made fortunes, but they rarely saved anything and usually started off on their trips in debt for all their trading goods. 'What good-hearted, jovial fellows they all were, honourable and brave, and enjoying their lives to the full.'[91] As far as profits were concerned, they had a precarious existence. J. S. Moffat doubted if any of the traders' stores paid 'in a proper sense'. Gifts had to be given to the court people, and the chief often took large quantities of goods without paying for years, if at all. Moffat felt that the traders who came in with a waggon or two of goods, sold out, and left were more successful than the resident traders.[92] But it is doubtful if many of these adventurers were ambitious commercially. One of the early concession seekers recalled: 'You did not require money here in those days. We lived on each other. A man would come and stay with you for a year and you thought nothing of it.'[93]

Their carefree attitude extended to the field of sex. They had no compunctions about sexual intimacy either casually or on a long-term basis.[94] Nor did the Matabele. Moselekatse was 'rather fond of annoying the missionaries by keeping them at his kraal for several days at a time, and offering them girls to compensate for the absence of their wives'.[95] The open status which inter-racial sexual intercourse attained is illustrated by the experience of Vaughan-Williams in 1889. On entering Matebeleland he was struck with the beauty of the young girls who were 'far from shy' and, he was informed, would offer themselves to any white man for two yards of blue cloth. Young girls tried to crawl into bed with the visitors. They were 'very persistent and seemed insulted when we cleared them off'. On another occasion Lobengula sent them three 'young, well set-up Matabele girls . . . [who] . . . looked like bronze statues'. By his own account he seems to have spent much of his time in warding off the attempts of 'these maids' to break down the resolve of the uncooperative visitor.[96] Other whites were more cooperative, and by 1890 miscegenation had so progressed that Lobengula called a meeting at Bulawayo 'of all the men, women and girls to discuss the subject of fornication' as he was becoming concerned about the number of half-caste children. The women, when accused of prostitution, were reported to have replied that the men sent them to the whites and 'then collared all the produce of their sins'. Sam Edwards, who had known the Matabele for more than thirty years, felt that the meeting would be of no avail for the girls 'must have limbo and beads and will risk their bodies to have them as per usual'.[97]

The existence of widespread moral laxity is confirmed by the correspondence of J. S. Moffat, British agent at Bulawayo from 1889 to 1892. A former missionary, he referred again and again to the 'abominably filthy' lives of the whites, 'living almost like natives, thinking their thoughts and imitating their ways'. In describing them individually he used the following terms—'utterly demoralized'; 'a mere native'; 'a very low lived man'; 'keeps a considerable native harem'; 'has some sense left and is not so saturated with Kaffir beer as most'; 'a moral invertebrate'; 'a drunken debauched life . . . capable of any falsehood or treachery'.[98] This language was no doubt unduly strong for Moffat saw these whites as barriers to the spread of the gospel, and as indulging in practices degrading to the white man. The extent of miscegenation, however, is not in question.[99]

6

While some of the traders, hunters, and explorers travelled with their wives, the main feminine element in British contact was found in missionary wives. The missionary, knowing the trials of an African existence, was governed as much by practical considerations as by sentiment in the choice of a marriage partner. A practical marriage meant one within the missionary group,[100] because a sense of vocation was as important for the wife as for the husband in tolerating the unromantic drudgery of difficult pioneer conditions on isolated outposts.

The presence of missionary wives had contradictory effects on race relations. The bachelor was debarred from influencing the female half of African society for several reasons. There was the argument brought forward by Harry Johnston that the suspicions of male Africans would be aroused if he spent too much time with African females, for the African regarded celibacy as either unnatural or dishonourable. This was supplemented by Johnston's belief that the bachelor missionary was not only liable to be restless and discontented, but that he might seek scandalous consolation and thus justify the suspicions aroused by his claims to celibacy.[101] These practical reasons for married missionaries were reinforced by the fact that the missionary, a representative of Victorian middle-class values, had strong inhibitions about discussing sexual matters with women. Since sexual morals were vital to his ethical code, this left a deep gap in the scope of his influence in African society. The frequent use of this argument in missionary requests for permission to get married indicates its importance.[102] From this viewpoint, the presence of dedicated missionary wives undoubtedly broadened the scope of missionary contact, although sisterhoods in the Catholic manner or devoted single women might have served equally well. A slightly different argument was that, at least in some tribes, the married missionary was held in 'higher estimation . . . by the natives than single'[103] and theoretically, therefore, possessed a greater influence than his bachelor colleague. In addition, the missionary himself was undoubtedly more settled if married and surrounded by his family.

These advantages were more than counterbalanced by other factors. The arrival of a wife was a mixed blessing in its contribution to the practical business of a mission station. The argument of Sir Bartle Frere, that marriage was a net gain to the missionary society for a missionary couple could do the work of more than two persons,[104] rested on the dubious assumption that the wife would be in good health and so bring strength to the mission cause. In reality, recurrent pregnancies followed often by miscarriages or especially difficult childbirth, meant that sickness and death were frequent. As Mary Moffat wrote, in consoling another missionary wife who was ill while nursing her child, 'it seems to be the lot of missionaries' wives to suffer from debility in this country, and thus we are much called to the exercise of passive graces'.[105] Her son J. S. Moffat, equally experienced with the problems of family life in the midst of tribalism, was sceptical of the value of wives.

> My convictions have grown deeper for years that our pioneering work ought to be done by men alone. It is useless cruelty to take a lady into an undertaking where she does no good beyond affording a spectacle of resigned and devoted suffering: and possibly a hindrance rather than a help to the cause she would die to promote.[106]

While marriage helped to settle the missionary, and placed a barrier in the way of his succumbing to the sexual temptations of a heathen environment, it simultaneously increased his responsibilities and gave him a dual loyalty—to the society and to his wife—loyalties which were not always compatible in the midst of the rigours of pioneer conditions. The approximation to African living conditions which the bachelor would accept, partly out of carelessness, was not acceptable to a married man and his wife. In addition, more time was spent in the privacy of the home, especially after the arrival of children. Captain Hore claimed that the presence of his wife and child on the mission station was a valuable point of contact and was helpful in bringing out the finer feelings of the Africans.[107] Yet children highlighted the dilemma which bedevilled race contact for those Britons concerned with diffusing higher ethical and spiritual beliefs among Africans. This was the fear that the intimate contact which such an objective demanded might imperil the missionaries' possession of the values they wished to disseminate. This danger of cultural contagion, especially pronounced with children, is indicated in Elliott's melodramatic description:

> as the little folks grew they readily, more readily than their parents, picked up the language spoken all around them. Ingrained, interwoven, of the very texture and fabric of that language, as ordinarily used, was filth unspeakable, filth unrecognized as filth by the speakers. The native girls, hired as servants in the home, taught the missionaries' children the nastiness current in their ordinary home talk, and thought no harm of it. Of course the little folks knew not the wrong that was being done them. But the seed was sowed in that most fertile of soils, a young child's mind, and unless counteracted and destroyed, a harvest of evil was inevitable.[108]

The missionary theory that the African should be shown an example of monogamous Christian family life was seriously weakened by the fact that marriage, by reducing the free time of the male missionary, by improving his living standards, and by emphasizing the dangers of contamination of children by the moral standards of tribalism, tended towards a separation of the races.

The arrival of wives affected race relations in an even more significant way. This is revealed by an incident which occurred when A. J. Swann of the L.M.S. was preparing to leave for the interior with his bride. An intoxicated African who had been offensive to his wife received a powerful blow from the outraged husband.

> 'Is that the way you treat black men?' I was asked by my wife. 'Yes,' I replied, 'it is, when they dare insult a woman of my colour—or any other colour, for that matter.' 'It was surely not a gentleman's blow, was it?' she added. 'Perhaps not,' I answered, 'but it was a sailor's, and I regret having had to teach him manners before you; but we have to travel hundreds of miles with these men, and the remembrance of that blow will deter every other scoundrel who may desire to overstep the bounds of propriety.' I think it did, for we had no trouble of any description afterwards.[109]

It is significant that although the crudities and rudeness of a drunken African were directed at Mrs. Swann, she was scarcely less surprised at the angry belligerent response of her husband than was the unfortunate recipient of his 'sailor's blow'. The incident illustrated a general tendency for the presence of white women to arouse a strong male protective instinct closely associated with an abhorrence for the idea of possible sexual relations between black men and white women. The result was an aggressive attitude in the British male which inhibited easy social contact between the races. Baker, one of the few British explorers besides Livingstone to travel with his wife, was contantly worried at the possibility that she might be left at the mercy of African 'savages'. He viewed women as the 'emblem of civilization', entrusted with the function of ennobling man, and he 'shuddered' at the prospect should his wife 'be left alone in savage lands' at his death.[110] The usually pacific Livingstone showed an aversion to rape or indignity to white womanhood no less strong than Swann or Baker.

> We would do almost anything to avoid a collision with degraded natives; but in case of an invasion—our blood boils at the very thought of our wives, daughters, or sisters being touched—we, as men with human feelings, would unhesitatingly fight to the death, with all the fury in our power.[111]

A similar reaction was displayed by the trader Westbeech when he heard that the Mashukulumbwe had robbed Dr. and Mrs. Holub and their party before they could make their escape.

> Had the Dr. not taken to shooting they would all excepting Mrs. H. have been murdered, and she to a white woman would have had a fate worse than death, for she would have been the slave of the one who captured her and entirely at his will. Of course, I should have gone and rescued her (or tried to) with my hunters, but only think how she would have suffered before any rescue could have got to her. I expect a fair quantity of niggers would have bitten the dust before we should have been satisfied, for we have not all Christian feelings, neither are we all saints, and I know my hunters would have been animated by their master and he most certainly is *not* a saint or would not have been in this case. . . .[112]

In the period preceding imperial control the number of white women was not large, but it is still worthy of notice that no case of rape by Africans has come to light. The fear of evil-intentioned African males seems to have been based more on a stereotype than on the actual situation. This fear also contained an image of British womanhood based on middle-class assumptions of female gentility, fragility, and purity. A. J. Swann, quick to protect his wife from any indignity, regarded white women in Africa as 'delicate flowers of civilization growing in the midst of general darkness and cruelty'.[113] Baker's protective instinct was based on similar attitudes, while H. H. Johnston's advocacy of married missionaries was marred by the feeling that contact with Africa would not be without unfortunate effect on young women nurtured in Victorian innocence:

> think of a modest girl . . . hitherto shielded with such jealous care from contact with anything coarse or impure . . . in fact, grown up stupidly

innocent; think of her suddenly thrust into a barbarous country where the inhabitants are naked and not ashamed, and where they exhibit a wanting knowledge of decency which to her English prudery must appear horribly indecent; where too, the women among whom she has come to minister will . . . talk glibly to her of matters that the most depraved of her sex in her own country would hesitate to mention; consider the effect of this ordeal on a mind innocent of evil, and you will realize that this unwholesome experience must necessarily be acquired at the cost of a certain loss of delicacy . . . so this rude contact with coarse animal natures and their unrestrained display of animal instincts tends imperceptibly to blunt a modest woman's susceptibilities, and even, in time, to tinge her own thoughts and language with an unintentional coarseness.[114]

Livingstone, with a different range of experience of British society, was less prone to equate British womanhood with such drawing-room innocence. He knew only too well the conditions in which the new urban poor lived, drawn into a devouring and dehumanizing industrial system. He argued, therefore, not that British womanhood would be scarred from contact with barbarism abroad, but that poverty at home precluded 'the healthy, handy, blooming daughters of England' from becoming the 'centres of domestic affections' and gave rise 'to enormous evils in the opposite sex, evils and wrongs which we dare not even name'. It was this 'monstrous evil', the barbarism of the poor produced by the industrial revolution which was the enemy, not the potential danger to delicate souls produced by contact with African savagedom.[115]

Nevertheless, contact with tribalism was an unnerving experience to British women. After her first meeting with the Matabele, Emily Moffat wrote to her father that the men jumped about 'and with great zest struck their spears on the ground' corresponding to the numbers they had killed. 'This was truly awful. . . . I turned to my waggon, wishing I could shut out such sights and sounds. I can't tell you what I felt, such a strange mingling of pity and fear, of despair and helplessness.' When her husband was away at a neighbouring town, and she was alone with many Matabele about, she wrote: 'And oh, Papa, I was frightened, for they are wild savage-looking people, and some are rather impudent.'[116] Mrs. Hore, wife of an L.M.S. missionary, recorded a similar uneasy feeling when left alone with the Zanzibar men on Kavala Island, but their 'steady and respectful conduct . . . soon gave me confidence'.[117]

Whether these feminine reactions of fear and trepidation were wide-spread and long-lasting cannot be estimated. It is clear, however, that the presence of women constituted a barrier to easier race relations for the white male who came to see himself as a protector of female honour. It is important to note that the depth of emotion aroused by the possibility of sexual relations between African males and British females was not paralleled in the case of sexual relations between male Britons and African women. The latter was regarded as degrading to the white race and hostile to the missionary cause, but it did not produce the wrath and emotion of its converse.

While incidents of sexual aggression by African males on white women seem to have been non-existent, instances in which white males played a leading part are more easily ascertained. The patriotic bias of most writers in this period produces a disproportionate emphasis on the responsible, humanitarian element in British contact— the missionary, the explorer, and the official. There were others. The sailors on the anti-slave squadrons have been justly lauded for their intrepidity in facing danger, and their zeal in anti-slave activities. The frustration, the boredom, and the heat surrounding their work, however, seem to have been relieved by more than the excitement of the chase. The sailors on H.M.S. *Gorgon* in the early sixties were known as robbers all along the coast. They were in

> the habit of *demanding* all they want along the coast, and in case of difficulty holding out half promises of payment until they receive the supplies. They then think it a good joke to refuse payment, little thinking how dangerous and impolitic it is to exasperate semi-savages, on whose mercy they are often thrown in the course of these 'dhow hunts'.[118]

When a 'prize' was taken the ordinary sailor's first thought was loot. He would sneak below deck and break open doors and boxes in his desire to pounce upon money and jewelry, while 'the sex to whom he is naturally so gallant, is not only disrespected, but roughly handled'.[119] This same crew, which had been assisting Livingstone on the Zambesi, was involved in an even more discreditable episode. On their way down stream, they got drunk, 'broke into the huts and seized the women. . . . One woman was abused five times.'[120]

At the 1871 Slave Trade Committee hearings Bishop Steere 'thoroughly believed' on the basis of African evidence that when the sailors went on shore 'they certainly leave . . . the impression of having insulted the natives', and he had 'very little doubt that when they land they sometimes get intoxicated, and that they then behave in a very rough and irregular way'.[121] Harry Johnston made a similar discovery in 1893. Johnston, who three years earlier had publicly stated that the 'average Briton inherits a certain amount of constitutional chastity',[122] found his average sadly pulled down by the British Blue Jacket, 'a fine looking animal, but very beefy and terribly given to alcohol, while in his fleshly lusts he is too unrestrained'.

This had provoked several cases of 'bad feeling among the natives' in British Central Africa. The women did not mind, but their husbands were annoyed 'because the blue jacket bestows his love unaccompanied by any payment in rupees', in this differing from the Sikhs who, although not paragons of chastity, 'arrange all their little affairs in the pleasantest manner and are very free with their rupees. The natives think a deal of the "A-indi" as they call them,' he concluded.[123] It is not without interest that the Arabs, whose sexual morals formed the basis for many a British diatribe, were seized with 'considerable indignation' at the conduct of an Englishman departing from Zanzibar who sold his 'black concubine . . . quietly to an Arabian official'.[124]

7

Isolation in the midst of tribalism created serious psychological problems for these early pioneers.[125] Relations among Europeans and between the races were beset with petty hatreds, personal animosities, and suspicion. In part this was due to malaria.[126] When an attack of fever was coming on, claimed Dr. Robert Laws, 'things look black and gloomy, the actions of companions are sure to appear distorted, and their motives apt to be misconstrued'.[127] It was doubtless this aspect of malaria which produced what the veteran missionary W. P. Johnson called a 'very trying' and 'fairly common' illness—an abnormal degree of sensitivity and suspicion among whites who became 'firmly convinced' that others were plotting against them.[128] In addition, there was the loneliness, the frustration, and the frequent irritability evoked by working with people of a different culture. The result was almost endemic quarrelling among these standard-bearers of civilization. The squabbles and misunderstandings among whites which marred Livingstone's leadership of the Zambesi expedition were far from being unique. In the first years of the mission work in Matabeleland the three missionaries[129] were divided into two hostile camps, and, although within sight of one another, communicated by chilly epistles, copies of which were sent to England for the edification of the mission directors.[130] At Panda Matanga, the resident trader Westbeech and the Jesuit Fathers 'a few paces away' did not speak to each other for months although living in complete isolation from other Europeans.[131]

The psychological impact of Central Africa on Britons unprepared for its hardships is revealed in the experiences and reactions of James Stewart, the youthful Scot who visited the Zambesi region in 1862–3 to investigate the prospects for a Free Church of Scotland Mission. He was overcome by almost unbearable feelings of despondency and loneliness as his hopes were shattered one by one:

my heart sinks within me at nightfall. The long darkness, no candles, no books, no conversation, much heat, and stifling smoke inside; swarms of impudent rats who rattle, scamper, squeal and chase each other through all the house, dozens of bats, and all such evil things as love the darkness and come forth to enjoy it, are the only things, you feel, that impress themselves on your senses and make you conscious of the rough mode of life you lead and the distance that lies between you and civilized life.[132]

He was filled with melancholy and self-pity as his thoughts reverted again and again to the civilized land he had left. Days spent with 'learned theologians, civic bigwigs and accomplished ladies', and evenings on the Champs-Élysées were scenes which flitted across his tortured brain. When he awoke one morning the sunlight playing on the leaves of a small lemon tree brought back his childhood. Nostalgically he began to recite Thomas Hood's 'I remember, I remember', as he recalled his boyhood days when all 'the beauty and freshness of the external world came in upon me like a flood of joy'. The contrast between early innocence and his African existence was 'so painful that [he] hid [his] face in the sheet and wished not to have waked'. His world of faith and hopes was sadly shaken as, racked with fever, he travelled amid scenes of desolation and tribal war. He was assailed by religious doubts as he tried to reconcile his belief in God with the series of deaths which plagued the U.M.C.A. at the time of his visit. He had come to Africa under the influence of Livingstone's optimistic descriptions of the possibilities of mission work in Africa. By the end of his trip his hero worship of Livingstone was dissipated. In a last burst of pique and anger at his fellow Scotsman he threw with all his strength 'into the turbid muddy weed-covered Zambesi [his] copy of certain "Missionary Travels in South Africa"'.[133]

Stewart's reactions were extreme, but the sense of despair he felt was not untypical. The Methodist missionary Charles New claimed that the initial sense of novelty and interest in strange surroundings was of short duration. Then 'a feeling of inexpressible desolation creeps over you—a feeling of exile; country, home, friends, social intercourse, religion, civilization, are all left behind'. Nothing remained but a 'dreary wilderness, strange suspicious people . . . barbarism everywhere, and . . . scenes of degradation and depravity'. For the missionary such a life was 'tolerable for the sake of the great work he has in hand'. Still, when the mail came the excitement was 'intense', and a visit from another European was an event to be cherished in anticipation and in memory.

To look once more upon a white face and the old type of features, to listen to your own language, to hear the news from those fresh from the scene of action, and to go on conversing and exchanging sentiments for hours upon all one has ever held dear, is an indescribable pleasure. The experience is almost worth being purchased by a few years of banishment.[134]

The 'strange feeling of loneliness . . . as I thought of home, and those I may never see again';[135] 'this is isolation with a vengeance';[136] 'only experience teaches one *how* dull one can feel. The mass of heathenism, too, is so *depressing* when there is no one with whom to share the burden';[137] 'it is one of the greatest hardships, nay, perhaps *the greatest*, we have to endure—the long intervals which elapse between our communications with home and vice versa';[138] such references, and they could be multiplied many times, leave little doubt of the tremendous significance of feelings of isolation and loneliness in the lives of these early pioneers.

This loneliness was cultural and racial, for these whites were seldom isolated from human contact. Cultural differences between Britons and Africans minimized the scope of common interests and emptied social relationships of large areas of value and significance for both parties. Admittedly there was a real friendship between Robert Moffat and Moselekatse,[139] and Livingstone was certainly drawn to Sebituane, the Makololo chief. On the whole, however, the friendship of a nineteenth-century Briton with a tribal African was not, except in a paternal sense, capable of satisfying human needs for sociability.

What the Briton lacked was the security of the familiar. There was for example, the frequently expressed desire simply to see a white face again, and then to converse with someone possessing a similar cultural background. It was the emotional insufficiency of relationships between the races which produced the tendency noted by W. P. Johnson as late as 1916 for life in Britain to seem more real than life in Africa, and for individuals to 'more or less arrange their life round the mail'.[140] Frontier hospitality sprang from the same emotional roots. Where whites were few and far between it reflected the desire for a type of culturally satisfying relationship impossible with the tribal African. When secular whites met on the road to Matabeleland the usual practice was to open a keg of brandy and remain together until it was empty.[141]

In this context of cultural isolation, certain symbolic activities acquired special significance as indicative of an attempt not to give in to the African environment. The pertinacity of Livingstone and Stanley in shaving and keeping clean,[142] and Harry Johnston's custom of dressing for dinner in the midst of the African bush,[143] had the effect of reassuring the individual in his self-identification with Britain and civilization. The Scottish missionaries had haggis on

New Year's Day and 'observed all the time-honoured ceremonies as if . . . at home'.[144] Robert Laws laid out the grounds of the first Free Church Mission in the form of a Union Jack.[145] Emily Moffat preserved another link with home by keeping her watch at English time after she had arrived in South Africa.[146]

This type of ritual adherence is standard among immigrant groups in alien lands. By itself it is not particularly indicative of any special difference in Central African conditions. There is, however, a large body of supporting evidence which indicates that many of these pioneers were seriously worried about their capacity to retain their cultural values. There was no peer group capable of sustaining civilized standards by social pressure and the constant reaffirmation of values which springs from interaction with individuals of similar outlook. To some extent the Arabs performed this function north of the Zambesi, at least in such matters as clothing and civility. That the Arabophile Richard Burton should claim that he was always 'at home when . . . amongst Arabs' and should speak of his pleasure and relief at hearing 'once more the voice of civility and sympathy'[147] was only to be expected. But even missionaries, in spite of the gulf of religion and divergent attitudes to slavery and the slave trade, could pass the time of day with the courtly Arab. The two groups shared a fellow feeling of being civilized among 'savages', and they had sufficient in common to idle away several hours over steaming plates of curried food.[148]

Apart from the marginal impact of the Arabs, the Briton was left alone in his struggle to preserve his civilized identity. 'Under a merciless sun, surrounded by an entirely hostile nature, they were confronted with human beings who, living without the future of a purpose and the past of an accomplishment, were as incomprehensible as the inmates of a madhouse.'[149] Some quickly and flexibly succumbed. In other cases the physical absence of a peer group led to an especially strong individual identification with his own culture, and an accompanying severe self-judgement on deviations from its moral imperatives. For missionaries the very contrast in the moral outlook of tribalism and Christian civilization turned Africans into a negative reference group. Their way of life seemed to symbolize the drastic outcome of a relaxation of self-control.

It seems that loneliness and the fear of being engulfed in savagedom affected missionaries with special intensity. With traders, hunters, and explorers there was the frequent satisfaction springing from the accomplishment of specific tasks—the purchase of ivory, the shooting of an elephant, and the continual conquest of space by the traveller. Their activities showed a rough correlation between performance and success. For the missionary, years of effort often produced no visible results in terms of conversions. Missionaries to the Matabele were faced with the 'unspeakably depressing' conditions of a trying climate, an apathetic people, an absence of success, and the constant strain of overwork.[150] Not only was the missionary denied the satisfaction of recurrent achievement, but he was less free in the range of responses he could make to tribalism. To have adapted his moral standards to those of African culture would have been a denial of his function, and would have been felt as a regression to a lower stage of human existence. He could not take advantage of the freedoms, in the field of sex for example, which for many traders and hunters partially compensated for the loneliness inherent in the absence of civilized men and civilized surroundings. He was also, unlike his secular contemporaries, denied the solace of alcohol and the brief but forgetful euphoria it could bring.

In Matabeleland the missionaries were faced not only with indifference to the gospel, but with the example of hunters, traders, and concession seekers who, in many cases, had few compunctions about lapses in sexual morality and drunkenness. Their conduct was not only widely held to be seriously detrimental to the mission cause, but it also emphasized the comparative uniqueness of the missionary attempt to retain his standards and the precarious grip by which those standards were held. As one missionary wrote to the Foreign Secretary of his home society:

> Oh Sir, have you felt the horrible deadening influence of personal daily contact with heathenism? I sometimes wonder how we can follow the Saviour at all when so circumstanced, and I am compelled to acknowledge thankfully and humbly 'By the grace of God I am what I am.' Surely there can be no position more discouraging to a Christian than ours, or more calculated to teach him his utter helplessness. Here we are severed from Christian Society, and surrounded by people, black and white, who appear to live mainly, if not entirely, to serve themselves, and who shut their ears to the warnings and callings of God. Physical discomforts here are utterly insignificant, but this severance is a sore sore trial. Nevertheless, by our Master's gracious and loving help, we will labour on, and hold the fort till He come.[151]

The missionary objective of assimilating the African into the Christian civilization of the west was accompanied by the troubling fear that the process might be reversed. This fear of being engulfed seriously inhibited missionary intimacy with Africans. The point was made graphically by Elliott of the L.M.S. In describing a colleague, Reed, who in the early years of Chartered Company rule in Southern Rhodesia lived in an African hut and ate African food, he wrote:

> His life presented in an acute form the experience of all missionaries to the heathen. He was pulling them up; they were pulling him down. He

was a man at the edge of a horrible pit of miry clay endeavouring to rescue them that were engulfed below. By his rope of sympathy he tried to raise them to the solid ground whereon he stood; their dead weight operated to pull him into their disgusting slough.[152]

The description of African life as a 'horrible pit of miry clay' and 'disgusting slough' reveals the fear of being submerged, sinking and losing individuality. The comparison of a mission station to an 'island of Christian civilization in an ocean of barbarism'[153] illustrates the same fear of being swallowed up, leaving no trace of past efforts. The same point was made by J. S. Moffat when in 1888 he advocated the desirability of the L.M.S. having a man permanently resident at the king's kraal and moving with him when a new royal residence was chosen. He felt that

> Such a man, to live alone, must be deeply imbued with God's Spirit in order to have strength to stand against the deadening and corrupting influence around him. I feel it during my comparatively short stay here [Bulawayo]; and I am like a man looking forward to getting back to the sweet air and bright sunshine after being in a coal-mine.[154]

Culture, in short, was infectious.[155] The greater the proximity to and involvement in tribalism the greater was the danger of contagion. One C.M.S. missionary, Pruen, argued that if the missionary was as careful of propriety in Central Africa as he would be at home, he might live among Africans for years without being offended or confronted with an improper gesture. Further, if he evinced no interest in hearing descriptions of the 'unholy practices of the heathen' he would hear none.

> In this way he will fail to describe a part, and perhaps a not unimportant part, of the life of the Central African; but it is a loss not to be regretted. Can a man touch pitch, and not be himself defiled?[156]

Appalled by what he regarded as sin and evil, the isolated missionary was simultaneously worried that contact with that sin which he desired to eradicate was personally dangerous.[157] The problem of the overthrow of evil was rendered doubly difficult by a revulsion from contact and a fear of contamination which worked in the direction of leaving the missionary in a position of splendid isolation. This helps to explain the especially strong missionary feelings of loneliness, the significance of links with the homeland, and the missionary tendency to ask for prayers that he might be kept from descending towards 'the poor pagans' who surrounded him.[158] The human desire for a variety of personal relationships was offset by a fear of losing identity. Part of Livingstone's solution was to remain detached and find relief in the beauties of nature. The more intimately

WHITE MEETS BLACK

he became acquainted with heathenism among the Makololo, the more 'disgusting' and 'inconceivably vile' he found it.

> Missionaries ought to cultivate a taste for the beautiful. We are necessarily compelled to contemplate much moral impurity and degradation. We are so often doomed to disappointment. We are apt to become either callous or melancholy, or, if preserved from these, the constant strain on the sensibilities is likely to injure the bodily health.[159]

'I shall not often advert to their depravity,' he asserted, and went on to compare his aloofness from the sin and corruption of African society with that of a physician seeking to alleviate and cure human misery 'without remaining longer in the filth than is necessary to his work'.[160] This technique was further extended towards the end of his life when, according to H. M. Stanley:

> He has lived in a world which revolved inwardly, out of which he seldom awoke except to attend to the immediate practical necessities ... then relapsed again into the same happy inner world, which he must have peopled with his own friends, relations, acquaintances, familiar readings, ideas, and associations; so that wherever he might be, or by whatsoever he was surrounded, his own world always possessed more attractions to his cultured mind than were yielded by external circumstances.[161]

On occasion it was argued that the very isolation and insecurity of a missionary existence produced an especially strong feeling of closeness to and dependence on God.[162] On the whole, however, it seems evident that the Catholic method of sending out teams of missionaries was much to be preferred to the more individualistic Protestant approach. The isolated missionary was in danger of breaking his heart. Lonely, and surrounded by individuals who mocked his beliefs by their actions and their indifference to his message, the solitary missionary could easily lose zeal, if not actually become a neurotic.[163] On isolated stations missionaries often lived lives of strained desperation. One L.M.S. missionary on Lake Tanganyika, finding that three of his colleagues were leaving for Britain, wrote strongly to the directors: 'In a country like this, so remote from civilization and where life is generally unsafe the solitary missionary may be easily persuaded to desert his post.'[164] Later, the only man in the field, he did leave for the coast, and was only stopped when he encountered a party of reinforcements for the mission.[165]

In the loneliness of Africa men quickly realized the fragility of their personal hold on civilization. This was the real problem facing those missionaries who felt they should simplify their existence and live among those they desired to convert. Some, such as W. P. Johnson, accomplished this difficult task. Others accepted the point of Mrs.

Hore, wife of an L.M.S. missionary, when she indicated the importance of 'civilized surroundings' to assist the missionary in personally retaining the standards he wished to communicate to the African. It was not impossible, she stated, for 'isolated representatives of civilization to be swamped in savagedom'.[166]

The missionary emphasis on civilization and commerce as agents for the regeneration of Africa was more than a discussion of the mechanisms of social change. It reflected also the personal needs and dispositions of missionaries. Hence the establishment of the African Lakes Corporation to supply the Scottish missions in the Lake Nyasa area. Livingstone's thesis that no permanent elevation of the Makololo was possible without commerce was related to his belief that a mission station could not exist without access to reasonably priced western commodities 'unless the missionaries should descend to the level of the Makololo'.[167] Many missionaries felt that without the cultural support derived from civilized surroundings their teaching function could not be successfully undertaken.

Recent observers have indicated that the success of missionary efforts in Africa was related to the creation of a western environment by imperialism and other forms of western penetration which undercut the utility of many aspects of tribalism.[168] 'In a heathenism become unbelieving,' wrote Warneck, 'is being developed a receptiveness for the Gospel of Christ.'[169] It is less frequently realized that in most cases a tribal environment not only militated against African acceptance of the ethical and spiritual beliefs of the west, but seriously endangered the retention of such beliefs by those who tried to purvey them.[170] It was this problem which explains Carnegie's otherwise curious remark that the success of the L.M.S. mission to the Matabele should be measured not only by conversions, but by the ability of the missionary to remain Christian in the midst of the pressures and temptations of heathen surroundings.[171]

8

In general, the paucity of whites in this period was productive of a significant degree of practical equality in race relations. Basically this reflected the facts of power. Few European objectives, whether of trade, the grant of a concession, permission to travel or hunt, or permission to establish a mission centre, could be achieved without the consent and willing cooperation of the appropriate chief. Thus much conciliation was necessary, varying from the practice of going through ceremonies of blood brotherhood with African chiefs to the purchase of assistance with propitiatory gift giving. With a powerful and amiable chief such as Lobengula, there were occasional festive social gatherings of eating and drinking in which the chief joined heartily, concluding with 'three hearty cheers' for this jovial ruler.[172]

Yet, within this generally egalitarian context there were important differences of attitude as to desirable variations of race contact. On the one hand the absence of a white community allowed an overt indulgence in status degrading practices inhibited by the explicit racial cleavages which accompanied imperial control. Simultaneously the isolation and numerical insignificance of these early whites evoked psychological factors working in the direction of emphasizing social distance. The problem of security reduced the desirability of familiarity by placing stress on the protective function of prestige. The missionary was influenced by this factor, but vocational necessities impelled him in the direction of minimizing external distinctions between the races. Secular whites often felt that the missionary was endangering the white position by his comparative reluctance to use force. Force is a method of operating cross-culturally when cultural differences preclude peaceful and voluntary cooperation. It is, however, only useful when the modification of behaviour desired is concerned with the externals of conduct. As such it could be used on mission caravans. It could not be used as an aid to conversion. Missionaries, generally more willing to tolerate indignities and to reach agreements by compromise, were reproached for their comparative leniency. Joseph Thomson, by no means a 'hard' traveller, felt that they spoiled the African 'utterly by their mistaken methods of kindness, and treat them too much as equals'. Convinced of the necessity for clearly establishing that one was not afraid of Africans, Thomson castigated a C.M.S. missionary living a miserable existence among the Taita tribe who were taking advantage of his pacific nature. Taking the matter into his own hands, Thomson administered a sound thrashing to rectify matters.[173] A similar distaste for missionary equality was displayed by Lugard who felt that some missionaries jeopardized the white position by the poverty of their surroundings, and by too pronounced a Christian humility.[174]

On the other hand the missionary vocation did not permit the type of intimacy allowed to traders and hunters who were not restricted by rigid adherence to an ethical code as to acceptable forms of race contact. The missionary, indeed, was bitterly critical of those whites who did not emphasize the moral uniqueness of white Christians in the midst of an environment of temptation. In fact, the missionary often felt that the close race contact which his vocation demanded might lead to a contamination which would imperil his Christian faith. His very isolation made it plausible for the missionary to partially order his existence on the basis of preserving his own beliefs and values rather than with the object of spreading them to the African.

It would, however, be misleading to assume that the analytical clarity of the above distinctions represented more than tendencies, which, often contradictory, varied from individual to individual, and with the same individual over time. These tendencies all existed, but the major characteristic of race relations in this period was their flexibility, their absence of clear cut definition, and the striking variations which they assumed.

III

CONTEMPORARY ANCESTORS

1

IN 1896 F. C. Selous asserted that 'deep down in his heart, whether he be a miner or a missionary . . . [the European held] . . . the conviction that the black man belongs to a lower type of humanity than the white'.[1] The justification for this deeply held belief might be questioned on grounds of value or of fact. It could be argued that the solidarity of tribal life was preferable to the social atomization created by a ruthless price system. In the area of fact it is often possible to point out that the data verifying inferiority are incomplete and distorted by evidencing hitherto overlooked achievements of a race conventionally regarded as inferior,[2] a technique which can be supplemented by astute indications of shortcomings in the culture of those who assume superiority.

All the preceding techniques, in their fruitless attempts to compare cultural achievements, are inherently unsatisfactory. In the first place there is the insuperable difficulty of devising fair criteria of measurement. Secondly, it is logically impossible to justify egalitarian race relations by any method of comparison, whether of values or of the achievements of different races within a given scheme of values. Comparison inevitably leads to an emphasis on differences, and on cultural or racial uniqueness productive of support for racially ordered hierarchical social systems.[3]

Condemnation of ethnocentrism is less important than an understanding of its basis as a social phenomenon. In this and the following two chapters, therefore, an attempt is made to analyse the British response to tribalism in terms of the interrelated attitudes which that response displayed, of the differences between British and African cultures, and of a variety of other factors which will emerge in the discussion. Ethnocentrism is a universal, but its manifestations are related to particular historical epochs and to members of specific cultures. Statements about tribal customs reflected an interaction between the observer and the observed phenomena. The basic step to an understanding of British attitudes involves a reconstruction of the framework of concepts and values which largely determined the British selection and subsequent interpretation of events and customs worthy of notice.

2

The Briton saw his world in terms of a broad three-stage hierarchy in which the white race, western civilization, and Christianity occupied the top rungs of the racial, cultural and religious ladders of mankind.[4] Western civilization, the pinnacle of human achievement, was followed by the complex but stagnant cultures of the Middle East and Asia whose artistic and architectural accomplishments, possession of writing, long history, and elaborate theological systems of reputable ancestry gave them superiority over the nonliterate, technologically backward, primitive cultures of Africa, the Americas, and the Pacific Islands. As the anthropologist E. B. Tylor stated, 'the educated world of Europe and America practically settles a standard [of civilization] by simply placing its own nations at one end of the social series and savage tribes at the other, arranging the rest of mankind between these limits according as they correspond more closely to savage or to cultured life'.[5] This hierarchy, in which racial position was derived from cultural performance measured by western standards, applied to and evaluated a broad range of differences between western and non-western man. In religion it stretched from paganism through eastern religions to Christianity. In economics a similar scale of evaluation accorded differential degrees of merit to subsistence tribal economies, developed but arrested eastern economies, and the productive capacities of nineteenth-century capitalism. In political terms there was a clear progression from tribalism, usually discussed in terms of tyranny or anarchy, through Oriental despotism to the European state system, culminating in the constitutional monarchy of Britain. Within these broad outlines there were innumerable subdivisions in such matters as marriage, clothing styles, conventions of beauty, attitudes to truth, and divers other aspects of human existence.

African society elicited almost none of that response which Seeley has indicated was present in the first generation of Anglo-Indians entering the 'new and mysterious world of Sanscrit learning', men who 'under the charm of a remote philosophy and a fantastic history . . . were . . . Brahminized, and would not hear of admitting into their enchanted Oriental enclosure either the Christianity or any of the learning of the West'.[6] While missionaries were obviously debarred from this degree of enthusiastic appreciation, they consistently reacted more favourably and with more excitement and interest to the complexity, ancient history, and richness of Asian cultures and religions than they did to those of Africa. In India, wrote Livingstone, there were widespread 'evidences of human labour' in contrast to Africa where 'the whole country looks, for all that man has done, just as it did when it came from the hands of its Maker'.[7]

Even within the general category of tribalism the Central African did not have high status. There were no impressive ancient civilizations of the calibre of the Aztecs or the Incas which might have served to restrain superiority feelings by the magnificence of their achievements. Unlike West Africa, there was a comparative absence of large indigenous states such as Dahomey, Ashanti, the Yoruba kingdoms with their urban inhabitants, or the Moslem states of the western Sudan. Further, Central Africa had little artistic tradition compared to the west coast. There was nothing analogous to the bronzes of Ife or Benin, or even Ashanti gold weights, to stimulate aesthetic appreciation. Even such common objects as crude fertility figures and tribal masks seem to have been rare. To the European the area lacked the partially saving virtues of barbaric splendour and colour. There was, in addition, a general insignificance of size and power displayed by African tribal systems. Central Africa was fragmented among innumerable tribes, the members of which often had little more community of feeling with each other than they did with the European.

The low racial status accorded to Africans was related to a variety of other factors less easy to indicate precisely. The Bantu were never idealized as were the American Indians. In addition, the British, unlike the Portuguese, had no historical experience of a dark-skinned people with a culture superior to their own.[8] Africans were darker than other tribal peoples, a factor which probably seemed to indicate greater biological difference. The symbolism of colour itself was undoubtedly detrimental to favourable European attitudes. The white–black dichotomy in western thought has equated whiteness with cleanliness, the light of day, moral purity, and absolution from sin. Black has implied sin, dirt, night, and evil. The colour contrast was also apparent in the frequent use of metaphors of light and darkness in missionary literature.[9] The coincidence of racial divisions with the moral distinctions implicit in these metaphors helped to make skin colour an identification mark for differing levels of moral and religious attainments.

The fact that the African lived in a tropical environment provides a further intangible element. The tropics evoked stereotypes of sensuality and indolence in contrast to cold climates which signified puritanism in morals and diligence in work. The Northern European assumption that inventiveness and creativity are responses to the more invigorating atmosphere of a temperate climate was coupled with the untenable assumption that a cold climate, being more difficult to master than a hot one, indicated the possession of the sterner virtues among those subjected to its rigours.

Finally there was the long history of attitudes associating the African with the institution of slavery,[10] the ownership and exploitation of one race by another, with its correlation between dark colour and low status, between menial labour and the African race. Richard Burton claimed that since Wilberforce the defenders and opponents of slavery respectively regarded the African as a 'Nigger' and as a 'Man and a Brother'.[11] Yet the 'Man and Brother' approach, seldom more than rhetorical, was dwarfed by the paternalism of the anti-slavery and the evangelical movement. The British attack on the slave trade engendered an idea that the African was a being to be helped rather than exploited, and by exemplifying British moral superiority provided a basis for wielding authority over the African. The anti-slavery tradition was an important component of humanitarian imperialism. The humanitarian in contact with Central Africa did not advocate social equality in racial contact, but rather the use of power and superiority for morally legitimate objectives. He was not only a convinced opponent of the slave trade, but a convinced proponent of the necessity and justice of European possession of power and authority.

3

Contact with Central Africa occurred at a time when technology was creating an increasing divergence of social and material conditions between western and tribal man which had a vital influence on racial attitudes and race relations. A growing military discrepancy—later to be summed up in the slogan 'Whatever happens we have got the Maxim gun and they have not'—seriously undermined the capacity of tribalism to survive in hostile contact with an aggressive white civilization.[12] More important than the objective technological superiority of western man was the set of attitudes which that superiority engendered. The bourgeoisie, as Marx stated in *The Communist Manifesto*:

> had been the first to show what man's activity can bring about. It has accomplished wonders far surpassing Egyptian pyramids, Roman aqueducts, and Gothic cathedrals; it has conducted expeditions that put in the shade all former Exoduses of nations and crusades.

The productive capacity which so impressed capitalism's sternest critic had a profound effect on British attitudes to racial contact. Not only did it evoke a racial and cultural pride hostile to egalitarian relations with tribal man, but the British appraisal of tribalism was markedly influenced by the values of a technologically advanced capitalist society. There was a tendency for evolutionary distance to be measured by technological distance, and then, by apparently indicating the immense distance in time by which British achievements were separated from 'savagedom', to be transformed into social distance.

The technological emphasis of nineteenth-century British culture indicated a relationship between man and his environment differing in kind from that of tribalism. This provided one of the basic measuring rods for the British evaluation of different cultures. Nothing, as Lord Bryce remarked, was more surprising to the European than the fact that savages left 'few marks of their presence' on their physical environment. He was struck in South Africa by the 'feebleness of savage man' which intensified 'one's sense of the overmastering strength of nature'. The savage, he argued, had 'no more right to claim that the land was made for him than have the wild beasts of the forest who roar after their prey and seek their meat from God'.[13] Bryce's view was standard. The occasional large town in Central Africa evoked favourable comment,[14] but African life was fundamentally village life at a subsistence level.

In general, the agricultural economies of Central Africa, although they may have been efficient within their 'limits of low production', as Gluckman points out,[15] did not impress Britons from a productive point of view. Neither the physical environment nor the tribal cultural pattern was conducive to the production of an economic surplus which would have allowed an evolving growth of living standards. Climatic conditions and the prevalence of destructive insect life made food storage almost impossible. The absence of the wheel and transport animals further limited potential productivity. But even the limited productive capacities possible with existing techniques were often not attained due to the insecurity engendered by the slave trade and inter-tribal war. If a village became wealthy by its industry, stated Rowley when speaking of the area south of Lake Nyasa, it would 'certainly be attacked . . . by a less industrious but more warlike neighbour'.[16] In some areas cattle raising and agricultural operations were reduced due to the risk of marauding raiders. Population was frequently sited for strategic rather than economic reasons with a consequent diminution of economic welfare. Famine was not a rare phenomenon, and accounts of parents selling themselves or their children into slavery in order to obtain food indicate the precarious economic basis of tribal existence. An absence of individualism dulled the acquisitive instinct, and individual incentive was often hampered by the jealousy of chiefs, or by communal attitudes which might lead to the burning of the stores of a too successful farmer as a sign of public disapproval. Mineral resources were untapped. Inadequate systems of communication minimized the economic advantages of a geographical division of labour. Finally, economic progress was held to be inhibited by the tyranny of custom, the subject of one of Burton's many diatribes:

> The Wanyika ... are so bound and chained by ... custom, that inevitable public opinion, whose tyranny will not permit a man to sow his lands when he pleases; so daunted and cowed by the horrors of their faith; so thoroughly conservative in the worst sense of the word, and so enmeshed by tribal practices ... that the slave of rule and precedent lacks power to set himself free.[17]

The apparent inability of the African to dominate his environment provided perhaps the basic proof of his backwardness. This was symbolized by the reaction to the winding African footpath. 'Whatever the cause,' claimed Professor Drummond, 'it is certain that for persistent straightforwardness in the general, and utter vacillation and irresolution in the particular, the African roads are unique in engineering.'[18] The straight line, a man-made construct, was indicative of order and environmental control. H. Duff, an early administrator in British Central Africa, displayed a deep racial elation in comparing his own 'railroad culture' with technologically backward tribal systems:

> nothing could more forcibly illustrate the difference between extremes of racial character than the picture thus conjured up—the European engineer forcing with incredible toil his broad and certain way, stemming rivers, draining marshes, shattering tons of earth and rock; and, on the other hand, the savage, careless of everything but the present, seeking only the readiest path, and content to let a pebble baulk him rather than stoop to lift it.[19]

The contrast between savage and civilized attitudes to nature was subtly illustrated by Stanley's comment when building a bridge across a stream: 'be sure it was made quickly, for where the civilized white is found, a difficulty must vanish'.[20] His complacent remark on an African bridge—'only an ignorant African would have been satisfied with its small utility as a means to cross a deep and rapid body of water'[21]—illustrated the ego-enhancing aspect of a contrast between whites and Africans in this area of cultural difference. Livingstone, struck by the backwardness of a continent where one never finds 'a grave nor a stone of remembrance ... the very rocks are illiterate, they contain so few fossils', felt that race played an important part in 'the present circumstances of nations'. He charitably added that the unhealthy coast climate, which had restricted intercourse with the outside world, was probably an important contributory factor in African backwardness.[22] Yet, in a teleological fashion common to missionaries, he wondered if the 'stagnation of mind in certain nations' might not have been designed by God so that the fruits of science and invention might be associated with Christianity.[23] Other Britons, such as Sir Roderick Murchison, President of the R.G.S., and Samuel Baker, less inclined to find divine explanations for secular circumstances, simply pointed out that the 'most remarkable proof of the inferiority of the negro, when compared with the Asiatic, is that whilst the latter has domesticated the elephant for ages and rendered it highly useful to man, the negro has only slaughtered the animal to obtain ivory'.[24]

The tendency to evaluate cultures in terms of their mastery of nature was complemented by an emphasis on a complex of secondary attributes which the successful functioning of an industrially advanced economic system demanded of its adherents. The most important requirement of the emergent capitalist system was the inculcation of values which placed a high premium on labour and individual efforts while denigrating laziness. The proper attitude was indicated by Carson of the L.M.S. who, after noting that African men spent 'much time in indolence', remarked that it was inconceivable 'how the practice of that vice in the African race can be supposed to conduce to happiness in them when it makes us so miserable'.[25] Work was not only regarded instrumentally with respect to the contribution it could make to material wealth, but was, as Max Weber indicated, a self-contained moral virtue independent of its productive implications. This work fetish produced a basic ambivalence of attitude to African poverty. Poverty was regarded as a removable evil. Yet if wealth occurred without serious effort, the necessity for arduous labour was minimized, an unsatisfactory situation for those who regarded the discipline of work as essential to the moral condition of man. There was, for this reason, a nagging concern lest a too generous nature induce content, minimize the stimulus to human effort, and lead to a leisured, and therefore retrograde satisfaction with things as they were. The intrinsic value of work was revealed by Bishop Smythies (U.M.C.A.) when he noted Africans east of Lake Nyasa clearing ground and cultivating 'on the steepest, and most stoney slopes' of a mountain side.

> This seems to point to one good which may come from the evil of African wars. If all was quiet and there was no fear of these marauding tribes and yet no civilization to quicken thought, in a climate where every

thing comes to hand so readily if there are only rivers as there are here, the people would have nothing to keep them from becoming more and more enervated. Whereas the dread of the enemy leads them at the cost of immense trouble and difficulty to build their houses high up in the mountains and clear and cultivate the most precipitous places.[26]

There was also the practical point raised by a missionary among the Wanyamwesi. He argued that their material wants were too easily supplied, and therefore although 'we do believe in the power of God's spirit' there was extreme difficulty in attempting to rouse 'those who are quite satisfied with their own condition'.[27]

The general attitude was that work, more for the sake of the virtues which it fostered than for the wealth which it created, was necessary to a well-ordered purposeful life. The ethical importance accorded to work is one thing; the question as to whether or not the African was idle or lazy is another. It is worth looking briefly at this latter question, as it illustrates the extreme difficulty of ascertaining answers to simple questions of fact. In most cases Central Africa was far from a tropical Eden where nature lavished her bounties with a generous hand. It seems reasonable to assume with E. C. Hore that unsympathetic observers described Africans as lazy with too much facility. He felt it ridiculous to describe as lazy a man who had personally made 'from Nature's absolutely raw materials' his house, his axe, and hoe and spear, his clothing, ornaments, his furniture, his cornmill, 'and all the things he has ... who, although liable often in a lifetime to have to commence that whole process over again, has the energy and enterprise to commence afresh'.[28]

Ultimately, however, any attempt to discover from contemporary materials whether the African was idle or energetic encounters a morass of contradictions. The reason for this is found in the fact that Britons adjusted their beliefs as to what social reality actually was in accordance with a variety of purposeful considerations.[29] Statements about the African as a worker often reveal more of the observer than of the observed situation. Charles New, in a general and characteristic missionary condemnation of tribal life, adverted to the drunkenness, lying, adultery, and mendicancy of the Wanika and then reprobated 'a leading feature ... the indolence of the men'. A few pages later he emphasized their willingness and capacity to work—colonists would find 'willing labourers for a fair wage in the Wanika'[30]—when it fitted in with his policy of trying to induce the British government, capital, and colonists to the area. Henry Drummond underwent a similar conversion. He claimed, after a short visit to the Lake Nyasa area, that 'Africa' was a nation of the unemployed due to a bountiful nature and a paucity of wants. After a casual indication that several weeks' work sufficed to grow a crop for a year's food supply, and a remark that the women did all the work preparing the food, he concluded that 'apart from eating, their sole occupation is to talk, and this they do unceasingly'. The soporific African, a voluntarily unemployed man who did 'nothing but lounge and sleep', became imbued with increasing vigour as Drummond turned his attention to the prospects of economic development under European guidance. He spoke favourably of African workmen on the Stevenson Road designed to join Lakes Nyasa and Tanganyika. Here the African worked 'steadily, continuously, willingly, and above all, merrily', for the princely sum of a yard or two of calico per week per man. The African was not only fit but willing to work and with the aid of capital and considerate employers 'who will remember that these men are but children', Africa could be added to the 'slowly growing list of the world's producers'.[31] There was, in brief, a marked tendency for the work capacity of the African to be enhanced in the context of the advocacy of white commercial enterprise.

Specific statements of 'fact' were also related to the general attitude of the observer to the African. A negrophile such as E. D. Young waxed enthusiastic over the integrity, loyalty, and hard work of the eight hundred Africans who carried the Free Church of Scotland mission steamer, the *Ilala*, past the Murchison Cataracts.[32] Samuel Baker, however, castigated African 'lack of industry', and wrote of the absence of progress in 'natives of tropical countries' who, 'enervated by intense heat . . . incline rather to repose and amusement than to labour'.[33] Although Baker and Young were commenting on different areas, the main difference is found in the predispositions they brought to the interpretation of African traits. Baker was consistently cynical and derogatory in discussing the African, while Young saw the African through the eyes of a humanitarian which at times led him into an unconvincing sentimentalism.[34] Statements by such men are more closely related to the general outlook which colours and influences their selection and interpretation of events than they are to the objective phenomena they are describing or evaluating.

Professor Gluckman has argued that 'unless the historian knows something of tribal politics and organization he cannot even evaluate the records left by travellers, missionaries and others'.[35] It is of equal relevance to insist that statements about the African not only vary from individual to individual, but the same individual will make apparently contradictory statements about an African trait as the context changes in which the statement finds its meaning. Statements of fact are coloured by considerations of purpose.

4

The work fetish as a basic cultural distinction between Britons and Africans was related to important differences of attitude to time. To a production-oriented society, the conceptual autonomy of time emphasized activity at the expense of leisure and thus was closely related to western attacks on the laziness of tribal man. Work sense was time sense.

With the growth of cities and the factory system, seasonal time, the cyclical rhythm of rural life, affected a diminishing proportion of the British population. In the city, time was dominated by the factory, which required punctuality and imposed a regular daily routine of work, commencing and ending with the precise demarcation of the factory whistle. As man regulated his activities by time, time acquired commodity value. Equally with time, space was quantified. The reduction of time-cost by labour-saving devices was paralleled by the reduction of distance by technological improvements in transportation. Space and time were intermingled in the concept of speed with its implication that moving slowly from point A to point B was time-wasting, and therefore money-wasting.

In contrast to the western arithmetic of space and time the members of tribal society did not break up space into equal units of miles, nor did they break up time into equal units, the qualitative content of which could be ignored in an enumeration of seconds, minutes, hours, days, and years. There was, for this reason, a conflict between a clock-watching society in which time was made up of qualitatively undifferentiated units of precisely equivalent duration, and tribal societies in which time was predominantly seasonal and recurrent rather than progressive.[36] These cultural differences constituted an important source of misunderstanding and provided further indication of African backwardness. The leisured African approach to travel was infuriating to the Briton who regarded time as a void to be filled with activity. The African, lamented John Buchanan in a typical traveller's complaint, 'has no idea of time. A delay of a day —even a week—is no matter to him, so long as he has food and drink; but time is as precious as gold to the Englishman who is anxious to get on.'[37] The incompatibility of haste and African cooperation emerges again and again in these early records of culture contact.[38]

Another difference productive of misunderstanding and anger concerned attitudes to truth. According to all accounts the African was addicted to that same 'want of accuracy, which easily degenerates into untruthfulness' which the Earl of Cromer asserted to be the chief characteristic of the Oriental mind.[39] Indifference to truth, according to one writer, was 'the most striking feature' of the African.[40]

Even a cursory glance at the literature of the period indicates that this opinion was almost unanimous among Britons and did not depend on the tribe they encountered.[41] Waddell summed up the Barotse pithily as follows:

> King David said in his haste, 'All men are liars,' but had he lived here, he might have said it at his leisure. Lies seem more natural to the Barotsi than the truth, and we have noticed, if they tell the truth, that it is more by mistake than good intention.[42]

The difficulty of eliciting reliable information from Africans was especially irritating to travellers. It was necessary, according to Selous, to coldly regard 'all savages in Africa' as liars, and never to take their word without independent verification.[43]

More charitable Britons, missionaries in particular, went beyond simple condemnation and attempted to explain the African attitude to truth. Hetherwick felt that the 'natural desire to please gives rein to much untruth',[44] a view with which Livingstone concurred.[45]

> The attitude the African assumes in the presence of a stranger is a defensive one, and may be stated thus. 'Who are you,' he seems to say, 'that I should answer all your questions. Why should I tell you all about ourselves, our country, our possessions, our government, our homes? How should I know what you are, or what your object is? For aught I know you may be a spy, and may turn out a bitter foe. You think I'm a fool, but I'm not. You want to know too much; don't you wish you may get it? If you think you are going to cheat me you are mistaken. Get the truth from me if you can.'[46]

These explanations were probably partially valid. In any case a significant advance had been made merely by indicating that African behaviour was explicable and subject to reasonable interpretation. It seems likely, however, that attitudes to truth, in the same way as attitudes to time and space, were integrally related to broad cultural differences between tribalism and nineteenth century industrial civilization. In small-scale societies, the minimal division of labour, coupled with a comparative uniformity of experience among members of the tribe, diminished the flow of information required to keep society functioning. The relative absence of social change minimized the necessity for constant individual and collective adaptation, and also enhanced the utility of existing knowledge as against new information. Further, members of tribal societies could test the reliability of information by their knowledge of the informant, for communications, to a much greater extent than in the nineteenth-century west, were between individuals who knew each other. In sum, the functional necessity for reliability in the transmission of information was undoubtedly less than in Victorian Britain. Modern Europeans have been trained to think scientifically, and the spread of literacy has tended to give exact meanings to words. Many primitive peoples, in contrast, have been trained to think poetically. While ambiguity of statement is generally deplored in the west, in primitive society the opposite may be true, and 'a faculty for making and understanding ambiguous statements may even be cultivated'.[47]

The quantification of time and space and the emphasis on accurate communication were part of a general reduction of random diffuse thinking demanded by industrial capitalism. The environmental control of western man was gained by accurate observation, an emphasis on facts, and a scientific approach which created a significant contrast in orientation between the western and non-western world.[48] The machine was incompatible with allegorical or fabled approaches to reality. In a technological society, breakdown or inadequacies in communications were as serious as breakdowns in the machine itself. More generally, truth became synonymous with strict accuracy; for an interdependent technologically advanced society could not function if imperfections in the transmission of knowledge went unchecked. As the growth of impersonality in human relations and business operations precluded knowledge of the source of many statements on which individuals had to act, the Christian basis for truthfulness merged with the reliability of statement required by technology to produce the fact-conscious precision of modern man. As man was adapted to the system he assimilated and came to value the requirements it imposed on him. He acquired, therefore, particular attitudes to time, space, truth, measurement, and accuracy, which he then used in his evaluation of the African. These attitudes were given their ultimate justification by the productive efficiency of the economic system whose successful functioning they sustained. To say that Africans had neither time nor space sense, that they were lazy, that they were chronic liars, was to say neither more nor less than that they were not living in technologically advanced societies.

In concluding this section it is perhaps useful to indicate the way in which these attitudes coalesced in the outlook of one man. James Stewart, a humourless introspective Scot, provides an extreme, yet revealing, example of biting castigation of the African in almost all aspects wherein he differed from the Briton in the above-mentioned attributes. His diary of his Zambesi journey in the early sixties disclosed a loathing and disgust at African customs little short of neurotic. His attitude was unrelieved by either humour, sympathetic understanding, or appreciation of the diversity of human custom. He was bitterly provoked by African indifference to truth. When his guides wanted to go to a village to get some tobacco they were a 'set of fools' whose attitude indicated that Africans never thought beyond the present. Elsewhere he stated that the 'uncalculating brain' of the African was not concerned about the future for he never thought of building a stone dwelling, and, like the Irishman, did nothing for posterity as posterity had done nothing for him.[49] It pained him to see a 'Kafir' make an uneven furrow.[50] He went so far as to argue that the whole human family could be significantly divided into those who built square houses and those who built round ones.[51] African 'laziness' infuriated him. When he witnessed a flogging he did not feel 'much pity. So inexcusable is that inexplicable and detestable laziness that you feel, as if you would not raise your arm to prevent the lash falling.'[52] According to his biographer he 'reverenced industry as the mother, nurse, and guardian of many virtues'. He held that Christianity and idleness were incompatible, and wrote proudly of the 'energetic Western races'.[53] His attitude to work was little short of obsessional. Absence of work was the 'most likely thing to drive a man into a state of drivelling imbecility'. The greatest kindness that could be done to the African was to force him to work by taxation 'whenever and wherever' possible. In the absence of this desirable medium of compulsion his jaundiced vision gave implicit approval to Yao destruction of Manganja villages. After all, 'the loss of an African village is little loss to the owners, and none to the world generally. They can soon rebuild, and anything that compels them to work is rather a blessing than a curse.'[54]

5

The idea of progress, popularly associated with the multiplying productivity evoked by the industrial revolution, markedly influenced British attitudes to African societies. The expanding economic system which it implied was related to British scorn for the subsistence economies of Central Africa. Progress implied the enthronement of reason over superstition, and hence was relevant to attacks on the practice of and belief in witchcraft. It also meant an increasing diminution of recourse to war as a method of solving group conflict, and thus permeated British attitudes to intertribal war. More generally it gave a goal to human endeavour, undermined sympathetic attitudes to cultural differences, and, with its emphasis on change, inhibited admiration for apparently static communities.

Among Britons there was virtual unanimity that the existing conditions in the interior were directly antithetical to that continuous upward advance which was regarded as the distinguishing feature of a progressive society. Speke thought it 'marvellous' that the African had lived 'so many ages without advancing... when all the countries surrounding Africa are so forward in comparison'. He argued that a government similar to that of the British in India was essential to raise the African from the backward state in which he lived.

> As his fathers ever did, so does he. He works his wife, sells his children, enslaves all he can lay hands upon, and, unless when fighting for the property of others, contents himself with drinking, singing, and dancing like a baboon, to drive dull care away. A few only make cotton cloth, or work in wood, iron, copper, or salt; their rule being to do as little as possible, and to store up nothing beyond the necessities of the next season lest their chiefs or neighbours should covet and take it from them.[55]

Sir Samuel Baker informed a British audience that:

> Central Africa ... is without a history. In that savage country ... we find no vestiges of the past—no ancient architecture, neither sculpture, nor even one chiselled stone to prove that the Negro savage of this day is inferior to a remote ancestor. We find primeval races existing upon primitive rock formation.... We must therefore conclude that the races of man which now inhabit [this region] are unchanged from the prehistoric tribes who were the original inhabitants.[56]

These were not exceptionally unfavourable portrayals of African existence. Sir Bartle Frere described conditions in the interior as a dreary waste of barbarism where ignorant armies fought meaningless battles rendering progress impossible:

> let me ask ... any one to picture to themselves what must be the state of nations with capacities not inferior to those of European nations, who have for some thousands of years, certainly for many centuries past, not known what it is to have a stable government which should endure for even a few generations round about it.... If you read the history of any part of the Negro population of Africa, you will find nothing but a dreary recurrence of tribal wars, and an absence of everything which forms a stable government, and year after year, generation after generation, century after century, these tribes go on obeying no law but that of force, and consequently never emerging from the state of barbarism in which we find them at present, and in which they have lived, so far as we know, for a period long anterior to our own era.[57]

In more prosaic language Livingstone emphasized this same absence of stability and duration in the history of African political systems.

> A Chief of more than ordinary ability arises and, subduing all his less powerful neighbours, founds a kingdom, which he governs more or less wisely till he dies. His successor not having the talents of the conqueror cannot retain the dominion, and some of the abler under-chiefs set up for themselves, and, in a few years, the remembrance only of the Empire

remains. This, which may be considered as the normal state of African society, gives rise to frequent and desolating wars, and the people long in vain for a power able to make all dwell in peace.[58]

Fraser, Laws, and Joseph Thomson commented in similar terms on this ephemeral nature of political power in Africa.[59] In general, this picture is accepted by anthropologists. Schapera points out that the Bantu tribe was basically an unstable political unit as tendencies to fission appeared to be stronger than tendencies to fusion.[60] This structural instability was exacerbated by the insinuation of a moving gunpowder frontier into societies incapable of self-restraint in the employment of the death-dealing rifle. The initial encounters of Britons and Central Africans occurred at a time when British self-confidence was at its peak, and African conditions were at their worst.

Even without the stimulus to ethnocentrism provided by the slave trade and tribal war any judgement of African culture against some ideal of progress could not fail to result in an unfavourable picture. Initially the components of progress were derived from British culture. Further, the concept itself was absent in African society.[61] To the African the passage of time did not dictate an ever increasing pace of social change. Time was a succession of events which could be placed with respect to each other, but could only with difficulty be placed against any abstract scale of measurement. For the individual, the ageing process was the successive assimilation of a certain number of predictable experiences[62] as one moved through the social structure from birth to death, rather than a process of self-striving and improvement.

Not only did the idea of progress inject an unfavourable bias into the evaluation of technologically static societies, it also made it difficult to believe that Africans had any direct connection with the occasional impressive ruins found in the interior. Mason has suggested that it was the prevalence of the progress concept which made it difficult for Europeans to believe the Shona people could have built Zimbabwe.[63] More generally, it could be argued that a willingness to believe historical facts varies with the impact which such belief would have on the legitimacy of the status position of the person or racial group concerned. Randall-MacIver, a scientific archaeologist who conclusively indicated in 1906 that Zimbabwe and other stone ruins of Southern Rhodesia had been built by Africans, pointed out that the results of his research were not of the nature expected by the general public, for 'popular opinion had confidently settled the question to its own great satisfaction' by attributing Zimbabwe and all similar buildings to 'an ancient people from the East'.[64]

The attribution of Zimbabwe and other Rhodesian ruins to the

African could have been explained without difficulty on the hypothesis that the Africans had fallen away from an earlier level of civilized attainment, or had lost in the process of time much of the original revelation vouchsafed to man. This theory of degeneracy, however, seems to have been held by only a surprisingly small number of Britons. Rowley claimed that Africans had failed 'in maintaining the standard of life which they occupied before they broke away from the great centre of the human race'. He asserted that 'signs of this degradation' could be seen in all their institutions, and that favourable aspects of African society were relics of the 'primitive good' not yet extinct.[65] Such views, however, were of remarkable insignificance, even among missionaries.[66] Far more common was the optimism of Livingstone who saw and devoutly believed in secular progress as a manifestation of God's continuing purpose.

In his famous Romanes Lectures in 1893 Thomas Huxley indicated that biological theories of evolution afforded no criteria for judging the progress of man. 'Let us understand, once for all,' he declared, 'that the ethical progress of society depends, not on imitating the cosmic process, still less in running away from it, but in combating it.'[67] In general, however, progress and evolution were interchangeable concepts. The harsh aspects of social Darwinism, the application of the 'survival of the fittest' to peoples and races, need not concern us here, but the set of ideas and values which evolution supplied for the interpretation of the position of the African deserves notice.

Evolutionary theories applied to human societies threw the prestige of science over the observable facts of growth and advance so strikingly displayed by the white race. The theory of social evolution relegated African societies to the early stages of human existence. Cultural history was seen as an increasing divergence from remote beginnings. Those who were held to have advanced furthest from the cultural infancy of a primeval past were the most evolved. Westerners, assuming these facets in which they themselves excelled were signal proofs of advance, saw themselves as the pinnacle of evolutionary achievement. The Africans were at the other end of the scale, a position which undermined any prospect of their societies being treated as worthy attempts to cope with the problems of human organization.

The bias of evolutionary assumptions is revealed in references to the 'rudimental mind of the savage',[68] and to the Africans as 'children —ungrown, primitive, survivals of the child days of the human race'.[69] Burton argued that 'the study of psychology in Eastern Africa is the study of man's rudimental mind, when, subject to the agency of material nature, he neither progresses nor retrogrades'.[70] This evolutionary framework for analysing the position of the African led the Rev. Edward Blyden, a West Indian with an intimate acquaintance with African conditions, and a perceptive observer of European attitudes to African society, to claim that a common mistake in considering the future of the African was to suppose

> that the Negro is the European in embryo—in the undeveloped stage—and that when, bye and bye, he shall enjoy the advantages of civilization and culture, he will become like the European; in other words, that the Negro is on the same line of progress, in the same groove, with the European, but infinitely in the rear.[71]

Blyden's point was exemplified in the writings of Professor Henry Drummond. Drummond asserted that the European could find the beginnings of his own past in African life, and added that if a human being playing with a toy spade is thereby proved to be a child, a nation working with a stone axe is thereby proved to be a child nation.[72] After a trip to the Lake Nyasa area he wrote:

> It is a wonderful thing to look at this weird world of human beings—half animal half children, wholly savage and wholly heathen. ... It is an education ... in the meaning and history of man. ... It is to have watched the dawn of evolution.[73]

This 'false evolutionism', as Levi-Strauss called it,[74] rested on a misinterpretation of history, and was markedly ethnocentric, but it did hold out the possibility of progress. Drummond felt that there was nothing in African society that was not found in modern civilization, and nothing in modern civilization which could not be found in embryo in 'the simpler life of these primitive tribes. To the ignorant these men are animals; but the eye of evolution looks on them with a kindlier and more instructed sense. They are what we were once; possibly they may become what we are now.'[75]

The idea of a progressive development from savagery to civilization was much older than Darwin or Lamarck, but evolutionary theory gave the whole sweep of history a new 'scientific' basis. The belief that complex social organisms had slowly developed from simple forms was complemented by the assumption that simple forms were designed, by laws of nature, to develop into complex social organisms themselves. The evolutionary anthropologist, comments Professor Lowie, demanded a sequence of events for every phase of human activity.

> As *Homo sapiens* was zoologically at the peak of the animal kingdom, so Western Europe in 1870 marked the goal of civilization. As the single cell was the hypothetical starting point for evolution, so a savage hovering on the border of bestiality must serve as the point of origin for culture. Since, however, that primeval man could no longer be observed,

modern savages were lightly substituted insofar as they differed from Victorian Europe. . . . A fatal fallacy of all this reasoning lay in its equation of modern primitive groups with the primeval savage.[76]

The basis of this 'embryo' attitude to African societies was eminently plausible if development meant increasing size in the units of social organization, a high degree of control over nature, the growth of bureaucracies, and an increasing complexity and interdependence in the social, economic and political order. The absence of these things, by analogy, indicated a replica of an earlier stage in the evolution of western societies. The fundamental mistake of the whole approach sprang from the ethnocentric evaluation of what constituted development. In addition, the difference between and complexities of 'primitive' societies were grossly over-simplified, while the facile comparison with the origins of western civilization was unsubstantiated by historical fact.[77]

While an evolutionary approach to social growth emphasized cultural distance between Europeans and Africans, it is possible that it exerted a small counteracting tendency by bringing Africans potentially closer to western culture than were Asians. Harry Johnston, a convinced devotee of the evolutionary school, asserted:

> with all his defects the Negro is more likeable, more akin to us of the white race in disposition, and far less alien to our civilization than is the cold, inscrutable, reptilian Chinese. In the course of two or three centuries I believe the Negroes of British Africa will only differ from their white fellow-subjects in the colour of their skins. But for some time to come the forefathers of these completely civilized men of colour will require to submit themselves to our guidance and control.[78]

On the one hand their cultural achievements meant that Asians were treated more seriously and with more respect than were members of African tribes who could more easily be regarded as children, or contemporary ancestors. On the other hand, perhaps Africans were more directly on the same line of development as the west, and although inexplicably retarded, perhaps due to the very poverty of their accomplishments, were potentially closer to whites in the long run.

Ultimately, however, it is unprofitable to conjecture widely on the impact of evolutionary theories on the formation of British attitudes, for the most striking aspect of the writings of these pioneers is the comparative absence of statements with an explicit evolutionary content. Indeed, it is highly significant that the discussion and debate which took place in the periodical literature in Britain on topics of marked importance to culture contact—monogenesis versus polygenesis for example, or the controversy between the proponents of progress and retrogression to which E. B. Tylor devoted much attention in his early anthropological writings[79]—might just as well have not occurred for all the impact they seem to have made on those who were actually experiencing contact with the tribal peoples of Central Africa at the time. Theorists such as Drummond and Johnston might weave elaborate hypotheses within an evolutionary framework, but the average Briton gave little indication that his attitude to Africans was premised on any clear assumptions about the nature of social evolution. The scattered references in missionary writings are casual and usually slightly scornful. The plain fact is that the conduct and attitudes of ordinary men cannot be explained as if they were by-products of controversial writings by intellectuals on esoteric subjects such as evolutionary theory.

In reality, the student of ideas will find little to interest him in the writing of the participants in culture contact in this period. Carefully constructed systems of thought dealing with the idea of race or the relative merits of various theories as to African origins are conspicuously absent. The material is scattered and fragmentary, and it is only by an artificial process of combination that an approximation to a general picture of the British reaction to tribalism can be created.

Almost all Britons would have agreed that the African was some sort of contemporary ancestor, but this was a simple deduction from apparently observable facts rather than a consequence of evolutionary theory. The strength of social evolution was its satisfying explanatory power with respect to the cultural attainments of Britons and Africans, but it was basically a supplementary rather than a causal factor in the formation of British attitudes. Livingstone, with little interest in, or knowledge of, evolutionary theories,[80] argued that in examining African society 'we are thrown back in imagination to the infancy of the world'.[81] Another missionary stated that the Old Testament was especially comprehensible to Africans, and that his own understanding of it had been deepened in Africa. The African's language and speech, he wrote, 'are those of the Genesis children. And comparing the contents of the early books of the Bible, with what we hear to-day from the child-people of Africa, we cannot fail to realize that they are in the same stage of civilization.'[82]

The essential point was not the existence of evolutionary theories, but the universal assumption that African society, whether seen in Biblical, evolutionary or simple historical terms, was analogous to some distant earlier stage of European existence. It was the analogy and not the theoretical concepts in which it was expressed which made anachronisms of African cultures. From this viewpoint, even the distinction between theories of evolution and of retrogression was insignificant. Both relegated the African to the bottom rung of the ladder of human achievement. Whether the African represented a degeneration from a former higher level of civilization or was simply a member of the human family who had failed to advance was surely of lesser importance than the ubiquitous evaluation that he was backward. The underlying assumption of the inferiority of tribal man and his culture was the point of origin of almost all British attitudes. This denial of equality of cultural status, an unwillingness to accept the legitimacy of marked cultural distinctions, reduced inhibitions for those who sought to civilize tribal man, as well as for those who callously destroyed him.

The most explicit indication of the denial of equality of racial and cultural status is seen in the very widespread comparison of the African to a child.[83] This comparison, which contained many of the assumptions of the social evolutionists, was well-nigh universal, while evolutionary references were rare. The reason was the obvious one that the child analogy was more comprehensible and within the realm of experience of all whites, while evolutionary theory was only vaguely understood by the non-expert.

6

Before discussing the child analogy several comments on the less frequent comparison of Africans to the lower classes in Britain are in order. For the humanitarian there was a tendency to regard Africans as an external proletariat making a claim on the public conscience comparable to that made by the working classes of Britain.[84] There was the same feeling of paternal or aristocratic responsibility. Both were deprived groups, and therefore both made claims on humanitarian and evangelical sympathies. The working class was at the bottom of the internal class hierarchy and the African was at the bottom of the world cultural and racial hierarchy, a conjunction of low status which encouraged placing the two in the same category. Livingstone, for example, frequently compared the African to the British poor. He asserted that the difference in position between Africans and Britons was as great 'as between the lowest and highest in England', and that if he were not a missionary in Africa he would be a missionary to the poor in London. On another occasion he compared himself to 'those who perform benevolent deeds at home' and his porters to the 'idle and ungrateful poor'.[85] Much of the descriptive language was also similar. When Bishop Steere talked of the frightful immorality of village life—'simply incredible'—he was in fact referring to rural England.[86] Burton, after castigating the 'sterile' intellect of the East African—'apparently unprogressive and unfit for change'—remarked that 'his intelligence is surprising when compared with that of an uneducated English peasant'.[87]

The significance of this comparison should not be exaggerated, for it was not widely used. Yet if the analogy was seldom conscious, there was a sense in which the humanitarian approach to Africa tended to implicitly assume that Britain as a whole stood in the same relation to Africans as a responsible upper class stood to the lower classes within the boundaries of the nation. The tendency for race relations to be patterned after class relations was indicated by the frequent assumption that the most important qualities required of those who aspired to positions of influence and control over primitive populations were found in the attributes of a gentleman. The gentleman concept, with its implication that the utilization of power should be suffused with moral purpose and restrained from abuse by inner controls, was, in an African setting, a direct transference of a successful pattern of responsible class behaviour within Britain. It was later to reach its apogee in the District Officer whose qualifications were related less to high academic attainments than to the intangibles of character.

The much more frequent comparison of Africans to children had a general basis in the hierarchical framework of concepts through which Britons viewed the racial divisions of the world. It had also a variety of secondary supports in the alleged possession by Africans of immature traits. Emotionalism and excitability were frequently mentioned.

> Usually their grief for their friends is intense. In this respect (as throughout the whole emotional side of their nature), they resemble children. They are easily impressed, but they do not keep grief longer than grief keeps them.[88]

Burton's reference to their impulsive nature was further evidence. The African, he asserted, will sacrifice his goat for a bauble, and then, 'childlike', tire of it and try to exchange it for another.

> The African preserves the instincts of infancy in the higher races. He astonished the enlightened De Gama some centuries ago by rejecting with disdain jewels, gold, and silver, whilst he caught greedily at beads and other baubles, as a child snatches at a new plaything.[89]

A further childish trait, the absence of forethought, was a recurring complaint of the explorer whose men improvidently consumed water or food heedless of future needs. H. H. Johnston echoed the complaint of almost all travellers:

> these East Coast porters, like most Africans, are utterly without prevision, and so long as they can satisfy the desire of the moment care little

to provide for future wants as yet unfelt. On long journeys, where there is no water on the road, you will experience the greater difficulty in preventing your men dropping and dying of thirst, because, although they may have started with an ample supply of drinking-water in their gourds —quite sufficient for the time required if carefully measured out—yet, in spite of warning and prohibition, they will squander the precious fluid, quench every slight attack of thirst, and consume it all in a few hours; then, during the long waterless tramp which ensues, they will wring your heart with the sight of their sufferings, and stagger along the dusty path with dry, swollen tongues, parched lips, and bloodshot eyes.[90]

Closely related to this was the view that the African had a happy-go-lucky nature. A. J. Swann asserted that Africans practised 'no moderation in anything! With one voice they seemed to echo the ancient saying, "Let us eat and drink, for tomorrow we die." '[91] Drummond implied that this carefree approach was a product of the African's lack of civilization:

> Hidden away in these endless forests, like birds' nests in a wood, in terror of one another, and of their common foe, the slaver, are small native villages; and here in his virgin simplicity dwells primeval man, without clothes, without civilization, without learning, without religion —the genuine child of nature, thoughtless, careless, and contented. This man is apparently quite happy; he has practically no wants.[92]

The happy child of nature stereotype was not without its danger to the missionary, for it laid him open to the charge of being a despoiler of primeval simplicity and innocence. Thus, although there were exceptions, the missionary tended to emphasize the evils of the tribal state. After his first journey to the Matabele chief Moselekatse, Robert Moffat refuted those who 'philosophize on the happiness enjoyed by man in his savage state'. They should, he said, visit a heathen warrior chief and hear of the cruelty and brutality inherent in the savage condition. They would then

> blush for their own natures, and weep for the ten thousand sighs and ten thousand groans which echo in these gloomy shades, and shudder at the innocent blood shed through the length and breadth of heathen lands; and then tell the world that such are happier in their native sins of robbery, rapine and blood.[93]

W. P. Johnson devoted almost an entire chapter of one of his books to refuting the assumption that 'the natives used to live like the people in Tennyson's Lotus Eaters in "a land where it was always afternoon"' until the missionaries came and disturbed it all.[94] It was clearly more helpful to the missionary cause to portray the African as a harried being at the mercy of malignant forces.

The comparison of the African to a child, used incidentally not only by laymen but by professional anthropologists,[95] reflected the natural human propensity to argue by analogy, and to categorize the unknown in terms of the known. It rested on a common ethnocentric inability to judge alien cultures in terms of their own values. All individuals will appear as children if observed and judged from a cultural background irrelevant to their way of life. Similar childish reactions would have been observed in Europeans forced to attune their actions to the intricacies of an African culture, but, as power and technological superiority were in western rather than African hands, adaptation did not proceed in that direction.

The child analogy was useful to whites for it denied to Africans the privileges reserved for adults. It both reflected and strengthened the idea that African cultures did not represent worthwhile achievements and were too loosely formed and inchoate to offer any significant resistance to an inrush of westernization. Most important, the analogy acted as a sanction and preparation for white control,[96] for its main implication was paternalism which denied the African the right of deciding on his own future. The paternalist view was succinctly expressed by the Rev. Alexander Hetherwick of the Church of Scotland in a speech made at the 1888 Centenary Protestant Missionary Conference in London.

> What now does Africa need? If Africa were standing on this platform she could not tell you; she does not know her needs. She might stand here and say, 'Give us the things we want; give us calico, give us gunpowder, give us all these articles that as traders you produce in your country.' But these are not Africa's real needs. It is only the Missionary who knows Africa's needs.[97]

As children the Africans were clearly incapable of protecting themselves from the evils of intertribal war, the slave trade, the despotism of the chiefs, and witchcraft, which beset them. The African, argued Lugard, 'holds the position of a late-born child in the family of nations, and must as yet be schooled in the discipline of the nursery'.[98] The wife of a missionary compared Africans to a 'lot of passionate children' mauling and fighting each other, who would 'with scarce an exception, instinctively hail with joy the advent of the adult power, which would secure them (though perhaps not without present reproof to some) mutual peace and happiness'.[99]

While the child analogy obviously reflected a low view of tribalism, it was not without its advantages to the African. Africa was bound to be drawn out of its isolation, and the African was patently unprepared for the new civilization to which he would have to adapt. The analogy contained a certain trusteeship element, and implicitly included the training, maturing, and eventual achievement of adulthood by the African. At a minimum it was preferable to the category of 'beast' or 'animal' which, by depriving the African of humanity, would, or could, have sanctioned brutality and cruelty. It softened European criticism by reducing the responsibility of the African for his acts. H. M. Stanley, although he felt that Africa was peopled 'not by timid Hindoos, or puny Australian aborigines, but by millions of robust, courageous men', was convinced that its European rulers should regard their charges as children; then the 'annoyances that their follies and vices inflict' would become bearable and comprehensible.[100]

Yet the analogy was inherently confusing. Individual Africans, like all other human beings, passed through the biological life cycle from childhood to old age without displaying what Europeans regarded as cultural maturity. Thus they were called children with the strength and cunning of men, or some similar confusing combination of attributes. Given the contradiction implicit in the analogy, only time would tell whether the childhood was ephemeral or inherent in the race. It was, therefore, a misleading analogy, for although races or cultures, like individuals, may be said to change and evolve, when they are in their childhood or adulthood depends entirely on what is considered as meaningful evidence of maturity. In addition, the analogy was logically opposed to equality between the races. The later colonial term 'boy' for males of all ages was as wounding to African self-respect as it was psychologically satisfying for Europeans.

Ultimately the comparison of Africans to children was simply a convenient short-hand way of expressing British self-confidence and superiority feelings and reflecting on African inferiority.

7

In any examination of British attitudes it is essential to keep in mind the inevitable bias involved in judging tribalism by values which originated in British society at a particular period in its evolution. The process of cultural conditioning which integrates an individual into his own society implants a particular way of looking at the universe productive of an almost inevitable failure to comprehend and evaluate alien cultures in terms which their members would accept as valid.[101] The impact of this cultural indoctrination extended from large pervasive themes such as the idea of progress, the rightness of man's control over nature, the consequent belief in technology, respect for the Puritan virtues of hard work, self-denial, thrift, foresight, and the Victorian family structure to the minutiae of cultural items such as the lip-ring and certain African eating habits. The lip-ring, a disc inserted in the lower or upper lip, or occasionally in both, protruded the lip outward from the face and bared the inside of the lip and gum. There is no evidence that Africans following the practice found it unnatural or repugnant. The British reacted to it with a combination of intense revulsion and incredulity.[102] An equally revolting custom from an aesthetic point of view followed the killing of an elephant or a giraffe by a white hunter. After he had shot four elephants, one hunter claimed:

> a scene that baffles all description was enacted. They rushed on them with knives, spears, battle-axes, and arrow-heads, fighting over their meat like hungry wolves. The beasts were soon ripped open, and I saw several of these men actually standing up to their waists in the entrails, pulling and tearing them out. The odour being too strong for me to endure, I withdrew to a respectful distance to windward, where I smoked a pipe and watched their operations. They yelled and fought over their work, and one or two were severely stabbed. . . .
> I have seen a fox thrown to a pack of hungry hounds more than once, and remarked how eagerly they fought for the hard-earned morsel, but they were nothing to these men. I never saw the savage nature so thoroughly developed. Each elephant had a mob closely packed round it, yelling and fighting like demons. . . .[103]

Such scenes, and there are numerous descriptions, seemed specific proof of savagery to the observer, who was alternately repelled and fascinated. Yet the widespread revulsion against these two customs, coupled with the emotional nature of the descriptive language used, does not validate the argument that they were in fact barbarous or savage, except in the tautological sense that the nineteenth-century Briton was induced by his cultural background to define them as such.

In themselves these two traits scarcely merit notice. They do illustrate, however, the cultural determination of values. To the anthropologist, western society represents only one of many possible forms of human organization. For these early pioneers the contrast between British and African cultures served to validate beliefs in their own cultural superiority. The strength of this ethnocentrism rested on the observable global nature of western and especially British influence and power. This inhibited understanding and sympathetic attitudes to the different orientations of tribal societies.[104] The individual Briton assumed that the difference in technological and other capacities between civilized and tribal man proved his own superiority without realizing the insignificant contribution of the average individual and the importance of other factors in determining the orientation of a culture and the type of abilities that it fostered. The British assumption that there were universal standards, that these standards resided in British culture, and that the merit of other cultures rested on their approximation to these standards, was not shaken by contact with Central Africa.

The initial bias of ethnocentrism was reinforced by the tendency of cross-cultural evaluation to be dominated by the need to preserve the ethnocentric pride of the observer. This resulted in the employment of a high degree of mental agility directed to the preservation of the hierarchical British view of the world against awkward and unwelcome facts. There was, for example, in evaluating African society, a truly remarkable lack of mention of the appalling living conditions of the urban poor of Britain. No reader of the literature on Central Africa would have any idea of the existence of the conditions described by General Booth in his massive survey of London, or later by S. Rowntree. The implicit and explicit comparisons of conditions in Britain with those in Africa consistently overlooked the unfavourable aspects of British society. There was also a tendency to use comments on cultural differences to provide comic relief to the reader and simultaneously reaffirm white racial and cultural superiority. The technique was illustrated by Speke:

> It is strange to see how very soon, when questioning these negroes about anything relating to geography, their weak brains give way, and they can answer no questions, or they become so evasive in their replies, or so rambling, that you can make nothing out of them. It is easily discernible at what time you should cease to ask any further questions; for their heads then roll about like a ball upon a wire, and their eyes glass over and look vacantly about as though vitality had fled from their bodies altogether.[105]

A further technique was to accord praise to individual Africans with an accompanying indication that such individuals were untypical of their race. In some cases there was simply an unwillingness to admit the existence of favourable traits which conflicted with racial stereotypes.[106] Or, when praise was given it was most lavish with respect to secondary virtues. The evolution of the stereotype of the faithful porter is especially significant in its indication that praiseworthy traits in Africans were those related to positions of subordination. The tendency for praise of the African as a worker to be related to pleas for capital, colonists, and imperialism reveals the same opportunistic method of praise giving.

There was, generally, a marked tendency in according virtues to Africans to restrict them to childish ones. No serious harm was done to superiority feelings by assertions that the African was a simple happy child of nature, for childish virtues in an adult world do not conflict with self-esteem. The same technique was used with Arabs and Portuguese whose hospitality was generously and highly praised; a favourable attribute, but hardly one capable of challenging British superiority feelings. Equally revealing was the propensity of some observers to admit the lenient nature of Arab slavery, but to use such a fact as a proof of Arab indolence rather than kindness.

It is particularly important to note the propagandistic context in which much white contact occurred and indeed found its justification. This is most strikingly apparent with respect to the missionary movement. At the public conferences held in England, an aggressive and virulent attitude was displayed to the non-Christian religions which were paraded before the audiences of the faithful and assailed in an arrogant fashion.[107] Abusive epithets were interspersed with references to the superiority of Christianity and its inevitable triumph. At a conference held in Liverpool in 1860, Tidman, Foreign Secretary of the L.M.S., refused to hear talk of mission failures. In Polynesia, he said, more than a quarter of a million human beings, 'if they could be regarded as such before the Gospel reached them —cannibals and murderers, have been brought under its influence', and then there was the case of Robert Moffat in Bechuanaland who found a 'race of the most degraded and savage creatures which could possibly be pictured to the imagination', and many were now Christians.[108]

The propaganda technique was relatively simple. The more degraded, backward and immoral the non-Christian world could be painted, the greater would be the difficulty of refuting the arguments for missionary expansion.[109] The dramatic contrasts of the worst features of heathenism with the most exalted aspects of Christianity exaggerated the distinctions between the Christian west and the non-Christian world.[110] R. N. Cust found much to condemn in deputation speeches, 'such as abuse of the poor Heathen races, their religious beliefs spoken of in terms of derision, and perhaps their objects of worship exposed to be laughed at'.[111] The missionary, whether in speech or writing, undoubtedly made a major contribution to that curious paternalism which combined a mixture of responsibility for the welfare and spiritual improvement of these African 'children', and a scorn and contempt for their existing level of cultural achievements. The message of the missionary was given special credibility not only because he was a first-hand observer, but because of the aura of heroism and adventure which surrounded his Christian work in 'Darkest Africa'. Simultaneously, the denigration of the non-Christian world was paralleled by a eulogizing of the nobility of individual missionaries which produced, on occasion, a selective interpretation of events little short of fraudulent.[112]

The missionary movement, in short, was a cause. As such it partook of the tendency to make truth, or at least published information, relative to a variety of needs which conditioned its momentum.

CONTEMPORARY ANCESTORS

Doubtless the Rev. J. S. Moffat exaggerated when he claimed that five-sixths of the interesting material in mission periodicals was only romancing by the missionary,[113] but there is no doubt that the need, among other things, to attract both candidates and funds was an important determinant of what should be said and what should be discreetly omitted.[114]

Whatever may have been the contribution of such propaganda devices to the revenue of mission societies and to their capacity to attract candidates for distant mission fields, they raised important problems for the individual missionary and for the movement as a whole. The gospel of love was inextricably tied to a propaganda system which used the militant language of war.[115] The propaganda which surrounded the missionary penetration of Central Africa differed little from a racial attack in tone and content. Christian universalism led to an intolerant and often indiscriminate condemnation of tribal practices in the name of divinely instituted patterns of conduct. The missionary was faced with the difficult psychological problem of simultaneously being loving and charitable to Africans while uprooting and eradicating many customs which the African cherished. This general difficulty was supplemented by missionary experience which often stifled the Christian sympathy for the African which the missionaries realized their calling required. The fact that a Briton was a missionary did not render him immune from pervasive racial attitudes to the African. The conflict between the divine command to love and an individual reaction of repugnance or dislike was resolved at a higher more abstract level by the assertion that one loved Africans, not for themselves, but 'for Christ's sake'.[116] This produced the type of missionary mentioned by Dewick who could give his life for his flock but was unable to treat individuals on a basis of natural human friendship.[117]

On the other hand, Christian universalism implied the spiritual equality of all mankind. The missionary, therefore, was not only dogmatic about the evil basis of many African customs; he was, in the face of criticism, equally dogmatic about the African's spiritual potential. He was often the most severe opponent of the African as he was, but he held out the prospect of admission to a new institution, the Christian Church, entrance to which was available on the fulfilment of fixed conditions. Theoretically, intolerance was only manifested towards ephemeral aspects not intrinsic to the spiritual man underneath and, not being inherent in racial factors, capable of alteration. These, however, were fine distinctions difficult to maintain in practice. For the missionary there was always the danger of hatred for customs sliding into hatred for those who manifested them. This dilemma was partly responsible for that curious and significant missionary phenomenon—the missionary who did not like Africans.[118] The missionary, in brief, attempted to distinguish between a man and his behaviour, loving one and hating the other. This, however, was not only an almost impossible psychological task, but was undoubtedly confusing to the recipient of such missionary concern who was respected not for what he was, but for what he might become, or for some spiritual centre of his person which did not manifest itself in overt conduct or inner belief.

8

British attitudes to the African provide a clear example of ethnocentrism in action. Comments on the inferiority of other persons or cultures are simultaneously comments on the superiority of the user or of his culture. When a Briton spoke of African inferiority, usually he was unconsciously enhancing his own ego, and confirming his own racial and cultural superiority. More specifically, all such statements helped to justify the undertaking of any European enterprise, religious, economic, or imperial, in which the African was an object. The imperialist, like the missionary, justified his intervention by placing strong emphasis on the insecurity generated by tribal war and the slave trade, and on the backwardness of the African. The simplest form of propaganda for missionary or imperialist entailed an exaltation of the virtues of the missionary movement or imperial nation and the placing of heavy stress on the cruelty, religious inferiority, cultural incapacity, or any other aspect of the indigenous societies which justified foreign intervention.[119] In general, therefore, the propaganda accompaniment of missionary and imperial contact exaggerated the differences between Briton and African.

IV

THE NOBLE SAVAGE

1

WITHIN the framework of attitudes discussed in the last chapter tribal man was simply a savage, a derogatory concept seldom prefaced with the adjective noble. At best, he was an object of pity to the humanitarian, or an object of salvation to the missionary. At worst, he was an object of scorn to be ruthlessly exploited or callously eliminated from the scene, as European settlers revealed in North America, South Africa, and Australasia that the superiority of civilized man was founded more on advanced killing techniques than on compassion or respect. Even where, as in tropical Africa, the climate saved the African from the fate of other technologically backward peoples, there was, on the whole, a significant absence of any feeling of respect, let alone admiration, for tribal man. Even those who stooped to aid their 'black brothers' did so out of feelings of Christian duty or aristocratic responsibility.

There was, however, a partial qualification of the preceding views in those Britons whose outlook was tinged with romanticism. This approach, which was of limited application, contained a modified appreciation of diversity and a comparative willingness to accord merit to ways of life not characterized by a desire for ever-increasing increments of material goods.

In itself, romanticism, an attitude to man and nature combining scientific curiosity and aesthetic appreciation, was a distinguishing feature between Britons and Africans. Samuel Baker found it impossible to explain to a Latooka chief why he wished to discover the Nile sources. 'Suppose,' said the chief, 'you get to the great lake; what will you do with it? What will be the good of it? If you find that the large river does flow from it, what then? What's the good of it?'[1] Other pioneers remarked on African insensitivity to flowers,[2] lack of curiosity about the Victoria Falls,[3] and a 'remarkable characteristic of the Negro race, as contrasted with the Asiatic or the European,

THE NOBLE SAVAGE

that beyond a slight interest in the sun or moon so little notice was taken of the heavenly bodies'.[4]

Romanticism, however, had a softening effect on British criticism of African shortcomings by introducing a certain tolerance and relativism into the British approach to African society. From a technological viewpoint Africans were simply failures eking out a miserable existence on a potentially fruitful soil. From a romantic approach their way of life acquired a certain justification as emphasis was placed less on their backwardness than on the fact that they were different. The savage became not so much a failed European as a picturesque oddity in his own right.

An infrequent but highly significant reaction saw wisdom in the social cohesion of tribalism, the absence of rugged individualism, and the African satisfaction with a modest level of material goods. Britons were not unaware of the communal generosity of tribalism, especially with respect to food. One woman visitor to the Shire Highlands, especially struck with this trait, wrote:

> Nothing strikes us more forcibly than the singular unselfishness of these poor savages, for both old and young share everything they get with one another, or those around them. Sometimes when I have given a child a biscuit, I have felt quite sorry to see the way in which the poor little thing has given a bit to all its companions, until many a time nothing more than a crumb remained for itself; yet there it was, as bright and happy as if I had given it a whole boxful to divide among them.[5]

Duff Macdonald of the Blantyre mission favourably compared the leisured African existence to the 'working at high pressure that meets us everywhere at home'. In Central Africa, he observed:

> There are no crowds of pale-faced men and girls rushing along almost mechanically in response to some factory bell. There are no poor clerks cooped up in dingy counting houses—no students with aching heads, trying to dispense with sleep. There are no careworn parents whose hard toil barely supports their children. The African has about him an air of stillness and repose that is in beautiful harmony with the scenery around. His life is not a struggle for existence. He does not care to work against time. Ambition does not drag him behind its chariot wheels. If we were to rank the Africans in classes, we should put down most of them as 'gentlemen in easy circumstances.' Their circumstances are easy not because their gratifications are many, but because their wants are few.[6]

He went on to castigate 'our boasted civilization'. What has it done for its adherents? he queried. His answer, nothing. 'Civilization' to Macdonald indicated the futility of supposing that progress and happiness were related to increased mechanical ability or a re-arrangement of human institutions. He felt, therefore, that the task of the white man in Africa was not to introduce the dubious merits of civilization, but simply to diffuse Christianity so that the African might possess in his rude condition the 'peace that passeth understanding'. This would exorcize the fears of tribal man who knew not whence he came nor where he was going.[7]

Walter Montague Kerr, an aristocratic traveller, was equally impressed with the idyllic nature of tribal life in areas where warfare did not turn man against man. As he approached the lower Zambesi from the south he came to the town of chief Chibabura where the people occupied themselves in supplying their daily wants, in herding their cattle and in building their huts. There was no ambition, he wrote, and glory was unknown, but 'contentment, the object of most of the aspirations of civilized life, reigned supreme in these heedless people's minds. Through the labyrinth of life, their path was clear, thoughtless and happy.' In what he called the 'rapid and deafening whirl of civilized life' man sought relief from the burdens and turmoil of his troubled existence, and yet some African tribes already 'live and move in this coveted simplicity; and in some respects they are to be envied'. Admittedly, in a human sense, their life was a failure, but in compensation 'their contentment—a feeling quite unknown in civilized brains—is great!'

> The traveller [he wrote of the Makorikori tribe] cannot help being impressed by the air of freedom which these primitive men and women breathe. They have a total want of anxiety; their children are as plump and round as distended bladders, no matter whether they are the offspring of a chief or of a slave.
>
> Suppose, for the time being, that the cultured blessings of civilization give place to matters material, how infinitely preferable does the life of a Makorikori appear when compared with the struggle of a poor man in a crowded city of Christendom! The children of the latter are penned in narrow slums; they grow up stunted in body and depraved in mind, and anon the deep lines of care or crime appear prematurely upon their youthful brows.
>
> The civilized poor man is not half so happy as the untutored savage, although the latter lives far beyond the sound of church bells. Can it be that heathen freedom and plenty in the wind-swept wilderness are preferable to civilized starvation in the polluted atmosphere of a rotten hovel? The subject is worthy of consideration.

His own answer was given in his concluding statement: 'Long may the gentle winds of peace and freedom caress your mountain home!'[8]

This type of reaction was comparatively rare among the early pioneers. Joseph Thomson revealed a similar attitude in *Ulu: an African Romance*, the story of a disillusioned young Scotsman and his romance with a Chagga maiden. Some of Thomson's published articles reveal a remarkably critical attitude to the benefits expected to

THE NOBLE SAVAGE

accrue to the African as a result of the introduction of western civilization,[9] but Thomson was anything but typical in his favourable portrayal of tribal man and his critical approach to his own culture.

These few observers shared a certain antipathy to western civilization coupled with a comparative capacity to find merit in tribal cultures expressing attitudes to life sharply contrasting with that provided by their own background. Significantly, they shared a partial reluctance to accept the desirability of introducing western civilization to the African. Finally, as far as can be judged, they were friendly rather than aloof in their relations with Africans. In fact very few Britons expressed so sympathetic an attitude towards tribal society; this is hardly surprising, for sympathy with tribalism seemed to involve a rejection of British cultural superiority. Objectively the major barrier to the acceptance of a relativistic approach to cultural differences lay in the disturbed state of the interior where peaceful Arcadias were few and far between. Only two tribal groups, the Wankonde and the Wataveta, fortunately preserved from the disruption caused by the slave trade and tribal war, lived in a bucolic simplicity capable of eliciting widespread favourable comment.

On his first exploring trip Joseph Thomson came upon the cattle-owning Wankonde who lived in large villages at the north end of Lake Nyasa. Their huts were tastefully constructed and scrupulously clean. Even the banana groves were swept in the vicinity of the villages. The men went naked and the women nearly so. They were a happy, friendly people, hospitable to strangers, and, until brutally attacked by a band of half-caste Arabs in 1887, largely immune from the ravages of the slave trade and inter-tribal war. Thomson, who visited them in the late seventies, was remarkably impressed, and presented a straightforward eulogy of the country and people, 'a perfect Arcadia, about which idyllic poets have sung, though few have seen it realized'.[10]

Other Britons were no less susceptible to the charms of Wankonde life. In fact, to see this tribe was to raise doubts about the desirability of introducing civilization. The people were 'particularly prosperous and happy . . . inoffensive and contented', according to Monteith Fotheringham of the African Lakes Company. He could 'not help thinking how much better they were than certain products of civilization at home'.[11] Like other Britons, Mrs. Jane Moir was much struck with the cleanliness and beauty of the villages. Had it not been for the necessities of trade, she wrote,

> how much nicer it would be to have all natives like these North-Enders with clean, well-oiled, or rather buttered bodies, instead of being swathed in filthy smelling calico, as most natives are who live near English stations![12]

THE NOBLE SAVAGE

It is indicative of the prevailing insecurity that only one other small settlement, Taveita, a mixed community of settled Masai and a Bantu group allied to the Akamba and the Chagga, who lived on the lower forested slopes of Kilimanjaro, was consistently given an analogous type of fulsome praise which implicitly questioned the justification of much of the social change many of the pioneers were bent on introducing. Their stockaded town with a republican form of government was a way station on caravan routes to the interior. General Mathews asserted that they were the 'best natives' he had ever met, 'very good looking, athletic', and, an important factor in view of their trading relations with passing caravans, 'no such thing as a thief to be found here'.[13] Joseph Thomson praised the people highly,[14] while Harry Johnston called the country an 'African paradise', and the people 'one of the pleasantest' he had encountered in Africa.[15] Another visitor, Thomas Stevens, doubted if all Christendom could produce a community of four thousand people 'so honest, so amiable, so gentle and so contented with themselves and all the world as these same Wa-Taveta'.[16]

This was high praise indeed, and it is worth noting that the peace, plenty, and happiness of these two tribes struck Britons so forcibly and evoked appropriate comments of respect, admiration, and even envy. There were other scattered instances of the 'happy savage', 'child of nature' analysis of African conditions; but by and large these stereotypes were seldom applied to specific tribes, not because they were unknown, but because there were few African Edens where their application seemed justified. Central Africa would have been taken over by European powers regardless of tribal conditions in the interior, but, had the way of life found among these two small groups been more widespread, it is at least conjectural that arguments for the introduction of civilization would have been somewhat muted,[17] or at a minimum would have sounded less convincing. The case for imperialism would have been much weakened had not cruelty and a glaring degree of social disruption been present to stimulate attempts at amelioration, and to provide a useful cover for less altruistic motives.

2

A main reason for the absence of idyllic primitive communities free from the troubles and cares of civilization was found in the aggressive policies of powerful martial tribes such as the Masai, the Matabele and the Galla. In the pre-imperial period the actions of these plundering cattle herders, the warlike external policies of such developed tribal groups as the Baganda and the Barotse, coupled with the growth in the slave trade as Arabs and Swahili penetrated ever farther into the interior, had a significant brutalizing effect on inter-tribal relations.

The tendency of non-anthropologists writing on African history to divide indigenous tribal systems into two broad categories of the raiders and the raided, is no doubt an unjustified oversimplification. Lewis Gann, in a brilliant article, has indicated the complexity of the factors which conditioned the response of individual tribes to the slave trade. Political organizations, military tactics, soil fertility, density of the population, complexity of the economy, and alternative methods of satisfying newly stimulated wants, were all important factors entering into the response of African tribes to the opportunities and dangers present in the growth of the traffic in black humanity.[18] While the same complexity was undoubtedly present in the whole range of inter-tribal relationships, there is a sense in which it is possible to make a simple and still meaningful distinction between dominant tribes and those which were essentially victims in the shifting, insecure world of the pre-imperial period. Even if such a distinction lacks the complexity required for a detailed anthropological study of tribal relations, it is undeniable that strength and military capacity became supreme virtues in this period. More important for our purposes is the fact that Britons tended to see tribal relations in the light of this simple distinction.

There was a fundamental ambivalence about British attitudes to the disturbed conditions in the interior. There was a real and deeply felt humanitarian reaction against the brutality, the loss of life, and the insecurity caused by the slave trade and tribal war. At the same time, there was a certain contempt for the weak and the defenceless, and a significant degree of respect for the powerful martial tribes largely responsible for the plunder and killings which repelled Britons.

There was a general preference for those tribes which dominated their environment, even if they did so by the instrument of war. On first meeting the Masai, 'the dreaded warriors that had been so long the subject of [his] waking dreams', Joseph Thomson exclaimed, ' "What splendid fellows!" as [he] surveyed a band of the most peculiar race of men to be found in all Africa.' A group of Masai elders, 'magnificent specimens of their race, considerably over six feet, and with an aristocratic savage dignity', evoked his admiration. The manliness, truculence, independence, and haughtiness of this tribe commanded his respect 'for, troublesome and over-bearing as they were, they displayed an aristocratic manner, and a consciousness of power, which seemed to raise them infinitely above the negro —as I had seen him.'[19]

Thomson's admiration for the Masai was shared by other whites.

THE NOBLE SAVAGE

As Captain W. H. Williams stated: 'I think most of us have a sort of sneaking regard for the Masai.'[20] The Galla, the Yao, and the various Zulu offshoots received, for similar reasons, a similar respect. Tribes of Zulu origin received consistently high praise from Britons for their masculine qualities of martial capacity, force, vigour, power, and energy. Robert Laws was much drawn to the Ngoni west of Lake Nyasa by their fine physical development, manly bearing and courtesy.[21] The Landeens, a Zulu tribe which levied tribute on the Portuguese stations on the Zambesi, were described by Rowley as a 'fine race', and as 'noble specimens of humanity'.[22] James Stewart, little given to praise, stated that some of the younger ones were 'Apollos for symmetry', and some of the more mature like Hercules 'in point of build and strength'. 'No effeminate cloth or calico of Manchester looms enervated or disgraced those warlike limbs.'[23]

The qualities which appealed to Britons were those associated with a confident assumption of power. The Landeens were 'splendid looking people . . . Goliaths to the poor Portuguese'.[24] The Galla had a 'manly appearance . . . [and were] . . . large and powerfully built'.[25] The Makololo whom Livingstone held in 'very great affection' were a 'jolly rollicking set of fellows with a great deal of the soldier in their character'.[26]

The converse of admiration for the strong and powerful was an attitude to the weak and the impotent verging on disdain and derision. Again and again this set of attitudes was coupled together. The size and power of the Galla tribe, a veritable 'imperial race', elicited eloquent praise from the Methodist missionary Thomas Wakefield, while at the same time he spoke with unconcealed scorn of the fragmented Wanika among whom he worked—a 'small, inferior, stagnant race' as he called them.[27] A similar contrast of attitudes was displayed towards the Yao and the Manganja by Rowley of the U.M.C.A. When the missionaries arrived south of Lake Nyasa in the early sixties the Yao, a warlike, partly Moslem tribe who had been driven from their own homelands in the north-east, were carving out living space for themselves among the disunited Manganja. The missionaries initially took up arms on behalf of the Manganja, but they soon realized the folly of continued interference and, at least in some cases, their feelings changed. Rowley began to prefer the Yao who had supreme 'contempt for the Manganja. . . . The dominant race . . . [was] . . . manifest in all their actions.' They were physically much superior to the Manganja whom Rowley described as an 'amiable, but a pitiably weak race, not ugly, but contemptible'. In revealing language, he observed: 'In dealing with the Manganja, the single sentiment of pity is ordinarily evoked; but a good Ajawa [Yao] one really likes.'[28]

THE NOBLE SAVAGE

The juxtaposition of oppressor and oppressed was particularly clear in the relationships between the Matabele and the Mashona in the area that was to become Southern Rhodesia. A recent writer has stated that 'the blood thirsty Matabele—the timid Mashona, delighted to be rescued from oppression . . . were the two pictures of the people of the country' general among the members of the Pioneer Column which marched into Mashonaland in 1890.[29] This stereotype undoubtedly derived much of its strength from the justification it shed over imperialist plans. It derived extra vitality from the frequent, and in most cases sincere admiration for the craftsmanship, industry, and intelligence of the Mashona. Knight-Bruce, for example, in advocating British protection for the Mashona emphasized these qualities and, in particular, their 'really astonishing' skill in smelting and other industries. With all their faults he felt they were considerably superior to the Matabele in character, and a more pleasant people with whom to deal.[30] Another proponent of imperialism claimed that the Mashona stood first in 'the industrial arts of a rudimentary civilization' of all the tribes south of the Zambesi.[31]

While a certain caution is appropriate in dealing with arguments which justified imperial control, the substantial sincerity of much of the early praise for the industrial skills of the Mashona can be accepted. Yet, at the same time, their Matabele oppressors participated in the admiration accorded to most warrior tribes and were held in high regard by many early pioneers. Their uninhibited savagery was not without its appeal. Their war dances were scenes of barbaric splendour in which the warriors looked magnificent. When standing behind their ox-hide shields in a semi-circle around their king, they presented 'as imposing a spectacle as any race of savages in the world'.[32] Of special importance was the fact that in their two chiefs, Moselekatse and Lobengula, they had strong powerful leaders for whom the early pioneers had not only respect, but what was far rarer, affection.

Even Knight-Bruce, with his preference for the Mashona, admitted that there was something about a pure Matabele which was 'outwardly very attractive. Their placid brute courage was very perfect.' He instanced as an example the killing of the king's brother who had become too powerful. When the executioner came, the intended victim was talking to a friend. ' "Do it quickly," [he said, and] he stood still while the man broke his head in with his bludgeon.'[33] Such qualities at least compelled respect, if not liking. The Matabele were men, proud and aloof, and although they revelled in pillage and bloodshed, they did dominate their environment, instead of being subject to it. They did not cringe before Europeans, and had it not been for the restraining hand of Lobengula in the eighties

THE NOBLE SAVAGE

there is no doubt that they would have killed the whites in their territories.

Praise of Mashona skills and admiration for Matabele courage seem to have co-existed in the pre-imperial period. After the arrival of the Pioneer Column, however, the former seems to have been replaced by scorn, while the latter continued unaltered. Marshall Hole claimed that few whites had any feeling 'other than contempt' for the Mashona. Their alleged cowardice meant that concern at their possession of guns was non-existent. When they rebelled in 1896 whites were both shocked and surprised, not only by Mashona brutality, but by the mere fact that these 'invertebrate native tribes' should even think of challenging white rule.[34] The Matabele, on the other hand, were regarded with a respect 'almost amounting to dread' by the early pioneers.[35] The difference was put succinctly by Frederick Ramon de Bertodano, Marques del Moral, shortly after word had been received of the Mashona rising at a time when the white community already had its hands full in putting down the Matabele rebellion. 'All of us anxious about the Mashonaland rebellion, no one likes the Mashona, dirty, cowardly lot. Matabele, bloodthirsty devils, but a fine type.'[36]

3

The tribes discussed in the preceding pages were, from the British point of view, savage, and the virtues they possessed were savage virtues. In the case of the Baganda and the Barotse it was their apparent civilized qualities which elicited admiration. For reasons of space discussion will be confined to the Baganda, although the Barotse also were rulers of a large kingdom, an African empire in fact, and westerners were impressed both with their system of government[37] and the intelligence and artistic skill of the people.[38]

Mtesa, the king of Buganda from 1857 to 1884, was a shrewd and intelligent man. He could read and write Arabic and he spoke several African languages. It was difficult to label as savage a chief who would 'discuss for hours abstruse points in theology, political economy, or philosophy'. A description of this monarch reveals the civilized atmosphere of the Baganda court.

> On a rich carpet lay Mtesa, supporting himself on his right arm on spotless linen cushions. He is a very fine man, about six feet high, and of well-proportioned build. . . . He was clad in a becoming Arab dress, richly embroidered with gold and silver braid; his head was covered with a tarboosh; and in front of him lay a large jewelled sword, with the hilt of which his long nervous hand played.[39]

THE NOBLE SAVAGE

The Baganda, with their high density of population, a social structure which encouraged mobility, an experimental approach to innovation, and a fertile soil, seemed to possess all the prerequisites for progress. It was felt that a people with 'so much good sense', and 'such a high state of order', would form a centre for the implantation of Christianity and civilization.[40] The superiority of the kingdoms of Baganda, Karagwe and Bunyoro made a forcible impression on all early travellers. The Baganda, Mackay asserted, 'are not savages nor even barbarians. They are out of sight far in advance of any race I have met with or even heard of in Central Africa; they are exceedingly neat-handed, far more so than the coast people, who call themselves alone "civilized".'[41] This superiority was shown in numerous ways. There were the 'wonderful roads which . . . often lead as straight as an arrow over hill and dale, through forests and across swamps, and, even in the more thinly peopled districts, are kept wonderfully clean and free from weeds'.[42] Unlike most Africans the Baganda clothed themselves from head to foot, and their garments were kept clean by frequent washing with soap. Their houses, especially of the upper classes, were large and roomy, and occasionally tastefully decorated. Harry Johnston remarked favourably that they were the first tribe in Africa to institute privies.[43] They were good metal workers, and were noted for the facility with which they imitated European techniques, a favourable and progressive trait. As Ashe's description indicates, the Baganda were no isolated, insignificant tribal group:

> Among the throng hastening to pay their respects to the majesty of Buganda were representatives of the Bahuma or Bakama, as well as chiefs from Busoga. The fair-faced Lubambula of Koki from the west, and the scowling Wakoli, paramount chief of Busoga, who divided with Luba—known as being the captor of Bishop Hannington—authority to the east of Buganda. Here too were obsequious smiling Arabs from Muscat—men who can smile and smile and be villains with it all; pale-faced Englishmen from the cold North; runaway Egyptian soldiers from the Soudan; adventurers from the east coast and Madagascar; mountebanks, minstrels, dancers, dwarfs.[44]

The relatively civilized aristocracy, the complex but comprehensible political structure, the elaborate court ceremonial and the extent of Baganda hegemony, elevated that tribe into a special category of attainment to British observers. The Baganda, although pagan, were different in kind from the poverty-stricken villagers of smaller tribes eking out a bare subsistence on less fruitful land. They lived in the midst of visible order with a political system, a military system, and a social structure possessed of sufficient resemblance to European feudalism—Felkin called it a 'perfect feudal system'[45]—to provide the Briton with a point of contact and understanding. Britons instinctively appreciated and felt they understood, whether rightly or wrongly is another question, a society which possessed both monarchy and aristocracy. The high praise accorded to the Baganda people rested primarily on the fact that they were felt to be closer to the west in terms of realized development and potential capacity than, for example, the Matabele or Manganja. The fact that the British placed the Baganda at the top of the ladder of African tribalism, however, represented neither a relativistic attitude to human achievement, nor an appreciation of cultural diversity. Praise of Baganda roads was simply an indirect reiteration of British technological control over nature. To have denied respect to the Baganda for this achievement would have been tantamount to self-criticism. In general, praise of the Baganda was no more than a reaffirmation of British values.

4

The preceding represents no more than an outline of the British reaction to the multiplicity of tribal groups in Central Africa. The salient features of the British response seem reasonably clear. They did not regard the interior of the continent as composed of one vast mass of undifferentiated savagery. Specific tribes were judged within the general framework of concepts and values discussed in the preceding section. In some cases accident probably played an important part in the reputations of individual tribes. Attitudes to the Makololo were closely related to their association with Livingstone. Livingstone's praise of Sebituane—'decidedly the best specimen of a native chief I ever met'[46]—and the sterling qualities of his porters, the famous 'faithfuls', contributed greatly to the renown of this tribe in Britain. An idealized myth[47] evolved around this tribe. A small body of Livingstone's Makololo who settled south of Lake Nyasa, thirty years later became a factor in the delimitation of Central Africa. The Scottish, in particular, looked on them with proprietary concern and regarded it as intolerable that they might fall under Portuguese control. 'Livingstone's Makololo were sacrosanct. To dare touch one of them was to rouse the righteous anger of every Scotsman—to whom Livingstone was a national hero.'[48]

Accidents apart, however, there was a high degree of consistency in British attitudes. One of the most significant aspects of their evaluation was the tendency for praise or contempt to mirror the existing distribution of tribal power in the interior. In general, praise went to the strong and the dominant, and, although their plight evoked sympathy, contempt was displayed for the weak, the disunited and the oppressed, with the exception of the occasional isolated small tribal group living in comparative peace and plenty. The preference for the powerful, especially if monarchical, tribes was in part a reflection of their convenience for European visitors. Thus Elmslie sympathized with Burton's view of the pleasure of arriving at the headquarters of a 'strong and sanguinary despotism'. After travelling through a series of petty chiefdoms it was a relief to enter Ngoni territory where one chief controlled a large area, thus greatly reducing the number of disputes and facilitating travel arrangements.

> Despotic rule [he claimed] is often the only kind suitable among uncivilized people. Until the people are governed by higher principles than those common among 'nature-peoples', a despotic ruler is a divine institution required to keep in check greater evils.[49]

A similar point was made by Ludwig Krapf. A gentle, kindly man, he had a certain affection for the Wanika who made up his flock; but when he visited the kingdom of Usambara he 'saw at once' that he was in a country where much better order reigned 'than in the lawless republics of the Wanika and Wakamba'. The condition of Usambara, he felt, would be critical, were it not for the iron hand of their chief. 'It were well,' he stated, 'if those quarrelsome and drunken republicans, the Wanika and the Wakamba, could feel, at least for a time, the power of an African lion-king!' As a traveller he noted the great boon of order over a wide area where a chief's word was law. Begging, the curse of all travellers, he also felt was much less 'in a despotic than in a republican country', once one had appeased the chiefs, 'those greatest of beggars'. When all travel arrangements were made for him in Usambara, he declaimed: 'Certainly a monarchy is thrice as good as a republic, whether it be savage or civilized!'[50] He felt that this distinction was also important in missionary strategy, as success was much more likely among monarchical tribes for strong chiefs, if propitiated, 'have it in their power to give the Missionary as many children as he likes for instruction; whereas things were different in republican states'.[51]

It is doubtful, however, if more than a supplemental explanation of the British preference for the powerful tribes can be found in such practical reasons. In the last resort the presence or absence of an independent spirit was the most important factor in determining British reactions to specific African tribes. Roger Price of the L.M.S. referred bitterly to the 'mania which Missionary societies have for getting at world-renowned "human butchers" such as Mtesa, Moselekatse and Sebitwane, passing by hosts of peaceful, industrious and much more hopeful people, in a Missionary point of view'.[52] In reality, the attraction which such leaders and their tribes possessed was not found in the 'butcher' element, which was in fact widely abhorred, but simply in their possession of manliness, dignity, and the martial virtues. The *Church Missionary Intelligencer* noted the 'strong flavour of chivalrous feeling . . . mingled with the most degrading and barbarous customs' of the Masai, and, the article significantly continued, it was this 'very admixture of savagery and nobility' which strengthened the desire to make them 'the warriors of the cross'.[53]

The point was made with striking clarity by A. F. Sim, U.M.C.A. missionary at Kota Kota on the west side of Lake Nyasa. He stated that the Nyasa tribes among whom he worked were not to be judged by other African tribes 'such as the Zulus, Matabele, etc., as they are very wanting in manly qualities. There is no *"fight"* in them.' He felt that their basic deficiency was a 'nerveless acceptance of what they are taught'. He admitted that they were industrious but not 'enterprising, nor great drinkers'. The real hope of the missionaries, he suggested, was with the Yao,

> the most unpleasant people possible. They drink, they slave deal, and do all sorts of abominations, but they are of independent spirit, and the British Administration knows this to their cost. They alone of these tribes give any trouble.[54]

It is possible that Darwinian ideas contributed to the favourable evaluation of the dominant tribes. Although these tribes caused much of the social disruption deplored by Britons on other grounds, this was counterbalanced by the fact that they were men. They excelled in the masculine virtues of force, power, vigour, and energy which had a particular attraction for these early pioneers, for they were the very traits they admired and which frontier conditions necessitated as a price of survival. A spirit of self-assertion, even though directed to the arts of war, seems to have produced a deeper respect than the more prosaic virtues of industry and hard work if they were unaccompanied by power. By and large British evaluations tended to follow the line of least resistance and to reflect social realities with respect to power between African tribes. Respect for the Zulu, the Masai, and the Baganda was analogous to the rise in status which has been noted for West Africans coincident on their progress to independence. From the British viewpoint, for a tribe to be weak and subjugated came perilously close to being contemptible.[55]

5

In this period of culture contact few Africans emerge as individuals. The available material, missionary biographies, travel books, and consular despatches, generally accords individual uniqueness only to Europeans whose activities are carried on against a background of comparatively indistinguishable Africans. This creates serious problems for the would-be impartial analyst. The general difficulty for a European of sympathetically entering into the feelings of tribesmen easily leads into an unconscious identification with the white participants in culture contact. This tendency is enhanced by the difficulty of identifying with Africans when they do not emerge as individuals. The possibility of bringing an individual African to life in a period dominated by European source material has recently been demonstrated,[56] but the obvious labours which such a task involved merely serve to underline the existence and nature of the problem. In the pre-imperial period it is almost impossible to treat more than a handful of Africans as individuals with personal idiosyncracies and characteristics. The major exceptions are the more famous African and Swahili porters, men such as Susi and Chuma, Bombay and Mabruki, and more important, several of the powerful chiefs who exerted a dominating influence on Central African history before European political control.

There was, at times, a tendency to treat African chiefs as objects of humour. This was illustrated by Alfred J. Bethell, an adjutant of the Bechuanaland Border Police. After a mocking and cynical introduction in which he intimated that he expected an African chief to be gorgeously clothed and surrounded by courtiers and impressive ceremony, Bethell stated that he found his preconceptions erroneous.

> I went to call on a King with a man who knew the proper way to do it. We called in after a long day's shooting, very dirty and tired, to see 'the old man'. On arriving at a circular mud hut, we hitched our horses on to a log and walked in. No one was to be seen, so my friend set to work to shout. Fancy shouting for a real live king! Presently a hideous old hag, with a small freehold garden on her, and clothed in an old skin that a London bagman would pass by in disgust, came in and told us that the chief had been unwell all day, but would come out and see us. This meant that he had been as drunk as Chloe for a week past. Soon a blear-eyed, filthy, smelly, disgusting, old drunkard came in, and sat down on the floor with a grunt. Then he asked for some tobacco. As we had only good tobacco, we said we hadn't any. Then he asked for brandy; subsequently for a coat, a pair of trousers, some boots, or a hat; and the interview finished by his trying to sell us a dozen of his wives for a bottle of brandy.[57]

Yet this attitude of humorous superiority was not conspicuous with respect to major chiefs. Bethell himself admitted that Chief Khama of the Bechuana tribe was a good man, not like a 'native'.[58] This technique, the isolation of chiefs from their race and background by those who felt compelled to admit their possession of praiseworthy qualities, was fairly common.[59] It was a method which limited praise to the individual mentioned and rendered it non-applicable to the group as a whole. Conversely, it indicated that the stereotype of the African was so unfavourable that only by indicating that it did not apply to a particular individual of high capacities was it possible to avoid contradiction.

In spite of this it is remarkable how many of the extant descriptions of African chiefs are couched in favourable and occasionally laudatory language.[60] This was most strikingly the case with the Matabele chief Lobengula, of whom it would not be difficult to write a long, eulogistic essay. In part, these favourable attitudes reflected white dependence on the king. The early pioneers knew that it was his restraining hand which held his warriors in check on the not infrequent occasions when they would have liked to blood their spears on white men. Admiration and respect, however, clearly went beyond the amount elicited by Lobengula's protective role. Numerous portrayals of his character emphasized his kingly bearing and his intelligence. His sense of humour and his willingness to engage in good-natured jest with the early pioneers were frequently observed.[61] Missionaries, who had little reason for sympathy with the Matabele after their long and unsuccessful years of mission work, almost unanimously exempted 'Loben' from their strictures on this warlike tribe. He was 'every inch a king', clean and courteous, wrote one missionary, and the 'heartiness of his handshake was something to be remembered'.[62] When the Matabele were finally overthrown in 1893, Matabele Wilson, who had lived in the country since 1888, and who knew Lobengula intimately, recorded in his diary that he was sorry for the king, as he thought most white people were, although for the Matabele as a whole he had not the slightest sympathy.[63] In supplementary notes appended to his diary over fifty years later, he added, 'if ever recognition was due to a fallen man it should be to Loben. A statue could be erected in Bulawayo to his memory as one of the greatest friends the white man ever had.'[64]

Mirambo, the Wanyamwesi chief, the 'Napoleon of Central Africa', as he was often called, also emerges from the obscurity of African history as a brave, dignified, and powerful leader treated with respect and admiration by whites. When J. P. Farler of the U.M.C.A. wrote to *The Times* in 1878 pleading for money to send a mission to this chief and his people, he called Mirambo 'a brave and liberal man without any of the superstitions of the African, [who] knows well the advantages of civilization'. Most important of all, he was said to be desirous of following 'the religion of the English'. The Wanyamwesi, readers of *The Times* were informed, were 'one of the most in-

THE NOBLE SAVAGE

telligent tribes of Central Africa', and 'great travellers' who 'have penetrated into countries yet unknown to us'. Farler had never met Mirambo, and his praise clearly reflected Mirambo's opposition to the Arabs,[65] but those who met him supported Farler's favourable description.

Stanley, who had aided the Arabs in their quarrel with Mirambo on his trip to succour Livingstone, met the warrior chief on his next trip to clear up some of the outstanding geographical problems of the interior. He was quite 'captivated' by this 'thorough African *gentleman*'. He noted in his journal:

> He is a man about 5 feet 11 inches in height, and about thirty-five years old, with not an ounce of superfluous flesh about him. A handsome, regular-featured, mild-voiced, soft-spoken man, with what one might call a 'meek' demeanour, very generous and open-handed. The character was so different from that which I had attributed to him that for some time a suspicion clung to my mind that I was being imposed upon, but Arabs came forward who testified that this quiet-looking man was indeed Mirambo. I had expected to see something of the Mtesa type, a man whose exterior would proclaim his life and rank; but this unpresuming, mild-eyed man, of inoffensive, meek exterior, whose action was so calm, without a gesture, presented to the eye nothing of the Napoleonic genius which he has for five years displayed in the heart of Unyamwezi, to the injury of Arabs and commerce, and doubling the price of ivory. I said there was *nothing*; but I must except the eyes which had the steady, calm gaze of a master.[66]

Southon, L.M.S. missionary at Urambo from 1879 until his death in 1882, probably had more intimate contact with this chief than any other European. Mirambo, he wrote, 'is far more intelligent than his followers and readily comprehends an idea which is far above them. Anything new, he eagerly inquired into and does not rest satisfied until he understands it.'[67] He praised his political astuteness, and stated that in building his empire Mirambo acted with a moderation and wisdom 'seldom seen in a native prince'. He created a loyal following among his new subjects by lavishing presents and prestige on the sub-chiefs who came into his kingdom as his hegemony expanded and by giving the commoners 'new rights and privileges . . . which raised them far above their former degraded serfdom'.[68] Southon's favourable attitude to this chief and his people was common among these early white pioneers.[69] Wanyamwesi porters, constantly encountered on the caravan route from the coast to Lake Tanganyika, impressed Britons by their physical endurance and their initiative. Joseph Thomson claimed that no matter where the Wanyamwesi settled they were sure to become an important factor due to their superior intelligence, mechanical skill, and love of trade.[70]

THE NOBLE SAVAGE

Although Mirambo and Lobengula have been singled out, it would be equally possible to present laudable descriptions of other African chiefs such as Mandara, the Chagga chief, Rumanika, the chief of Karagwe, and Lewanika, the Barotse ruler. Livingstone's comment is apposite: 'After a great deal of intercourse with different rulers, we have been unable to discover the grounds on which "sensation writers" have managed to envelop African Chiefs with an air of ridicule.'[71]

The comparatively favourable attitudes displayed to some of the major chiefs had several causes. The imperatives of leadership in all societies exert a tendency for capable men to attain positions of political power. It is also likely that the disturbed condition of the interior placed a premium on above average attributes of courage and intelligence. In addition to exceptional abilities these men were in command of much more information than tribal commoners and had more intimate and frequent contact with foreigners. For these reasons the major chiefs were closer to the white man in terms of experience and knowledge, a factor which provided a basis for respect and a certain meeting of minds. Further, the impossibility of dealing with such men as Mirambo and Lobengula by the simple exercise of authority, as with the caravan porter, made communication a two-way process, and meant that their actual qualities were readily observable. Finally, respect for chiefs was respect for power. British attitudes of respect and disrespect closely followed the distribution of power within tribes as well as its distribution among tribes which, as already noted, led to an appreciation of the strong and powerful tribes and a contempt for the weak and the impotent.

6

Admiration for the aristocratic dignity of the Masai or for the sterling attributes of such warrior chiefs as Mirambo was one thing. They were the strong. Acceptance of the system of which they were a part was an entirely different matter. Central Africa was in the throes of anarchy as tribalism adapted to a new environment in which the arts of peace were of diminishing utility. The disruption of the slave trade and tribal war carried on with more deadly weapons of destruction wrought havoc in the interior and destroyed any prospect of the 'happy savage' thesis finding significant acceptance among British observers. Conditions were such that any approach imbued with cultural relativism seemed a dereliction of responsibility and a refuge for the cynics or the indifferent. The most convinced proponents of imperialism were those who had seen the turmoil evoked by the destructive conduct of men, Arabs, Portuguese, and Africans themselves, whose power was devoid of long-run humanitarian intent. Not only were tribal authorities incapable of controlling, but they contributed to the carnage and brutality which so shocked the responsible element among the early British pioneers. Tribal morality was outmoded by its incapacity to meet the challenge of the destructive possibilities of the improved military technology which flooded the interior with western guns and powder. Parochial concepts of group membership became anachronistic when the power to kill or capture accompanied an increase in opportunities to turn human beings into items in exchange transactions. Battered by the slave trade and tribal war, Central Africa required the restraining hand of imperialism to turn the energies of its inhabitants to more constructive pursuits.

V

THE IMPOSSIBILITY OF CULTURAL RELATIVISM

1

THE moral justification for imperialism, the objective verification of the savagery of the African, and, to the British, the most striking proof of their own civilized nature, was found in the endemic conditions of tribal war, the cruelty with which it was waged, and the apparent impossibility of improvement without outside intervention.

> The good old rule, the simple plan,
> That he should take who has the power,
> That he should keep who can.[1]

Such was Duff Macdonald's summary of conditions south of Lake Nyasa, an area where a law of the jungle analysis was consistently employed by the British. Indeed, in the early sixties there was a widespread assumption that imminent extinction faced the Manganja tribes caught in the midst of the invading Yao, Portuguese half-caste slavers, and a small body of Makololo left behind by Livingstone.[2] Admittedly this area was somewhat exceptional in the severity of its troubles, but conditions elsewhere did little to belie the British assumption that force was the essential arbiter of tribal fortunes.

East of Lake Nyasa the Gwangwara and the Yao did little to facilitate the growth of the arts of peace and industry. The former attacked and destroyed the U.M.C.A. mission station at Masasi in 1882, raided as far as Kilwa and held the town to ransom, and plundered and looted the villages on the Lake Nyasa coast opposite Likoma Island. The vicious circle bred by insecurity in this area was sadly noted by W. P. Johnson who explained a Yao raid on a Nyasa village by the desire of the raiders to obtain food and resources in order to hold their own against an even more powerful Yao chief,

THE IMPOSSIBILITY OF CULTURAL RELATIVISM

Makanjira, further to the south.³ West of the Lake various Ngoni settlements, stretching from Chikusi's Ngoni in the south to Mombera's warrior bands in the north, caused equivalent havoc with their military tactics of the short stabbing spear, cowhide shields, and a mobile food supply in the form of cattle. Elmslie claimed to have seen an army of Mombera's warriors 'ten thousand strong, issue forth in June and not return till September, laden with spoil in slaves, cattle and ivory, and nearly every man painted with white clay, denoting that he had killed some one'.⁴ Further north, on the Nyasa-Tanganyika plateau, numerous villages in ruins and others surrounded by stockades indicated the insecurity wrought by the Bemba, 'a marauding tribe, dreaded almost from the shores of Nyassa to far up the Eastern shore of Tanganyika'.⁵

The raids of the powerful warrior tribes, the Masai, the Galla, and the marauding Zulu offshoots—Matabele, Ngoni, Landeens, Gwangwara, and Maviti—almost covered the entire area stretching from Bechuanaland to Ethiopia. There was no hope for civilization, so Kirk informed the Foreign Office in 1884, as long as these 'plundering tribes' looted and killed throughout the interior. They 'carry ruin over the whole of East Africa'. No one was safe, and no district secure, for 'sooner or later, the savages come, kill all and cause a desert'. He believed they had done more to stop civilization and ruin Africa than even the slave trade, and until 'completely broken up and kept in check by some strong hand it is useless to hope for an advance of civilization'.⁶

The Masai might well be the epitome of fighting manhood, admired for their physique, courage, and martial prowess, but Kirk, reporting their activities near Tanga in 1885, stated 'their only occupation is lifting cattle and murder'. The first task of any government on the mainland, therefore, would be to wage 'an aggressive war which to be successful must annihilate every vestige of the present Masai system'.⁷

Many Britons were appalled at the ferocity of tribal war and the heavy losses of life which it entailed. The highly emotional nature of the British reaction partially reflected differing attitudes to cruelty and the conventions of war. The killing of women and children and the application of torture were especially repugnant to Britons, yet they were typical practices of African raiding parties. A concession seeker in Matabeleland was told by one of his 'boys' how a Matabele *impi* tortured an old woman to death. First they tied grass around her, and then set it alight 'when she would not respond to the pricks of the assegai'. When she broke loose she was stabbed to death while these 'devils would stand around and laugh at her'.⁸ On another occasion he was told by some of the older Matabele of the days when

THE IMPOSSIBILITY OF CULTURAL RELATIVISM

they were young men 'and had not to go as far as now, hundreds of miles to find an enemy'.

> they would go out on the veldt with their assegais, and hunt all kinds of people and wild animals, and bring them back to the king and [their] homes in triumph. They compared themselves as they were then to their young men of today who go out with a gun, and kill things at a distance. 'Truly our hearts were bigger than theirs.'[9]

The devastation of the Matabele raids, with the killing of people, capture of new recruits, and looting of cattle, eventually created a no man's land around their kingdom necessitating an extension of their raiding operations into ever more distant fields. What this meant in human terms can be given in the words of a European observer who visited the Batoka country after a Matabele raid:

> they had plundered the fields, burnt the villages, mutilated and massacred the men, impaled the women, hung up little children by the feet and roasted them, satisfied their thirst for carnage, and committed nameless atrocities which the pen refuses to describe.[10]

The Barotse and the Baganda were placed a step above the 'savage' by most Europeans, but their raids for cattle and slaves were no less brutal or shocking to white observers. They culminated in long trains of captives filing into the royal capital amidst a wildly excited population eagerly awaiting the results of the distribution of the spoils.[11] The callous methods employed in the civil wars which raged in Barotseland after the assassination of Sepopo in 1877 astonished even experienced frontiersmen. The trader Westbeech described conditions in a letter to his friend J. Fairbairn, just after Lewanika had returned and retaken the country:

> women, children, and all belonging to the rebels were assegaied. Women in the family way were just split open and left to die on the flats, others made fast, children and all and thrown into the lagoons in order to feed the crocodiles. Hundreds have been polished off and it's still going on.[12]

There was a vast gulf between the comfortable security of British life and the turmoil and struggle for existence in Central Africa. The slave trade and the cruelties of tribal war were not abstractions but visible, sickening realities. Thus, when Bishop Mackenzie heard that Livingstone and members of the U.M.C.A. mission party had interfered with a slaving gang in the Shire Highlands, he was doubtful about the wisdom of their action. When he found that a sick baby had had its brains dashed out against a rock because the mother could not carry it fast enough, he quickly changed his mind and thanked God for such a countryman as Livingstone. Mackenzie was never

THE IMPOSSIBILITY OF CULTURAL RELATIVISM

able to erase from his mind the picture of a man 'being stabbed to death'.[13]

War was far from being the only factor which aroused humanitarian concern with respect to cruelty and human suffering. A variety of tribal punishments were highly repugnant to the British. A quote from Mackay reveals an extreme case among the Baganda:

> Death is almost invariably the punishment for adultery, as also for theft on a large scale. The culprits are executed by having their throats cut, just as goats are slaughtered. In some cases they are taken to a distance from the capital, generally to the side of some swamp. Their bodies are then smeared over with butter, or frequently with the gum of the incense tree, and they are hung up alive over a slow fire till dead, the executioner and his slaves meantime sitting by, smoking and drinking, and jeering at the wretch in agony. But, strange to say, all these extreme measures fail to put a stop to theft and other crimes which are every day being perpetrated. Women have their backs seared with red-hot irons, and only recover after months of doctoring. Ears are cut off for very trifling offences, especially among boys. The extraction of one or even both eyes is a very common mode of punishment. Noses are also cut off; but perhaps the most hideous form of mutilation consists of cutting away the whole of the lips, leaving the jaws and teeth exposed. I have known the hands and feet to be all cut off, and the poor victim left thus to die by the roadside, his offence having been the theft of only a pot of beer valued at less than a shilling! If a thief is found at night in any one's garden, he is simply speared to death, no inquiries being made about the matter.[14]

Mutilation, which was also practised by such major chiefs as Lobengula, Kazembe, and Msidi, aroused very strong British reactions. Human sacrifices, for whatever purpose, were regarded as murder sanctioned by folly. Finally, and more important because more widespread, there was the belief in witchcraft and its consequences, which for the captured witch often included burning at the stake 'before a howling, cursing crowd'.[15]

In addition to the general condemnation of a practice which Britons believed violated all principles of reason and justice, there was a very widespread tendency, as Rowley pointed out, 'to regard the witch-doctors generally as impostors'.[16] The discovery and punishment of witches was regarded as a fraudulent Machiavellian technique employed by chiefs or witchdoctors to accomplish some personal end such as getting rid of the unpopular or gaining possession of the goods of the wealthy.

In spite of their general assumption that witchcraft was morally wrong and socially harmful, Europeans were unable to decide on whether or not witches existed. Some Europeans, living in an atmosphere of infectious belief, picked up the superstition themselves.

THE IMPOSSIBILITY OF CULTURAL RELATIVISM

Others scorned the possibilities of witches having an actual existence or possessing the powers with which they were credited. Finally, there were those such as Maples who could not make up their minds on whether or not witchcraft was a fact, but insisted that it was a sin and a crime.[17]

Attitudes to witchcraft were distorted by a cultural inability to distinguish between the practitioners of malicious witchcraft and the witch doctors who protected the community against evil witches, and rooted them out. To the African this distinction was fundamental. To the British, reluctant to believe in the existence of witches or the possible efficacy of mystical methods of inducing sickness, death, or misfortune, there was naturally no need for protection against these non-existent entities and, by a further extension, witch doctors were assumed to be frauds battening on the unrealistic fears of gullible populations. This general inability of whites to distinguish between witches and witch finders was reflected in later colonial regulations which condemned the entire practice, and by so doing led, in the opinion of numerous observers, to an actual increase in insecurity as Africans were no longer able to openly protect themselves against the doings of evil-intentioned witches.[18]

The observable brutality of inter-tribal relationships, and an apparent delight in cruelty, were of major importance in substantiating British beliefs in African savagery. Ideas of progress and a confident frame of mind engendered a feeling of moral rectitude which, to the mid-twentieth century citizen with two global wars in his immediate background, seems indicative of a naïve age of innocence. In a discussion at the 'Club' in Bulawayo during the Matabele rebellion, the Marques del Moral wrote that 'no one excused the barbarity of Zulu methods of killing but most of us agreed it was absurd to try and judge such by standards of civilization'. More than fifty years later the chronicler of the discussion added a footnote to the above entry in his diary. With Buchenwald, Belsen, and Russian slave camps as examples of 'civilized' conduct, he pointed out that modern man had made 'mental torture . . . a fine art and added to physical torture something undreamt of by savages'. Zulu methods were definitely preferable. 'So much for "civilized" warfare!' he concluded.[19]

The general British reaction of a simple deeply felt abhorrence for the cruelties of tribalism, coupled with implicit assumptions of moral superiority, was modified by several variables. One was a sense of history which, by indicating that white men too had burnt witches and performed other bestial acts, minimized the moral gulf between white and black and induced a certain tolerance.

An important and undoubtedly widespread tendency was a grow-

THE IMPOSSIBILITY OF CULTURAL RELATIVISM

ing impassivity, an inability to be deeply stirred. David Picton Jones indicated that this blunting of sensitivity was one of the most painful effects of constant European sickness:

> Where the suffering was greatest, there generally was to be found the greatest coldness and lack of sympathy. Men seemed to be tired of seeing sickness, and to want to shake off all responsibility in regard to it. When they were told: 'So and so is dead', little interest or feeling was shown. All they would say, possibly, would be: 'Who will be the next, I wonder?' Yet I cannot believe that they were quite so unfeeling as sometimes they appeared to be.[20]

This attitude was even more apparent with respect to African suffering. Inhumanity and cruelty were part of the prevailing atmosphere, and when it was not possible to alter the situation, the result often was a slow, unconscious, but gradual acceptance. Rowley had seen so much death from famine in the Shire Highlands that he could watch men and women die 'almost with indifference', although even at this stage the sight of long famished children wrung his heart.[21]

In some cases the response was cynical lack of concern. In 1890 Colenbrander wrote from Bulawayo to the Secretary of the B.S.A. Co. that he had nothing to report and everything was quiet. Lobengula 'has been killing a good few witches but this does not concern us'.[22] An early concession seeker described how he walked into the body of a strangled woman hanging from a tree: 'I never heard why she was killed. I never worried. It was no concern of ours.'[23] A slightly different version embodied the assumption that those who were being killed were worthless anyway. 'The world would not have lost much if the whole of the Mashona were gone to make room for a better people. They won't work and if by any chance some do, you can never tell the moment he will run away, without giving you the least warning,' wrote Wilson, reflecting on the Matabele-Mashona strife.[24] Finally, there was the explanation provided by evolutionary science. W. M. Kerr was highly sympathetic to Africans but in travelling through Mashonaland he came to the conclusion that the Mashonas were a declining race 'exemplifying strongly the Darwinian doctrine of the survival of the fittest'. Unable to resist the 'stronger blood' of Zulu tribes, he felt they were probably doomed to disappear from the world's stage and become but a memory.[25]

Yet, when all the qualifications from modified acquiescence or Darwinian explanation to cynical indifference have been noted, the basic fact remains that cruelty and suffering were undoubtedly the most important factors in producing a British reaction against the *status quo* in the pre-imperial period. The white man, stated Ward, no matter how long he stayed in Africa, could never completely conquer

THE IMPOSSIBILITY OF CULTURAL RELATIVISM

his 'repugnance to the callous indifference to suffering that he meets with everywhere in Arab and Negro'. Life was for the strong and powerful. On a caravan the dying were left by the wayside, while the weak dropped out of the ranks and the caravan passed on leaving them to a lonely fate.[26]

No complicated arguments for white intervention in the affairs of Central Africa were required beyond the basic one of humanity. The humanitarian task itself was simple. The words which Bishop Knight-Bruce applied to the Matabele were of general application:

> The Theology which the Matabele . . . will have to learn for the next quarter of a century will *not* be (what some clergy seem devoted to teaching) what separates one Christian Body from another; but that it is wrong to take all the babies of a village by the heels, and break in their heads against the ground: that there can be no Heaven for the warriors of a tribe who assegai women in cold blood; and that to murder, lie, and steal are not qualities to be proud of.[27]

2

The basic tragedy of Central Africa was that its descent into intertribal anarchy was aided rather than impeded by the Arabs and the Portuguese who, at that time, formed its main link with the outside world. Neither Arabs nor Portuguese were capable or desirous of easing the socially necessary transition which the forces of historical change demanded of the African. An examination of these two groups and the British attitude to them is helpful therefore in understanding Central African conditions and the British image of themselves as agents and precursors of social change.

David Livingstone penetrated the interior in the hope of finding tribes untouched by the vices of civilization. That this was a vain hope was soon indicated by his travels in the fifties among the Makololo and the tribes they had subjugated on the upper Zambesi. To satisfy their desire for guns the Makololo had sold slaves to the Mambari,[28] to Silva Porto, a Portuguese trader from the west coast, and to some Arabs from Zanzibar.[29] Slave-dealers from both coasts had made contact in South Central Africa while the geography of the interior was still only dimly known in Europe. At the two terminal points of his crossing of Africa, St. Paul de Luanda and Quilimane, Livingstone was in Portuguese territory where slavery and the slave trade were time-honoured institutions. As the evolution of Livingstone's own thought indicated, the conduct of the Arabs and the Portuguese fed British feelings of moral superiority, and rendered easy of acceptance the assumption that if Africans were to be placed on the road to progress the agents of that transformation should be

THE IMPOSSIBILITY OF CULTURAL RELATIVISM

British. With their recently acquired hatred of the slave trade, the British judged these non-indigenous elements primarily with respect to their influence on the African. Their connivance in the traffic in men not only indicated their moral incapacity as agents for the reformation of Africa, but, even without the supplementary evidence provided by tribal war, conclusively refuted any suggestion that the African could be allowed to work out his own destiny.

When Livingstone arrived at Quilimane in 1856 the East African coast was politically divided at the Rovuma River. The southern part, down to Delagoa Bay, contained isolated Portuguese enclaves whose poverty, impotence, and general backwardness were grandiloquently but ineffectively veiled under such romantic names as Inhambane, Mozambique and Ibo. To the north the coast was dotted with Arab towns stretching from Cape Delgado to Warsheikh. For centuries before Mohammed the Arabs had been trading on the coast and transporting goods across the Indian Ocean by dhow to both India and the Middle East. By the fifteenth century an Arab-African coastal civilization had evolved which, at least on a material level, would have stood comparison with any of its European contemporaries. In the early years of the sixteenth century the Portuguese, backed by their superior weapons, overthrew what Frere was later to call this 'ancient and probably progressive Indian and Arabian civilization'.[30] The Portuguese, in wresting dominance of the Indian Ocean from the Arabs, brought the entire coast under their sway, but their rule was baneful in its effects.[31] After two centuries of intermittent revolts and reprisals the Arabs succeeded in throwing off the Portuguese yoke in the north, and by 1740 a tacit delimitation of the coast had been made at the Rovuma River. On the northern half of the coast the Arabs and Swahili never fully recovered the advanced level of civilization achieved by their ancestors, but after 1840 they did initiate a vigorous commercial expansion which took them deep into the interior. In terms of energy they far surpassed their recent Portuguese conquerors whose pretensions to empire were mocked by the apathetic fever-ridden white colonists on the coast and inland on the Zambesi.

Portuguese decadence was obvious to all who visited the east coast in the mid-nineteenth century. The small settlements were stagnant and the colonists demoralized. National zeal and ambition were inconspicuous qualities in the isolated residents cut off by distance and indifference from their homeland. The administration was apathetic and corrupt. Official salaries were small, and frequently much in arrears. Soldiers of the same rank often received unequal recompense. Few of the inhabitants had any real stake in the country. 'What do I care for this country?' an enterprising Tete merchant said to Livingstone; 'all I want is to make money as soon as possible, and then go to Bombay and enjoy it.'[32] The easy road to personal wealth was to participate in the slave trade. Lyons McLeod, British Consul at Mozambique for a short time in the late fifties, stated that Portuguese officials knew the terms of their appointments—'a small salary and the opportunity of making a large fortune by the slave-trade'.[33] As the sale of slaves to foreigners was forbidden, a lucrative and widespread system of bribery evolved to ensure that the law was not enforced. One governor was reported to have made £80,000 out of the slave trade in one year.[34] When Livingstone opened up the Shire Highlands the immediate result was an incursion of Portuguese slavers, one party of which worked for the Governor of Tete, the brother of the Governor-General of Mozambique.

Portuguese participation in the slave trade elicited almost savage British denunciation, coupled with a tendency to attribute Portuguese degradation to their involvement in this crime against humanity.[35] Yet the Portuguese treatment of slaves as domestic servants, on the *prazos*, and in small private armies possessed by many of the colonists does not seem to have been particularly brutal or harsh. Livingstone admitted that the Portuguese treated their slaves well, although the half-castes acquired a reputation for cruel slave-handling.[36] As in the case of the Arabs, however, a recognition of the comparative leniency of the institution of slavery could not justify the havoc caused by the trade itself—a trade in which supplying the domestic market was only significant when external markets dried up.

Although slavery and the slave trade constituted the basis of the humanitarian onslaught on Portuguese Africa, other aspects of the colonists' way of life were singled out for condemnation. They lacked energy and were usually carried in *machillas*, a display of effeminacy and weakness repugnant to the British. With few Portuguese women on the coast, miscegenation was normal. Harems were common on the *prazos*, and the honourable regard for offspring which Livingstone had noted in Angola was absent.[37] Promiscuity—the morals of the country were worse than Sodom according to Livingstone[38]—facilitated the spread of venereal disease which was almost universal.[39] Sexual freedom was accompanied by alcoholic excess in an attempt to relieve the boredom of a forsaken and sickly existence.

The Portuguese provided a clear example of tropical degradation. The climate, disease, an unbalanced sex ratio, an uninterested motherland, and an absence of vigorous willing migrants had the not unexpected effect of undermining morale and morality. There was almost no religious provision for the colonists and missionary work was insignificant. At Zumbo Livingstone noted that the church bell had become a fetish, and travellers observed that the Zambesi boatmen chanted a ditty about 'Mother Mary' which had come down the ages, but actual mission work seems to have fallen into the same state of indolence and decay which affected other aspects of Portuguese activity. The colonists and the local administration had neither the means nor the desire to improve their own condition, let alone that of the African.

The Portuguese way of life elicited neither sympathy nor understanding. Instead, it evoked a mixture of scorn, contempt and occasionally hatred. It provided an opportunity for satisfying an almost lustful indulgence in verbal aggression. 'Surely,' wrote E. D. Young, 'if dissipation, wretchedness, and vice ever were personified to the full in human form, they are to be seen in such men! More sickening examples I never witnessed than amongst these unfortunate wretches.'[40]

A later generation might argue that the Portuguese knew how to 'handle the Natives' with their firm policy,[41] but throughout most of the nineteenth century Native ability to handle the Portuguese was more apparent. The Landeens, a Zulu tribe, came periodically to levy fines upon the inhabitants of Sena as they considered the Portuguese a conquered tribe. The other inland stations on the Zambesi also existed on sufferance and were periodically sacked in the absence of payment of sufficient tribute. The Rev. Wm. Monk informed the British public with biting sarcasm that the Portuguese 'pedlars in human flesh' get beaten 'even in their wretched wars with the natives ... and many pay blackmail to be allowed to cultivate the soil or trade at all'.[42] Neither in conduct nor in power did the Portuguese impress British observers. After a few years of slaving, asserted Bartle Frere in 1873, there was little trace by which one could recognize the descendants of the 'hero nation' of Prince Henry and King John.[43] He pointed out that the Portuguese had failed to attach to themselves either the affection or the respect of the Africans on the mainland. 'Out of sight, they are out of the Mind of their so-called Subjects,' he informed the Foreign Office.[44]

Along the banks of the Zambesi the real power of Portugal rested on the private armies of semi-independent half-castes, men often of ability and capacity who amassed wealth, military followers, and black concubines from a variety of tribes for their pleasures.[45] Although frequently entitled *Sergento Mor* or *Capitao Mor*, and armed by the the Portuguese, these men recognized Portuguese authority in but a nominal fashion. Men such as Mariano alternately fought with Portuguese officialdom and conducted private slaving expeditions in the interior.[46] On his unsuccessful trip to get a treaty from Msidi for the Katanga region, Joseph Thomson ran across a 'ruthless half-caste Portuguese expedition' taking hundreds of young women and

THE IMPOSSIBILITY OF CULTURAL RELATIVISM

children as slaves to Zumbo. He claimed that it would be almost impossible to make Europeans believe the 'enormous extent' to which depopulation had gone on throughout the Loangwa basin. Compared to the Portuguese half-castes such as Matakenya, Thomson felt that Tipu Tib and his fellow Arabs belonged to the Aborigine's Protection Society.[47] With the exception of the doubtful support of these semi-independent brigands and their retainers, government along the Zambesi, declared W. M. Kerr in 1886, was 'wholly a question of price and purchase'.[48]

The Portuguese possessed few of the attributes necessary to command respect. Their hospitality was often highly lauded, but that was all, and hospitality was not an imperial virtue. There was little evidence of the national propensity for understatement in the virtually unanimous scorn, sarcasm, and contempt heaped on the Portuguese by a variety of British observers. The implicit contrast of British zeal, energy, and humanitarianism with Portuguese apathy, indolence, and indifference to the lot of the African evoked an imperialistic response among Britons. To assume that the Portuguese had a significant part to play in the regeneration of Africa seemed either whimsical or outrageous to those who surveyed these relics of decaying grandeur. Livingstone claimed that it was impossible to describe the 'miserable state of decay into which the Portuguese possessions . . . have sunk'.[49] He wrote bitterly of their 'sham sovereignty', 'unwarranted assumption of power over 1360 miles of coast', 'exaggerated and obstructive tariff' and added that their presumption of power was the 'curse of the negro race on the East coast of Africa'. England, he felt, would perform 'a noble service to Portugal by ignoring these pretences to dominion . . . by which, for the sake of mere swagger in Europe, she secures for herself the worst name in Christendom'.[50] Other Britons were no less vehement. Kirk had no sympathy for the petty, greedy system of the Portuguese and was happy to belong to a nation powerful enough to regard them as but an insignificant obstacle to British plans.[51] James Stewart was equally hostile. At Cape Town, even before he had set eyes on the east coast, he wrote in his diary of the 'accursed' Portuguese rule, and their 'trumpery pretensions' to a coast they did not control. Should the interior, he queried, be left to these slavers and tyrants? 'Was it after this fashion that we dealt with these civilised barbarians the Chinese? . . . Nay, truly. My own private opinion is this, the sooner it comes to a little bit of a twist between the two nations the better.'[52]

Admittedly the Portuguese record was far from prepossessing, but they were judged by standards they did not profess. Their colonizing ability had been directed to Brazil and they had never regarded

THE IMPOSSIBILITY OF CULTURAL RELATIVISM

themselves as founders of a land empire in East Africa. They had come to trade and to guard the security of the route to the East, and they were scathingly criticized for not developing the hinterland or ameliorating the lot of the African. In addition, the coastal districts and the thin line of settlement along the Zambesi were feverish and unhealthy.[53] The interior could not be developed until modern means of transport facilitated commerce by overcoming the uneconomic dependence on the porter, or the use of the shallow and unreliable Zambesi. Further, Portugal was a small country incapable of extensive settlement schemes in a difficult tropical environment. Voluntary migrants from the mother country preferred Brazil, and the bulk of the colonists in East Africa were transported criminals and political exiles. Finally, there was a certain incongruity, at least in the initial stages of nineteenth-century British contact, for casual visitors to castigate the admittedly sparse achievements of Portugal when other European states held themselves aloof from prospects of imperial power in tropical Africa.[54]

Yet the moral basis of evaluation used by the humanitarian and missionary element in British contact was not affected by such considerations. Portuguese incapacity as agents of African amelioration emphasized British superiority feelings, and justified intervention on grounds of superior virtue. These attitudes were noticeable in the writings of Captain Owen after his surveying voyages on the east coast in the twenties.[55] They were intensified after the experiences of Livingstone, continued throughout the pre-imperial period, and culminated in the late eighties in the typical attitude of British imperialism that the Portuguese, having done nothing for Africa, had little right to serious consideration when the division of the continent among the powers of Europe took place.[56] A comment widespread in Africa and Europe—'let the Portuguese have only the territory where the whites can't live'[57]—summed up the bundle of attitudes which had evolved around Portuguese Africa.

Moral disapproval was accompanied by scorn for the ineffectiveness of Portuguese power. Eventually, Frere informed the Foreign Office in 1873, the question would have to be faced as to what rights the government of Portugal had to the country beyond the points where alone they held possession and authority.

> They are clearly unable to afford protection or exercise any single right of sovereign authority along most of the coast intermediate between their garrisons on the coast,—or a single march inland from most of their custom houses. Where are we to find the legal frontiers of their possessions and where may we begin to treat with other powers?[58]

In this passage Frere was referring not only to the Portuguese, but also to the position of the Arabs to the north. The Sultan of Zanzibar and his mainland 'empire' faced a no less critical audience than the Portuguese.

3

Unlike the Portuguese, the Arabs were responding to the economic opportunities of Central Africa with considerable vigour. After Sultan Seyyid Said concentrated his attention on his African dominions, Zanzibar became the focal point of an expanding commercial system based on ivory and slaves which, in the half century preceding European control, covered the interior north of the Zambesi with a network of caravan routes and small settlements from the coast beyond Lake Tanganyika into the Congo. Under the guiding genius of this Moslem prince, Zanzibar, an ideal focus for Arab power with its proximity to the mainland, possession of a deep harbour, and a supply of pure water, grew rapidly in importance and prosperity. This was reflected in an increasing European interest in that island in terms of consular representation, commercial enterprise and missionary activity. It was here that the great caravans, financed by resident Indians, were fitted out for the interior. Here was the slave market where black humanity was examined and purchased for the clove plantations of the island and for shipment to the Middle East and elsewhere.

Although a numerically significant Arab-Swahili penetration of the mainland only occurred under the stimulus of the nineteenth-century demand for ivory, there had long existed a reasonably continuous cultural diffusion of coastal influence into the interior. For at least a century before European control the Yao had acted as middlemen and traders, bartering ivory, beeswax, tobacco and slaves with the coastal Arabs for guns, gun-powder, cloth and beads. The Wanyamwesi had manned caravans from the coast to the Lake Tanganyika regions for generations. In 1879 Hore of the L.M.S. wrote that the 'Oriental element' was 'largely diffused' throughout East Central Africa, not only in the person of the Arab, but also by the 'usage of generations as a part of the very nature of the natives'.[59]

As far as the interior is concerned, Hore's statement was probably an exaggeration. It was, however, highly applicable on the coast where, as a result of racial mingling between Arab fathers and African mothers, a new race and a new language had grown up over the centuries. After long years of intermarriage there had evolved a coastal Swahili civilization, a racial and cultural fusion of Arab and African. The Swahili were Moslem, but they seem to have understood their faith in only a rudimentary manner, and did not find it incom-

THE IMPOSSIBILITY OF CULTURAL RELATIVISM

patible with a continuing element of tribal belief. Beyond this social diffusion of their religion, the Arabs, like later generations of white settlers, do not seem to have concerned themselves with proselytization. Not only had Seyyid Said instituted a policy of religious toleration in the interests of commerce, but there is evidence that the slave trade muted Arab religious zeal. The making of converts would have diminished the number of those their religion permitted them to enslave.[60] Krapf felt that their 'usual fanaticism' was checked by their prosperity and their intercourse with heathen tribes.[61] Islam was undoubtedly affected by its contact with tribalism. Charms and talismans were widely used in what missionaries regarded as a bastardized version of the Islamic faith. The daughter of Seyyid Said admitted that superstition 'reigns supreme', and added that the inhabitants of Zanzibar were 'irresistibly' attracted to the occult— 'the less comprehensible a circumstance, the more probable its reality'.[62] An 'increasing love of ardent spirits'[63] provides a further indication of a slackening of religious purity and fervour. Whatever the reasons, many of the Arabs were apathetic about their religion. They were willing to speak of its decay with 'perfect equanimity'. Some even affirmed 'with the most complete indifference' that when the Turkish empire was destroyed Islam would become a thing of the past.[64] Numerous observers noted the unique Moslem tolerance for Christian missionaries. On the island of Zanzibar, wrote Kirk in 1875, 'Christian bells are rung along side of the Mohammedan Mosques and the chants of the Roman Catholic Mission almost drown the prayers of the Faithful without a remark. Every form of worship is tolerated whether it be the various rites of sects of Mohammedans that elsewhere cannot meet in peace or the idolatry of the Hindoo.'[65]

In the interior the Arabs and Swahili sought neither converts nor political power. They created no Moslem states comparable to those of the western Sudan. They grew wealthy as commercial adventurers without the necessity of acquiring political hegemony. Well armed and adaptable frontiersmen, they opened up Central Africa with a network of caravan routes which, had European political control not intervened, might have carried them to the west coast. Along these routes, way stations which often became flourishing settlements were established. In 1861 when Livingstone visited Kota Kota on the west side of Lake Nyasa the Arabs had few attendants. When he returned in 1863 they had in their village and adjacent territory some fifteen hundred persons.[66] During his visit to Taborah in the fifties Burton noted that the Arabs lived comfortably, and imported various goods from the coast.[67] Ujiji, smaller and less luxurious, possessed Swahili carpenters, sandal makers and gunsmiths, and was a flourishing market area for the lakeside tribes with barter supplemented by a bead currency. When the Congo Free State forces captured Kasongo they found a profusion of European luxuries, including candles, sugar, matches, silver and glass goblets and decanters. Even the 'commonest soldiers' of the conquering forces slept on silk and satin mattresses in carved beds with silk mosquito curtains. The granaries of the town possessed 'enormous quantities' of rice, coffee, maize and other food. Well-planted gardens contained a variety of fruit illustrating the 'splendid work which had been done in the neighbourhood by the Arabs'. In Kasongo and Nyangwe every large house was fitted with one or more bathrooms.[68]

These levels of luxury indicated a tendency for trade to merge into settlement. One missionary asserted in 1881 that many of the traders at Ujiji, Taborah and Nyangwe seemed 'to have given up all thought of returning to the coast'. They could not bear its restraint, he claimed, and were always glad to get back into the interior again where 'they have more freedom to do as they please and find themselves with more power than they could ever expect to attain to in their own country'.[69] Cameron cited a typical case in Muinyi Dugumbi, the headman at Nyangwe of the Wamrima from the Bagomoyo district, who, 'finding himself a far greater personage here than he could ever hope to be in his native place, gave up all idea of returning to the coast, and devoted his attention and energies to establishing a harem'.[70]

While evidence is difficult to obtain it seems that half-castes were more likely than pure Arabs to settle in the interior. The pull of Zanzibar was obviously less for these men and the attractions of the interior were correspondingly greater. Faced with the prospect of being Caesar in a village or second at Rome, many of them preferred the former. Paradoxically, the diffusion of coastal influence into the interior diminished the influence of the Sultan. At the same time as Kirk was building up the Sultan's power on the island of Zanzibar the scattered dispersion of his subjects created increasingly independent centres of power in the interior tribes. The tentacles of influence from Zanzibar became increasingly difficult to exercise as the distance from the coast increased and duration of stay in the interior grow longer.

The Arab and Swahili capacity to plant oases of civilization in the interior, coupled with their easy-going race attitudes, led many Britons to regard them as valuable pioneers of civilization, well suited in terms of race, culture, and religion to play a key part in the elevation of the African. Yet this approach was vitiated by the fact that one of the predominant aims of British policy in Central Africa, the gradual restriction and eventual abolition of the slave trade, ran

THE IMPOSSIBILITY OF CULTURAL RELATIVISM

counter to a basic aspect of Arab life. Slavery, sanctioned by the Koran, was an integral part of Arab society. As the daughter of Seyyid Said stated: 'whoever wants to be regarded as wealthy and important in the East must have an army of servants.'[71] On Zanzibar and Pemba the production of cloves fostered by Said led to a recurrent demand for slaves as the low plantation birth rate did not replenish slave numbers. The first British Consul in Zanzibar, Atkins Hamerton, claimed that many of the landed proprietors of these two islands has 'as many as from four to fifteen hundred slaves'.[72] Early in 1842 he wrote:

> All each and every one [of] the subjects of His Highness the Imam of Muskat are concerned in the slave trade, being holders of slaves, every person in proportion to his means, each man possessing from five slaves to five hundred; and from which number they sell as many as from time to time they require to realize whatever sum or sums of money they may happen to want. A man's wealth and respectability in the dominions of the Imam of Muskat is [sic] always estimated by the number of African slaves he is said to possess. The meanest of the Imam's subjects in Oman, Zanzibar and the coast of Africa, whether an Arab, a half-caste Arab, or a freed man, such free man being a Mussulman, never dreams of doing any sort of labour, when he has once got sufficient money to purchase a slave or slaves. . . . He has but one care on earth —how to procure the means of obtaining slaves.[73]

Thirty years later Frere noted that slaves all along the coast were important articles of commerce and investment, handled without any feelings of legal or moral responsibility by most coastal natives and their Arab rulers.[74] As in the case of the Portuguese, Arab involvement in the slave trade evoked the wrath of British humanitarians. A picture was created of idyllic African societies, a prey to the dawn raids of treacherous Arabs.[75] This was helpful to British prestige, missionary propaganda, and the attainment of imperial aims, but it possesses only partial truth. Such a picture, by reducing history to the level of a national ego enhancer, ignores the complex interaction between various tribal groupings and Arab and Swahili pioneers. Hore of the L.M.S. admitted that the 'degradation, misery, and death' associated with the slave trade were undeniable, but correctly added that the African should share responsibility. Slavery, he insisted, was 'a most complicated system, the details of which require years to understand'.[76]

In the first place it is clear that the pursuit of ivory was the essential motivation which drove Arabs half way across the continent. On grounds of logic alone it is self-evident that the Arabs did not travel past hundreds of thousands of Africans closer to the coast in order to reach the Congo River in search of slaves. Yet for economic reasons the slave trade was closely integrated with the ivory trade. They complemented each other nicely. The slaves not only provided porterage for the precious tusks, but were themselves saleable when the caravan reached the coast. While ivory was the predominant factor in the Arab drive across the continent, their readiness to purchase slaves created an incentive for Africans to procure them even if they did not make a practice of deliberately generating intertribal wars as anti-slavery propagandists asserted. They also spread gunpowder and guns which increased the ferocity of tribal war by enhancing the destructive capacities of societies living at a subsistence level.

The slave trade was not an alien imposition, but in many cases a cooperative endeavour between Africans and Arabs. Domestic slavery was widespread in African societies and tribal ethnocentrism facilitated the enslaving and selling of members of alien tribes. Africans, indeed, often expressed astonishment and disbelief when Europeans refused to purchase slaves,[77] or in the case of women, even accept them as gifts.

The fundamental problem of Central Africa derived from the fact that in many areas man was a disposable asset.[78] An exchange of slaves was a common practice among chiefs.[79] The Arabs sold slaves for ivory to the Manyuema cannibals west of Lake Tanganyika who 'fattened them up for eating'.[80] The Portuguese not only exported slaves but also sold them for ivory 'to a tribe that lived far inland, and who, having been unfortunate in war with the Matabele had lost to their conquerors most of their women and children'.[81] The Bakuba in the Congo purchased male slaves 'for the sole purpose of killing them at funerals'.[82]

The practice of slavery was exceptionally widespread. Porters on caravans dealt in slaves while bringing supplies to the L.M.S. mission stations near Lake Tanganyika. When the missionaries protested their agents in Zanzibar pointed out the inevitability of slave-dealing 'if Swahili are employed in a country where slaves are a more popular form of investment than Consols would be at home'.[83] Runaway slaves formed colonies north of Mombasa and then became active participants in the slave traffic themselves.[84] Slave selling was often a product of economic necessity. In some districts famine often resulted in local kidnapping and the sale of the captives in exchange for food.[85] Slavery was simply a fact of life which often seemed to imply no particular degradation for the enslaved. This was especially true of internal tribal slavery which was usually mild and with no significant 'difference of condition between the bond and the free'.

All lived alike, all followed the same occupations. A stranger passing

THE IMPOSSIBILITY OF CULTURAL RELATIVISM

through their land would not know, from anything he saw to remind him of it, that there existed amongst them such a distinction as bond and free. . . . slavery as it exists amongst the agricultural tribes of East Central Africa, when left untouched by foreign influences, is productive of no great harm. It does not degrade morally, and it scarcely seems to inflict a stigma socially. . . .[86]

Pilkington of Uganda related the story of a young boy who had been purchased by one of Stanley's porters for four yards of cloth and 'seemed rather proud of having been worth so much'.[87] The complexity of the situation was best revealed in an incident mentioned in the correspondence of Charles Livingstone. He reported the case of an African who sold himself to a kind Portuguese master for three pieces of calico, and with the proceeds forthwith bought himself a wife and a boy.[88]

In brief, the 'buying and selling of humans was a universal practice',[89] a factor which helps to account for the comparative absence of hostility to the Arabs. This does not mean that the slave trade was always carried out by peaceful means; nor that its victims were indifferent as to whether they remained in their villages or were seized and transported to the coast. The horrible slaughter witnessed by Livingstone at the market-place in Nyangwe,[90] the brutal and treacherous raids by half-castes on the Wankonde culminating in a fiendish massacre,[91] serve to indicate the atrocities which the slave trade sometimes brought in its wake. There was, inevitably, even under the best of circumstances, much callousness and cruelty involved in the breaking up of kin ties, the frequent change of masters, and the weary hungry march to the coast to be followed by a necessary learning of a new way of life among strangers. Yet it remains essential to place the whole nefarious business in its context and to indicate that the responsibility for the existence and continuation of slavery and the slave trade cannot be attributed to one specific racial group. Those in Europe who purchased products made of ivory and paid no concern to the processes by which it was obtained are not entirely blameless.[92] Criticism of Arabs and Africans cannot justifiably ignore the lack of alternative means of transporting goods in the interior, and the absence of a labour market which would have freely supplied the plantations of Zanzibar and Pemba and the caravans to the interior with the labourers these endeavours required. Finally, it is not without relevance to point out the almost standard use of coercive taxes by European administrations to force Africans on to the labour market when the responsibility for a labour supply was placed in their hands. These points do not constitute a defence of the sordid practice of the sale of human beings. They do, however, indicate that in Central Africa the practice was a response to certain

THE IMPOSSIBILITY OF CULTURAL RELATIVISM

economic problems and that it occurred within a cultural framework which facilitated its ready acceptance.

The ubiquity of slave trading in the interior meant that measures of repression at the coast or treaties with the Sultan of Zanzibar could only stop a part of the trade. In the first place, as Arabs and Swahili settlement grew in the interior, more and more slaves, employed in Arab or Swahili households or in agricultural work, never reached the coast at all but spent their working lives at Ujiji, Taborah, Kasongo or elsewhere.[93] Then the internal slave trade 'that so universally prevails in Africa between the various native tribes'[94] was immune from the efforts of the British anti-slave squadron in the Indian Ocean. It was this aspect of the trade which caused Alfred Sharpe to assert that it was the African who was constantly selling his fellows to the Arabs, 'and it is the *native* who is the great upholder of the Slave Trade'.[95]

To many of the major chiefs of the interior the Arabs were not alien intruders, but eagerly coveted arrivals who distributed much desired guns and powder, cloth and beads, and other trinkets in exchange for slaves and otherwise worthless ivory. To the Yao, the Arabs and Swahili were technical and economic agents of great value. Mirambo, the Wanyamwesi chief, saw them as bitter enemies intent on destroying his hegemony over an area stretching from near Taborah to Lake Tanganyika and northwards to Lake Victoria. Yet, in spite of the missionary backing he received, Mirambo was a slaver himself, and cooperated with Arabs and Swahili when it was to his advantage. He employed Swahili artisans in his capital at Urambo. Even in the midst of his struggles with the Taborah Arabs, he found Arab unity insufficiently strong to prevent some traders from supplying him with guns which could then be used against the co-religionists of the sellers. As such situations make clear, the interaction between Arabs and Africans was a complex process in which responsibility for the growing insecurity of life in the interior cannot be readily affixed to any one group. Even the L.M.S. missionary A. J. Swann, a fiery opponent of the slave trade, could recognize the peace and security around the settlement of the Arab Kabunda at the south end of Lake Tanganyika.[96] It was not Kabunda's presence, but his departure for the coast which evoked an increase in slaving. He left a vacuum behind which became the scene of small-scale slaving and raiding on the part of renegade Wanyamwesi, slaves of a deceased Arab, neighbouring Bemba, and the Walungu themselves.[97]

Yet, if analysis of the slave trade and slavery serves to indicate its complexity, it remains evident that its most important effect was a marked increase in suffering and insecurity for those unable to defend themselves. In general, the increased wealth and power of the few—Arabs, chiefs, and members of dominant tribes—was purchased at a heavy cost, paid largely by others.

But after the slave had been torn from his kindred, and if he survived the long march to the coast, he experienced a comparatively mild form of servitude under kindly if somewhat indifferent Arab masters. There was very broad agreement that the Arabs were lenient with their slaves.[98] An exercise of ingenuity by Devereux and Rigby evoked the assumption that lenient slave treatment merely proved Arab apathy and indolence, thus transmuting an absence of harsh treatment into proof of sloth.[99] This simply indicated the observable mildness of the institution of slavery to even critical observers. In discussions with Sultan Barghash over the abolition of the sea-borne slave traffic, the Rev. Percy Badger, interpreter for Sir Bartle Frere, admitted 'upon the almost unanimous testimony of well informed foreigners' that the slaves at Zanzibar were well treated.[100] Consul Pelly, after visiting Arab plantations in the early sixties, thought the slaves were comfortable, well-hutted, adequately fed, with clean homesteads, and a demeanour anything but servile.[101]

To a considerable extent the British attitude to slavery was based not only on a humanitarian and Christian respect for personality, but also on the growth of economic individualism, a market economy, and a diminishing acceptance of the type of traditional bond of responsibility and obligation which had prevailed between master and serf in medieval times. The absence of a social, as distinct from an economic, relationship between employer and worker in Britain undoubtedly tended to mean that the social context which bound African slaves and Arab masters into a reciprocal relationship was difficult for Britons to properly appreciate. The actual mildness of the reality of Arab slavery was obvious to all observers, but the reality conflicted with the stereotype of sugar and cotton plantation slavery —a factor which inevitably confused thought, understanding and discussion on the subject. Livingstone glimpsed the gist of the matter with his usual perspicacity:

> The Arabs are said to treat their slaves kindly, and this also may be said of native masters; the reason is, master and slave partake of the general indolence, but the lot of the slave does not improve with the general progress in civilization. While no great disparity of rank exists, his energies are little tasked, but when society advances, wants multiply; and to supply these the slave's lot grows harder. The distance between master and man increases as the lust of gain is developed, hence we can hope for no improvement in the slave's condition, unless the master returns to or remains in barbarism.[102]

In other words, the saving grace of slavery in Central Africa was the pre-capitalistic, 'non-progressive' social context in which it occurred.

THE IMPOSSIBILITY OF CULTURAL RELATIVISM

Legal ownership was not used in the interests of ruthless economic exploitation. The gradations of slavery were subtle and manifold. The status of an individual slave often improved throughout his lifetime—perhaps culminating in manumission and exaltation to the status of a slave owner. It remains a striking paradox that the British who fought to eventually overthrow the institution of slavery were less friendly to the African, and less likely to treat him as a human being, than were the Arabs against whom they raised the cry of freedom. The attack on slavery represented hatred of a concept rather than love of its victims.

Many of the British, in fact, possessed little short of an obsessional hostility to the slave trade and slavery. The conviction that the slave trade was an anachronism in a world undergoing constant improvement automatically placed the British, as judges and deliverers, in the vanguard of the moral progress of the world. Concomitantly those communities which defied Britain, 'the chief instrument in the hands of Providence'[103] for its abolition, were unenlightened, medieval, and backward, deserving of little sympathy, if not objects of scorn and contempt.

In addition, the institution of slavery was considered incompatible with economic growth. As it rested on an immoral use of human beings there was an assumption that it could not be rewarded in the same manner as hard Christian effort without making a mockery of the moral meaning of the universe. The increase in the wealth of Zanzibar, which reflected the enlightened policy initiated by Seyyid Said, was, for this reason, incongruously attributed to the presence of Europeans by the Methodist missionary Charles New.[104] The existing prosperity of Zanzibar, Britons argued, was but a fraction of that which would ensue from the adoption of free labour. In any case, it was unthinkable that the degree of affluence attained by Zanzibar justified the depopulation of the interior. The British, missionaries in particular, saw themselves as purveyors of attitudes which would significantly stimulate economic growth while at the same time destroying the great moral evil of slavery.

Further, it was a widespread assumption that the Arab virtues of manliness, energy and simplicity had been swamped by their aristocratic life as owners of slaves. The East African Arab, argued Frere, was far removed from his ancestors in Arabia, 'men of war from their youth', who grew up amongst fierce tribes in a harsh, rugged environment. His descendants in Zanzibar and on the coast, surrounded by slaves, lived a life of 'indolent ease' which had destroyed the more energetic virtues characteristic of the Arab.[105] The same point was made by Rigby, who added black concubines to the list of causal factors in Arab 'degeneration'.[106]

THE IMPOSSIBILITY OF CULTURAL RELATIVISM

The question of sex to which Rigby referred cannot be ignored as a factor in British attitudes to the Arab. In general, the harem and progress were considered incompatible as sexual indulgence seems to have been associated with a reduction of energy available for other purposes. This is seen in Pelly's comment that Sultan Majid

> has probably indulged too frequently, and at too early an age, his sexual passion, and to this fact I surmise His Highness may attribute a good deal of the softness of his brain and character. As a man, he is doubtless a poor specimen.[107]

Among missionaries the Arab attitude to sex produced a reaction only slightly, if at all, less condemnatory and hostile than Arab association with the slave trade.[108] If bitterness of verbal denunciation is a trustworthy guide a strong case can be made that the difference in sexual morals was the key factor conditioning the missionary attitude to Islam.[109] To the missionary, the seventh commandment was the keystone of morality. He upheld the virtues of the monogamous middle-class family of Victorian Britain. In the marriage relationship the base desires of the male were given a legitimate but restricted outlet falling far short of sexual indulgence. Women were exalted, and home was regarded as the fount and origin of the gentler social virtues. A wife was a helpmeet who offset and softened the rougher masculine qualities by her more spiritual nature and outlook. Sexual indulgence and polygamy, held to be closely related, were not only repugnant to the Christian ethic, but antagonistic to social and moral progress which were assumed to be integrally associated with systems of monogamous marriage in which sexual passion played but a minor role. Not only was Islam directly antagonistic to these assumptions, and therefore incapable of regenerating Africa, but, more serious, its looser sexual ethic was held to be one of its greatest attractions to Africans.

The sexual morals of the Arab evoked scathing vituperation from missionaries. Bishop Steere, a highly cultivated man, and a great Swahili scholar, felt that polygamy and divorce had made Moslem marriages 'something lower in the scale of morals than even illicit connections in England'. To keep their husbands, Moslem women had to stoop to the 'same sort of arts' as those by which a mistress keeps her lover, with the result that a London street-walker had a 'higher and better ideal of life than the great Mohammedan ladies', for she knew her way of life was disreputable and hoped to escape from it. He added the more practical point that polygamy 'is based on the cynical avowal that vices are for the rich. When one man has twenty women, somebody must certainly go without.'[110] The U.M.C.A. periodical *Central Africa* favourably quoted the letter of

THE IMPOSSIBILITY OF CULTURAL RELATIVISM

a naval officer from Zanzibar stating that the mind of the average Moslem was 'about the foulest thing' he knew. 'They revel in sensuality and the after dinner recreation was invariably recitations from the Koran, interspersed with the foulest and most bestial stories.'[111] To the Christian propagandist Islam was viewed as sensuality sanctioned by religion, even the afterlife being 'a paradise of sensual delights'.[112] Moslem society was considered to be masculine dominated, with women being but objects of gratification and lust. Given the contrast to the Christian ideal it was perhaps not unexpected that even the more cultured of the missionaries should stoop to verbal abuse rather than analysis when discussing Islam, and should resort to vicious contrasts between the person of Christ and that of Mohammed. Islam, stated Bishop Tozer, is

> a kind of horrible parody of religion, pandering to every passion and lust, and utterly misrepresenting God and goodness. That Mahomet must have been a coarse, vulgar, treacherous man to invent a system which could lull his followers into security, and yet leave them as far from God as ever.[113]

The combination of indulgence in sex and indulgence in slavery, both of which represented to Britons the treatment of other human beings as objects, placed the Arab in direct conflict with two of the most fundamental values of the humanitarian element in these early pioneers. W. Cope Devereux, with a sailor's bluntness, summed up the Arabs as

> ignorant, cowardly and false; their only thoughts being their black concubines, stomachs, slaves and dollars, their present sensual enjoyment, and a repetition of it in a more voluptuous form hereafter in the Prophet's Paradise.
> That they have any fellow-creatures to study, improve, lift up, love and to be loved by them, is foreign to all the ideas of the modern Arab. Affection has no place either in his heart or his vocabulary.[114]

A final factor used as a basis for the criticism of the East African Arabs was the nature of their political system and the absence of a governmental basis to their expansion into the interior. Arab attitudes to political control on the mainland produced a spotty patchwork system of Arab power localized around the coastal towns and the interior settlements. Even along the coast, observed Consul Pelly in 1861, the Sultan's power was 'very slight and undefined'. 'He exercises over the coastal and agricultural tribes and mixed breeds of the low shore a certain degree of authority, but does not tax them or advance any governmental claim to the soil.'[115] Over a decade later the situation was unchanged, for Frere noted that on no part of the coast could the Sultan's power be said to be more than 'skin-deep'.

THE IMPOSSIBILITY OF CULTURAL RELATIVISM

It was not easy, he pointed out, 'to convey to an European mind a correct idea of the very superficial character of the Sultan's authority away from Zanzibar and out of reach of his ships'.[116] Shortly after this, when Sultan Barghash visited England, Kirk pointed out that his suite contained two distinct groups. There were 'really intelligent men' who would be useful to his Highness, while others were included as they were too influential and dangerous to be left behind. The Sultan's dominions, Kirk added, were held together by a 'vis inertiae seemingly peculiar to the people of East Africa'. Any disturbing element was capable of fragmenting the whole coast into isolated districts 'under no law'.[117]

The various Sultans, in spite of a few spasmodic aberrations, were satisfied with the existing state of their mercantile empire. They were, as Professor Coupland has made clear, basically merchant princes rather than rulers of a state in the western sense. The Sultans possessed shares in the caravan ventures to the interior, reaped revenues from custom duties, and, by the sending of presents to influential chiefs in the interior, attempted to keep trade flowing smoothly. Beyond that they were unwilling to go. Again and again they were vainly prodded by successive British consuls to display some overt political interest in the mainland. Official British correspondence from Zanzibar constitutes a long lament over the unconquerable Arab political apathy.

The British, however, were asking the impossible. The operation of their policy was based on the cultivation of an influential relationship with the Sultan and from this position the exertion of pressure to secure acquiescence to British demands. The personal prestige of the British consul was ultimately backed by naval force. The fact that the locus of Moslem and Arab influence was on an island, that the city of Zanzibar was a port, and that the Sultan's possessions were predominantly coastal, greatly increased the effectiveness of threats of force when a conflict of interests could not be solved by negotiation. Thus the slave trade treaty of 1873 was signed while Zanzibar was under naval blockade. The illness of a Sultan, with the possibility of a disputed succession, was the signal for a British man-of-war to move into the harbour to preserve peace, protect British lives and property, and, most important, to secure a favourable succession. The Sultan was placed in the position of many an African chief of later days, a position where he was compelled to satisfy conflicting loyalties and demands placed on his influence and powers. British pressure, however, was incapable of inducing the Sultan to establish a framework of law and order on the mainland.

Arab indifference to mainland hegemony reflected not only absence of desire but, and here was the fundamental limiting factor

THE IMPOSSIBILITY OF CULTURAL RELATIVISM

in the extension of Arab political domination, institutional incapacity. The far-flung areas over which Arab caravans roved could not have been ruled by the Arab political system. Their political and administrative institutions were insufficiently developed for imperial rule. An almost total absence of bureaucracy made any talk of extended administration utopian. There was no treasury, properly speaking; accounts were but rarely kept and there was no budget. The monies collected from customs and other sources went to the Sultan who paid some of it out 'indiscriminately' and stowed the remainder in sacks in the cellar.[118] Even on the island of Zanzibar there was no state as such,[119] and no recognized and accepted law of succession to facilitate a peaceful transfer of power at the death of a Sultan. When Seyyid Said died only British intervention prevented serious strife between rival factions for his legacy, and it was found necessary to separate the Muscat possessions from those in East Africa. When Seyyid Barghash died, his successor, Seyyid Khalifa bin Said, was almost totally unprepared for his job as Barghash, fearful of plots, had kept him imprisoned for six years and then forced him to live in isolation in the country. It was difficult enough to operate the existing Arab political system within the restricted boundaries of Zanzibar and the coastal cities. Beyond this the system could not go.

With the exception of the settlements on the main trade routes, Arab power and influence in the interior were personal to leading Arabs and their retainers who moved slowly from place to place. Such a system was well adapted to the pursuit of commercial gain in a disturbed area, but was antithetical to the stability and continuity of power within defined areas which, to the British, was essential to the meaning of government. British scorn for the nature of Arab power in the interior reflected basic cultural differences as to the nature of government and influence.

4

A comparison of British attitudes to Arabs and Portuguese reveals a striking similarity in many of the traits singled out for criticism. In particular, sexual morality, involvement in the slave trade, and an apparent incapacity to make any effective administrative contribution to the establishment of law and order in the interior provided common grounds for criticism. Behind these there was the fundamental humanitarian reproach that the activities of these two groups were not predicated on any acceptance of responsibility for ameliorating the lot of the African. The slave trade provided sufficient proof of this. In addition, neither Arabs nor Portuguese were particularly

THE IMPOSSIBILITY OF CULTURAL RELATIVISM

active in attempting to spread their religious faith to the pagan African. The comparative absence of anti-Catholic attacks in British discussions of the Portuguese undoubtedly reflected the paucity of religious work being undertaken among either colonists or Africans. Islam, on the other hand, was attacked again and again with polemical vigour. The reasons for this were threefold. Islam, if not a missionary religion in Central Africa, was attracting new adherents essentially by the process of cultural assimilation which characterized Arab-African relations. Secondly, there was a deep fear that the moral proximity of Moslem ethics to African values gave Islam an inestimable advantage over Christianity in the struggle to replace paganism. Finally, the bitterness of missionary criticism was an emotional and propagandistic response to the fact that a significant number of Britons, dubious of African capacity to imbibe the high ethical and spiritual content of Christianity, regarded Islam as a religion peculiarly apposite for the elevation of tribal peoples at the bottom of the ladder of human achievement. It is significant that no one argued that the Portuguese had any important part to play in the civilization of the African. The Arabs were at least treated as worthy opponents. Contempt was the standard attitude to the Portuguese.

In the context of the accepted necessity of civilizing the African, the Arabs and the Portuguese were judged and found wanting. In the same context, Africans were felt to be incapable of any fundamental steps on the road to social improvement by their own unaided efforts. The general British attitude to tribalism has already been discussed. Here it only remains to reiterate the truly appalling conditions prevalent in the interior. It is no doubt true that most Africans, most of the time, were engaged in peaceful activities. But Central Africa, whether taken as a whole or in specific regions, was the scene of bloodshed and death of a frequency which must have caused an enormous loss of life. The ethnocentric attitudes of individual Britons fade into insignificance when contrasted with the attitudes and conduct of African tribes to each other. The appellation 'dogs', used by the Barotse to describe the Mashukulumbwe among whom they pillaged and raided, was typical of the attitudes of the haughty powerful tribes whose aggressive tendencies were such a deplorable feature of late-nineteenth-century Central Africa. The brutality and cruelty of the strong indicated little respect or concern for the preservation of other tribal cultures. Tribalism, whatever its advantages, was simply incapable of controlling the inrush of new forces—the demand for ivory, the demand for slaves, the diffusion of guns and powder—which rendered tribal morality incompatible with the survival of societies which gave restricted answers to the question of whether or not they were their brothers' keepers. On the whole it seems clear that in the shifting environment in which tribal man was increasingly called upon to make decisions and to act, the result was a brutalizing of human sensitivity.

VI

BRITISH, CHRISTIAN, AND WHITE

1

THE British attitude to Africans, to Arabs, to the Portuguese, to an acceptable order of race relations, and to the role of the white man in Central Africa was integrally related to their attitude to themselves. The point of origin of British attitudes and conduct was a cultural and racial pride which reflected the dominant global position of Britain and the white race. Statistics of population growth, industrial expansion, rising per capita real income, burgeoning exports, and growing foreign investments gave quantitative and therefore irrefutable proof that Britons were the vanguard of a new era of human history. They saw an ever expanding stream of achievement, power and influence emanating from the white peoples of the earth. The importance of this factor can scarcely be over-emphasized. The nineteenth century witnessed the apogee of white hegemony in the world. The world was being westernized and to be British was to be in the forefront of the process—a fact which evoked a heartening assurance of racial and cultural abilities. The *Daily News*, commenting on Livingstone's crossing of Africa and his subsequent hero's reception in Britain, claimed that it was impossible not to feel

> a thrill of exultation at the thought that, literally, the whole earth is full of our labours—that there is no region in which our industrial enterprise, our skill in arms, our benevolent eagerness to diffuse the blessings of civilization and pure and true religion, have not been displayed.[1]

A racial distribution of power seemed to be an inviolable law of the universe.[2] Confident beliefs in progress had not been shattered by the impact of two world wars on the psyche of western man. It was an era in which the mere fact of being British was felt to be indicative of superiority and virtue, especially in such a backwater as Central Africa where the comparison was with the indolent, corrupt Portuguese, the sensual, slaving Arabs and the primitive, pagan African.

Pride of nationality was especially evident in British explorers,[3] hence the naming of Victoria Falls by Livingstone, Albert Nyanza by Baker, and Victoria Nyanza by Speke.[4] Nationality was a stimulus to courage and daring. When the youthful Joseph Thomson suddenly found himself in charge of an expedition to the interior after the death of his leader, he reasoned: 'with my foot on the threshold of the unknown, I felt I must go forward, whatever might be my destiny. Was I not the countryman of Bruce, Park, Clapperton, Grant, Livingstone, and Cameron?'[5]

There was at times a tendency to assume that Central Africa was, and should remain, a special British preserve whether in humanitarian, economic, or imperialistic areas of activity. This helps to explain Livingstone's desire to rectify the erroneous impression that a young German, Roscher, had discovered Lake Nyasa prior to his own arrival at the south end of the lake,[6] and his perturbation at the inability of the C.M.S. to obtain English rather than German missionaries to staff its mission inland from Mombasa.[7] It helps to explain the cavalier and ungenerous reception accorded Stanley after his discovery of Livingstone, an event which indicated that an American newspaper, the *New York Herald*, had displayed more resourcefulness in aiding the great traveller than had his British compatriots. The President of the Royal Geographical Society, Rawlinson, disseminated vicious and ludicrous remarks, including the aspersion that it was 'not true that Stanley had discovered Livingstone, as it was Livingstone who had discovered Stanley'. More bluntly, Horace Waller asserted that only the 'steel head of an Englishman could penetrate Africa'.[8]

The British possessed the psychological security of living in a world where the power of their own nation was an almost global phenomenon. In practical terms this power was not operative in the heart of Africa, but it still existed in the minds of Britons who travelled beyond its reach. When Samuel Baker and his wife were in trouble with the 'Turks' in the Sudan, Mrs. Baker (a Hungarian) told them they 'did not know what Englishmen were; that nothing would drive them back; that the British Government watched over them wherever they might be, and that no outrage could be committed with impunity upon a British subject'.[9] In the late eighties British missionaries could demand government protection as part of their heritage and rightly assume that their demands were capable of fulfilment.[10] Such feelings, based as they were on the individual's estimate of the power

BRITISH, CHRISTIAN, AND WHITE

and influence of the nation to which he belonged, would have been incongruous to a Spaniard or a Greek. To the Briton they were justified as an accurate reflection of the natural order of the universe.

The optimism and confidence of the Victorian age reached its peak in David Livingstone. He had a simple and yet profound belief in human progress in a world 'rolling to the golden age'. He proudly noted the prosperity of his own era wherein persons of average means wore 'finer clothes than Lords did in the time of Queen Elizabeth', while even those in the workhouse had more comforts than rich African chiefs. He was indeed little short of exultant at the 'glorious future for our world'.

> Surgical operations are performed without pain, fire is obtained instantaneously, and it is probable that before long we shall burn water instead of coal. Intelligence is communicated instantaneously, and travellers are conveyed on the ocean and on the land with a celerety [sic] which our forefathers could not comprehend and which Africans now consider fabulous...
> An electrical machine attached to a kite will bring down rain from a cloud, and this may be so improved as to call down copious showers when needed.[11]

Not only was progress a self-evident fact to Livingstone, but it was inextricably tied up with his optimism about the future prospects for Christianity. In the midst of the preceding passage descriptive of secular advance he stated:

> And when we view the state of the world and its advancing energies in the light afforded by childlike or call it childish faith, we see the earth filling with the knowledge of the glory of the Lord, aye all nations seeing his glory and bowing before him whose right it is to reign.[12]

Livingstone was one of the most tolerant and observant missionaries in nineteenth-century Africa. A sense of humour, a feeling for history, a concern for humanity, and a devout Christian faith kept him remarkably free from arrogance and vulgar pride. It is, therefore, all the more relevant to notice the very deep sense of satisfaction which he felt for his British background. From British women whom he regarded as the most beautiful in the world, to British merchants whom he thought the most upright and benevolent in the world, to the more general approbation that the British were 'the most philanthropic people in the world',[13] and 'perhaps the most freedom-loving people in the world',[14] his reflections reveal little questioning of the virtues of British character or the achievements of British culture. He felt that it was 'on the Anglo-American race that the hopes of the world for liberty and progress rest'.[15] His cultural and racial self-assurance were summed up in his instructions to a subordinate on the Zambesi expedition:

> We come among them as members of a superior race and servants of a Government that desires to elevate the more degraded portions of the human family. We are adherents of a benign holy religion and may by consistent conduct and wise patient efforts become the harbingers of peace to a hitherto distracted and trodden down race.[16]

Race, state, and religion were fused into a composite whole. It was a good time to be white, British, and Christian.

2

The specific self-image of the missionary must be viewed in the broad context of the numerous factors and beliefs to which he related his function as an agent of Christianity. The essence of missionary activity can be summed up in the words used by T. M. Thomas in his application for missionary service with the L.M.S.

> I am anxious to be instrumental to carry the gospel to the poor pagans, that, by making known unto them the way of life, darkness—idolatry and cruelty may disappear from their land and enable them to enjoy the immeasurable and unspeakable blessings which my countrymen do.[17]

The dissemination of the gospel message found ready justification in a variety of biblical injunctions, and in the simple desire of devout Christians to spread the spiritual and ethical system in which they believed. In addition, several interesting and important supplementary arguments were adduced in support of the sending of men and money to the dark places of the earth.

One of the more widespread arguments was simply that among the heathen the needs were great, the labourers were few, and the potential harvest large compared with the situation at home. This basic argument was of great importance for it indicated that all men had the right to hear and the capacity to understand and accept the word of God. Christian universalism based on implicit egalitarian assumptions provided the key rebuttal of those who asserted that the Christian's main responsibility was to his own nation, or that the religious potential of non-western peoples was inadequate to the task of comprehending such an advanced religion as Christianity. The very existence of the missionary presupposed the belief, constantly reiterated in missionary periodicals, that Christianity was suited to all men in all places at all times.

Fundamentally the missionary refused to accept the existence of a conflict between the claims of the heathen at home and the heathen abroad. They were not at all competitive, for it was a standard thesis that mission work in foreign lands was not only symbolic of the health and vitality of the Church, but that it had a stimulating effect on the clergy and laity at home and thus led to an increased concern for the poor and irreligious in Britain. Propagandists for the missionary cause laid great stress on the thesis that Christianity could only prove and maintain its spiritual strength by continual extension. From this viewpoint a non-missionary religion was a contradiction in terms, and expansion became the first law of existence.[18]

A rationale for missionary activity with special reference to Africa was found in the former profitable connivance of Britain in the great evil of the slave trade. This, it was widely argued, called for atonement by especially pronounced endeavours in the task of converting the African. The Church of Scotland declared that her mission to the Lake Nyasa area was

> her first contribution of Christian love to the people who have been for ages the miserable victims of blood and violence. It is the first step which she has taken to make some reparation to the African people for the unnumbered wrongs which our forerunners perpetrated upon them.[19]

These concepts of guilt and atonement, debt and repayment, were also used by the editor of Livingstone's *Cambridge Lectures* when he asserted that Africa had particular claims on the established church, 'the Church of the nation . . . [which] . . . is bound to help in making national reparation'.[20] Livingstone himself longed to see the British nation relieved from the 'guilt and stain' of supporting American slavery by purchasing slave grown cotton and sugar, and felt the necessity for repayment for the 'wrong we have done to Africa'.[21]

Atonement for national sins meant the necessity of doing good to compensate for evils formerly indulged. The 'we must be good because we have been bad' argument was supplemented by the argument that 'we must be good because we are prosperous, powerful, and globally influential'. The possession of privilege and power not only created special opportunities for spreading the gospel, but engendered an onerous 'sacred responsibility' for so doing.[22] A variety of relationships between worldly measures of progress and power and missionary expansion constituted recurrent items in missionary publicity. Secular progress not only fed racial and national pride, it also contributed significantly to religious pride, increased Christian self-confidence, and made of material advance a basic measure of religious purity. It also evoked a religious provincialism, 'the attitude that almost everything worth while being done for missions was being accomplished by Anglo-Saxons'.[23] The thesis that the Anglo-Saxon race, and especially its British representatives, had been granted a special missionary destiny was a recurring factor in missionary publications. One speaker compared the British population to Noah and his family. 'The world,' he declaimed, 'is deluged with superstition, and ignorance and wretchedness; and we are in our ark of Christianity, voyaging upon this deluged world.' With the assistance of missionary reports it was possible to look out on the 'mighty surface of the sea of superstition' gradually receding through missionary effort. Eventually the 'deluged world' would emerge from 'the desolating flood all beauteous as paradise, fragrant with every Christian virtue, and vocal with the praise of the Most High'.[24]

More important than the fact that national and racial pride easily slipped into religious pride, was the attempt of the missionary movement to arrogate to itself specifically, or more generally to Protestant Christianity, credit for progress and power in non-religious aspects of existence. In the grandiloquent phrases of the Rev. Wm. Monk:

> Those Christian missionaries who first came to the British Islands before St. Augustine, as well as he, found our forefathers half-clad savages; and what has Christianity after the lapse of ages made us now?—The greatest nation standing in the forefront of the civilization of the most astonishing age of the world's history.[25]

This correlation of Christianity with progressive, wealthy, and expanding countries, and the converse association of other religions with poverty and backwardness, was not considered fortuitous. To many it illustrated the existence of 'an overruling Providence awarding to national communities prosperity or adversity according as they fulfil or fail to fulfil the duty which they primarily owe to the Most High'.[26] This meant that the inadequacy of non-Christian religions could be inferred from the national or racial insignificance of their adherents and the material poverty of the populations in which they were dominant. If Morocco, Egypt, and Turkey were backward and poor, the cause was surely their adherence to the monstrous heresy of Islam.[27] Could one then expect to find healthy, advancing societies where paganism was the prevailing religious form, as in Africa? Rowley claimed that a great famine in 1862–3 in the Shire Highlands was due to the absence of a Christian social system. The famine deaths were the results of 'imprudence', or 'the inevitable consequences of heathenism'. If the inhabitants had been Christian there would have been 'law and order, security for person and property, and stores of food to fall back upon when the crops failed'.[28]

Not only was the rise of the British nation to affluence and power related to an historical allegiance to Christianity, but the retention and expansion of British secular pre-eminence depended on continued fidelity to the faith of their fathers. Thus the Mayor of Liverpool, addressing a U.M.C.A. annual meeting in 1868, surveyed the prosperity of England, 'a small country . . . [like] . . . Israel of old, which was chosen to be master of the earth because of its smallness'. Only the blind could not see that this prosperity was due to the fact that in Britain, 'more than any other' country, the Gospel had had 'free course', and the British people had endeavoured to extend it to distant lands. By continuing along these lines of Christian duty, 'England's God would protect and bless her, and they should go on prosperously'.[29] In the same city eight years earlier the Bishop of Oxford had asserted that if England rose to her opportunity to 'spread the faith in its truth' the God of wisdom and the God of battles would preserve 'her virgin soil from being tainted with the foot of an enemy' and that generation would be able to hand on to its descendants not only the higher gifts of a pure faith and abundant worship, but also the 'lower gifts of prosperity and power'.[30] In 1849 the *Church Missionary Intelligencer* included an article on 'The True Strength of Empires—a Lesson from History'. After discussing the downfall of past empires, the article stated:

> Our merciful Father still bears with us, and looks for fruit; still condescends to employ us as heralds of salvation; and is even yet enlarging our boundaries, as a token that He will still further employ us, if we only rise to a due sense of our duty and our safety. Only look at the vast accession to our colonial empire since we have begun, however feebly, to be a Missionary nation! Must not the Christian mind see something of cause and effect here? . . . Our dominion is greater than that of Rome. O that all British philanthropists and statesmen would ask, *Why?* On the fulfilment of the duty of evangelizing the world is suspended the promise of all blessing and fruitfulness at home.[31]

In sum, material prosperity and global influence were held to be blessings for fidelity to the true faith. They reflected Christian allegiance, and if this allegiance should weaken or become corrupted its attendant blessings would also surely diminish. Thus missionary writers asserted that the Indian Mutiny was God's chastisement of the British nation for the respect which it had accorded to Hindu and Moslem religions and the concomitant lack of zeal in spreading Christianity.[32] Material wealth, national power, and global influence indicated that the British collectively were an elect group. The secular blessings they enjoyed were divinely granted and their retention depended on adherence to their accompanying condition, namely the diffusion of the gospel. The correlation of the sacred and the secular allowed the missionary, at least in theory, to undercut secular opponents of missionary work by the assertion that secular advances were, under divine scrutiny, by-products of missionary zeal among the heathen in Africa, Asia, and elsewhere. Towards the close of the eighties it was pointed out with proud complacency that 'it is to the race which is sending the blessings of Christianity to the heathen to which God is giving success as the colonizers and conquerors of the world'.[33]

3

The missionary saw himself not only as a member of a superior race possessed of an advanced culture, but also, and more important, as an adherent of a cause commanded by God and backed by divine assurance of success. The very magnitude of the mission movement, with emissaries of the gospel scattered over the globe, was a major source of strength to individual missionaries. Those who read the mission periodicals were able, as Livingstone did, to 'exult in the glorious prospects which God is working out for our world in this nineteenth century'.[34] When Mirambo, the famous Wanyamwezi chief, expressed ignorance of the objects of the L.M.S. missionaries he was told of the inhabitants of the South Sea Islands who, forty or fifty years earlier, 'were like the Wanyamwezi and worse but that many of them now are like good white men and that we hoped to see Wanyamwezi made like unto them'.[35]

In addition to the psychological infusion of strength deriving from membership in a crusading global movement, the missionary derived sustenance from a variety of beliefs specifically associated with his vocation. There was initially the simple clear-cut view of human affairs which cast aside confusion and complexity by the emphasis on the one meaningful division of mankind into believers and non-believers. Missionaries were told that their work was 'the noblest thing which human life can offer', and that 'a man cannot have a true-hearted missionary soul if he does not think that the cause . . . is not only commanded but will prevail'.[36] The missionary had a feeling of importance and cosmic significance which enabled him to deprecate talk of the sacrifice of a mission existence by pointing out the satisfying nobility of his vocation. Mackay of Uganda claimed that he would not give up his position for all the world. 'A powerful race has to be won from darkness to light. . . . Who would not willingly engage in such noble work, and consider it the highest honour on earth to be called to do it?'[37]

More important than any of the above was the main tenet of the mentality of the Christian missionary, that the universe was purposive in its very nature. The missionary related his activities to the fulfilment of a divine and inevitable historical process. He believed that prayer was effective, that God was an active intervening agent on his behalf, and that he was an important collaborator in the implementation of God's plan for man. Both God and the direction of history were fused in the missionary mind as supports to the inevitable extension of the gospel.

This produced an almost unshakeable faith in ultimate success which gave courage and fortitude and helped to overcome feelings of despondency and despair. In a sermon to his missionary colleagues in 1883 Robert Laws stated:

> we know that all the regions around Lake Nyassa and round the other great Lakes shall yet be the Lord's. God has said the heathen shall be given to his Son for an inheritance and the uttermost parts of the earth for his possessions. Christ has given us our marching orders to go and evangelize the nations of the earth, baptizing them in His name. We are to go forward and teach them. This is what we are doing. We know what is to be the result of the fight. We have to do our duty in it. Duty is ours, success and results are God's.[38]

The long years spent by Livingstone in Africa at the cost of incredible suffering and hardship, and the labours of less renowned missionaries, provide strong proof of the psychological efficacy of beliefs in divine support and the unique missionary approach to the measurement of success or failure. The conviction of eventual success was psychologically reassuring, and paradoxically meant that one could carry on undeterred by apparent failure. It was all in the hands of God. Livingstone regarded himself as a 'fellow worker with God', and consequently that God would protect him—'we seem immortal till our work is done'—as he carried out divinely sanctioned tasks. Immediately after an earnest discourse on the future judgement awaiting man, Livingstone's heathen audience disconcertingly commenced a great beer drink. 'The earth shall be filled with the knowledge of the glory of the Lord,' reflected Livingstone. 'That is enough. We can afford to work in faith, for Omnipotence is pledged to fulfill the promise.'[39]

Still, there was a conflict between the idea of duty and the idea of inevitable success,[40] especially if the latter implied rapid and numerous conversions. The prevailing optimism fostered a tendency in England to look for results, while missionaries in difficult mission fields were concerned with duty. Thus Robert Laws deprecated the misguided beliefs of the home church that a mission was a failure which had produced no converts. No one had a right to demand results, he stated, and missionaries 'have no sympathy whatsoever' with such a view.[41] Yet, the missionary was human, desirous of certainty, and eager for results. This was well expressed by an artisan missionary of the L.M.S. working among the Wanyamwesi:

> I sit and wonder sometimes. 8 long years at Urambo and little or nothing to show. I ask myself—Is it me? is it the plan on which I work?

is it the people? or what is it? Lord open our eyes, show us where the fault lies, and give us a remedy: what I do I do for the Lord, and the success I know is as sure as the promises he gave.[42]

New arrivals, fresh from the exciting and invigorating meetings attending their departure, were often sadly disillusioned by the paucity of results in the field. One young L.M.S. missionary in the Lake Tanganyika area was unable to 'express the disappointment' occasioned by his first realization of the apparently insignificant Christian impact after 'so many noble lives and so much money had been spent here . . .'[43]

Faith could exist without results, but it was immensely strengthened when they appeared. An intense conviction of the inevitability of triumph was not incompatible with ecstatic joy at the appearance of the first convert or the first African clergyman. As W. P. Johnson observed: 'In one way we took an exaggerated view of the importance of our first baptisms.'[44] Such events, and they were few and far between, were red-letter days in the lives of the missionaries.

Yet faith had an autonomy of its own and could exist without substantiation. Within the framework of assured success and certainty as to the rightness of his aims the missionary was capable of long effort unattended by visible results. The basic questions: Should the work be continued? Is God really with us? Do we have a right to attempt to alter old-established customs and institutions? were seldom asked. As fundamental articles of belief they were simply taken for granted. The self-criticism which such questioning implied would have had a paralysing effect on missionary zeal, and, as a result, it was psychologically impossible for the missionary to undertake.

While the belief in inevitable success had biblical support it was in part a reflection of a confident missionary optimism induced by western political and economic supremacy and the widespread beliefs in progress which rapid social and technical changes had evoked in the British middle classes. For many Britons these factors led to a religious ethnocentrism which assumed a rapid conversion of Africa once the self-evident virtues of Christianity were presented to the heathen. This confident attitude reached its apogee in 1896 when the 'Evangelization of the World in this Generation' became the watchword of the missionary students of the British Isles.[45]

In Central Africa, however, trials, tribulations, and an absence of visible results were more apparent than signs of a progressive evolution towards a Christianization of the African. All such problems, however, were taken care of by the assumption that although the ways of God are benevolent, they may be inscrutable, and hence not to be judged or condemned by man. The deeply felt necessity of interpreting events as the workings of God's will, as manifestations of divine purpose, allowed the missionary either to ignore the inexplicable as beyond man's comprehension, or to interpret seeming incongruities in a forced and ingenious fashion. This produced a pattern of belief practically incontrovertible by events.

Arnot, a member of the Plymouth Brethren, lost his temper when his carriers demanded meat. His gun accidentally went off and shattered the point of his left forefinger which he then cut off at the joint, a proceeding which effectually cooled his anger.

> Indeed, I was compelled to rejoice at the mercy of God. Two verses came forcibly to my mind: 'You only have I known of all the families of the earth: therefore I will punish you for all your iniquities'; and 'the Lord loveth judgement, and forsaketh not His saints.' I have given way time after time lately to fits of temper, with no one by to rebuke me. I acknowledge His great goodness and pity towards me in thus rebuking me. My men cannot understand my joy.[46]

When Livingstone's medicine chest was stolen, an event of grave seriousness, he attempted to console himself with the thought that such things happened 'by the permission of One who watches over us with most tender care'. Although unable totally to reconcile himself to his loss he pointed out that it might turn out for the best 'by taking away a source of suspicion among more superstitious charm-dreading people further north'.[47] His comment on the incident when he was shaken by a lion and had his elbow broken was equally revealing:

> The shake annihilated fear, and allowed no horror in looking round at the beast. The peculiar state is probably produced in all animals killed by the carnivors; and if so, is a merciful provision by our benevolent Creator for lessening the pain of death.[48]

This attitude constituted a deep-seated facet of Livingstone's pattern of thought. Significantly, when he was bitten by a tampan, a species of large tick, the bite of which is especially painful and irritating, he pointed out that if the swarms of this insect were viewed as the 'production of a Benevolent Father the plague must be considered as the necessary effect of our being parts of one grand system, in which each ministers to the gratification of the other'.[49]

These last two comments by Livingstone reveal a fundamental aspect of his attitude to nature and to God. He had an almost lyrical interest in the beauties of nature coupled with a capacity for accurate scientific observation. He saw everywhere a benevolent interdependence between all forms of life and their environment. The design which he found in the universe was the product of, and verification of, the existence of a divine intelligence. A description of the 'indescribable charm' and the 'calm beauties of nature' led on to a discussion of an 'ever present intelligence', and significantly concluded that we 'must feel that there is a Governor among the nations who will bring all his plans with respect to our human family to a glorious consummation'.[50] The perfection of nature led to God and by extension to the fulfilment of God's plan for man.

Livingstone's attitude to nature was part of a general teleological attitude which the Christian missionary carried to Africa. With this pervasive attitude the missionary had a special set of concepts to analyse the data of experience in a manner which facilitated the rationalization and interpretation of events so that basic items of faith were reinforced rather than shaken by apparently untoward incidents.

Thus Robert Laws was extremely puzzled as to why the interior of Africa had so long remained unknown. The explanation was blindingly simple. God could not trust the European with such knowledge 'until the Christian conscience had awakened to the sin and cruelty of slavery' and slavery had been abolished in the United States.[51] Ignorance was divinely ordained until knowledge could be used with compassion. Rowley of the U.M.C.A. saw the justification for the trans-Atlantic slave trade and slavery in the United States in the assumption that the conversion of Africa could best be undertaken by coloured people. Superficially a blot on western history, these events in reality had been part of a divine plan to bring Africans into contact with Christianity, thus preparing them to return to their continent and lift it out of barbarism.[52] The East African slave trade, with all its 'horrors and ... violations of the laws of humanity', argued Ludwig Krapf, was surely part of God's 'inscrutable purposes'. He tried to console himself with the reflection that conditions in the interior were such that even this 'vile traffic' might be considered an advance. Krapf also thought that Providence had brought the Portuguese to the eastern coast of Africa and had impelled the Gallas forward to prevent the 'fiery and proselytizing Islams' from overrunning Equatorial Africa.[53]

Such teleological explanations, which indicate the extreme difficulty of fitting the brutal facts of history into a purposive framework, frequently reveal more of the missionary than of the reality he interprets. Given the assumption that the universe was endowed with unfolding purpose, the corollary that events should be seen and interpreted in terms of that purpose, inevitably followed. This produced a tendency to look for 'signs' and facilitated and evoked an almost irresistible propensity to rationalization. Both Krapf and New claimed that it was Providence which prevented them from encountering the warrior Masai by divinely delaying their travels when on trips to the interior. Livingstone felt that an unexpected delay at Cape Town was providential by saving him from being at his residence at Kolobeng when it was destroyed by the Boers.[54] The missionaries not only worked for God, but God worked for them. Arnot of the Plymouth Brethren had an especially trusting faith in God's positive action on his behalf and cites case after case of divine intervention to show the heathen the power and reality of the white man's God. In Barotseland a dog, which was being taken by a messenger to the chief Lewanika, ran away. Arnot prayed for the dog's return, for the thought struck him 'that this was an opportunity given me to prove the power of the God I had been speaking ... about two nights before'. When the dog returned, the 'news went all through the town that the teacher's God had sent back the king's dog. ... Quite a lively interest sprang up.'[55] Arnot claimed to have no personal plans at all, but to trust entirely in God for guidance in the choice of a mission site.[56] He had an especially strong belief in divine intervention, a predisposition which may have been related to his independence from a home organization in his early journeys and his pronounced isolation from white contact.[57] While the occasional traveller or explorer, such as H. M. Stanley, was at times no less prone to see the hand of God in events both large and small,[58] this was basically a missionary phenomenon.

It is easy to be cynical about a set of assumptions capable of eliciting assertions that the Opium War in China was the working of Providence to divert Livingstone from his first missionary choice of China to Africa.[59] As one critic put it, there was a 'wide indulgence in Prophecy, and use of the Divine Name', loud assertions that God was on the side of the missionary, and an 'intimate acquaintance with the Divine Plans, which is most presumptuous'.[60] Yet such beliefs were obviously of vital significance to the missionary movement and to the individual missionary. Lonely and embattled men faced with heathen indifference and a hostile climate derived sustenance from the conviction that their work had divine backing and would inevitably triumph. Short-run failure could be tolerated when long-run success was guaranteed. Death and sickness lost some of their sting when martyrdom was the seed of the new church and the individual had the 'bright hope of a glorious destiny hereafter'.[61] Human plans, often unwise from a worldly outlook, carried special conviction and were pursued with extra tenacity when subsumed under the rubric of divine support.[62] Problems did not disappear, but at times they could be explained away on the assumption that God had designed them for some purpose unknown to the limited outlook of mortals, or they could be borne with resignation in the light of the knowledge that one walked with God.

4

The reader of these records of early race contact is immediately struck by the chronic oversimplification which Britons brought to the discussion of almost all of the complex problems of existing and potential race relations and social change. To some extent this was inherent in the initial and groping stages of culture contact. The inadequacy of this as a complete explanation is readily seen, however, from the fact that these simplifications consistently placated British conceit and indicated, in diverse ways, African recognition of British or white superiority.

One of the most revealing assumptions was that a white-dominated racial structure would automatically evolve at the inception of race contact. Africans, it was held, recognizing their own inferiority would readily and happily shake off the tribal fetters which bound them as they contentedly accepted positions of subservience under new white overlords and protectors. The facile assumption that whites were as gods in an African setting was given classic expression in the glib nonsense of Professor Henry Drummond:

> Why a white man, alone and unprotected, can wander among these savage people without any risk from murder or robbery is a mystery at home. But it is his moral power, his education, his civilization. To the African the white man is a supreme being. His commonest acts are miracles; his clothes, his guns, his cooking utensils are supernatural. Everywhere his word is law. He can prevent death and war if he but speak the word. And let a single European settle, with fifty square miles of heathen round him, and in a short time he will be their king, their lawgiver, and their judge.[63]

Drummond's thesis that the white was the one-eyed man in the country of the blind was based on a short visit to the Lake Nyasa area in 1883–84. 'The mere presence of a white man', he asserted, 'is considered an absolute guarantee of safety in remoter Africa. It is not his guns or his imposing retinue; it is simply himself. He is not mortal, he is a spirit.' The hypothesis he propounded in his travel diary was regrettably belied by the experience of his own porters, four of whom, unacquainted with their master's preconceptions, had run away the previous night rather than accompany him into a strange land.[64]

There were numerous versions and gradations of these psychologically satisfying beliefs which usually reflected cynical and derogatory attitudes to African culture.[65] Those who denied the 'African's recognition of the European's superiority' were talking 'egregious nonsense', claimed Richard Burton, and 'everyone who has studied the natural history of man must have the same opinion'.[66] Stanley asserted that once brought into contact with the European, the African

> is awed by a consciousness of his own immense inferiority, and imbued with a vague hope that he may also rise in time to the level of this superior being who has so challenged his admiration. It is the story of Caliban and Stefano over again. He comes to him with a desire to be taught and, seized with an ambition to aspire to a higher life, becomes docile and tractable....[67]

A typically superficial contribution to the discussion was given by the negrophobe Sir Samuel Baker. He stated that there were no human obstacles to exploration in 'those wild countries', for Africans were 'passionately fond of music'.

> I believe the safest way to travel ... would be to play the cornet, if possible without ceasing, which would insure a safe passage. A London organ-grinder would march through Central Africa followed by an admiring and enthusiastic crowd, who, if his tunes were lively, would form a dancing escort of the most untiring material.[68]

In the hands of E. D. Young these chauvinistic absurdities were raised to the level of policy pronouncements on the slave trade in the Lake Nyasa district. Young was reasonably experienced in African conditions. He had been with Livingstone on the latter part of the Zambesi expedition; he had led a search party which indicated the falsity of rumours of Livingstone's death; and he guided the United Free Church of Scotland party to the shores of Lake Nyasa in 1875. Experience, however, was irrelevant to his beliefs which were a product of his overestimation of British virtues, assumptions that Africans desired white rule, and an obsessive hatred of the Portuguese. He was tireless in reiterating the ease with which the slave trade around Lake Nyasa could be stopped. The 'mere appearance of a small group' of determined Englishmen,[69] or a 'proper exhibition of authority' by a boat and a small armed force which would not have to fire a shot, or again 'one glance at the muzzles of two or three mountain field pieces would ... settle the whole question', or ten men and a steamer to end the diabolical traffic,[70] comprised his simple solution to the slave trade problem in the Lake Nyasa district. So well does the English name stand, he claimed, that a 'handful of Englishmen' would in a few months find themselves surrounded by a 'very large population' which they could then lead in the arts of peace, industry, and legitimate commerce.[71]

Another traveller, Verney Lovett Cameron, scorned the idea that the rights of African chiefs should or need be respected. He doubted whether there was a country in Central Africa where the people would not soon 'welcome and rally round a settled form of government. The rule of the chiefs over their subjects is capricious and barbarous, and death or mutilation is ordered and carried out at the nod of a drunken despot.' Africans, he claimed, were prone to collect around any place where they might find security from the 'constant raids of their enemies', and, 'throwing off the yoke of their own rulers, [they would] soon fall under the sway of the strangers', who would have to be prepared for the exercise of magisterial powers.[72]

The stereotype of African readiness to burst the bonds of tribal custom and accept new overlords in their desire to escape from oppression was not entirely without foundation. Runaway slaves in the Mombasa area certainly found the freed slave station of Frere Town a blessing. The Manganja were justifiably delighted when the U.M.C.A. took up arms on their behalf against the Yao. In cases where their life was imperilled by tribal custom, individuals understandably saw white settlements as a possible refuge. But these are all explicable for specific reasons. The element of truth is further minimized by the numerous areas where such flocking around the white man's banner did not occur. The dominant tribes such as the Masai, the Matabele, the Yao and the Ngoni showed remarkably little propensity to beat their swords into ploughshares and fall at the feet of the white-skinned intruders. Further, Africans in disturbed areas were just as prone to gather around Arabs, or Makololo in the Shire Valley, or half-caste Portuguese, as they were around Britons. In such cases security was the predominant consideration and the nationality or race of those who could afford it was secondary.

The fundamental error was the elevation into a general law of responses which only reflected specific conditions in specific areas. The belief in the automatic nature of African acceptance of white overlordship was also based on the false supposition that African tribes, as Cameron indicated, were largely governed by the despotic use of force and terror, and that Africans were unwillinging adherents of the political institutions which controlled them.[73] The basic fact was that Britons, viewing race relations in the form of white leadership and African subordination, falsely assumed that their perception was universal rather than particular to themselves.

5

Missionary assumptions about the ease with which Christianity could be disseminated indicated an analogous type of oversimplification. The missionary movement possessed many of the characteristics of radical political movements. This was shown in the enthusiasm with which mission ventures were undertaken, the assumption of inevitable success, the underestimation of the opponent, and in the belief that rapid social change was possible. For his important and onerous task as an explicit agent of social change the missionary had only a theological training mingled with conventional stereotypes about savages and tribalism.[74] Frere noted in 1874 that the missionary was lamentably ignorant of other religions.[75] This ignorance was still being castigated in 1902 when James Stewart advocated more missionary knowledge of foreign religions and cultures:

> It is not too much to affirm that amongst those who go abroad at present, probably more than one-half would fail to distinguish with any degree of accuracy the three . . . great religions [Brahminism, Buddhism and Confucianism], or even give an accurate account of African fetichism. The answer would probably be little more than what any educated layman can give.[76]

One reason for missionary ignorance emerges from a quotation by Wardlaw Thompson, Foreign Secretary of the L.M.S.

> Ignorant, degraded, corrupt, their life darkened by their belief in evil spirits and witchcraft, cursed by the slave trade, the inhabitants of Central Africa make their mute but powerful appeal to the Church of Christ to come over and help them.[77]

The implication of this statement, that the missionary possessed something the African wanted, was simply untrue. The phrase 'mute but powerful appeal' and Elmslie's assertion that Christianity was the fulfilment of an 'inarticulate and unuttered' cry[78] reveal the confusing, contradictory, and misleading nature of missionary phraseology. Missionary after missionary had to discover to his sorrow that these were no more than unreliable figures of speech: the initial reaction of the African to the gospel was complete indifference. The missionary desired to Christianize the African. This was often distorted into the entirely different belief that the African wanted to be Christianized. The basic fallacy of this approach lay in the assumption that the inferiority of African culture, self-evident to Britons, was equally obvious to Africans. It ignored the cultural determination of values, seriously underestimated the involvement of an individual in his culture, and by implication asserted that the process by which peoples accepted new norms of conduct and a changed conceptual understanding of the world and their position in it was one of rational thought by individual men. On the other hand, the assumption that there was an 'inarticulate and unuttered' cry for religious change meant that the missionary knew what was good for the African even if the latter did not. It was the religious counterpart of an imperial mentality. It contained the germs of theocracy in exactly the same way as Rousseau's general will contained the germs of dictatorship.

A second and more fundamental reason for ignorance of African cultures was the almost universal belief in the cultural immaturity of Africans with the accompanying assumption that their cultures, inchoate and fragmentary, need not be regarded as serious barriers to the introduction of social change. Frere, who denigrated missionary ignorance of non-Christian religions, significantly argued that Africans were 'peculiarly docile, and everywhere tend rapidly to assimilate themselves to any more highly-civilized race with whom they may be brought into contact'. He admitted that there would be considerable difficulty in getting them to understand any kind of abstract idea, as their own religion was little more than a 'childish vacancy of belief, and materialism more or less marked'. There would be, however, no real opposition to missionary endeavours.

> The Africans have, so to speak, no fixed belief, but a multitude of bad habits and baseless fears. They have absolutely no inheritance of knowledge, either in morals or creeds, but ample power to acquire such knowledge when presented to them; and the few who have a chance of profiting by European or Asiatic education seem quite as apt scholars as the ordinary run of children in other continents.[79]

General Rigby, sometime British Consul at Zanzibar, was confident that Africans could be civilized by education far more easily than the Asian races, for they 'have no religious prejudices to overcome, and have a feeling of veneration which makes them easily susceptible of teaching'.[80] The very paucity of African cultural achievements was a hopeful sign to the optimist by diminishing African resistance to the introduction of alien ideas and ways of life. This approach had special cogency for the missionary movement. Baffled by the complexity and obduracy of Asian religions, it became almost axiomatic that the simpler, non-literate, technologically backward societies of Africa would prove more responsive to missionary effort. The conversion of the African, stated Rowley of the U.M.C.A., would be easier than that of the Hindu or the Chinese who possessed a system of religion, 'a regular philosophy for which they think no problem in life too hard', 'a living antagonist not readily overthrown'. Africans, in contrast, were 'dense, dark, barbarous, and degraded', incapable of giving reasons for their beliefs and actions beyond 'it is the custom of our country'. 'The idea which gave life to their former customs has, in most cases, been forgotten,' he complacently concluded.[81]

A similar view was indicated with extreme clarity by H. Duff, an early administrator in British Central Africa who was much influenced by evolutionary ideas. He contrasted the achievements of Africans and Asians and remarked of the African that

> He has no links with the past. In a certain sense he may truly be said to have no past. He has evolved for himself nothing lasting, nothing elaborate in any domain. His ideas are vague and formless. His nature is as plastic and impressionable as a child's—a blank sheet whereon we may write as we will, without the necessity of first deleting old impressions.[82]

This type of approach relegated African cultures to the position of anachronisms which, consequently, had no future and little power of resistance to the law of progress. It was a 'simple question of time to see all . . . [African customs and beliefs] . . . relegated into the land of oblivion'.[83]

A basic reason for white ignorance of tribalism therefore sprang from the implicit assumption that there was really nothing to study. Tribalism did not represent a way of life in any significant sense, but simply a generalized category of inferior attainment. The gulf was too great for Britons to enter with imaginative sympathy into the life of tribal man. Partly for this reason the British did not see tribalism as an ordered system of human relationships but simply as despotism or anarchy. The very backwardness and cultural poverty of tribalism inhibited the paying of any serious attention to its complexities. The absence of visible or tangible expressions of African culture in the form of substantial buildings, monuments, and other indications of an engineering mentality, provided not only a basic proof of African inferiority, but, by apparently indicating the virtual absence of any culture as the British understood the term, contributed to the assumption that tribalism was especially fragile.

In addition, the recency of contact, the initial linguistic difficulties, the fleeting and ephemeral nature of contact for the non-resident group, and the high turnover from sickness and death among resident whites such as missionaries made an impartial spirit of enquiry and a developing coherent body of knowledge almost impossible of attainment. Anthropology at that time was still an infant study and its attention was less directed to problems of ordered social change than towards comparative and evolutionary studies. Anthropological field trips did not become common practice until the early years of the twentieth century, and armchair anthropology did not provide any organized body of knowledge to act as a corrective to oversimplified approaches to tribal cultures and problems of social change.

6

It seemed so easy, so sensible, and so natural for the African to grasp the religious and cultural opportunities offered by these emissaries of the west that few seemed to have realized the magnitude of the change they were asking of the African, or the complexity of their task as agents of a revolutionary transformation of the life pattern of a people. The presumed ephemerality of tribal customs justified an absence of concern as to their basis and interrelationships. That tribal cultures were integrated, that they were possessed of emotional value for their adherents, and that as a consequence the problem of social change was highly complex and deeply disruptive of an existing network of social relations—these aspects of the contact situation were simply ignored. That later British colonial policy would be based on the system of indirect rule with its sociological and conservative approach to social change finds no forerunner in the attitudes of these early missionaries.

Inexperienced youthful missionaries, fresh from theological college, and ignorant of the cultures they were bent on overthrowing, frequently incurred responsibilities they were incapable of properly assuming. Some missionaries, such as Roger Price and T. M. Thomas, with their upbringing in rural Wales, were perhaps better able to understand some facets of tribal belief and custom than their urban-bred colleagues. Price, comments his biographer, was raised in an agricultural environment of peasant farmers in which 'witchcraft and sorcery were still a reality'.[84] This degree of accidental preparation, however, does not justify the general inadequacy of missionary training.

The missionary as a dispenser of firmly held beliefs and values was, in an important sense, more inhibited from appreciating African life than were his secular compatriots. His *raison d'être* might conceivably have been imperilled by too sympathetic an understanding of the culture he was bent on eradicating in large part. Among missionaries there was always present to some extent the feeling that studies of comparative religion, or anthropological approaches to other cultures, might undermine the uniqueness of Christianity and weaken missionary zeal.[85] This argument should not be pressed too far, however. The duration of missionary contact, the fact that he had to be concerned with Africans as people rather than as objects, and his Christian sympathy, occasionally led to an anthropological spirit of enquiry into the life surrounding him. Livingstone, Duff Macdonald, W. P. Johnson, H. Rowley, and T. M. Thomas all displayed in varying degrees sympathetic and understanding approaches to African society which were reflected in their writings.[86] In fairness, it must also be added that anthropologists who later undertook sympathetic field studies of tribalism worked in a different environment and social context than their predecessors. In the first place they took paludrine which diminished fever with its notorious tendency to make men irritable and critical. More important, they worked in a framework of law and order supplied by imperial governments. Had they worked in the pre-imperial period they would have been, perhaps, less prone to spend their time dispassionately elaborating kinship relationships if the peoples they studied had been likely to disappear from the face of the earth after an attack by a Zulu impi.

Be that as it may, the assumption that zeal and theological training sufficed often put the missionary in an impossible situation. Most missionaries, though perhaps not all would have admitted it, were placed in the position graphically described by J. E. Hine in referring to his arrival at the Yao town of Unangu. It was, he candidly confessed, a 'rather overwhelming position' to be among a multitude of people without knowing their language, and completely ignorant of their 'ways of thought and customs and traditions'. How the gospel message could be presented in such a way that it would be intelligible to his hearers he did not know 'in the slightest degree'.[87]

VII

REVOLUTIONARIES BEFORE THE REVOLUTION

1

RELATIONS between the races in this early pioneer period were groping and unstable. Neither side correctly understood the other. Most of the British were poorly equipped for either the intellectual understanding of tribalism, or for any degree of empathy with the way of life which it represented. They did encounter, however, whole communities which helped them to place the African in a cultural setting. The African, in contrast, saw only isolated individuals, predominantly youthful males engaged in a limited range of activities. He had no basis in the contact situation for obtaining any rational or coherent picture of the background from which these whites came, and he could not overcome these deficiencies by recourse to the written word. He was, inevitably, almost totally ignorant of the nature and power of European civilization. This mutual ignorance, more pronounced on the part of the African, meant the existence of a vast gulf between the self-image of each group and the image possessed of it by the other group. These discrepancies in perception and understanding injected a high degree of instability into early race contact.

Africans were insatiably curious as to the nature of these strange beings: so much so that whites frequently compared themselves to wild animals on circus display, and reacted with irritation and frequent loss of temper to the zoo-like absence of privacy. African curiosity was mingled with apprehension and suspicion.

> There must be something in the appearance of white men [wrote Livingstone] frightfully repulsive to the unsophisticated natives of Africa; for, on entering villages previously unvisited by Europeans, if we met a child coming quietly and unsuspectingly towards us, the moment he raised

his eyes, and saw the men in 'bags', he would take to his heels in an agony of terror, such as we might feel if we met a live Egyptian mummy at the door of the British Museum. Alarmed by the child's wild outcries, the mother rushes out of her hut, but darts back again at the first glimpse of the same fearful apparition. Dogs turn tail, and scour off in dismay; and hens, abandoning their chickens, fly screaming to the tops of the houses. The so lately peaceful village becomes a scene of confusion and hubbub, until calmed by the laughing assurance of our men, that white people do not eat black folks; a joke having oftentimes greater influence in Africa than solemn assertions.[1]

These fears may have had some basis in tribal legends. W. M. Kerr, who travelled from Bulawayo to Lake Nyasa in 1884, claimed that nearly all Africans had the 'common story that the white man is cannibalistic in his humours'.[2] Further north there is evidence that the Arabs and Swahili actively propagated malicious rumours. A group of half-caste Arabs who preceded Burton and Speke on their journey to Lake Tanganyika spread the following ill-intentioned reports about the white travellers:

They had one eye each and four arms . . . they caused rain to fall in advance and left droughts in their rear; they cooked water melons and threw away the seeds, thereby generating small-pox; they heated and hardened milk, thus breeding a murrain amongst cattle; and their wire, cloth, and beads caused a variety of misfortunes; they were kings of the sea, and therefore white-skinned and straight-haired . . . as are all men who live in salt water; and next year they would return and seize the country.[3]

Further indications of the prevalent suspicion are found in the frequent reports of magic tests being undertaken in order to see if the omens were favourable before a chiefly audience was granted to a Briton, or even before he was allowed to enter tribal territory. Whether the main source of suspicion and fear was located in traditional legends, Arab machinations, or simply spontaneous trepidation in the face of the unknown, race relations were frequently initiated in an atmosphere of mistrust and nervousness.

Uncertainty and anxiety were aggravated by a spate of misunderstandings inevitable in the initial stages of race contact.[4] Numerous items such as cameras, sextants, theodolites, magic lanterns, and magnifying glasses had to be used with special care lest they bring on some unjustified charge of attempting to bring harm to an individual. To the uninformed observer activities torn from their cultural context often appeared incomprehensible, dangerous, or simply foolish. An innocent, simple act of affection could have serious repercussions. The wife of Robert Laws, the Free Church missionary, patted the son of Mombera, the Ngoni paramount, on the head. The boy became ill and died. Shortly afterwards a headman died. At a meeting of the Ngoni council the missionaries were accused of the deaths, and two of them were held prisoner until the mwavi poison test could be undertaken on fowls in order to prove their innocence or guilt. Fortunately, as the poison was vomited, the missionaries were considered blameless.[5] This type of incident, however, clearly indicated the complexity of cross-cultural relationships, and how easily 'from ignorance, a stranger may give offence'.[6] Recurrent misunderstandings reveal the probing experimental nature of this early culture contact in which neither mutual understanding nor mutual acceptance of an ordered framework of race relations was present.

2

Simple misunderstanding was far from being the only source of tension in race relations. Africans refused to accept the missionary image of himself as a harbinger of peace, good will, and divine revelation. The indignities experienced by W. P. Johnson are indicative. He was pelted with corn cobs, had his dinghy seized by villagers when he was hard up for cloth to pay for milk, was unceremoniously expelled from the town of the Yao chief Mataka for his alleged association with anti-slave-trade measures undertaken by the British navy, and was tied up and physically maltreated on two separate occasions by Yao chiefs.[7] Admittedly his experiences were extreme, but numerous other instances serve to indicate the element of conflict inherent in the arrival of small groups of whites into the midst of tribal struggles for power and survival. The dominant tribes were almost unanimous in resisting missionary attempts to work among their subject peoples.[8] The Free Church of Scotland missionaries at Bandawe on Lake Nyasa found that the oppressed Tonga, in whose midst they settled, saw the missionaries as protectors and refused to let them leave lest Mombera's Ngoni come and destroy their lakeshore villages. The Ngoni, for their part, were furious at the missionaries for settling in their raiding grounds, and attempted to persuade them to move to Ngoniland, leaving the Tonga as prey for their warriors.[9] East of Lake Nyasa, the Gwangwara, wishing to test the mettle of these white-skinned intruders, looted and destroyed the U.M.C.A. mission station at Masasi.[10]

The most important element of conflict reflected African resistance to many of the revolutionary objectives pursued by the Christian and humanitarian element among these early pioneers. One of the most striking aspects of the conduct of these early pioneers was the intrepid, even foolhardy, manner in which they intervened in situations repugnant to their moral code. The cruelty of foreign cultures is always conspicuous to outsiders, and condemnations of the slave trade, of intertribal war, and of the apparent injustice of witchcraft, are not in themselves unusual. What is important is that a crusading approach to eradicating these evils was felt to be an essential component of Britishness. This was especially the case with the slave trade,[11] which for most Britons was the fundamental social evil of African life. As revelations of the magnitude of the trade gradually became apparent, it became, for humanitarians, the dragon of Central Africa only awaiting its knightly slayer. Missionaries often left Britain with the object of undermining the slave trade in the forefront of their minds,[12] and this was naturally reflected in their actions. When Bishop Mackenzie intervened in the slave trade south of Lake Nyasa, Livingstone explained his strategically mistaken policy on the ground that while the Bishop was averse to using arms his action was one which 'very few Englishmen' would have failed to undertake.[13] When in 1880 and 1881 a controversy arose over the reception of runaway slaves by the C.M.S. at Frere Town, one of the missionaries hotly refuted the assertion that such slaves should be returned to their owners and that missionaries should not deal in such issues. 'We are Englishmen,' he retorted, as well as missionaries, 'and cannot consent to fold our hands and see poor miserable wretches ill-used and put to death for no other crime than running away from savage masters.'[14]

These were no isolated examples of humanitarian fervour. John Moir told a mission audience that one look at a slave caravan would make their 'hearts ... boil—as every Englishman's must at such a sight', and would provide a powerful incentive to increased missionary endeavour.[15] A similar statement was made by E. D. Young[16] whose 'hatred of slavery amounted almost to an obsession'.[17] Robert Laws was 'wild with anger'[18] whenever he saw evidence of the slave trade. He and Young, in spite of explicit instructions to the contrary from their mission headquarters, boarded an Arab dhow on Lake Nyasa to search for slaves and were prepared to fight if necessary. Laws argued that however much non-interference might be theoretically the correct course to follow, this was almost impossible for the 'free-born Briton' with his hatred of the 'horrid traffic in human flesh and blood'.[19] In brief, hostility to the slave trade was exalted at times to the status of a national characteristic, a burning passion too strong to be controlled by rational calculation. In addition, missionaries tried wherever possible to put down the ravages of intertribal war by negotiation, by prayer, by open and courageous denunciation of chiefs who engaged in it, and even by active participation on behalf of the weaker side. Finally, there were frequent attempts to save the lives of individuals when tribal customs such as witchcraft, the making of sacrificial human offerings at the death of a chief, or simple indifference with respect to the aged or infirm seemed to be leading to unjustified and unnecessary deaths.

The attitude behind these actions emphasized duty, responsibility and a high moral standard which has been sadly lacking in the annals of conduct between the white and non-white races. A recitation of similar incidents leads easily to the assumption that early British contact was an unblemished record of noble conduct with a fairly consistent stream of benevolence flowing into the interior. Even leaving aside those Britons who were not motivated by altruistic considerations, this picture would be difficult to sustain.

In the first place the assumption that actions undertaken for humanitarian reasons would inevitably have beneficial results was, in many cases, of doubtful validity. Duff Macdonald of the Blantyre mission came to the conclusion that the Church of Scotland reception of runaway slaves 'had alienated many excellent men who might have been our best friends, and who were better able to rule slaves than we'.[20] To the African who believed in witchcraft, humanitarian intervention to save the lives of wizards appeared not only quixotic but positively cruel. When W. P. Johnson reproved some villagers for tying up and punishing some of their fellows for allegedly bewitching their dying chief,

> a young man sprang up and began to speak thus: 'These white men have no pity! Here is our old chief dying by inches, bewitched, and they would have us sit still and do nothing—not catch the wizards and not torture them!' He spoke earnestly and evidently had the meeting with him. He held forth for half an hour and we felt out-numbered and beat a rapid retreat to the ship [on Lake Nyasa].[21]

The definition of progressive change clearly depends on the vantage point of the observer. To the Arabs the British attack on the slave trade was an unrealistic and unreasonable interference with a necessary institution and the way of life which it supported. In the negotiations between Sir Bartle Frere and the Sultan of Zanzibar leading up to the ending of the sea-borne traffic in slaves, the Arabs, from the Sultan down, exhausted their ingenuity in an attempt to get the British to mitigate their demands. Sultan Barghash, in resisting Frere's pressure for a new treaty, argued passionately and melodramatically: 'We are in your hands, if you persist all the Arabs will die and die through your instrumentality and I would not wish it so. For if 200 people were shut up in a house and no food brought will they not die?'[22] At one meeting between Kirk and the Sultan, old Seyid Suleiman bin Hamed laid his hand on Kirk's arm 'and in the most earnest manner with tears in his eyes said "I have heard nothing of what has passed. I am now old and deaf, but if Government press this matter, I myself will live to reach London, and Paris, and New York and claim a hearing and justice for the Arabs".'[23] The answer to this type of argument was simple and was reiterated throughout the interviews. Percy Badger, interpreter to the British mission, admitted that hardship would be caused the Arabs, but asked the Sultan 'by what right do you impose tenfold greater hardship on the wretched Slaves who are torn from their homes, wives from husbands and children from parents,—to alleviate your distress?'[24] Or, as Frere put it, in commenting on the preceding, he 'did not think draining the life-blood of the mainland would repair the ruin of the Islands'.[25]

Similarly, the idea of peace was anathema to tribes whose economy was partly based on loot and plunder, and whose young men found in war an outlet for wild and brutal passions. Lobengula and Mombera, respectively chiefs of the Matabele and the Ngoni at the northwest end of Lake Nyasa, rebutted advocates of social and religious change with the counter argument that God had made the differences between nations, and intended them to continue. In Mombera's words, God gave knowledge of letters to the whites and spears to the Ngoni.[26] The warrior Gwangwara who were visited by W. P. Johnson were equally adamant in justifying their way of life. They repudiated the missionary's thesis that God wanted them to cease war and tribal raiding and live at peace with all men.

> We cannot do that. God has given us this work of war: He has told us to fight with everybody and to try and make all serve us. Let the European fight with us and if he conquers us, then we will acknowledge that his words are true and that God is on his side; then we will do what he tells us, and help him to pray to God. Our work is war, nothing else.[27]

A deep-rooted habituation to tribal raiding for cattle, slaves, and simple blood lust was not to be given up in response to the verbal denunciations of a few isolated missionaries. To the strong and powerful, peace was a revolutionary concept. It meant that the Masai way of life was an anachronism; that the Yao should negotiate peacefully with the Manganja for land which they required and could take by force; that the Matabele should cease the periodic raids from which they derived cattle, new recruits for their military impis, and the satisfaction of proving their manhood.[28] In the Hobbesian conditions of the interior to ask such renunciation of the strong was to ask the impossible.

Still, the defence of injustice by those who are its beneficiaries is not surprising, and does not transmute evil into goodness. No responsible argument for the continuation of the slave trade and tribal war is possible. Only the cynic or the indifferent could place them under the rubric of cultural relativism. Their effects in terms of social disorganization and loss of life were so grievous that they were probably beyond the recuperative capacity of tribal societies which, at the best of times, existed at a precarious subsistence level. The motivations which led to the attack on these institutionalized inhumanities must therefore be accorded the highest praise. It is no doubt true that the propagandistic accompaniment of the attack on the slave trade and tribal war exaggerated the cruelties of Arabs, the brutalities of tribal war in which death was bloody and usually at close quarters, and by implication helped to evolve distorted stereotypes of western and white virtue and humanitarianism. Yet, great movements of social improvement are seldom carried out in an atmosphere of academic caution and scrupulous respect for precision of statement. An excess of zeal is an essential requirement for their existence.

It is, however, necessary to consider the revolutionary scope of the changes which humanitarians sought to introduce into African society. As the missionary constituted the core of this humanitarianism it is desirable to examine the revolutionary nature of the task he assumed. This is important for the obvious yet frequently ignored reason that in the west we only effectively realize one side of missionary endeavour. We send missionaries rather than receive them. We possess little emotional understanding of the feelings of those who are confronted by an isolated alien who denies the validity of their most cherished beliefs, scorns their traditional customs, refuses to abide by their conventions of human relationships, and expects his astonished hearers to give up a major part of their way of life and accept his. The missionary who believed he was carrying out a divine imperative, and who saw himself as the harbinger of love and good news, was a seditious stranger to the believer in polygamy, witchcraft, ancestor worship, initiation ceremonies, bride price, and numerous other values and customs both integral and peripheral to tribalism.

The message which the missionary brought conflicted at numerous vital points with the practices and values of a large part of tribal life. To preach the gospel to the Matabele, commented John Mackenzie, was to condemn their entire social system.[29] The point was elaborated by another missionary:

> the greatest hindrance of all to our work here is to be found in the *constitution* and *polity* of the tribe. The Gospel goes dead against everything which distinguishes them as the Amantabele tribe. (*a*) It destroys all despotic power, makes men intelligent, thinking and responsible beings who seek for judgement and justice. It takes from the King all Divine power attributed to him and attributes it to God alone—(*b*) It

destroys entirely their military standing whose sole object is bloodshed and death, to devour and live on other tribes. Every year they send marauding parties to the weaker tribes to kill the aged and even little children—& to take captive all the young and middle aged as well as all their cattle and property. (c) It destroys all polygamy and also that much to be dreaded enemy of all human life and liberty—I mean witchcraft. These are the monuments of this nation in which they glory. To take away Divinity from the king is to make him only a man, and to take away his despotic power is to make him in some measure subject to his subjects. Deprive them of their military standing and how shall they multiply their numbers and add to their already numerous herds of cattle. To take away their plurality of wives is to take away their personal property and to do away with witchcraft is to deprive them of their most effective means of getting rid of all whom they hate and who may stand in their way. These are not matters of faith but of sight and touch and dearer to them than their life's blood.[30]

The idea of equality was a disturbing concept to the chiefs of hierarchical societies, and both Moselekatse and Lewanika protested vehemently when missionaries asserted that all men, chiefs included, were equal in the sight of God.[31] This struck directly at a key support of political power in such societies by undermining the sanction of awe and reverence which surrounded the person of the chief.[32] It was an invitation to civil disobedience. The missionary was a rival to the chief. 'I tell the people my own words,' was the reply of Moselekatse to a missionary who complained of his difficulty in getting audiences for his mission services.[33] Among the Barotse and the Matabele the power of the chief and his prerogative of indicating appropriate tribal attitudes to the new teaching were obstacles to the acceptance of Christianity by ordinary tribesmen.

The egalitarian assumptions of Christianity also involved a denial of tribal slavery and slave selling to outsiders and were, therefore, economically disruptive to those tribes which regarded the slave trade as an important source of livelihood, socially disruptive where slave holding was an important aspect of status, and politically disruptive where power, to a large extent, was a function of numbers of followers. In general terms, an emphasis on the equal dignity of all men regardless of their tribal affiliation was incompatible with the very basis of tribalism in which the concept of neighbour was very sharply delimited by ties of group membership.[34]

A further problem area for the diffusion of Christianity concerned marriage, sex, and the treatment of women. A typically blunt missionary appraisal of the status of women was given by the Methodist Charles New. 'The social condition of women ... is something fearful, and will hardly bear looking at. A woman here is a toy, a tool, a slave in the very worst sense; indeed she is treated as though she were a mere brute!'[35] Behind this polemical, exaggerated abuse there was the missionary ideal of Christian marriage as it existed in the middle classes of Victorian England and which the missionary desired to transplant to Africa. As one writer recently observed,[36] the tendency to argue that women did all the hard work, in agriculture for example, while their men idled away the time was a middle-class judgement which conveniently omitted mention of the domestic drudgery performed by servants in middle-class homes.

The ideal marriage was to be monogamous, life-long, freely entered into by both partners, sexually restrained, devoid of extramarital sex relations, and suffused with a love which fluctuated between the platonic and the romantic. This marriage pattern was not only desirable in itself, but in addition, it was felt that the whole social fabric of civilized life was based on its existence and that social progress was impossible in its absence. Not only has this type of marriage been comparatively rare in time and space, as Radcliffe-Brown reminds us,[37] but it conflicted at numerous points with African attitudes.

There was a basic distinction between marriages in which creation of an elementary family of father, mother and children was the predominant consideration, and marriages which had significant continuing meaning for the kinfolk of both of the participants. Since each marriage system was harmonious with the wider social system of which it was an integral part, it becomes obvious that the successful transmission of the western pattern to Africa depended on important structural changes in society, changes which were absent in the pre-imperial period.

Two aspects of African marriage customs, polygamy and lobola, were regarded as directly antithetical to the missionary ideal. Polygamy in Central Africa was an almost universally accepted custom, even if practical considerations—the difficulty of raising cattle for the marriage payment to the wife's kin, and the numerical equality of the sexes—prevented it from being of universal application. Polygamy was functional for the solution of a variety of problems. In societies where the preparation of food and beer was a laborious task, it was almost essential for the entertaining required of chiefs and other persons of importance.[38] Polygamy was also a useful diplomatic device which enabled chiefs to establish a network of friendly relationships with key segments of their own tribe and with neighbouring chiefs. The very high value placed on children encouraged the addition of a second wife if the first proved barren. Polygamy also helped to solve the social problem of widows and other women who for one reason or another might otherwise have had difficulty in obtaining mates or support. Finally, not only was polygamy a mark of prestige—Mtesa was reported to have 'seven thousand so-called wives'[39]—but there can be no doubt that the sexual variety it provided and the possibility of always having a youthful attractive wife constituted important arguments for its existence. Africans, as Edwin Smith pointed out, do not in general regard sexual intercourse 'as being in itself an evil thing, a sin'.[40] For all these reasons, undiluted monogamy as advocated by the missions encountered serious opposition.

Missionaries frequently held that polygamy constituted the main barrier to the acceptance of the gospel. To the British polygamy implied a loveless marriage relationship and an emphasis on sex which were held to give Islam a special advantage because of its greater concordance with African ethics. It might also be mentioned in this context that missionaries were usually bitterly opposed to certain forms of initiation ceremonies which they regarded as obscene and leading to sexual excess, and various forms of dancing which were regarded as licentious. In their attempts to eliminate such customs they often acted with a reckless zeal productive of little advance towards their objectives.[41]

The antagonism between monogamy and polygamy rested on a real conflict of views and interests. Another equally serious conflict, but one largely based on misunderstandings, concerned the custom of lobola, the payment of cattle or services to the bride's kin. This practice, which was interpreted literally rather than symbolically, was consistently misconstrued as wife purchase and was labelled a 'mercantile transaction',[42] a 'purely business arrangement',[43] 'a mere affair of buying and selling',[44] and so on.[45] Anthropologists have sufficiently exploded this misconception for any extended comment to be necessary. Even in this period some missionaries[46] were breaking through the barrier of misunderstanding and seeing that 'bride-price' fulfilled a variety of functions. It was in reality a form of compensation to the kin who had lost a member. It created a bond between the two families, was an indication of respect for the new wife, and a partial assurance that she would be fairly treated as her family held cattle as a security. It was an arrangement which helped determine the position of children in the social structure and gave to the husband and his kin certain rights formerly possessed by the kin of the bride. It contributed to stable marriages by giving the kinfolk firstly an incentive to see that the morals of young girls were carefully watched before marriage, and secondly a continuing interest in keeping the couple together lest the 'bride-price' have to be returned should the husband be dissatisfied. In sum, the marriage payment was 'the objective instrument by which a "legal" marriage [was] established'.[47]

There is some truth in the simple assertion that the misunderstanding of this African custom simply represented a failure to transcend an understanding of marriage arrangements derived from a background of British culture. It was, however, more than that, for it illustrated the recurrent and very important point that misunderstandings of African customs consistently showed a tendency to be unfavourable and derogatory. This misunderstanding, like so many others, turned out to have harmful effects. Missionary attempts to abolish 'bride-price' actually increased marital instability and lowered morality.[48]

The antagonism between the requirements of Christianity and many tribal values was exacerbated by the arrogance of the missionary in matters little if at all related to his message. Some missionaries went to the length of attempting to eliminate even minor customs, such as the lip-ring. Others carried their hostility to beer drinking to the point of smashing beer pots when a gathering of Africans was in the midst of what they regarded as a harmless and time-honoured carousal, an action which so irritated one group of Africans that they retaliated by forcing the offending missionary to drink beer at the point of a spear.[49]

Intervention to stop tribal war, eradicate the slave trade, stop beer-drinking, or end the wearing of the lip-ring were all interconnected. They sprang from the assumption that the African did not know what he needed. Only the missionary did. The missionary, aggressively self-confident and convinced of the superiority of his own way of life, felt little compunction about interference with customs differing from those to which he was habituated. Ignorance, as a wise Bishop later pointed out, made it far too easy for the missionary to condemn what he did not understand. Before the 'immense assistance of anthropology' became readily available, sweeping condemnations were often made which produced far-reaching and deleterious results.[50]

It is readily admitted that an element of caricature is involved in viewing the missionary only in terms of arrogant interference with tribalism. In extenuation it is suggested that an uncritical approach to the agents of western civilization is too easy for the European to adopt. He brings to any analysis of western expansion the seldom explicit assumption that since his culture is by definition good, its extension must also be good. This value judgement is itself a matter of debate; but even granting its correctness this need not imply a total acceptance of the methods by which western civilization has been spread. The attitude of its purveyors is obviously closely related to the depth of its acceptance by non-western people.

The changes which missionaries sought to introduce were revolutionary not only in terms of some of the basic social values of tribalism, but also, in many respects, were alien to African religious concepts. In the Christian sense the African possessed no feeling of sin, a lack which made salvation meaningless. The first step therefore was to create the sense of burden and guilt entailed by sin, for only then would the gospel make headway. The Christian idea of God, the concept of the soul, the idea of the afterlife and its relation to conduct and belief in this life—all these had to be introduced as new ideas, or, at a minimum, grafted on to existing religious constructs.[51]

The radical nature of the clash between tribal religious values and Christianity was aggravated by an apparent absence of any conscious or explicit attempt to utilize existing religious beliefs as a basis for the introduction of Christianity. There were exceptions. Rowley argued that inasmuch as Christianity was a spiritual life system, and African beliefs contained the basic idea of sympathy between the natural and the supernatural, there were 'the possibilities of highest spiritual advancement' in the African.[52] He argued strongly for the use of the existing fabric of religion to ease the introduction of Christianity.[53] Chauncy Maples also advocated the use of this technique,[54] while a later U.M.C.A. bishop, Hine, went to the length of wondering if perhaps primitive tribes were not more closely in touch with the spiritual powers in which the early church had believed than was the modern white man.[55] The occasional expression of this idea, which perhaps significantly tended to be found among Anglicans, probably did not mean much in practice. It is noteworthy that the basic attitude to African culture and religion was simply that they were too inchoate and immature to form serious obstacles to the introduction of the Christian message. In any case, not only was the application of this sociological approach especially difficult in the fumbling early days, but there were numerous areas of conduct and belief which the missionary, in spite of a theoretical respect for the religious 'gropings' of the African, regarded as barbarous and un-Christian, and therefore incapable of fusion with Christianity. Even sympathetic missionaries such as Duff Macdonald remarked that superstition crushed the very soul of the African.[56]

On occasion missionaries openly destroyed the religious charms of the African. Mackay of the C.M.S. purchased a charm, which he then proceeded to burn with the aid of a magnifying glass.

'Can your great witches make fire out of the sun, like I have done?' I asked. 'No, no.' 'Then, you see, I am cleverer than these gods whom you worship.' 'Yes, you make magic,' they said. 'Well, you say there is magic in this charm which I have bought?' 'Yes.' 'Well, let us see'; so putting the great charm into the heart of the fire, it was reduced to ashes in a few moments, half of the bystanders running away in horror, the rest standing round, hoping every moment that some terrible judgement would come upon me for my sacrilege. 'Now the devil is dead,' I said, 'and you all see that I have told you true, that there is no saving power in charms, and that God alone can save us.' 'You are a god,' some said; while others said, 'You are the devil.' They have the two words, but they fear and worship the devil only. This is one of the many such-like stories of the kind which I might narrate.[57]

Whatever the utility of this technique as a device of proselytization there can be no doubt that it indicated little attempt to use the existing religious fabric and assimilate it into the Christian philosophy and outlook. A slightly different illustration of a lack of missionary sympathy with tribal religious practices is given in a letter by T. M. Thomas of the L.M.S.

> We have received some orders of late from the King and some of his wives, one of which is this. The mother of this town (as she is called and as some one of the King's wives in every Town is called), sent to me to tell me that I must not dig my garden today because they were going to bury the bones of the dead in this mountain in order that the rain might come, for if I put a spade in the garden on that day I would certainly be guilty of keeping away the rain. To this I replied that to bury not only the bones but also the flesh of the dead and that not at a certain season but whenever the soul departed from the body seemed to me much better than to leave them to be eaten by birds and wolves, that it was strange to me they were not taught by their own nature and feelings to do so always. But to bury or not to bury had nothing to do with the rain, that to dig or not to dig was no cause to bring or send away the rain. The rain would come just the same and since they were so erroneous in their views concerning the causes of rain I could not think of sinning so great a sin against him who had the rain and all other things which were goodly for man in his hand as to pay any attention whatever to what they said and that if they wanted to convince me of the propriety of their proceedings that day and of the truth of what they said they must bring reasons instead of meaningless traditions and dreams.[58]

In the same letter Thomas wrote of a severe reprimand he had given to Moselekatse for allowing the Matabele to trade on Sunday. The chief was informed that he had committed a great sin

> not against me remember, but against the great God. And remember this thus sinning against God you fight against him and if [you] begin to fight against God take care for you will most certainly repent of your foolishness.[59]

In sum, the moral and spiritual values of Christianity were in basic conflict with significant tribal values, and Europeans lacked the power to impose their values. Missionaries, inadequately trained and often possessed of an arrogant outlook, encountered insurmountable obstacles in their attempts to spread the Christian message in an environment not conducive to religious change. The problem was that missionaries were not preparing the African for life in tribal society and no alternative society existed at this stage of culture contact.

Finally, the very individualism of Protestant Christianity was in opposition to the close and intimate identification of the individual with his group life characteristic of communal forms of tribal organization.[60] The idea of personal salvation preached by missionaries presupposed a division between religion and other aspects of social living. Where, as in African societies, activities were not compartmentalized into various segments but were highly compact and interrelated, it was asking the impossible to assume that the individual could isolate himself from his social environment and adopt a religion differing in fundamental matters from that of his fellows.

3

In view of the preceding it is not surprising that reports of mission successes in the pre-imperial period were almost non-existent. Initially, the missionary was met with a blank complacent indifference to the Christian message. Biblical assertion to the contrary, Ethiopia was not stretching out her hands unto God. This was soon discovered by Ludwig Krapf, the first modern missionary in Central Africa. After his first public service he had the 'humbling experience' of the Wanika declaring they would come again only if they were given food to eat. When he told the Wanika that they were sinners and transgressors he was warmly repudiated, and when he spoke of the evil in the heart of man to two old Wanika women, one self-righteously called it slander while another stated that she had come to ask him for a garment and not to hear his speeches.[61]

Krapf's experiences were typical. Missionary anticipations of easy success were quickly eroded by experience in the field. At one of the first missionary sermons on Likoma Island 'the principal men began shouting and gesticulating—one old fellow in particular was very demonstrative. Another headman said that preach God's word as we liked they would be drunkards and quarrelsome to the end!'[62] Elmslie of the Free Church of Scotland stated that his sermons were often accompanied by hotly contested dog fights, and sometimes a listener would intervene with the remark that it was all lies, that they had heard enough of the gospel and now wanted to be given cloth.[63]

African indifference to the moral and spiritual aspects of the west was in strong contrast to their much greater interest in the material and technical attributes of western civilization. This was clearly indicated by a small point, the ubiquity of African begging which, according to Elmslie, was 'almost maddening' at times.[64] Compared to his heathen neighbours, the poorest Europeans lived in aristocratic opulence.

> Chiefs [south of Lake Nyasa] fawned upon Europeans or rather on their goods. They would promise anything or everything for the present of an old coat.... The sneaking beings were found to be a perfect nuisance. They put themselves on the footing of beggars, and the most unpretentious of the Europeans had to treat them as such.[65]

Begging was part of a selective African preference for the non-moral aspects of western civilization. The missionary whose message was initially treated with an indifference verging on contempt was often highly appreciated for his medical skills. By virtue of their medical knowledge some missionaries got on close and intimate terms with African chiefs.[66] The remarkable friendship of the Matabele chief Moselekatse for Robert Moffat was undoubtedly related to Moffat's ability to relieve the chief of the discomforts of dropsy. When he bade Moffat farewell after one of his visits from Kuruman the chief said:

> You gave medicine to the sick and you have cured my beloved wife. All the doctors in the land have been called. They could do nothing. I pay and feed doctors, but they are fools. My wives say, let us have Moshete [Moffat].[67]

Although there were dangers involved should an operation fail, a favourable African response to western surgical techniques and medicines was a widespread characteristic of early race contact.

Superiority in the arts of healing was surpassed in the arts of killing. Guns and powder constituted the most popular trade goods then flooding the interior. In the disturbed conditions of Central Africa strength and fighting capacity became supreme virtues, and consistent attempts were made by African chiefs to turn these new arrivals into military assets in the struggle for existence. In the unsettled parts of Africa Britons were constantly subject to 'proffers of alliance, offensive and defensive'.[68] When the U.M.C.A. took up residence on Likoma Island in Lake Nyasa one of the first demands of the local chief was for guns. When the request was refused and he was told that the missionaries were bringing religion only, he gloomily replied that that would not help him against his powerful Zulu enemies, the Gwangwara.[69] The arrival of the C.M.S. missionaries in Buganda was assumed by Mtesa to mean a growing influx of European weapons,[70] an aspect of westernization which had intrigued him since the arrival of Speke in 1862. Even the Matabele, who continued to fight with their short stabbing spears and shields up until the

Matabele rebellion, displayed a consuming interest in western guns and powder.[71] Robert Moffat, whose medical skills were so highly regarded by the Matabele, increased his acceptability by willingly mending guns for the tribe.[72] There is no doubt that Matabele acceptance of the L.M.S. missionaries in 1859, whose way had been cleared by an earlier visit of the elder Moffat, was related to hopes that the whites would be willing purveyors and repairers of these new weapons.[73] The missionaries were understandably dubious about the role in which they were cast. J. S. Moffat refused to yield to the demands that he mend guns.[74] He reflected that there was no means so potent as gunmending to gain influence, but he considered it immoral to provide a haughty warrior race with improved methods of destruction. In the end, however, he reluctantly acquiesced. It was somewhat more than disheartening to come to preach the gospel of peace and find oneself coveted for mending the weapons of war. 'My ideas of missionary work,' he informed his father-in-law, 'are very different from what they were; perhaps I have "come down a peg". Be it so—and some day I hope these poor Matabele will understand why it is we do these things for them.'[75]

In addition to guns and powder African chiefs frequently demanded 'medicine', meaning that 'peculiar medicine which every white man is supposed to possess, and which acts as a charm against hostile invasion'.[76] Rowley, of the first U.M.C.A. mission to Magomero, claimed that the white men's capacities were simply incredible to the Manganja tribe without some supernatural explanation. They believed, for example, that it was impossible to escape from the white man for the telescope brought people back again. They credited the mission members with possession of strong witchcraft and fetish powers, and besieged them with demands for medicine to defeat their bitter enemies, the Yao.[77] At times it was almost impossible to convince Africans that such medicine did not exist. When the people of Taveita demanded charms and medicine from Joseph Thomson to prevent Masai attacks, Thomson's efforts to disabuse his petitioners of the idea that he had any special power were treated with incredulity. He was constrained to brew some Eno's fruit salts which the people drank with fear and trembling. He then photographed the various gates of the stockades guarding the town with much ceremony and firing of guns in an attempt to convince the inhabitants that he had done his best.[78]

These demands for medicine reflected not only the unscientific tribal idea of causation but, more important, the selective tendency of Africans to utilize these white arrivals for the fulfilment of objectives harmonious with tribal values. Thus, in Barotseland the missionaries warded off a threatened outbreak of smallpox by widespread vaccinations,[79] and the L.M.S. missionaries inoculated cattle at the request of Moselekatse, the Matabele chief.[80] T. M. Thomas indicated the variety of activities which an adaptable missionary could perform in the midst of a still functioning tribalism.

> When the people were killed with hunger during the years of drought I shot hundreds of large game for them . . When the lung sickness broke out and carried away thousands of their cattle I laboured beyond measure to save them. When the king's wagons, guns, &c., broke, I mended them. When the people themselves suffered from affliction, or in any other way, I did my best to relieve them of their pain and distress.[81]

The heathen, he asserted, 'will not believe in a Sunday religion, neither will they trust an inward love only, they must have it out of one, ere ever they can understand it'. He added that he had cured one sub-chief of dropsy, the 'prime minister' of gout, and then helped Moselekatse to recover from fever and ulcers on the foot.[82] Thomas, with his Welsh background, fitted easily into frontier conditions. He was remarkable both in his talents and in his willingness to place himself at the disposal of the Matabele. After he had spent nearly two decades in the country he was given the task of transporting the aged keepers of royal charms and medicines to the king's headquarters and back to their homes. He realized there was something incongruous in a missionary being

> entrusted with a naked old heathen and a whole heap of dirty black sticks and plants in one's waggon . . . but the natives, poor things, could not bestow a much greater honour than this upon any man; and we saw no object in hurting their feelings and intentionally insulting them.[83]

He realized, however, that the degree of tolerance which the Matabele had for the missionaries was in large measure due to the utilization they could make of them.

The position which Thomas was able to gain among the Matabele indicated that the European, even if his moral and religious precepts were largely ignored, was always a person of some consequence in pre-imperial Africa. At Masasi the U.M.C.A. missionaries were in the position of 'well-to-do squires'.[84] When Duff Macdonald arrived to take charge of the struggling mission effort of the Church of Scotland he found that many of the artisans were preparing to leave the mission as they preferred to become traders and petty chiefs.

> All the artisans [he remarked] had an enormous influence in the country. In the service of the Mission, they had hundreds of native workmen under their charge. In a private capacity each had one or two black butlers, not to speak of cooks and clothes-washers! Some were large landed proprietors on their own account.[85]

REVOLUTIONARIES BEFORE THE REVOLUTION

It cannot be too strongly emphasized, however, that the capacity of the white to gain influence in certain situations did not imply any widespread African recognition of the desirability of rejecting tribal values. The clearest indication of the African attitude was shown in the attempt of some chiefs to use the white man as a transmitter of the technical arts of western civilization, for it was in this field that Africans most readily noted their inferiority.[86]

Between these early pioneers and chiefs there existed in microcosm a relationship analogous to the modern form of technical assistance supplied by the west to the developing countries. Mtesa of Buganda consistently tried to turn the presence of Europeans to his own benefit. In 1875 H. M. Stanley, by an ingenious device of a floating fortlet, helped him to defeat the Wavuma. With this background he initially regarded the C.M.S. missionaries as technical agents of the west who would aid him in the building up of Baganda power. In the field of foreign policy Sir John Gray has made it clear that Mtesa brilliantly used the various European visitors to his country in the interests of preserving the independence of his nation. A sympathetic attitude to Christianity waxed as threats from the Moslem Turks from the north seemed dangerous to his security, and waned as those threats diminished. From his apparent conversion to Christianity, a piece of kingly acting which 'splendidly duped' H. M. Stanley, to his custom of holding theological debates on the relative merits of Islam and Christianity with the resident Protestant and Catholic missionaries, his attitude to Europeans was governed by the basic consideration of maintaining the independence of the kingdom he had inherited from Suna. Even in death the European presence served his needs as he was buried in a coffin made by Mackay.

A similar adroit use of Europeans was made by Mirambo the Wanyamwesi chief, who had rebuilt the dissolving Wanyamwesi empire by personal ability. This was particularly true in his relations with the L.M.S. missionary Dr. Southon who arrived in 1879. Southon soon constituted himself technical adviser and political assistant to Mirambo. He made gun cases, repaired chairs and musical boxes, removed tumours from Mirambo's arm, doctored his people, acted as his secretary in correspondence with Zanzibar, and used his influence to help prevent an attack by the forces of Sultan Barghash after Mirambo had accidently killed two Englishmen, Carter and Cadenhead, in a battle on one of his military expeditions.[87] Mirambo, who had long engaged in intermittent warfare with the Arabs over control of the trade routes to the Great Lakes, had made known his desire for missionaries before the L.M.S. arrived. He welcomed Southon and successfully used his many talents. Southon, a good handyman, a resourceful physician, and an inveterate optimist, was well fitted for his role to which he applied himself with vigour and the more diligence because of Mirambo's opposition to the Arabs and their religion which, of course, was anathema to the missionaries. The relationship, although there seems to have been a mutual admiration between the two, did not extend to the spiritual and moral sphere where Southon's influence had no appreciable effect. Over a year after Southon's arrival, Mirambo, on being directly asked, admitted having no idea as to the real objectives of missionaries.[88] Ten years later, both Mirambo and his erstwhile adviser having died, the same reports of a complete lack of interest by the Wanyamwesi in the gospel were being forwarded to London by the missionaries.[89] As one missionary put it—the people were interested in the missionaries only for what they could get out of them.[90]

The fundamental, yet frequently ignored, point which these situations illustrate is simply that culture contact is a two-way affair. Throughout Central Africa Europeans and Africans saw each other in terms of their own cultural values and attempted to employ each other for the satisfaction of needs and desires dictated by their own experience and background.[91]

4

In retrospect it seems clear that no major changes in the conditions of the interior were possible in the absence of some imperial control. The enthusiasm of the mission meeting in Britain often seemed somewhat utopian to the missionary in the field. Forty years after his meeting with Livingstone on the Zambesi the Rev. James Stewart was led to sadly reflect that 'the world has not altered, but our views of it have. The wonder is, that so great a mistake was ever made as that of regarding conversion of the world from heathenism to Christianity as an easy matter.' He reiterated as a matter of course that Christianity was intended to be, and would become, the universal religion of mankind.[92] The prospect, however, no longer seemed imminent. It had become one of those far-off divine events towards which the whole creation slowly moved.

The picture of a dominant superior culture which, in contact with a primitive tribal system, swept all before it and remained unaffected in the process, is never true of any situation of culture contact. This was especially the case in the pre-imperial period when the number of whites was too minute and their dependence on African society far too great for social change to flow uninterruptedly in a western direction. As long as their environment was overwhelmingly tribal, the incentive for Africans in any large numbers to change their moral and spiritual beliefs was, as the missionary very quickly discovered, highly limited.

Nevertheless, moral influence was not completely lacking. There is some evidence that Stanley's exhortations had an impact in mitigating the harshness of Mtesa's rule in Buganda.[93] In Matabeleland, in spite of the absence of missionary success in the area of conversions, the moral teachings of Robert Moffat seem to have had a softening effect on Moselekatse's rule.[94] Then, too, explicit religious change, if not widespread, did occur. The missionaries gathered small bands of adherents around their stations, often of low status or for some reason disaffected from the tribe. There was a scattering of converts and a diffusion of Christian principles among the socially disintegrated communities of freed slaves where the missionary made use of the opportunity presented by the separation of Africans from their political communities, and the power and prestige which were related to his responsibility for their care. Finally, there was the major Christian breakthrough in Buganda. Mtesa might well have duped Stanley, but the C.M.S. pioneers who followed up Stanley's request for missionaries arrived in an area where they found a marked receptivity to their message. Nothing indeed is at first glance more surprising than the fact that the Baganda, regarded by Europeans as the most advanced and civilized people in Central Africa, proved the least capable of resisting the religious impact of the outside world. Baganda society reeled under the triple blows of Islam, which had arrived with the Arab traders in the early forties, evangelical British protestantism represented by the C.M.S., and French catholicism represented by the White Fathers who arrived a year and a half later in 1879. The reasons for this remarkable success for Christianity are too complex to treat here. In any case, they have been examined by other scholars.[95] It is sufficient to indicate that there were special historical factors present in the Baganda situation, a certain disenchantment with the status quo, a social structure peculiarly mobile for Africa and well adapted for the making of individual choices, an experimental attitude, and a political kingdom in which religion and politics were far less closely interrelated than is customary in tribal forms of governmental organization.[96] The Christian Baganda, with their willingness to accept martyrdom, proved the depth of their faith and, in spite of the sorry religious wars which later set Baganda against Baganda, proved the capacity of Christianity, given the right set of conditions, to strike deep roots in the minds and hearts of Africans. By so doing they provided a proof for the sceptics that the high ethical and spiritual system of Europeans was not destined by some divine or natural law to pass its historical course within the restricted confines of the white race. Nevertheless, the success of

Christianity in Buganda was exceptional and special circumstances were clearly responsible for it. Elsewhere the missionary story was one of sowing without reaping.

Traders and hunters could be more easily incorporated into African society than the European missionary. Their activities were more comprehensible to Africans and their vocations were not revolutionary with respect to tribal values. They were ready to give what was wanted without making impossible demands in return. To a hungry village the resourceful European hunter could be a godsend. Traders provided chiefs with welcome opportunities to accumulate some of the material aspects of western civilization. Msidi, the Wanyamwesi ruler of Katanga, for example, collected an astonishing variety of goods from Portuguese, Arab and African traders. In addition to flint-lock guns, powder, cloth and beads, his collection contained

> tins of meat unopened, musical boxes, concertinas, guns and pistols, all kinds of opera glasses, scientific instruments (generally out of order), trinkets of every imaginable description, watches and jewellery; also cast-off clothing, varying in quality and colour from the sombre blue of the London policeman's uniform to the gorgeous dress of some Portuguese governor.[97]

Several writers have pointed out that traders strengthened the power of the chiefs,[98] and Arnot has suggestively stated that the rise of African empires was closely related to the capacity of some tribes to gain possession of a supply of guns and powder.[99] As guns flowed into the interior in increasing numbers they posed both an opportunity and a danger.[100] They gave important military advantages to their recipients, and African chiefs tried to ensure that these new weapons of destruction did not find their way into the hands of their enemies.

Guns, calico, medical aid, the goods of the trader, and the flesh from the kill of the hunter—these were all acceptable supplements to the African's existence. To give up polygamy, ancestor worship, tribal warfare, and a quasi-religious reverence for chiefly authority at the bidding of a handful of strangers constituted impossible requests for most Africans. These were only to be seriously questioned when imperial control shook the very basis of tribalism and created an environment conducive to social and religious change.

VIII

HOW CAN SAVAGES BE CIVILIZED?

1

IN the last seventy years Africans have undergone a social revolution of almost unequalled magnitude. Yet when European contact commenced there was no indication of the speed with which this process of adaptation was to occur either in the responses of Africans or in the expectations of Britons. The African could not foresee the signposts of the future in the isolated missionary preaching strange ethics or the feverish traveller asking unreasonable geographical questions. The British could not predict the absorptive capacity of these 'savages' for the values and techniques of the west. The British, however, if justifiably ignorant of the future of the African, were far from indifferent to the necessity for introducing significant impulses for social change in the interior.

To the cynic, the African had nothing to lose but his barbarism. Before Richard Burton left England to take up a consular appointment in Brazil he was given a farewell dinner by the Anthropological Society of London. Lord Derby proposed the toast:

> He has done his share in opening savage and barbarous countries to the enterprize of civilized man, and though I am not quite so sanguine as many good men have been as to the reclaiming of savage races, one has only to read his and all other travellers' accounts of African life in its primitive condition, to see that whether they gain much or not by European intercourse, at any rate they have nothing to lose. (Laughter.)[1]

Burton not only did his share in opening up Africa, he also, with his biting humour and scornful pen, contributed more than his share to the assumption that the African could scarcely be worsened by increased intercourse with Europe.[2] Yet, if other travellers painted

HOW CAN SAVAGES BE CIVILIZED?

less gloomy pictures, they did little to foster the thesis that Africans should be left to their own devices. Livingstone presented exceptionally balanced accounts of African conditions, but his writings contained frank pleas for increased white intervention, including imperialism, on humanitarian grounds.

The desirability of white intervention might have been refuted either on the ground that the African was capable of self-improvement, or that contact with whites would lead to the same extinction which seemed imminent for the North American Indian, the New Zealand Maori and other tribal peoples who seemed incapable of survival when brought in contact with white men. Neither of these possibilities was deemed applicable to the African.

The assumption that change was required but was not self-generating was practically universal. For Africa to join 'other nations in the march of progress', asserted the Methodist missionary Charles New, 'she will have to be put in motion, an impetus will have to be given her by some more civilized people—by westerns, and probably by the English'.[3] The evolutionist Harry Johnston was equally convinced of the necessity for an external stimulus.

> By their own unaided efforts I doubt whether the Negroes would ever advance much above the status of savagery in which they still exist in those parts of Africa where neither European nor Arab civilization has as yet reached them. There they are still to be found leading a life which, in its essential features of culture and social organization, is scarcely altered from what it was four thousand years ago, when the black men and their simple arts and savage surroundings were truthfully limned in Egyptian frescoes. The Negro seems to require the intervention of some superior race before he can be roused to any definite advance from the low stage of human development in which he has contentedly remained for many thousand years.[4]

Somewhat paradoxically the African was not only culturally backward but was held to possess biological strength, racial tenacity, and survival capacity. There was none of that danger, Rev. C. T. Wilson asserted of the Baganda, 'which exists with regard to many savage nations, of "improving them off the face of the earth".' He claimed that in common 'with the whole Negro race', they must possess an enormous amount of vitality to have survived the drain of the slave trade and constant tribal war.[5] Fears over the extinction of African populations were occasionally expounded by anti-slavery propagandists such as Cameron,[6] but, in general, the African, given in Livingstone's words, 'that imperishability which forms so remarkable a feature in the entire ... race', was seldom compared with other vanishing aborigines.[7]

The combination of biological tenacity, cultural backwardness, and

HOW CAN SAVAGES BE CIVILIZED?

the social disruption of life in the interior provided the strongest possible set of factors in favour of white intervention by maximizing the possibility of good and minimizing the possibility of evil occurring from a high degree of white contact. Thus, in 1877, Sir Rutherford Alcock, the President of the Royal Geographical Society, dismissed social Darwinian ideas of the inevitability by which the 'stronger and more civilized will supplant the savage—and that it is vain to struggle against this fatality'. This hypothesis, he claimed, was irrelevant, for there was no vice or disease with which Africans were not already familiar. 'The field is already occupied by evil, and is only open to good.' The danger of extermination by civilizing was insignificant, for not only was the climate basically inimical to Europeans, but the vast numbers of Africans, which he estimated at one hundred and eighty million, were 'a cultivating and hardy race, with the instincts of labour, tenacity, and resistance'.

> Men of European race will not kill them off, as they do the Red Indians by destroying their prey, nor as they did the Caribs by working them to death, or the Australians by giving them drink, or the South Sea Islanders by introducing new forms of disease, and carrying them off in a new born slave-trade. None of these dangers are to be feared now for the Africans.

The evils most to be feared, he continued, existed already in Africa, and 'cannot be aggravated by any foreign influence which can be employed in the present day'. There was, therefore, no reason 'for leaving millions of the African race, and so vast a portion of the habitable globe, a prey to barbarism, intensified by all the revolting horrors of a slave-trade which we did so much ourselves . . . to sanction and encourage'.[8] In the last resort the only important reason for individuals or nations staying out of Africa was absence of desire.

The questions as to what form external intervention should take, and what objectives should be sought, were less easily answered. The fundamental problem was that Africans, regardless of their own wishes, were inexorably bound to be drawn out of their tribal way of life, and brought into a new relation with the outside world. These early pioneers were the forerunners of an expanding western civilization which was in process of moulding the world largely in its image. Illiterate, technologically backward populations with parochial concepts of group membership, with no understanding of their position relative to the forces encroaching on them, were destined to be assimilated to a new and more complex environment created by external impulses. For the peoples concerned, a change of such magnitude was inevitably bound to cause a high degree of disruption and social stress.

HOW CAN SAVAGES BE CIVILIZED?

The most striking tendency in British discussions of the methods and possibilities of introducing social change into Central Africa was the recurrent oversimplification of the nature of culture contact and the problems which would face tribal peoples as they became involved in a web of relationships with the outside world. This intricate sociological problem of the utmost importance was largely discussed in abstract terms. What, for example, did the application of evolutionary theories to culture growth imply as to the feasibility of rapid social change? Was it possible for Christianity, the religion of the Anglo-Saxon, to make contact with primitive man, or was it necessary for primitive man to be civilized first before he would be capable of comprehending the religion of the advanced west? If Africans constituted a child race, what was the reason for their backwardness? Were they inherently backward, or were they capable of evolving into what the British regarded as cultural maturity? The importance of such questions was that they constituted significant social facts inhibiting or facilitating various approaches to the problem of the 'civilization' of the African. Yet, they were verbal rather than real questions discussed in terms of a variety of possible relationships between a profusion of omnibus concepts such as evolution, civilization, higher and lower religions, legitimate commerce, primeval man, progress, and retrogression. The now discredited idea of race constituted a basic element of confusion with its implication of the fixity, or at best slow changing, nature of cultural traits. The inability of Britons to treat the African as a human being whose colour and culture represented differences of degree rather than of kind made it impossible for them to treat the problem of social change in a pragmatic fashion.

Christianity, commerce, civilization, colonization, and imperialism became the great catchwords of those who concerned themselves with the future of the African. As slogans, they were thrown casually into writings and speeches with a bewildering frequency, illustrating Voltaire's maxim that language was designed to conceal rather than reveal thoughts. Eventually, as Joseph Thomson cynically but astutely argued, they became magic incantations endowed with a sanctity under the cover of which almost any kind of nefarious practice could be undertaken.[9]

2

In the writings of David Livingstone these concepts were woven into a consistent if somewhat visionary scheme for the regeneration of Africa. His ideas deserve special consideration for several reasons. He was possessed of exceptional common sense and clarity of thought.

HOW CAN SAVAGES BE CIVILIZED?

His observations, perhaps because of his medical training, were remarkably scientific in tone and accuracy. Secondly, the duration of his experience gives his words a special authority in a period when white contact was often ephemeral. Further, he epitomized in his life and in his writings the humanitarian relationship to Africa in its finest form. Finally, Livingstone's public reputation far surpassed that of any other Briton in this period, a fact which gave to his theories on the techniques of social change a particular importance in this formative period of British attitudes to Central Africa.

Livingstone, first and last a missionary who out of Christian love resolved to devote his life to 'the alleviation of human misery',[10] conceived his Christian objectives very broadly, and the methods of their attainment included far more than gospel preaching. In his belief that the missionary enterprise included 'every effort made for the amelioration of our race'[11] he indicated a desire for a wholesale application of the best of British culture to lift the African from superstition, poverty, and all the evils which beset him in his tribal condition. The essential prerequisite to the implementation of his plans was, as his own life exemplified, exploration; the discovery of highways into the interior so that the missionary, trader and colonist could pass rapidly through the fever-ridden coastal delta and feed a host of civilizing impulses into the hinterland. Colonization and commerce, no less than missionary activity, were fundamental to his plans for the social regeneration of Central Africa.

His economic beliefs were founded on the gospel of free trade which accompanied the growth of British industrial supremacy in the first half of the nineteenth century and triumphed over protectionism. He saw trade as an essentially Christian phenomenon, equating the laws preventing free commercial intercourse among nations with the remnants of western heathenism, and he claimed that the Christian teaching that all men were friends and brothers was the complete antithesis of protectionism.[12]

He was more concerned with the social than the economic benefits of trade for he regarded commerce essentially as a powerful agency for the diffusion of civilization. An increase in trade would work towards peace by the creation of interdependence among tribes and nations. The role of Christian commerce in Africa, therefore, was to demolish the isolation engendered by the parochialism of heathenism and to make the tribes feel themselves to be mutually dependent on and mutually beneficial to each other. On a wider scale commerce would bring the African 'into the body corporate of nations, no one member of which can suffer without the others suffering with it'.[13] The improved communications resulting from trade would also enlarge the area of individual freedom and put a limit to the exercise of arbitrary authority. If tribes had more intercourse with each other a good influence would be exerted on tyrannical chiefs who would hear what other tribes thought of their misdeeds, and oppressed populations, with new knowledge of liberty in nearby areas, could flee from suffering and cruelty. The cash nexus too was felt to have a liberating effect. On the Zambesi expedition he insisted that the African workers be paid directly, for by that means 'a most important doctrine is widely inculcated, and in process of time each man comes to feel that he owes subjection to the head chief alone and is otherwise a free subject'.[14] A final supplementary argument was that the increased prosperity derived from trade, if associated with missionary efforts, would identify the gospel with temporal advancement, and thus increase its attractiveness.

He practised what he preached. In his travels he exhorted the people to trade, explained how cattle could be milked, and brought fruit trees from Angola to the Makololo in order to increase the variety of their productions. He attempted unsuccessfully to get the Makololo chief Sekeletu to give up his personal monopoly of all the ivory in the country. 'Let it be known that every one who kills an elephant is entitled to one tusk, which may be sold to the trader . . . and thus all the ivory will be attracted to one spot and the traders too will be attracted hither.' Tribute from the conquered tribes should be made nominal allowing a growth in trade in which all could participate, a development which would lead to a milder rule and establish more amicable relations between conquerors and conquered.[15]

The fundamental argument for commerce, however, was found in the abolitionist assumption that legitimate trade would destroy the slave trade. The demand for foreign goods could be met by ivory and other products of the interior thus undercutting the necessity for the traffic in human beings.[16] He felt that British merchants could come up the Zambesi in the months from June to September and 'soon drive the slave dealer from the market'.[17] This was before he found the Kebrabasa Rapids an insuperable block to the navigation of the Zambesi above Tete, but the Shire River leading out of Lake Nyasa to the Zambesi directed his thoughts to that region and he argued that a small steamer purchasing the ivory and cotton above the Murchison Cataracts and around the lake would soon render the slave trade unprofitable.[18]

Not only would the African slave trade be undermined, but the iniquitous British involvement in American slavery by the consumption of slave grown sugar and cotton could be overcome by putting the fertile areas of the Shire Highlands to productive use. The trade which Livingstone hoped would spring up as a result of his efforts would be mutually beneficial to both Africa and Britain. If Africa supplied raw materials to Britain in exchange for manufactures, both sides would gain in the process. Africa, he felt, was especially suited to the meeting of British needs for it was capable of producing an 'unlimited supply' of agricultural produce, such as cotton, coffee, sugar, indigo, oil, fibrous tissues, and wood, and he foresaw 'no probability that the future of Africa will present that rivalry in manufactures which even now enables the Americas to consume a large quantity of their own cotton', a feature which, in time, might 'materially diminish the supply of that commodity which England so imperatively needs'.[19]

As Livingstone trudged across Africa his mind was constantly concerned with finding some means of improving the condition of the British poor. As his thought evolved he increasingly saw the solution in an extensive emigration from the overcrowded British Isles. His initial interest in emigration was personal. In his early letters from Bechuanaland, before he acquired fame, he continually exhorted his parents to eimgrate as had his brother Charles (to the United States). He felt that emigration from England 'must take place . . . sooner or later by millions . . . the world will teem with the Anglo-Saxon race'.[20] In letter after letter he informed his parents that the world had been made for man, and that God had provided more than sufficient productive, fertile land to allow individuals to escape from the backbreaking toil which produced meagre results in the slums of Britain.[21] His recommendations soon went beyond the narrow bounds of family and embraced the British lower classes. Finally, as his travels took him deeper into the interior, he began to place increasing emphasis on Africa as a likely area for large scale British settlement.

He saw in south Central Africa 'so much of this fair earth . . . unoccupied, and not put to the benevolent purpose for which it was intended by its Maker'.[22] South of Lake Nyasa he reflected on the misery of the poor in Britain, while in the Shire Highlands 'our Heavenly Father has so abundantly provided fruitful hills and fertile valleys'. The honest poor, not the 'blackguard poor',[23] or the 'ragamuffin poor',[24] with whom he thought humanitarians had been overly concerned, could find in Africa ample opportunities to live a devout Christian life.

These settlements would perform a dual function. Not only would they relieve distress in Britain, but they would bring the African into contact with communities of God-fearing settlers who, by their Christian example, would have a far more profound effect on the imitative African than the isolated efforts of individual missionaries. In effect he equated the British colonist with the missionary. He even toyed

HOW CAN SAVAGES BE CIVILIZED?

with the idea of the 'old monastery system without the celibacy'.[25] 'Christian families' sent out as missionaries by their richer friends would save the 'expensive machinery' of missionary societies and by their lives would draw the African into the Christian fold.[26] Such communities would bring peace, for thousands of

> industrious natives would gladly settle round . . . and engage in that peaceful pursuit of agriculture and trade of which they are so fond, and, undistracted by wars and rumours of wars, might listen to the purifying and ennobling truths of the gospel of Jesus Christ.[27]

In spite of numerous references, the type of white community for which Livingstone hoped remains obscure. On the one hand he claimed that the usual idea of a colony could not be entertained with respect to Africa, for Englishmen could not compete in manual labour 'of any kind' with the natives:

> but they can take a leading part in managing the land, improving the quality, increasing the quantity and extending the varieties of the production of the soil; and by taking a lead too in trade and in all public matters, the Englishman would be an unmixed advantage to every one below and around him, for he would fill a place which is now practically vacant.[28]

In this context the British were clearly seen as leaders, and the assumption is that only a handful of whites would be involved. Yet at other times he referred to the migration of whole communities, 'the families of the godly going forth with their ministers, their elders, their Christianity'.[29] On one occasion, when discussing colonization, he observed: 'How many millions might flourish in this Africa, where but hundreds dwell.'[30] Africans, he asserted, need not be 'torn from their homes in order to contribute to the wealth of the world'. There was also

> room and to spare for English emigrants to settle on and work the virgin soil of the still untilled land of Ham . . . no more need the English poor be crowded together in unwholesome dens, debarred from breathing the pure air of Heaven. There is room for all in the wide and glorious domains of the Lord, the king of all the Earth.[31]

As the preceding indicates, Livingstone was intent on making a major impact on the problem of poverty and its attendant evils in Britain. The fundamental dilemma of how colonies of British poor could be fitted into a society where the only European function was that of leadership was never satisfactorily resolved. The main reason for this confusion is simply that Livingstone was intent on simultaneously solving the problems of Africa and significantly alleviating poverty in Britain with one master stroke.

The civilization Livingstone was desirous of introducing into

HOW CAN SAVAGES BE CIVILIZED?

Africa combined hard work and practical morality with the Bible, 'the Magna Charta of all the rights and privileges of modern civilization',[32] as its basis. His Christianity was neither ascetic nor theoretical. It was not even overly denominational. It was a practical down-to-earth ameliorating Christianity, more concerned with results than with dogma. The sturdy Christian colonists, the increased diffusion of knowledge and prosperity based on commerce in conjunction with the work of the missionary, would harmonize in the production of a Christian African civilization.

The broad scope of Livingstone's approach to the solution of African problems illustrates his emphasis, not on the individual, but on the community. The difficulties facing individuals were due to the drawbacks of their environment, and an isolated missionary was not the proper instrument to introduce a change of the requisite magnitude. The ideal to be worked for, rather than actual conversions, was the widespread permeation of society with better principles and a higher moral tone. Thus his missionary emphasis was on diffusion. He deprecated comfortable mission stations which made the missionary less mobile. Missionary concentration and permanence in one spot were wrong for they limited the spread of Christian ideas, the indirect but most valuable aspect of mission work. Missionaries, he felt, should not stay overly long with an unpromising tribe, but should leave and broadcast the message in other areas. In brief, he desired to uplift the whole social and moral fabric of African life. When this had been done, and poverty, ignorance, and inter-tribal hostility had been eradicated, an environment conducive to the making of individual Christians would have been created.

One reason for the broad scope of Livingstone's views was that he saw Africans as 'suffering' rather than 'perishing'. This automatically gave his missionary impulse a broad humanitarian basis and led to his concern for ameliorating all aspects of African life. He saw the individual's relation with his culture and thus realized that it was an entire social system which had to be altered in Africa where there was not, as in Britain, an 'atmosphere of Christianity and enlightened public opinion, the growth of centuries', to influence conduct.[33]

All things considered, Livingstone's theorizing represented perhaps the most thorough attempt in this period to present an ordered analysis of the methods to be employed in putting the African on the path to advancement. His thought was unsullied by serious inhibiting doubts about the capacity of the African to improve his position. His breadth of vision, and his kindly, if paternal, relationship with Africans, marked him as an example of contact which has been all too rare in the meeting of the white man and his differently pigmented, technologically backward neighbours. Yet, in spite of all the

HOW CAN SAVAGES BE CIVILIZED?

well-deserved plaudits which have been lavished on this Scotsman of humble birth, his theories of African advance suffer seriously from an oversimplification which largely robs them of value. His importance lies in the realm of character and in his unprejudiced, tolerant approach to the African rather than in his theories of social change.

Ultimately Livingstone's vision of a conjoint attack by missionaries, colonists, and traders on the problems of Africa was only saved from internal contradiction by the inveterate optimism which suffused his writings.[34] He was a true child of the nineteenth-century climate of opinion which saw man advancing ever onwards and upwards in an unending chain of progress, which he personally equated with the working of God's will on earth. His ideas on the beneficent effects of commerce reflected his sanguine beliefs in the generally progressive and harmonious nature of the universe. Trade was to benefit both Africa and Britain. There was the implicit assumption that 'good' trade would drive out 'bad' trade. This, in turn, was based on an optimistic assessment of human beings with its supposition that Africans were unwilling participants in the slave trade, and would have rather earned the guns, beads, and calico they coveted by more honest, and perhaps more earnest toil. To Livingstone trade was an ethical rather than an economic concept. As Macnair has said: Livingstone meant 'business conducted on Christian principles by Christian men'.[35] As British merchants were 'as a whole, decidedly the most upright and benevolent in the world',[36] they were clearly the appropriate agents to produce that uplifting effect which was held to be inherent in legitimate commerce. The production and export of cotton would undercut the slave trade in the Shire region, relieve Britain from the stigma of dependence on slave-grown American cotton, and bring the African into an interdependent relationship with the civilized world. Colonization would facilitate the Christianization of the African and simultaneously relieve the suffering of the honest poor from the slums of Glasgow and London. Only an uncritical optimism enabled Livingstone to balance such multiple objectives harmoniously within a single scheme.

It was Christian trade, Christian colonists and Christian civilization which were to rejuvenate Africa. From a practical point of view the adjective Christian which kept his various themes together constituted their main weakness. Once actual trade and traders, and actual colonists, were compared with his Christian ideal, it was readily seen that their relationship was by no means intrinsically harmonious. The penetration of Africa was not the planned experiment required for the fulfilment of Livingstone's policies. Riff-raff vied with missionaries for influence, and 'legitimate' trade had to compete with European gin seller as well as Arab slave buyer. In the absence of rigidly controlled immigration to Africa his community of saints from the honest poor was inherently unrealistic. Yet, even if it had been possible, the transition from tribalism to a way of life dominated by western standards and values was inevitably bound to be a disruptive process. This was not foreseen. Here Livingstone shared a blindness ubiquitous among the early British—an inability to realize that tribal cultures, even in a period of social strain, were replete with emotional values for their adherents and integrated in a harmonious fashion. The mere fact that change was necessary often led Britons falsely to assume that the process by which it was to be brought about would be easy, and led them to overlook the social problems it would bring in its wake.

3

While few missionaries evolved such elaborate schemes for African advance as David Livingstone, there was widespread agreement that the missionary task included far more than the inculcation of a spiritual change by gospel preaching. In the first place Christianity and civilization were almost inseparable concepts. To say that people were not Christian implied that they were uncivilized; to say that they were uncivilized implied that they were not Christian.[37]

This coupling of Christianity and civilization, less a conscious act than an unconscious, unquestioning identification or intermingling of the two in the mind of the missionary, was a basic factor in making him a purveyor of western culture. In a letter to his society, Carson, an artisan missionary of the L.M.S., discussed the advantages of employing Africans in order to teach ideas of discipline and concentration, and then added:

> and lastly but not least the more they learn of the arts and customs of civilized life the more easy it is for them to understand the truths of the bible. The bible was addressed to civilized people, and its language is couched in terms that relate to the relations and arts of civilized people, to be ignorant of which is to [be] without that knowledge which makes it possible to express the unseen in terms of what is seen. I do not think that nothing of the gospel can be understood by the untutored native, but I do know that the great difficulty in explaining it to them is their inability to comprehend what to us is known, and to them unknown of the world, and so made the means of comprehending the unseen. The effective way to remove this difficulty is to make them practically acquainted with our customs and arts. Happily we are compelled to do this for at the beginning industry was wedded to revelation for man's spiritual welfare when God cursed the ground for man's sake, and so the exigencies of life compel us to employ the people to work for us.[38]

HOW CAN SAVAGES BE CIVILIZED?

The real point of Carson's analysis was not, as he imagined, that Christianity and civilization had always been coterminous, but his incapacity to recall the diversity of social and economic conditions with which Christianity had existed before the nineteenth century. The problem was in his inability to distinguish the Christian from the non-Christian content of his own thought, rather than the inability of the African to understand an inherent civilized content of Christianity which, on examination, always turned out to be synonymous with nineteenth-century British values. For those missionaries unable to see the distinction, cultural imperialism was an inevitable accompaniment to proselytization. Admittedly it may be only theoretically possible to extract the 'essence' of a religion from the general cultures of its purveyors. The difficulty of the task, however, did not deter some missionaries from making the attempt, and a more widespread recognition of the nature of the problem would have been salutary.

The unwillingness to attempt a divorce between Christianity and the nineteenth-century west partially reflected a belief in the social benefits of Christianity and the thesis that rewards of prosperity and power flowed from fidelity to the Christian religion—both standard items in the missionary credo. The neat fit between Christianity and the progressive west, in conjunction with the absence of secular progress in non-western countries, gave the missionary tangible proof of the efficacy of his belief, buttressed missionary ideas of the social value of Christianity, and made it difficult and almost contradictory for him to isolate his message from his culture. This was especially true in Africa where the low level of existing cultural achievements gave special emphasis to the argument that it was necessary to accompany Christianity with the arts and sciences of civilization.[39] If Christianity and a low level of civilization could not co-exist in the same society it was necessary for the missionary to civilize those he was Christianizing.[40]

The civilizing side of mission work was especially pronounced in the first U.M.C.A. mission to the Shire Highlands and the later Scottish missions of the Church of Scotland and the Free Church with their strong emphasis on industry, agriculture, and crafts. While few other missions actively undertook a similar explicit civilizing role, this seems to have reflected inadequacies of staff rather than conviction. Only the U.M.C.A. after the appointment of Bishop Tozer had a consistent and well thought out mission philosophy which deliberately emphasized the specifically Christian nature of the missionary task.

In a sense, the absence or presence of industrial training on mission stations was irrelevant, for most missionaries believed that to spread Christianity was, in itself, to spread the basis for social and economic progress. The Wanika, argued Charles New, were too inert and lazy to do anything. However, after they had imbibed the Gospel 'their activity and enterprise shall be aroused; they will then devote themselves to the arts of civilization, and these hills and dales shall smile with plenty'.[41] The idea that Christianity would evoke aspirations for a higher life by arousing individual dignity was elaborated by Pruen of the C.M.S. He felt that the grown African wanted neither to be civilized nor to work.

> The only prospect . . . is by first getting him converted . . . he will get desires toward higher things than he naturally seeks after. . . . Whether a civilized African would receive the Gospel more readily than an uncivilized one, I do not in the least know. But my small experience . . . certainly gives me the right to expect that the Christian African will embrace civilization a great deal more easily and naturally than the heathen one. To attempt to civilize the African before attempting to convert him is, I think, to put the cart before the horse.[42]

Missionaries disseminated a Christianity which was less a solace for a life of sorrow and suffering than a radiant social blessing which would immensely improve the lot of man on earth. There was a marked propensity of missionaries to attribute to Christianity those facets of western growth and progress which seemed beneficial to the prestige of the religion they wished to disseminate. When Africans were impressed with Mackay's construction of two steam engines and other contrivances from 'an incongruous mass of iron and brass and bolts', but slow to believe that they themselves were capable of doing such work, he told them 'that we were once naked savages like themselves, and carried bows and arrows and spears; but when God began to teach us, we became civilized'.[43] This curious but typical missionary assumption that the capacity to construct steam engines reflected the Christianity of their builders inevitably meant that the Christianity they spread would have a similar content, and by logical extension would create a similar progressive civilization. It was, however, always ambiguous whether or not material prosperity and social advance resulted from the converts' changed attitude to work and resources, or whether they were blessings for fidelity to the true faith. While the human efforts of the Christian converts were clearly involved, the results of these efforts also partook of the blessing of God on the principle that God would reward his true believers. What does not seem to have been envisaged was the possibility that Christianity could co-exist with material poverty or technological backwardness.[44]

These beliefs in visible tangible benefits for adherence to a specific faith were obvious reflections of their time and place of origin.

HOW CAN SAVAGES BE CIVILIZED?

The justification of things eternal by the social and material conditions of their believers, a recurring strand in Protestant belief, rests on the assumption that there is a reflex action between the spiritual and the worldly sphere, and that religions, like other aspects of human behaviour, should be judged by their fruits. For the nineteenth-century missionary it was reassuring to verify the efficacy and divinity of religions by the secular measurements of prosperity and power. In retrospect, however, it can be seen that the association is unfortunate. When conditions change, when prosperity and power occur independently of Christianity, or when Christianity finds problems of poverty and backwardness intractable, the foundations of faith are imperilled by a one-sided analysis of social causation.[45]

A final factor leading to a missionary emphasis on a civilizing role was a growing conception of a benevolent God, 'the advancing views as it were, of God's character', as Robert Laws phrased it,[46] coupled with a marked decline in the belief in eternal damnation for the heathen. Robert Moffat, who commenced his career among the Bechuana in the early years of the nineteenth century, believed in an after life of 'everlasting torment' or 'everlasting destruction', and informed Africans that if they died 'in ignorance of the Saviour, [they would] die miserably and go to perdition'.[47] This belief seems to have waned in the last half of the century, and references to an eternity of hell fire are but seldom found in the records of missionary contact with Central Africa.[48]

At the annual conference of the L.M.S. in 1876 one speaker noted the doubt which contemporary thought was introducing with respect to future punishment of sin:

> There was a time—I daresay it is within the recollection of most of us here—when the principal motive appealed to at the public meetings of this Society . . . was the eternal doom that awaited the nations that knew not God. That time has gone by. The very phrase 'the perishing heathen', I do not remember to have heard for years. We seldom hear anything at our missionary meetings of the danger or the judgement which the nations that die without Christ incur from Christ's hands. . . . It was once assumed that, because they were heathen, without a doubt they would perish everlastingly. It seems now to be assumed equally without doubt that because they are heathen they shall be saved everlastingly.[49]

The decline of the 'perishing heathen'[50] meant that distinctions of culture and civilization grew relative to distinctions between the saved and the unsaved. The specifically spiritual aspect of the missionary task became only part of the broader task of ameliorating the whole environmental context in which tribal man lived.

For all of the reasons mentioned in this section the missionary

HOW CAN SAVAGES BE CIVILIZED?

tended to see a close connection between Christianity and civilization and also tended to see his own role in terms of a civilizing function. This association of Christianity and civilization raised important practical and theoretical issues which will be discussed in the following sections.

4

The special environmental context of nineteenth-century missionary activity raised what Gustav Warneck called the 'culture question', a question far more complicated for men of his generation than it had been in apostolic or medieval times:

> In both these earlier periods there was no such difference of culture between the subjects and the objects of missionary work as is the case now.... The modern missionaries ... go from nations whose superiority in culture over the heathen nations of the present day—even the so-called culture peoples, such as the Hindus, the Chinese, and the Japanese —is absolute.[51]

While the isolated missionary struggled with this 'culture question', and despairingly sought to make some religious impression on the indifferent African, a variety of critics argued that he was undertaking a hopeless task.

To Samuel Baker, the discoverer of Lake Albert and the Governor of Equatoria from 1868 to 1873, the association of Christianity and civilization indicated the folly of missionary endeavours to spread the gospel among savage races. Baker's background was not conducive to favourable attitudes to the non-white peoples. The family fortunes were based on large properties and sugar plantations in Jamaica and Mauritius. Baker, 'conservative, race-conscious, and class-conscious', imbibed from his father 'an immovable prejudice against stay-at-home philanthropists'.[52] Before turning to Africa as a field for his personal exploits, he had managed the family sugar plantations in Mauritius, and had spent some time in Ceylon where he displayed, a sympathetic biographer has noted, an intolerance, 'to the point of harshness with the backward Cingalese'[53]—an attitude to racial contact which he carried to Africa.

A strong and fearless man, Baker was a great believer in the civilizing capacity of force and despotism. There was a certain variation in his views, but he was invariably cynical about African ability, consistent in defending the use of force, and tireless in reiterating the necessity of extirpating savage idleness. He was scornful about missionary work, declaring: 'As to Christianity! the name is profaned by coupling it with the Negro.'[54] In his published writings he compared Africans of the Nuer tribe unfavourably with his pet monkey, and labelled the Kytch tribe 'mere apes'[55] for they trusted entirely to the production of nature for their subsistence. In a scientific aside he attributed the lack of suicide and insanity among Africans to their animal existence in which 'the brain . . . exercised as a simple muscle of the body . . . is never overstrained by deep thought or by excessive study'.[56] At Latooka he recorded in his diary for April 10, 1863:

> I wish the black sympathizers in England could see Africa's inmost heart as I do, much of their sympathy would subside. Human nature viewed in its crude state as pictured amongst African savages is quite on a level with that of the brute, and not to be compared with the noble character of the dog. There is neither gratitude, pity, love, nor self-denial; no idea of duty; no religion; but covetousness, ingratitude, selfishness and cruelty. All are thieves, idle, envious, and ready to plunder and enslave their weaker neighbours.[57]

Baker's jumble of stereotyped prejudices was partially based on a climatic theory of history. He argued that the power and intelligence of man would have 'their highest development within certain latitudes, and the natural passions and characters of races will be governed by locality and the temperature of climate'. The natural energy of all countries was held to be influenced by climate, and civilization, being dependent on energy, 'must accordingly vary in its degrees according to geographical position'.

> The natives of tropical countries do not progress: enervated by intense heat, they incline rather to repose and amusement than to labour. Free from the rigours of winters, and the excitement of changes in the seasons, the native character assumes the monotony of their country's temperature. They have no natural difficulties to contend with,—no struggle with adverse storms and icy winds and frost-bound soil; but an everlasting summer, and fertile ground producing with little tillage, excite no enterprise; and the human mind, unexercised by difficulties, sinks into languor and decay.[58]

These character traits, initially dictated by climate, apparently became permanent aspects of racial endowment. The English, no matter in what part of the globe they were found, 'exhibit the industry and energy of their native land'. The African, on the other hand, could never escape from his natural instincts of a 'love of idleness and savagedom' unless 'specially governed and forced to industry'. It was all part of the 'great system of creation' and its 'mysterious laws' against which, therefore, it was folly to struggle.[59]

Although Baker asserted that Central Africa was 'peopled by a hopeless race of savages' for whom 'there is no prospect of civilization',[60] he was willing to entertain, in his more generous moments, faint hopes of the improvability of the African. Force was the fundamental prerequisite. The country first had to be annexed, and a firm but paternal government established. The 'only government suitable for the first root of law in a savage country is despotism'.⁶¹ This meant 'the musket and the bayonet . . . the precursors of permanent trade in savage countries. . . .' Superior force, if well directed, had an important civilizing influence in evoking the 'first seeds of civilization . . . [after which] the young plant can . . . be nurtured'. The course of development was summed up as exploration, then a government 'represented by military occupation, which results in war'; then 'victory, which brings peace and annexation', followed by the development of commerce, under a despotic government.⁶²

Given his racist outlook the 'man and brother' theory was not only abhorrent to Baker, but in its failure to recognize that the 'negro . . . is a distinct variety', it was based on the 'grand error of equalizing that which is unequal'.⁶³ The proper place for the African was as a worker for the white man, if necessary by compulsion to overcome instinctive idleness. As Governor of Equatoria at a salary of £10,000 a year, Baker's programme included forced labour. 'No man shall be idle under my rule,' he wrote to a friend. He would first free the Africans from slavery, and then, an indication of Baker's odd interpretation of African freedom, 'insist upon their working for themselves'. Every tribe was to be 'compelled to cultivate a certain amount of corn and cotton, in proportion to the population'. A 'vigorous authority' would constantly be on guard lest they 'quickly relapse into a hopeless apathy and indolence'. The produce of this vast Equatorial plantation was to be exchanged for British manufactures.⁶⁴ The stimulus of commercial intercourse carried on under the surveillance of a despotic white regime would increase African wants, thus necessitating increased production. In this process, with wants and African efforts increasing at an equal rate, the basis of civilization would be laid, and the savage would have to 'become industrious; industry being the first grand stride towards civilization'.⁶⁵ By this process the African would slowly be raised in the 'scale of humanity'. Until this had occurred the missionary, however earnest, could only wait while others built the foundations on which his 'superstructure' was to be erected. Christianity, argued Baker, could not exist without civilization, which, in turn, depended on commerce. To defy this obvious relationship would merely lead the philanthropist and missionary to 'expend their noble energies in vain in struggling against the obtuseness of savage hordes'.⁶⁶ He preferred not to speak of civilizing savages, feeling that 'improvement' was more appropriate and less presumptuous. He was not optimistic, but conjectured that 'perhaps after some centuries, we may expect a certain class of civilization among negroes'. It would doubtless be an 'immense period' when it took Britons eighteen hundred years to attain their civilization, even considering the fact that at the time of Caesar the British, 'although savage, were far superior to any tribes of Africa'.[67] Throughout most of this long transitional period the role of the missionary, and all others whose vision was distorted by mawkish sentiments, should consist of simply waiting on the sidelines while white despots ruthlessly drilled the African in the preparatory arts of discipline, industriousness, and obedience.

5

Baker was unique in his candid espousal of harsh racial doctrines. His attitudes were based, however, on a deep-seated British belief that the low cultural attainments of the African created special problems for those who wished to civilize him. The root of this problem rested on the assumption that civilized man and tribal man were at opposite ends of the ladder of human achievement, and the accompanying question of whether or not a fruitful transfer of cultural goods between such extremes was possible. Could Christianity, the acme of religious endeavour, make effective contact with cultures and religions at the bottom of the evolutionary ladder? Or was Islam a necessary preparatory stage for the acceptance of Christianity, or perhaps even the limit of potential African capacity? The fundamental question—did laws of social change exist, and if so, what were they?—was of supreme importance. If the laws of human development dictated that man could only progress by slow evolutionary stages, the missionary was doomed to failure. Missionaries excepted, there was a basic ambivalence of attitude about the desirability or possibility of disseminating western culture, or even Christianity, to the African. Pessimists such as Richard Burton claimed that while it might seem an easy task to overthrow the 'loose fabric of wild superstitions' of tribal man for a more advanced system of religious belief, in practice the opposite was the case. Religion was the 'mental expression of a race', and to assert that 'the Bible made England or the Koran Stambul' was to propagate a fallacy.[68] On this assumption, religious beliefs of a higher or lower nature were specific to the capacities of various races, rather than causal factors in their cultural backwardness or possible future elevation. This approach implied the folly of attempting to telescope centuries of social change by the mechanism of conversion and, therefore, undercut the universality of Christianity by the plain implication that, although it might be the highest form of religion, it was restricted in its application to the superior races.

For those who doubted the possibility of the civilization of the

HOW CAN SAVAGES BE CIVILIZED?

African being directly undertaken by European preceptors, the logical solution was to assert that at least part of the task should be handed to an ethnic group superior to the African but inferior to the European. By this stratagem the racial, cultural and religious distance between the African and his mentor would be reduced, a factor which would ease the process of African advance by simplifying the steps by which it was to occur. Such was the thesis of Harry Hamilton Johnston, a devout evolutionist and the first Commissioner of British Central Africa.

Johnston was hopeful about the prospects of African advancement, although as evolution indicated, it would necessarily be slow. He did not believe that direct racial contact between such extremes as the African and the white man could be fruitful. Nor did he believe that the biologically unadulterated African race could successfully advance above its existing cultural level. He was driven inevitably to the conclusion that a racial middleman was required to inject a dash of superior blood into the backward and brutish African.

> On the whole I think the admixture of yellow that the negro requires should come from India, and that Eastern Africa and British Central Africa should become the America of the Hindu. The mixture of the two races would give the Indian the physical development which he lacks, and he in his turn would transmit to his half negro offspring the industry, ambition, and aspiration towards a civilized life which the negro so markedly lacks.[69]

Johnston desired to build an interdependent multi-racial society in which each race carried out the functions appropriate to its racial and cultural capacities. The white man was to govern, instruct, and supply intelligence. The Indian, clever but lacking initiative and the capacity to govern, was to act both as a racial and cultural middleman—a link between the races and a biological lever to raise the African. He would also undertake work which was too intelligent for the African and too costly or unhealthy for the white. The black man was at the bottom. He was to serve and labour in the menial posts. It was, in a way, a simplified version of the British class system with white aristocrats, 'yellow' middle class, and black proletariat.[70] It was an impressive piece of intellectual chess, a depressing illustration of the scientific mentality, and a frightening example of social engineering based on dubious racial propositions.[71]

In the opinion of a number of writers the role which Johnston visualized for the Indian was already being performed in Central Africa by the Moslem Arabs and the Swahili. Critics tended to describe Islam as a dying faith, lacking energy and incompatible with the spirit of the age. Livingstone commented adversely on an alleged lack of proselytizing activity by Moslems,[72] thereby denying Islam membership in the ranks of the great missionary religions. The use of missionary sources, however, is inclined to do less than justice to Arabs and Swahili. Men like Ahmed bin Ibrahim, who chastised King Suna of Buganda for his cruelty, would have been an ornament to any religion.[73] In any case it was an observable fact that Islam was gaining adherents in the interior. As early as 1860 Ludwig Krapf had written of the powerful influence of Islam in Eastern Africa. He predicted it would become 'still stronger, and the heathen and Christian populations be involved in a mighty conflict with it'. He also noted numerous examples of Moslem efforts to convert the African.[74] Frequently it was to the Arab's advantage to have religious allies among tribal groups in the interior. The Yao, slave suppliers to Arab traders, were such a tribe and Moslem influence was strong among them. In addition, many slaves were initiated into Islam and often became independent caravan leaders in their own right. The much criticized Swahili, while they may have been deficient as theologians, strongly felt that they were Moslems and were impervious to Christian attempts to convert them. A further element of worry to the missionary was the fact that powerful African chiefs such as Mtesa of Buganda, Mandara the Chagga chief, and some of the Yao chiefs such as Makanjira were already capable writers of Arabic.

The most striking example of Christian-Moslem conflict occurred around the southern half of Lake Tanganyika. The L.M.S. missionaries, who plunged with crusading fervour into an area where Arab and Swahili influence was marked, and who aspired not only to preach the gospel and convert the heathen, but also to save them from the iniquities of the slave trade, found to their distress that the African preferred the religion of his oppressor to that of his would-be saviours. From the outset the mission had employed Moslem Wangwana from the coast and Zanzibar to do the work of gardening, building, and carpentry on the mission station. While the missionary busied himself learning the language his Moslem workmen acquired a 'really wonderful' influence over the local people.[75] By the time the missionary could make himself understood he was surrounded by semi-Moslems, converted by his own workmen.[76] As Jones was later to write to the Foreign Secretary of the L.M.S.: 'We have been bringing up Mohammedans, while we were fondly imagining that we were laying a foundation of solid Christian work.'[77]

The struggle between Islam and Christianity became a prominent feature of missionary thought. Although social relations between Arabs and missionaries were often friendly, there was an undercurrent of Arab hostility from the very onset of white contact. Overt or veiled Arab and Swahili opposition was a recurring missionary problem. In the eighties Moslem missionary activity was intensified. There was a growth of hostile feelings to Europeans and attempts to seize political power at various points in the interior.[78] To the missionary paganism receded into the background and Islam loomed larger and larger. In a sense paganism was felt to be no more than the passive material over which each of the two great contending religions, Islam and Christianity, struggled for supremacy.

The missionary not only had to struggle directly with Islam, but he had to defend the wisdom of his struggle against a variety of opponents. Unlike the pagan African, the Arab and his religion elicited a modicum of respect and at times a certain admiration from the British.[79] Gibbon had accorded praise to Islam. Mohammed had been one of Carlyle's heroes, and the gifted Richard Burton verged on being an adherent of the Islamic faith. Admittedly the Arab involvement in the slave trade incurred the wrath of humanitarians, but even hostile attitudes were very rarely invested with the contempt and sarcasm accorded to the African. There was, if nothing else, a certain glamour and romance attached to the minaret and the muezzin. Zanzibar, curtly described by Henry Drummond as 'Oriental in its appearance, Mohammedan in its religion, Arabian in its morals . . . [a] cesspool of wickedness . . . a fit capital for the Dark Continent',[80] was a colourful port to Frederick Elton to be defended against 'revilers of the picturesque'.[81] The missionary W. P. Johnson commented that although Zanzibar may have been filthy, 'to me, and I think to others of us, it localized the Arabian Nights'.[82] More dangerous to the missionary than such romantic appreciation of the exotic was the advocacy by a number of intelligent, articulate and persuasive writers that Islam as a religion and Arabs as a racial group were peculiarly well adapted to play a key role in the civilization of the African. Since their arguments tended to follow a common pattern, only a few will be considered in detail. They were all, in some degree, cultural relativists, less prone than the missionary to make western achievement the measuring rod for all mankind, partly because they were somewhat doubtful of the achievement itself, and partly because they were prepared to adapt their standards in different situations.

To Bosworth Smith, a Harrow School master, the superiority of Christianity was not in question, but the laws of social change were. Might it not be, he queried, that the superiority of Christianity was the great barrier to its spread? Christianity, he asserted, was a dynamic individualistic religion, suited for the progressive Aryan races. Islam, a religion of stability, was suited for backward races and stationary societies. Thus Islam was not a competitor, for it succeeded where Christianity was unable to get a footing. It was, he claimed, the nearest religion to Christianity, and he was tempted to call it the Christianity best suited to the East. In Africa, where Islam was yearly spreading by 'giant strides', the African was received as an equal into a vast fraternity in which he found a dignity and self-reliance contrasting strongly with the servility and dependence of the Christian African who still felt himself to be 'an immeasurable distance' from Europeans. In general, Smith's view of the laws of social change upheld the superiority of Christianity but minimized its potential for expansion by the assertion that its exalted virtues rendered it unsuitable for backward races. Its 'proper home [was] in the Western world, among the inhabitants and progressive civilization of Greece and Rome'.[83]

Smith had an influential friend and skilful ally in Dr. Edward Wilmot Blyden.[84] A West Indian, Blyden went to Liberia as a youth, became Liberian Minister of Education, and later Liberian Plenipotentiary at the Court of St. James. His basic thesis was that Islam was a preparation for the diffusion of Christianity in Africa. From his background of West African experience he compared the stimulus given to African society by Islam with the comparative failure of Christianity. He argued that the very qualities rendering Anglo-Saxons irresistible as conquerors—'that unrelenting sternness, and uncompromising hardness—disqualify them for the subtle and delicate task of assimilating subject races and winning their confidence and affection'. He believed that the African had a unique cultural contribution to make, and for this purpose a tolerant Islam was preferable to an ethnocentric Christianity which would force the African to be an imitation. He was deeply perturbed at the racial element in Protestant Christendom, and pointed out that if a pariah became a Moslem he could rise to the throne, while if he became a Christian he remained a pariah still. He thought that western literature was saturated with anti-African prejudice. He noted that curious and contradictory attitude of the humanitarian white who 'under a keen sense of the wrongs done to the Negro, will work for him, will suffer for him, will fight for him, will even die for him, but he cannot get rid of a secret contempt for him'. Blyden argued that the diffusion of Islam would diminish such harmful psychological attitudes due to the greater respect accorded to the Moslem African, and would also obviate the tiresome task of coping with a multiplicity of African languages by its introduction of Arabic. Islam would also provide theological preparation with its monotheism, and cultural preparation by introducing reading, writing, architecture, commerce, and other attributes of an advanced culture not found in tribal life. To Blyden the basic enemy was paganism, and in its destruction Islam was an ally. Mohammed, in fact, was the servant of Christ. He added the telling and irritating point that if the divinity of a religion could be inferred from the racial diversity of its adherents, then no religion could prefer greater claims than Islam.[85]

The distinguished and persuasive advocacy of Islam offered by these two writers was anything but palatable to the missionary movement. The seeds of decay went even further in 1887–8 when an Anglican divine, Canon Isaac Taylor, sparked off a bitter and vitriolic controversy over the relative merits of Christianity and Islam as apposite agents to regenerate Africa. The controversy commenced when Taylor, at short notice, gave a paper on Mohammedanism at a Church Congress held in Wolverhampton in 1887. To the astonishment of his audience he did not present the usual condemnation of Islam, ending with a plea for greater effort against this false sensual religion. He not only asserted that 'over a large portion of the world Islamism as a missionary religion is more successful than Christianity (Sensation)', but he claimed that this was inherent in the very nature of the two religions and was indeed desirable. Islam 'though quite unfitted for the higher races . . . is eminently adapted to be a civilizing and elevating religion for barbarous tribes. Christianity is too spiritual, too lofty. Islam has done for civilization more than Christianity. (Oh, Oh).' How little, he asserted, missions have to show for the 'vast sums of money and all the precious lives lavished upon Africa!' Christian converts were reckoned by thousands, Moslem converts by millions.[86] His essential argument was that higher religions were for higher races, and lower religions for lower races. It was a question of 'cerebral development'.[87] In his own pungent words: 'We cannot expect African cannibals to rise at one bound from the worship of lizards to an intelligent comprehension of the Athanasian creed.'[88]

Joseph Thomson entered the controversy on the side of Canon Taylor. He contrasted the 'petty results of three hundred years of Christian contact' on the west coast with the 'immense civilizing work of the reviled religion in the Central and Western Soudan'. The trouble with missionaries was their 'astounding blindness and obstinacy' in persisting in 'senseless and impracticable methods, ever attempting to graft the higher, nay the very highest conceptions of the Christian religion upon low, undeveloped brains incapable of their comprehension, not to speak of their assimilation, trusting, however, in Providence to do the watering and give the increase'. Thomson, perhaps because he was a geologist, was inclined to favour evolving rather than abrupt social change. He concluded that the missionary could produce but a veneer unless he learned the necessity of preaching from the level of the savage.[89]

Thomson's contributions to discussions of African affairs were consistently presented with candour and a minimum of prejudice. He possessed a gift for satire and trenchant criticism, but he struggled successfully against a tendency to simplify problems in the extreme fashion common among his contemporaries. Although he was impressed with the energy, nobility, and devotion of missionaries, he was unrepentant in his advocacy of the necessity of a simplified Christianity being presented to the African. Though he praised Islam he did not think it was more suitable than Christianity for the African. It was only more suitable than Christianity as taught.[90] He felt that Christianity would never succeed unless it adapted itself to African conditions and divested itself of the theological accretions of centuries. Thus he ridiculed the U.M.C.A. priests with their emphasis on ritual.[91] In Edward Coode Hore of the L.M.S. he found his ideal missionary—'a man who did not waste his time wandering about with his Bible in his hands, trying to teach the natives to talk mechanically about things they could not comprehend', but a highly moral man who lived his Christianity and could teach the African to build better boats, dig their fields to more advantage, and generally see to their material wants. The men required for mission work were men 'readier with their hands than their tongues'.[92]

In part the dispute between the missionary and his opponents rested on a difference of objec   The advocates of Islam were often not concerned with Chri∶   zing the African, but with the more limited objective of improving him. The fact that Islam produced some social advance was sufficient proof of its merits. From the missionary viewpoint it was preferable that Africans remain in degraded paganism rather than participate in the social and religious advantages of Islam. Although Islam was an advance, the essential consideration to the missionary was that it constituted a barrier to real progress,[93] which for the individual was measured by salvation, and for society by the degree to which it was permeated with Christian values.

In political terminology it was a dispute between radicals and conservatives. The basic assumption of the opponents of the missionary enterprise was that social change could not occur rapidly and that successful influence could only be exerted in contact situations between near equals in cultural attainment. In essence the defenders of Islam argued that conversion, like politics, was the art of the possible. Their defence of Islam often reflected unfavourable views of African capacity as well as favourable views of the Moslem religion.

The conservative approach was clearly presented by the explorer Verney Lovett Cameron:

> with regard to education and civilization, we must be satisfied to work gradually and not attempt to force our European customs and manners

HOW CAN SAVAGES BE CIVILIZED?

upon a people who are at present unfitted for them. Our own civilization, it must be remembered, is the growth of many centuries, and to expect that of Africa to become equal to it in a decade or two is an absurdity. The forcing system, so often essayed with so-called savages, merely puts on a veneer of spurious civilization; in the majority of cases the subject having, in addition to the vices of his native state, acquired those belonging to the lowest dregs of civilization.'[94]

Sir John Willoughby thought likewise. After a hunting trip to the Kilimanjaro region, he wrote that the natives were 'childlike and of a singularly low order of intelligence'. He felt that slavery, 'properly supervised', would be no hardship to them, as their capacity of 'being improved up to a point of understanding needful to fit them for higher callings' had not been demonstrated. 'So-called civilization by conversion will not do it, as under such conditions the low class native simply deteriorates into the utter blackguard.' He added cynical comments on the policy of the U.M.C.A. since the death of Bishop Steere. All practical enterprise was dead, and instead of the girls being taught to cook and the men to work 'the observance of ritualistic exercises' seemed the chief occupation of the missionaries on Zanzibar. He especially deprecated missionary work among Moslem Africans, inducing those 'with a religion which they understand and which suits them, to exchange it for one which does not'.[95]

These criticisms of the missionary movement and the advocacy of Islam for the African were bitterly resisted. Since Darwin's *Origin of the Species* public attacks on Christianity and in particular on missionary work had been frequent. In the sixties there had been verbal exchanges with the Anthropological Society of London which had given prominent place to Richard Burton and Winwood Reade with their pro-Moslem heresies.[96] The bluff Bishop Wilberforce had been decisively vanquished by the incisive mind of Huxley in 1860, but when Livingstone died his lonely death a decade later new recruits for the cause of missions had come forth regardless of man's descent from primates. Missionary societies had grown accustomed to fighting a dual battle with heathens abroad and sceptics at home. To them the religious relativism of the advocates of Islam was simply heretical and impossible of acceptance.[97]

The missionary attitude to Islam was aggressively hostile, illustrating the 'all-too-familiar maxim in ecclesiastical history, that they who differ least in religious matters hate the most'.[98] Missionary writers and speakers 'girded their loins', attacked the credentials of their opponents, prominently played up mission successes, and insisted that the 'Gospel . . . we preach is as well adapted to Africa as to India, to India as to Europe; it is a Gospel which is suited to every continent and island upon the face of the earth—to either hemisphere and to every habitable zone.'[99] The comparative missionary optimism as to the eventual success of his task was perhaps less a reflection of a generous assessment of African capacities than a requirement of the faith—a belief in the special efficacy of the gospel as an instrument of social and religious change among even the least advanced members of the human family. Whatever its basis, it consisted of an unyielding claim that the Christian message could make effective contact with the tribal African. As Pruen of the C.M.S. observed, the African could not be a Christian without God's help, but then neither could the Englishman.[100] In any case the matter was not disputable for, as missionary writers somewhat wearily reminded their critics, they were executing a divine mandate.

The intellectual follies of such writers as Smith and Blyden were only to be expected in an imperfect world. Smith, the *Church Missionary Intelligencer* pointed out, had no real claim to be heard on the subject, for he had not seen so much 'of the practical working of Mohammedanism as one of Mr. Cook's tourists obtains in the course of a midsummer's vacation'.[101] Blyden's writings, 'the production of a Negro . . . proved what we have always stoutly maintained —that . . . the Negro can assert his position among the other members of the human family', but it was clearly impossible for intelligent men to agree that 'the professors of a creed which justified slavery, and who had always shown themselves forward beyond others in slave-dealing' were either forerunners of Christianity or capable of showering vast blessings on benighted Africa.[102] As for Canon Taylor and the praise which he had heaped on Islam, the major opponent which he and his fellow L.M.S. missionaries faced, A. J. Swann wrote:

> I assert its effect on the natives in Central Africa is to make them *professionally* savage and [it] places them hopelessly beyond reformation; it turns them from a being who knows certain things displease a supernatural Being . . . to a creature who is taught to believe the *Deity* the Creator God, can allow any amount of vile actions and periodically forget the same at the mention of his name: *this is what it does*! no matter what Taylor or the Devil may say.[103]

This polemical vituperation was not unrelated to the missionary inability to convert Moslems. Capitalism was acceptable to the Marxist for he knew it contained the seeds of its own destruction, but the missionary could find no dialectical logic to comfort him in his struggle with Islam. The argument that Islam was a half-way house on the road from paganism to Christianity was denied by the hard fact of missionary experience—that Islam was almost impregnable. There was a 'strange venom' in Islam, asserted Mackay. How-

HOW CAN SAVAGES BE CIVILIZED?

ever superficial its hold on a formerly pagan people, subsequent conversion to Christianity was almost impossible.[104] There was also the complex theological problem of fitting the emergence of Islam into God's plan for the universe. It was inferior to Christianity and yet it had appeared later in time. Surely the greater should follow the less. The frequent assertion that the appearance of Islam in the seventh century was a divine chastisement for the decadent state of the Christian Churches in North Africa and the Middle East in that period partially served to make its origin explicable,[105] but was of little practical assistance to the embattled missionary twelve centuries later.

The missionary was happy to agree with his critics that the success of Islam among tribal Africans was related to its inferiority,[106] an explanation which left the exalted nature of Christianity untouched. He gained, however, little solace from the assurance that his failure was due to the superiority of the ethical and spiritual doctrines which he attempted to disseminate. Like other men, he preferred to be convinced by success.

He was compelled to admit that he laboured under special racial and cultural disabilities in transmitting his message to primitive peoples. Islam, it was widely conceded, possessed important advantages in the easy-going race attitudes of its Arab and Swahili purveyors, and the assimilating nature of their culture. 'Englishmen', noted Steere, 'generally have a much less kindly feeling towards a free negro than the Arabs have toward their slaves.'[107]

The competition between Arab Moslems and white Christians raised important issues of race relations which merit examination because of the light they throw on British attitudes. The varying composition of the mixed Swahili race, from almost pure African to pure Arab, provided ocular proof of a bridge between African and Arab, paganism and Islam, and clearly indicated the graduated assimilative process by which Islam was diffused in Central Africa. Miscegenation was open and natural to the Arab. Concubines chosen from slaves became almost equal with Arab wives after the birth of a child, and little distinction was made among the children.[108] Arab systems of marriage and concubinage helped establish contact and obliterate racial lines. To the British miscegenation was furtive,[109] and half-caste offspring were usually scorned. An attitude of contempt for the half-caste, who was frequently held to partake of the vices of both races, was typical of these early pioneers, and even more so of later settler communities. Miscegenation was associated with racial degeneration. No missionary thought of marrying an African woman. He went home for a wife and when he returned the paraphernalia of western society surrounding him increased. Missionary marriages decreased the prospect of race contact on a basis of equality. There was a basic conflict between British repugnance at the thought of racial mixture and the desire of the missionary element among humanitarians to spread the Christian aspects of British culture among Africans. Religious universalism was poorly served by biological exclusiveness.

Christianity produced a deeper break with African society than did Islam. With its emphasis on individual salvation it had little message for the community and was thus antithetical to the integration of religion and society characteristic of tribalism. It emphasized the isolation of the convert, and was far more likely to create antagonism among his kinsmen. Islam demanded no radical change from the African and was compatible, not only with polygamy, the most striking illustration, but with 'the greater part of tribal custom'.[110] Between Islam and tribalism there was a highly flexible cultural fusion. Islam tended to spread slowly and gradually by intermarriage, and the prestige of the Arab and Swahili aristocracy of the coast.[111] For a minimum alteration of life habits, considerable secular and psychological advantages were acquired by the African Moslem. He derived self-respect from membership in a 'recognized civilization', and also, given its diffusion in the interior, valuable social and economic advantages in his travel and trade activities.[112] Islam had a less rigid set of criteria for membership than Christianity, and the right of admission was in the hands of ordinary believers vague about dogma and not overly concerned about its significance—factors which greatly increased its adaptability.

In significant contrast to Islam the spread of Christianity was entrusted to agents of large expensive bureaucracies, a clear indication of the compartmentalization of religion in western society, and hence a basic aspect of its weakness, for it did not spread automatically along with the culture of which it was a part. The fact that it was spread by specialists trained in the requirements of dogma and belief for converts also had important effects. One of their main concerns, the preservation of the purity of the faith by a strict adherence to standards, militated against flexibility and made it impossible for a fusion of tribal values and Christian ethics and beliefs to arise in areas deemed significant by missionaries. Their function was not to adapt standards to society, but to bring men and societies into accordance with divinely transmitted standards. For this reason the early missionaries strongly emphasized the need for a disciplining religion to bring the African out of the morass of impurity in which he lived. Bishop Steere went so far as to argue the special value of monasteries for their 'strict discipline . . . which leaves scarcely anything to the discretion of its junior members, might be the very training for our unstable Africans [whose] vanity is easily puffed up when they find themselves teachers'.[113] Less extreme views showing the same tendency to favour a lengthy disciplining probationary period, and a distrust of sudden avowals of Christianity made under the stress of emotionalism which, it was widely believed, formed a conspicuous part of African character, were widespread. The necessity of this approach was argued in terms of the special environmental temptations faced by the convert who was likely to face ostracism from his own society and who lacked the support of any public opinion to maintain him in his new way of life. The dangers were exacerbated by the belief that Africans were subject to specific weaknesses of character—'wanting in backbone' in Pruen's phrase[114] —which were inimical to a too ready grant of religious independence. The general effect of these arguments was to make the reception of Christianity an arduous process for the African, hedged in with qualifications and restrictions. The spread of Islam was almost diametrically opposite.

The problem which faced the missionary had several facets which can be analytically distinguished, although they were closely related in practice. There was the factor of feelings of racial superiority which contradicted by their exclusiveness the universality of the Christian brotherhood that the missionaries proclaimed. The only way to overcome the barrier which race posed for the effective presentation of the gospel was to raise up an African ministry to provide living proof of the independence of Christianity from race or colour. The existence of an African ministry would provide an irrefutable denial that Christianity was the white man's religion. Africans would also be more capable of understanding the thought patterns of their fellows, would know how to present the Christian message in a comprehensible language, and could live alongside their fellows differing in nothing except their Christianity. The creation of an African clergy and the raising up of an indigenous church were, in any case, the essential aims of the missionary movement, but it seems clear that they were pursued with peculiar urgency due to the difficulties encountered by Europeans in effecting the type of contact with the African which the spread of the gospel necessitated.[115]

The second main aspect of the problem rested on the greater moral and spiritual gap between Christianity and heathenism than between Islam and heathenism. Fundamentally this was insoluble for the missionary was unwilling to alter the content of his Christianity to make it especially attractive to heathens. What was possible, and it was here that there was a divergence of opinion and practice, was for the missionary to attempt to separate his Christian message from the civilized context in which it was found and to disseminate to the best of his ability Christianity alone. In spite of the difficulties which such a task involved, some missionaries, to whom attention will now be directed, made the effort. By so doing they attempted to make the significant gap between the races exclusively religious and thus smaller than the civilization plus religion gap over which most missionaries attempted to lead the African.

In discussing this group it should be pointed out that their ideas and actions were not specific responses to the competition of Islam. They were, however, responses to the 'culture problem' which Islam dramatized, and with which this section commenced.

6

William George Tozer, the second U.M.C.A. bishop, was one of the few Britons who deliberately repudiated any inherent connection between Christianity and the late-nineteenth-century western culture in which it was embedded. Tozer has been an unjustly maligned figure in the history of the European penetration of Central Africa. His missionary career showed no outstanding successes and, unlike many others, he made no important contributions to the study of African languages or to the geographical unveiling of the interior. His views on the nature of the missionary task, however, were important and consistent.

> What do we mean when we say that England or France are civilized countries and that the greater part of Africa is uncivilized? Surely the mere enjoyment of such things as railways and telegraphs and the like do not necessarily prove their possessors to be in the first rank of civilized nations. We claim to have been a civilized people long before these things were in use, and mere superficial distinctions of this kind cannot go to the root of the matter.... Nothing can be so false as to suppose that the outward circumstance of a people is the measure either of its barbarism, or its civilization.... The Church of Christ ... has no commission to bring all nations to any other uniformity than that of the faith.[116]

He found a main weakness of missionary work in 'an avowed desire to obliterate everything connected with the convert's nationality'. How, he asked, could the Church of God flourish and spread itself among non-western peoples if in addition to employing a foreign ministry 'open war' was made 'against everything' which reflected the uniqueness of their separate nationality? Tozer set himself to oppose resolutely this ethnocentric trend, arguing the wisdom of disturbing the habits and modes of thought of the potential Christian only to the minimum extent required by the truth of Christianity.[117]

In part his approach indicated a respect for African customs. He

HOW CAN SAVAGES BE CIVILIZED?

felt it would be of dubious value to 'Anglicize the people' in matters of food, clothing, and other cultural traits, and noted: 'It is wonderful how much wisdom after a time you will discover in the use of customs which at first sight seem barbarous.' He saw his function as the making of African Christians, not the production of 'black Englishmen'.[118]

Tozer was the first of a succession of U.M.C.A. bishops and missionaries who attempted to make a distinction between civilization and Christianity, and tried to blend the latter with a tribal way of life. As Steere wrote:

> You know that the one great thing that we desired [was] to train up the Africans to teach their own people. We felt that an exotic Church was a thing that would perish before any cold blast, and that it was necessary to put it upon a sound native basis. We have, therefore, from the first steadily set our faces against any denationalization of the people of Africa. For this purpose we have been anxious to teach them in their own language, to accustom them to their own style of food and dress, as far as we could, in order to raise up a race of people who should not feel that they were strangers amongst their brethren, and a race of ministers who should be able to exist upon the common food of the country, so that those who heard them might be able to maintain them.[119]

As a result the U.M.C.A. played down the industrial[120] and European element in its mission work. The missionaries adopted a life of spartan simplicity in which the diminution of external differences between whites and blacks was designed to render race contact more intimate and understanding on both sides.

The reasons why the U.M.C.A. missionaries did not see themselves as agents of western civilization are complex. The fact that the mission headquarters were at Zanzibar possibly played a minor part. Missionaries in the interior tended to exaggerate the virtues of civilization, partly as a defensive reaction against their tribal surroundings, and partly because their experience did not provide them with information on the deplorable conduct which has typically characterized secular Europeans in contact with tribal peoples. At Zanzibar the reality was at least somewhat more apparent. Steere gave evidence before a House of Commons Committee on the immorality of British sailors engaged in the suppression of the slave trade. He also talked grimly of the 'Planters' ideal of Native Races',[121] a concern which was to trouble other missionaries when secular representatives of the west began to arrive in increasing numbers, but which for the moment was a danger only dimly apprehended.

It is, however, clearly necessary to look for much deeper factors to explain the important distinction between the missionary who saw his function in terms of the steam engine and the Bible, and one who saw his in fairly exclusive religious terms. It was, in a way, analogous to the difference between a total assimilation policy characteristic in theory of the Latin colonizing powers and the indirect rule policies later devised by Lugard and Cameron and embedded in the very core of British colonial policy in Africa. It is impossible to offer more than tentative explanations for this difference in temperament which manifested itself in differences in policy. The indirect rule analogy provides a partial insight, for not only did that policy contain respect for tribal cultures, but it implicitly contained serious doubts not only as to the capacity of the African to assimilate western standards, but of the wisdom of letting him make the attempt.[122] It is dangerously easy to confuse cultural conservatism with the cultural relativism of the anthropologist. Missionaries, for example, have been rightly praised for their linguistic work, and one scholar has asserted that no stronger proof for their comparative respect for tribalism could be found.[123] Another explanation, however, may well have been a reluctance to spread English. One L.M.S. missionary who advocated the teaching of English ran up against the prevalent idea that 'English speaking natives are rogues'.[124]

At times the preservation of, and respect for, African customs was transmuted into an unwillingness to allow the African to follow western customs of his own volition. Thus in 1899 J. E. Hine, Bishop of Likoma, informed a U.M.C.A. conference of the grave danger that had arisen due 'to the increasing spirit of dissatisfaction' on the part of the African clergy who were showing a tendency to copy European habits of life in food, clothes, and other customs, tendencies which violated mission policy, and were being resisted by the European members of the mission. He cogently argued the necessity for maintaining simplicity of life on the ground of the danger involved in separating the African clergy from the standards of their parishioners and thus weakening the prospects of an indigenous church.[125] It is possible, however, to suggest, if not to prove, that this represented an unwillingness to reduce cultural distinctions between Africans and Europeans as much as to prevent distinctions arising between indigenous clergy and their flock.

The Anglo-Catholicism of the U.M.C.A. was an important contributory factor. A study of similar differences in missionary attitudes between Anglicans and nonconformists to tribal society in Fiji has led J. D. Legge to emphasize the importance of the Anglican concept of the Church as a necessary instrument of salvation, a universal organization able to encompass all men regardless of their station and the type of their society, an approach evoking emphasis on doctrine and ritual. The nonconformist, he argues, was more concerned with the relation of the individual conscience to God, and therefore more prone to lay emphasis on ethical matters.[126] This inevitably produced an intolerant attitude to tribalism.

This was not the only factor. The U.M.C.A. missionaries were drawn from the upper and upper middle classes of British society, and they tended to be well educated, frequently at the better public schools, followed by Oxford or Cambridge. Their educational and class background probably helped to induce a certain appreciation of diversity with an accompanying tolerance and comparative respect for other cultures. Significantly, 'aristocrats' in Central Africa, both secular and clerical, men such as Kerr, Jephson, and Knight-Bruce, tended to express comparatively favourable attitudes to African culture. Yet, as Jephson indicated, this could be coupled with the assumption that Africans were incapable of becoming Europeanized,[127] and with a distaste, which existed even at this early date, for the African who 'aped' the European in such matters as clothing.[128]

An apparent respect for African culture may veil a disrespect for African capacity, or a distaste for the breaking down of cultural distinctions. The Scottish missions with their emphasis on civilization displayed less respect for tribalism, but their approach was possibly indicative of a greater optimism as to the capacity of the African to asssimilate a range of western values and traits which would eventually place him on a level of equality with Europeans in more than spiritual matters. This, however, is dangerous ground for which explicit evidence is sparse. In part the U.M.C.A. attitude may have reflected the assumption that the training of backward peoples was an affair for gentlemen, and that mechanics and agriculturists were likely to be devoid of the appropriate moral qualities for such a delicate task.[129] Finally, the upper-class background of the U.M.C.A. missionaries with a relative lack of involvement in industry and commerce was probably partially responsible for a certain detachment about some of the ideals of progress and prosperity which animated other Britons.

Whatever the reason, the U.M.C.A. as a body was unique in its approach to African culture and society. Duff Macdonald, the anthropologically inclined Scottish missionary, held similar views—'undoubtedly, a native might become a very good Christian, and still be content with his small hut and his coarse fare'[130]—but the standard missionary approach was that civilization and Christianity should go hand in hand, as seen in the industrial training establishments of the Scottish missions, in the regeneration of Africa.

In historical perspective it can now be seen that those whose respect for African culture, whatever its basis, led to an emphasis on the preservation of tribalism were basically unrealistic. A qualified

HOW CAN SAVAGES BE CIVILIZED?

admiration for African society could perhaps ease the transition to a large scale society which Africans perforce had to experience, but it could not prevent that change from taking place. The troubles of contemporary African nationalist leaders are not unrelated to the sympathetic respect paid to tribal systems which time was to render obsolete.

7

The Christianity which missionaries proposed introducing into Central Africa proves on analysis to be an elusive concept with varying meanings. The same is true of discussions of the 'civilization' of the African, and the mechanics of commerce and colonization which were to help bring it about. Civilization was conceived in remarkably down-to-earth and non-philosophic terms. There was an almost complete absence of the concept of the 'soul' of civilization, and no mention of some ineffable psychic core of culture which was to be transmitted to the African. At times civilization seemed to mean no more than the buying and selling of the market place. The equation of civilization with commerce rested on the elementary assumption that civilization consisted of the material goods diffused by commercial transactions. When missionaries pointed out that the Matabele were advancing in civilization they meant simply that the wearing of European clothing was becoming more common.[131]

The simple fact was that the British looked at nature from the viewpoint of commercial exploitation. From explorers who conceived an economic survey of the land over which they travelled as one of their major functions, to the missionary who sent examples of potential marketable produce to his society in order to interest prospective investors and merchants,[132] the value of commerce was continually stressed. A commercial emphasis was a cultural imperative for members of an advanced industrial society.

That commerce had generally beneficent effects and was an important agency of civilization was one of the most fundamental and deeply rooted British beliefs. As the discussion on Livingstone has shown,[133] the prospective economic relationship between Britain and Central Africa was designed not only to serve Africa, but to make a major contribution to the solution of a diversity of economic problems facing Britain. This economic emphasis was especially pronounced in the propagandistic support for imperial policies in the eighties and nineties.[134] Africa was seen as an outlet for surplus capital, a new source of raw materials, a protected market, a population safety valve, and as providing positions for the unemployed 'sons of gentleman', 'a very numerous class' according to Cameron.[135]

HOW CAN SAVAGES BE CIVILIZED?

While some writers, Joseph Thomson being the most prominent, were far from optimistic about the economic prospects of Central Africa,[136] their realism was submerged beneath the Eldorados of less accurate observers. V. L. Cameron, one of the most ardent exponents of imperialism on economic grounds, referred to 'almost unspeakable richness', 'vast fortunes', and 'incalculable wealth in tropical Africa'.[137] Matabeleland was described by another writer as a country which would prove 'the largest and richest gold field that the world has ever seen'.[138] According to Marshall Hole such eulogistic descriptions were not without effect, for the early pioneers contained men 'otherwise sane' who expected to find chunks of gold in quartz reefs and assumed that panning in the river beds would certainly produce 'nuggets in every bucketful'.[139]

Our concern here, however, is directed to the role commerce was expected to play in the regeneration of Central Africa, rather than to the economic benefits expected to accrue to British settlers or to Britain from the economic development of Central Africa. One Briton after another uncritically lauded commerce as a basic factor in the diffusion of civilization.[140] The prestige of commerce was indicated by the strong support it received in missionary quarters. One missionary wrote that if he had private means he would probably leave the mission and engage in a fair and honest trade with the Africans in the belief that a Christian trader would have an immense power for good.[141] Mackay of Uganda asserted that history showed plainly that isolation produced degeneration, while intercourse with other nations tended to elevation. All Africa, he claimed, 'is a standing testimony to the destructive power of isolation'. Hence the necessity for improved communications and the introduction of Christian merchants.[142] While the missionary movement tended to lay stress on the civilizing impact of Christian trade, the reverse, a pointed indication of the advantages to commerce flowing from missionary work, was also present.[143] Indeed, this recurrent intermingling of the sacred and secular was one of the most striking characteristics of missionary writings in this period.[144]

In addition to the general civilizing impulse which commerce was to give to backward peoples, it was further held that legitimate commerce would oust the slave trade from its hold in the interior. This belief enjoyed the unquestioning acceptance usually accorded to dogma. It was sanctioned by its association with the British antislavery movement. Yet its validity was, to say the least, doubtful. The question must remain hypothetical in Central Africa for, aside from the African Lakes Company and the isolated efforts of individual traders, there was no attempt to put the thesis to the test of practice. It is significant, however, that the African Lakes Company did not declare a dividend in the first decade and a half of its existence, and that individual traders such as Cotterill found their attemps at legitimate trade partly vitiated by the hostility of slave-trading chiefs.[145]

It seems clear on grounds of economic logic alone that there was no valid reason to assume that an increase in legitimate trade would have destroyed the traffic in black humanity, or the slavery which was its ultimate cause. Had legitimate trade been attempted on an extensive scale—by which no more can be meant than the presence of traders who refused to purchase slaves in exchange for the western goods coveted by Africans—it is possible that an increase in slavery and consequently of slave-raiding might have resulted. The presence of western merchants might have led to an expansion of coffee, sugar, or cotton production; but this might have increased the demand for slaves to work on plantations newly established by African chiefs or budding entrepreneurs in the interior in the same way as the emergence of clove production on Zanzibar increased the demand for slaves to meet plantation labour needs. On the other hand, if free labour proved more efficient in producing the exchange goods required to purchase western articles, the willingness of African chiefs to sell their fellows would have diminished. This would have undercut the supply of slaves and therefore raised their price if demand from other sources had remained constant, resulting in a decline in slave-raiding. Yet, even had free labour proved more productive than slave labour, the prestige factor involved in slave possession, especially household slavery and concubinage, would have still exerted pressure for a continued slave supply, and, had the increased wealth resulting from the expansion of legitimate trade in the interior been unequally distributed, this form of demand probably would have increased. The only predictable reduction of the slave trade would have occurred if an expansion of legitimate trade increased standards of living in the interior, thus diminishing that part of the trade caused by individuals selling themselves into slavery in order to avoid famine.

On the whole, the economic impact of legitimate trade on illegitimate trade is indeterminate. If alternatives to slaves as exchange goods for western articles had not been readily developed, the presence of 'legitimate merchants' would have been simply irrelevant. As long as there were willing buyers and willing sellers of slaves, some would have been forthcoming at a price determined by market forces. It would seem more appropriate to ask whether legitimate trade could successfully compete with the slave trade. Where two trading competitors exist in the same market the economic advantages clearly lie with the one who is not restricted as to the goods he can purchase and sell—a principle which would have worked to the advantage of slave-traders. West Coast experience is instructive, for one of the main complaints of British merchants, after they had been personally debarred from participation in the slave trade, was that they were unable to compete with foreign traders not so debarred—a clear indication both of the remunerative nature of the trade and of the inability of legitimate commerce to make serious inroads in a market when its agents were prohibited from purchasing one of the key articles of sale offered by the middlemen coastal tribes.[146] The experience of the United States, with the necessary employment of force to bring the American South to heel, is also indicative of the tenacity of the institution of slavery in the midst of legitimate commerce.

Basically questions of the slave trade and slavery were related to morality rather than to economics. From an economic point of view the adjectives 'legitimate' and 'illegitimate' were meaningless, and merely serve to confuse the issue. They did indicate, however, the moral basis of the British approach to the two competitive forms of trade. As the question at issue was moral, it is not surprising that there was a paucity of economic arguments brought forward to prove the capacity of legitimate commerce to oust the slave trade. 'It had become axiomatic that good trade would drive out bad,' states a recent student of the subject, 'a sort of Gresham's law for commerce.'[147] Influenced by the idea of progress, humanitarians felt they lived in a world sympathetic to their objectives. In the midst of the resultant optimism, the inevitable triumph of the good—'legitimate' trade—did not require explanation. Slavery and the slave trade were looked on as anachronisms which, by definition, would be unable to compete with more highly evolved and progressive forms of commercial intercourse. It was an aspect of the same optimism which evoked easy beliefs that higher religions would replace lower ones, and higher cultures, lower ones. These were matters of faith rather than investigation, and they were held with the distinguishing zeal which faith imparts. They reflected generally hopeful assumptions about the way the universe was moving, rather than actual theories of how human institutions change and evolve.

The widespread agreement on the civilizing effect of commerce and the special contributions it could make to the overthrow of the slave trade reveals the abstract nature of the discussion as to the appropriate methods to be used in ameliorating African conditions. This abstract approach pervaded the whole framework of concepts by which Britons analysed the problem of changing conditions in the interior. Unless it is constantly remembered that much of the theorizing on the role of commerce and colonization was singularly unrealistic the reader of the available literature will unconsciously imbibe the largely visionary picture of social change which many Britons held.

The confusion produced by this type of thinking can be most readily seen in the basic ambivalence and contradictions in missionary attitudes to commerce and colonization. Although at times missionaries were prone to assert that Christianity should precede civilization in Central Africa, they often came to realize that by their own unaided efforts they would be unable to exert sufficient influence to significantly alter the tribal systems within which they worked. What was needed among the Matabele, asserted Thomas Morgan Thomas of the L.M.S., was the settlement of 'a number of industrious, upright, and God-fearing men' scattered throughout the country. This would produce marked improvement in the social and religious condition of the tribe and 'by the blessing of God upon the efforts of such colonists, Central Africa would soon undergo mighty changes for good'. For this reason, Thomas was pleased about the gold discoveries in Mashonaland in the late sixties, and the consequent prospect of more Europeans coming into the country.[148] His colleague, J. B. Thomson, claimed however that the gold fields did not look very promising and 'I hope they will never come to anything, for if they do it will be the ruin of the natives'.[149] A few years later when Thomson was appointed to the L.M.S. mission to the regions of Lake Tanganyika, he wrote to the Directors advocating a line of trading stations from the coast to Ujiji. The traders were to be little 'centres of light' to the people by their spiritual example as well as reducing the costs of establishing and working the mission by acting as forwarding agents. He felt that it was exceptionally important for the Directors to pick these men and grant them some initial assistance, for traders of the wrong type exert

> a very baneful influence on the Natives and greatly retard missionary work. I have felt this very much in my experience in this country. If a class of men could be got who observe Sunday, lead pure and moral lives and abstain from fornication and conduct business upon sound and honourable principles, they would do more in the furtherance of mission work than can be well imagined.[150]

The problem which bedevilled the missionary attitude to colonization and commerce was the dichotomy between the desire for communities of God-fearing white Christians and the fear that in fact future settlements of whites would be conspicuously deficient in men possessed of the Christian characteristics described by Thomson. The ideal settlement for which Thomas hoped, for example, contrasted strongly with his description of some of the white traders and hunters already active in Matabeleland, men who had tired of the restraints of civilized life and who sought a 'more genial home among lawless barbarians'.

> Let loose, giving full scope to their evil inclinations and sinful habits, they become very degraded, and soon exceed, in immorality, the heathen themselves.... Of many vices the Amandebele knew comparatively little before their contact with these degraded Europeans, who, not content with plunging into these depths of wickedness, and becoming the tutors of the natives in flagrant vice, also set themselves to oppose the Christian Missionary, and to counteract his influence over those among whom he labours.[151]

In Matabeleland, where secular contact in the pre-imperial period was more significant than in any other part of Central Africa, the conduct of some of the traders and hunters was chronically brought forward by L.M.S. missionaries as one of the main hindrances to the diffusion of Christianity. It would be 'simply impossible' claimed one to indicate the 'extent of the injury traders and hunters do to our work'. Only the previous year some gentlemen hunters and some traders 'degraded themselves by their drunkenness and immorality at the King's town, so that they excited the contempt of the natives they professed to despise'.[152] Although commerce was theoretically desirable, was the irreligious white, trafficking in liquor, personally addicted to drink, and above neither brutality nor concubinage in his relations to Africans, not a serious drawback to missionary work? Were traders who spread rumours of tribal war in order to prevent other traders from coming into their trade territory and competing for ivory and ostrich feathers really aiding in the spread of civilization?[153] Was the trader who engaged in a drunken quarrel with a chief over an ivory sale, shot and killed the chief, and was then speared to death, an asset to the missionary cause?[154] The answers to such questions were obvious, and they illustrated the distinction between the legitimate commerce desired and some of the actual commerce that prevailed.[155]

Attitudes to colonization revealed a similar confusion. The type of colony for which the missionary hoped, as well as the type he dreaded, must be seen in relation to his own function of building a Christian civilization in Central Africa. There was the recurrent emphasis on upright, honourable Christian gentlemen who would not use their superiority for selfish purposes, and, by sheer force of personal moral example, would lead the African gently away from the chains of tribalism with its superstition, poverty, and moral turpitude.[156] This colony, comparable to the dreams of Livingstone, was less a plan than a vision inherently incapable of fulfilment except under theocratic conditions with strictly regulated immigration. The weakness of all discussions of colonization was in the inability of its advocates to discover the procedures for implementing the type of colonization they deemed desirable.

As imperialism loomed ever closer, the contrast between ideals and reality became painfully evident. Elliott of the L.M.S. appealed to the Foreign Secretary of his society in 1890 to 'help to the limit of your power . . . [in obtaining the] . . . Christian settlers, Christian traders, Christian gold diggers [who] will be the need of the good time coming' in Southern Rhodesia.[157] According to Lord Bryce, the European community of that territory in the early days of Chartered Company rule contained an especially 'large proportion of well-mannered and well-educated men'.[158] The local press, especially *The Bulawayo Sketch*, frequently commented on the superior quality of the population to that of the typical frontier area.[159] Yet an examination of that same press in the first six years of the life of the new colony reveals almost no concern whatever for the welfare of the Africans. The ubiquitous cry was for labour, and the African was seen almost exclusively as an economic asset, to be procured by force and held by force if necessary. Coupled with the preceding was a cynical attitude to Exeter Hall and stay-at-home philanthropists. The 'main reason we are all here is to make money and lose no time about it' was the pithy comment of *The Bulawayo Sketch* on the pioneer attitude.[160]

The colonists, in spite of their comparatively high calibre, did not prove to be the lay missionaries which the L.M.S. agents had hoped. They were so 'impatient to be rich' that they demanded that the Africans

> be compelled to work & that instantly & in response the Govt turned itself into a Slaves Registry Office with limitation that the slavery should be for only a limited period of each year & should be paid a monthly wage but giving the labourer no choice as to employer, work or wage.[161]

The L.M.S. missionaries who had seen the hand of God in the arrival of the Chartered Company soon began to see the hand of the devil in the conduct of many of the whites towards the Africans. Although the Matabele power had been broken 'the devil has had reinforcements in the person of many a white man, whose deeds are too filthy to be recorded'.[162] Rees felt that the less white people around the mission 'the better it is for us and our work'.[163]

The transformation in the missionary attitude to colonization and commerce was inevitable given the unrealistic nature of their early aspirations. A preference for good men over evil men was undoubtedly to be commended, but it did not constitute a theory of social change. Indeed it is worth suggesting that it constituted a substitute for effective analysis of the problems of social change. If

HOW CAN SAVAGES BE CIVILIZED?

good men could be obtained, surely all else would follow. This emphasis on character was not only a particularly British approach to the problems of culture contact (later institutionalized by the British Colonial Service), but, although it was the most elementary item in the humanitarian proposals, it was inherently unrealistic. This was revealed in case after case of contact both in the pre-imperial era and in the early years of white administration.

In his scheme for a white colony on Kilimanjaro, Harry Johnston advocated that a

> careful selection should be made, so that no debauchees, or drunkards, or fanatics should disturb the peace of the rising colony, nor break the pleasant intercourse which at present exists between the native and the little known white man.[164]

While nothing was to come of his Kilimanjaro plans, Johnston was later to comment regretfully that the ideal white-black relationship in the eyes of the first group of settlers in British Central Africa, over which he presided as Commissioner, would have been 'a country where the black millions toil unremittingly for the benefit of the white man'. The settlers would feed the Africans and not treat them brutally, 'but anything like free will as whether they want to work or not, or any attempt at competing with the white man as regards education or skilled labour would not be tolerated'.[165]

The conduct of the white settlers in this territory was one factor which influenced Robert Laws to select his site for the educational and training institutions of the Livingstonia Mission at the northwest end of Lake Nyasa, about as far away from the white settler community as possible.[166] The Church of Scotland, centred in the very heart of white settlement at Blantyre, harshly criticized settler conduct and engaged in a vendetta against the members of Johnston's administration for their alleged immoralities.[167] Johnston, however, although he had hoped for whites who would be 'spruce, temperate, clean and pleasant-mannered, struggling with me to keep up a higher tone of society in this embryo colony by dressing for dinner in nice, white dinner jackets and behaving like quiet, low-voiced gentlemen',[168] had remarkably little control over the personnel of his early administration, let alone over settlers, and was forced to take them where he could find them.[169] In a similar fashion the African Lakes Corporation, established to solve the supply problems of the Scottish missions and also to undercut the slave trade by the purchase of ivory, was compelled by financial stringency to recruit 'waifs and strays in Quilimane and men dismissed by the Mission', with an inevitable lowering of white prestige.[170] Another observer, E. C. Hore, asserted that several of the employees consisted of men

HOW CAN SAVAGES BE CIVILIZED?

'discharged from missions for immoral conduct or incompetence or from ships at Quilimane as incorrigible ruffians', some of the younger ones being 'very anxious to "pop off a few niggers" '.[171]

As noted above, even mission societies were unable to ensure a high standard of conduct among their own personnel.[172] As long as settler contact was potential rather than actual, the Bible-reading settler was a useful concept in avoiding contradiction between missionaries and the future representatives of an alleged Christian civilization whom the missionary desired to aid him in his work. The ideal-type Briton was also useful in keeping the moral conduct of those who believed in it at a high level, but it became ludicrously inappropriate when applied wholesale to the likely characteristics of future colonies of British settlers. Almost all sense of reality was lost and colonies were conjured up containing Christian gentlemen and Christian yeomen tilling the soil in a relationship of friendly paternalism to the Africans they initiated into a higher civilization. The settler pursuing economic gain did create economic wealth, but he also brought with him race prejudice and the colour bar. In Nyasaland, points out Professor W. K. Hancock, it is 'unfortunately true' that resource poverty which precluded white settlement, and the racial impartiality for which that territory was long noted, 'are phenomena not entirely disconnected from each other'.[173]

When the actual settler made his appearance under the protecting aegis of imperial rule, the missionary, by a natural evolution, became the chief spokesman for the African, and aroused anger among settler whites. Only by distinguishing themselves from the new arrivals could the missionaries ensure that the contrast between the precept and the practice of the Christian nations and their representatives did not render their position anomalous. To the extent that missionaries refused to assume the function of acting as a counterbalance to the small settler groups which eventually appeared, especially in the Rhodesias and Kenya, they admitted that the brotherhood which Christianity contained was not strong enough to overcome the arrogance of the civilization in which it was found. This is not meant to suggest that settlers did not perform useful functions, or that their treatment of the African was especially deplorable. The point is simply that the settler, as was only to be expected, fell far short of the completely unrealistic missionary aspirations as to his nature, and, by so doing, shattered the utopian missionary vision of social change in which Christ-like settlers were to perform important and altruistic roles.

IX

THE BEGINNING OF A NEW ERA

1

IN the closing years of the nineteenth century, Europe speedily and easily took over control of Central Africa. Although the often difficult and long process of pacification which attended the establishment of European administration indicated that not all Africans lightly gave up their independence, the outcome was never in doubt. Any possibility of successful indigenous military opposition foundered on African technological inferiority and the tribal divisions of the interior which destroyed the prospect of united action against the newcomers.

The conditions which elicited the changes in European attitudes from indifference to eager competition for imperial hegemony in Africa are not relevant to the purpose of this essay. It is, however, important to note the presence of a consistent vein of imperial sentiment among those Britons personally conversant with Central African conditions long before any official British interest had been aroused.

Africans, asserted John Hanning Speke in 1863, required a government 'like ours in India' if they were not to be replaced by superior beings or destroyed by the slave trade.[1] A year earlier Livingstone had hopefully enquired of Lord John Russell as to whether his task as British Consul included the annexation of territory in the Lake Nyasa region. He was firmly rebuffed.[2] His imperial response to the conditions prevalent in the area south of Lake Nyasa in the early sixties was shared, however, by others who saw, and found themselves powerless to combat, the chaos and insecurity of this strife-torn region. James Stewart argued that the best hope for African advance rested on breaking the power of the chiefs and incorporating the people with colonists under the 'mild and merciful sway of British government'. He visualized 'another race, like the Roman but with greater differences, overspreading the world, giving laws and learning and commerce and Christianity'.[3] Horace Waller, later to edit Livingstone's *Last Journals*, was equally convinced of the value of some form of white rule, 'an idea founded on the state of the country as we first came into it and living amongst such a crumbling set as the Manganja people is bears it out thoroughly'.[4]

In the seventies a similar divergence existed between official apathy in Britain and expressions of imperial zeal among Britons in Central Africa. Bartle Frere, in the midst of his endeavours to negotiate a new and more restrictive slave-trade treaty with the Sultan of Zanzibar, indicated the official British attitude. He wrote that there was a 'tempting opening for an Empire in East Africa at the disposal of any great Naval power', but intimated that Britain had no such objectives.[5] In discussing the 'civilization of the Continent', he stated that the scope of the task was far beyond the powers of any one nation, and that he would gladly see some of it delegated to other nations 'which, like the Germans or Italians, have a desire to extend their spheres of national activity, whilst there is not much room for expansion left to them nearer home'.[6] In 1878 a lack of official interest was again revealed when a projected concession by the Sultan of Zanzibar of almost complete control of his mainland dominions to a company headed by Mackinnon, the Scottish shipping magnate, was secretly vetoed by the Foreign Secretary, Lord Salisbury.[7]

At the same time as the British government was continuing its traditional refusal to involve itself directly in the administration of mainland territories, requests for such action continued to be made by Britons with experience of African conditions. In 1877, Cotterill, the son of the Bishop of Edinburgh, who was attempting to introduce legitimate trade into the Lake Nyasa region, expressed the wish to the British Consul at Zanzibar 'that at no distant period, this inland region may be placed under the British flag'.[8] At roughly the same time the explorer Verney Lovett Cameron made a spirited plea to the Royal Colonial Institute for British rule in Central Africa. He hoped that the day was 'not far distant when we shall see the Union Jack flying permanently in the centre of Africa, and not merely passing through it, as when I carried it there'. Although he did not believe that much of Africa was suited to manual labour by whites, 'especially of the Anglo-Saxon race', he believed that 'Anglo-Saxons may direct the course of labour in that country, and employ it so as to make it of great use to the British Empire'.

> Now this country, if not taken in hand, one day or another must become simply an overgrown wilderness, and its valuable products will be lost.

THE BEGINNING OF A NEW ERA

It will become more difficult day by day to prevent the growth of these [slave trade] crimes, until the country is taken in hand by a strong and determined Government, or by some great company, like the East Indian Company, which would have the power of governing, and be able to carry on its work in a perfectly upright, independent, open manner, and in a way such as would defy the cavillings and the evil speaking of anybody and everybody in the world.

Africans, he asserted, were an industrious people, but due to constant internal wars they were going back instead of advancing 'in the race of civilization', and would continue to do so until 'the country is opened up' by colonization.[9] In pursuance of these objectives Cameron had secured treaties placing the basins of the Congo and the Zambesi under British control, subject to the discretion of the British government. His actions aroused no official interest. He then tried to institute a chartered company for Eastern Africa, but was told that the day for such things was over.[10]

It was not until the close of the eighties that official British policy converged with the opinions of Britons experienced in African conditions on the necessity of imperialism.

2

The statement of the Earl of Cromer with reference to Britain's task in Egypt provides an appropriate point of departure for a discussion of the basis of imperial thought among the early pioneers.

One of the first qualifications necessary in order to play the part of a saviour of society is that the saviour should believe in himself and in his mission. This the Englishman did. He was convinced that his mission was to save Egyptian society, and, moreover, that he was able to save it.[11]

In Central Africa there were several factors involved in the creation and widespread acceptance of this type of imperialist approach. Of basic importance was the absence of alternatives for the attainment of humanitarian objectives. On the East Coast the British noted with scorn the general lack of vigour and vitality in the Portuguese colonies south of Cape Delgado. As factors making for civilization and a higher morality they seemed practically beneath contempt. Their officials were underpaid, sexually loose, and they generally connived at, where they did not openly participate in, the slave trade. On the northern part of the coast the Arab and Swahili settlements, like those of the Portuguese, were but precarious enclaves with little or no dominion over their hinterland. The Arabs did have an expanding economy, but again like that of the Portuguese, it was too intimately associated with the slave trade and slavery for admiration to be a frequent reaction. Some writers did see the Arabs as potentially important assets in the civilizing of the African, but in general both of these non-indigenous elements appeared in the guise of agents of destruction rather than as aids to progress. Their conduct helped convince Britons of their own moral superiority, and almost automatically evoked the idea that British intervention, either governmental or by individuals, could not fail to be an improvement.

Finally, it was clear that indirect pressure and piecemeal measures were inadequate. The attempts of Samuel Baker and General Charles Gordon, acting under the authority of Khedive Ismail of Egypt, to annex the sources of the Nile, eliminate the slave trade, and introduce law and order into the vast areas of Equatoria were rendered hopeless by distance, administrative incompetence, corruption, and an absence of sympathy for their anti-slave-trade measures among their subordinates. The Mahdist rising of 1883 wrote finish for a decade and a half to any European influence in this area. On the east coast a series of increasingly restrictive measures against the Arab slave trade, culminating in the treaty of 1873 and the proclamation of 1876, underlined the fact that the legal abolition of the trade and its actual ending were two different things, for the obvious reason that the impetus to end the trade came from Britain while those whose livelihoods were affected were Arabs and Swahili. British policy with respect to the Arabs was most effective at Zanzibar, reasonably effective on the coast and minimal in the interior. A naval blockade could secure written acquiescence to an abolition of the sea-borne slave trade; Kirk could get a recalcitrant governor removed from a coastal port, and could effectively intervene at Mombasa when the position of the British missionaries established there was threatened, but he could not ensure an extension of Arab government in the interior, nor could he have controlled the nature of that government had it developed. The Zanzibar policy, British-inspired, had to be implemented by Arabs—and since there was little community of interest in attitudes to the slave trade, its effectiveness was severely restricted by the geographically limited possibility of applying coercion by naval pressure.

Underlying justification for imperialism was found in several attitudes basic to the British outlook. The belief that man should vigorously exploit his natural environment easily slid into the assumption that since their productive techniques were backward Africans had no right to keep out more advanced peoples with more developed capacities to exploit the resources, both real and fancied, with which Britons invested the interior. The African, in the words of Harry Johnston, 'was living like an animal, miserably poor in the midst of boundless wealth'. Under European guidance this wealth could be developed to the mutual benefit of both parties.[12] It was in keeping with this attitude to economic growth that, shortly after the defeat of the Matabele by the pioneer troops from Mashonaland, a Bulawayo newspaper displayed a cartoon split into two sections. The first section, containing a picture of the old kraal at Bulawayo, was entitled 'Then—Idleness', and the second, a picture of European Bulawayo, 'Now—Industry'. The cartoon as a whole was displayed under the heading 'Le Roi est mort,—Vive le Roi!!'[13]

Of essential importance as a rationale for imperialism was the almost universal British belief in the inferiority, whether racial, cultural, or both, of Africans, the group which imperialism was to deprive of control of its own future development. As W. C. Devereux succinctly phrased it in arguing the desirability of white rule in the early sixties, 'a negro nation . . . should be governed by whites'.[14] Devereux's assertion rested on a variety of facts and beliefs. There was, initially, the simple fact of example. In other parts of the world small numbers of whites possessed political power over non-white races. India provided an obvious illustration of what could be done. There was also the widespread comparison of the African to a child which was supported by, and supported in turn, a number of secondary and supplementary attributes—emotionalism, an absence of forethought, a lack of time sense, space sense and truth sense. The alleged incomprehensibility of African mental processes to whites formed a further proof of immaturity. The child analogy itself was consistent with the assumption that Africans were contemporary ancestors, or were, in some fashion, comparable to the lower classes in Britain. The specific meaning of these analogies differed, but individually and collectively they relegated the African to a position of inferiority, thus justifying any enterprise in which he was to be treated as an object. They clearly contributed to the climate of opinion sanctioning imperial control.

The child analogy made African self-rule an anomaly. The conditions of the interior destroyed all moral basis for its continuation. The books of the great travellers portray an area riven by tribal war and the slave trade. The latter, as was frequently observed, was far from being an alien imposition on African society, while tribal war was an acceptable adjunct of existence for those capable of reaping benefits from its operation. African participation in the major evils besetting the interior, the consequent incapacity of tribalism to work out its own salvation, and the non-ameliorating nature of Arab and Portuguese contact automatically justified outside intervention on humanitarian grounds.

The humanitarian argument for imperialism was both widespread and deeply held. After a trip through Matabeleland and Mashonaland

THE BEGINNING OF A NEW ERA

Bishop Knight Bruce, undoubtedly with the experience of the recently established Bechuanaland Protectorate in his mind, strongly advocated white rule.

> I consider [he said at Vryburg, Dec. 8, 1888], that of all the protections which the English nation has accorded to oppressed peoples, none could be more righteous than a Protectorate over the Mashonas. It would be exercising an act of righteousness such as I think would surround the English name with a new and abiding halo of humanity and kindness ... there is a nation called the Mashona, a gentle, industrious and skilful people, being cut off, man, woman and child with no chance of escape and no hope of succour; that their slaughter went on last year, and will go on again this year ... and there is no refuge nor help. I do say that England ought to and must interfere, but I do say this—that it would be an act of which England might be proud for ever if she would exercise a proper protection over that unfortunate country from any nation which might wish to reign over it.[15]

The same juxtaposition of atrocities and cruelty with a plea for imperial control is found in the writings of Ashe, C.M.S. missionary to Buganda. After describing an attack by Mtesa on Karagwe after the death of chief Rumanika, he continued:

> And so the caravan of captive women and children went on, leaving the Kagera River behind choked with the corpses of husbands and brothers who had died in their defence, the way marked by the emaciated bodies and whitening bones of helpless children who died on the terrible march. This is Africa left to herself. Livingstone, Stanley, and Cameron have told us what Africa is when left to the Arabs. If such recitals as these have any meaning, it is that the most powerful appeal is made to civilized nations to take the African tribes under their fostering care. It is an appeal to England to do for Africa what she has so triumphantly effected for the peoples of India.[16]

In the prevailing conditions of insecurity the humanitarian case for imperialism was practically irrefutable. It is, however, clear that humanitarian concern for the African was, in some cases, far more prevalent in the propaganda of imperialism than in its inner motivations. In December, 1889, Frank Johnson, a young prospector, and his colleague Maurice Heany made an agreement with Cecil Rhodes to overthrow the Matabele in a sudden assault by about five hundred men. Johnson planned a moonlit raid on the king's kraal, culminating in the 'killing [of] Lo Bengula and smashing each military kraal .... Or ... I [Johnson] might dig myself in at Gubulawayo with Lo Bengula and his entourage as hostages' while negotiations for the transfer of the Matabele territory to the Chartered Company were undertaken.[17] The plan, which failed to come off when word of it reached the British High Commissioner at Cape Town, was

THE BEGINNING OF A NEW ERA

clearly designed to speed up the opening of the country to European prospectors and administration. Clause three of the agreement mentioned breaking 'the power of the Amandebele as to render their raids on surrounding tribes impossible, to effect the emancipation of all their slaves and further, to reduce the country' so that mining and prospecting operations could be undertaken in peace and safety.[18] In plain language it was murder. As Johnson wrote in an unpublished chapter of his autobiography, the humanitarian objective 'looked well and would have appealed to the Nonconformist conscience, then a great power in England, when the inevitable row took place'.[19]

A similar cynical attitude was revealed by Harris, the secretary of the B.S.A. Company, in a letter to Colenbrander, the company's agent in Bulawayo:

> I hope they [the Matabele] do raid the Barotse. All these raids and deaths and murders ought to be entered into a book, so that we may always be able to prove justification and their being a cruel damnable race.[20]

Indications of diplomatic deference to humanitarian sentiments were also evident in the early years of administration in British Central Africa. Wordsworth Poole, the young medical officer of the administration between 1895 and 1897, wrote that if the Africans refused to pay hut tax for protection they did not want

> there is war, and we kill their men and burn their houses and collar their cattle and ivory and cloth and beads and their women whom we call slaves and to whom we give papers of manumission, which papers are found afterwards thrown away in heaps, for obviously a paper saying that 'so and so has been freed by me this day—signed so and so' is really not much use to a free woman. But Exeter Hall and the old ladies and the missionaries at home think a lot of it and haven't the slightest idea who is a slave and who is not, but it all pays. It is with many winks and digs in the ribs and chuckles that we read the effusions of the Rev. Horace Waller and others in the papers from home.[21]

His governmental experience, he asserted, had taught him the worth of an 'original document'. One can imagine 'a stupid old historian taking infinite pains to get to the original Foreign Office despatches and thinking that at last he had hit on the truth, the plain and uncontroverted truth'.[22]

Broadly speaking the climate of belief and opinion among these early pioneers which sanctioned imperialism was internally consistent. The useful cover which humanitarian pleas gave to imperial ventures in Central Africa provides a partial explanation for the frequency of their expression. Equally revealing of the underlying factors influencing belief and expression is the surprising absence of mention of social Darwinism in discussions of race relations or as justification for imperial control.[23] The 'survival of the fittest' doctrine was occasionally used to describe tribal war, and other aspects of evolutionary assumptions were used to argue the possibility of Africans becoming westernized, or conversely to argue the inevitable slowness of such a process. On the whole, however, it is the absence of any application of theories of nature 'red in tooth and claw' to British African relationships which stands out. This was related, it may be conjectured, to a variety of factors. In the first place the predominantly missionary composition of British contact meant that emphasis was less on the rights of the strong than on their responsibilities. Secondly, traders and hunters could operate within the existing framework of tribal societies with reasonable success. They required no arguments to justify repressive policies against the African. Thirdly, and of special importance, the prospects for large-scale European settlement, especially north of the Zambesi, always appeared doubtful to many of the early pioneers with experience of African climatic conditions and the prevalence of deadly disease.

The Africans, unlike the American Indian or the Australian aborigines, were expected to play a permanent role in future economic development. Consequently, theories justifying their extermination lacked utility, and accordingly were not employed. In essence, the use of evolutionary theories stopped at the point where their employment might have been detrimental to European interests. Fundamentally the definition of the 'fittest' was by no means clear in Central Africa, a fact which members of a racial group experiencing great difficulty in adapting themselves to tropical conditions were unlikely to forget. It is significant that social Darwinism only emerged into tentative and short-run significance during the racial struggles in Southern Rhodesia in the early years of Charter rule when it appeared that a self-contained European community might be feasible, and when European hatreds[24] had been aroused by the barbarities of the Matabele and the Mashona in the rebellions in the mid-nineties.[25]

A basic aspect of the imperial frame of mind was a general assumption of British moral superiority, with the accompanying belief that the possession of the virtues of responsibility, trust, and integrity legitimized intervention and the seizing of power over the backward peoples of the earth. The attack on slavery and the slave trade, for example, not only indicated British humanitarianism in action, but it associated the right to power with moral fervour; in effect, with being British.

The missionary contribution to this attitude should not be overlooked. Throughout the nineteenth century the great British missionary societies grew in importance until practically the entire non-western world became an area of missionary concern. This automatically exalted Britain as the point of origin of these benevolent enterprises, and led to an increased flow of information, couched in unfavourable terms, about the nature of non-western societies. Eulogistic missionary biographies flooded the market with tales of heroism, martyrdom, and nobility, and thus sanctioned the expansion of Christianity and indirectly of British civilization in general.

In terms of his vocation it was imperative for the missionary to assume the inferiority and inadequacy of paganism. At the same time he was compelled to defend the spiritual capacity of the African lest he render his own position anomalous. From this viewpoint the universalism of the missionary movement was of intrinsic importance in the westernization of Africa, for it represented an open-ended facet of western contact. Christianity provided access to a culture pattern which was bound to conquer by virtue of technological superiority. In theory the missionary function was essentially self-annihilating, for the surest way of convincing the sceptical that Christianity was not an alien religion was to raise up an African ministry to provide ocular proof to the heathen that Christianity was more than a special form of white witchcraft or divination.

Yet, if in the long run the missionary was his own grave-digger preparing his own obsolescence, in the period under survey, by his very presence as an agent of western civilization in the midst of the dark places of the earth he represented an unofficial symbolic imperialism which helped in the creation of a climate of opinion justifying imperial takeovers. There was often a conflict between the universalism of the Christian message and the racial attitudes of its purveyors. There was, indeed, a curious racial pride involved in the fact that a religion designed to overcome racial barriers was being disseminated by the Anglo-Saxons.[26] There was, further, the striking parallel between the missionary emphasis on expansion, on finding proof of Christian vitality in foreign ventures, and similar conceptions which informed imperial thought.[27]

Missionaries made fundamental contributions to the undermining of ideas that African societies had any right to a continuing existence. This aspect of the missionary movement was related not only to their moving revelations of the cruelty and insecurity of life in the interior, but to the more general point that, by his existence as well as by his actions, the missionary strengthened the attitude that cultural differences were to be eliminated rather than cherished or respected. By evaluating a broad range of distinctions between tribalism and civilization and in effect decreeing the destruction of those which conflicted with the wide compass of his approach to morality and social customs, the missionary helped to create sanctions for the use of power to eliminate other distinctions. The missionary was a symbol of the rightness of cultural aggression. From this viewpoint the universalism of Christianity simply meant an organized attack by one religious faith on the others. The missionary adherence to universalism coupled with a widespread ignorance of non-Christian religions and social systems was the spiritual analogy of imperialism[28] with its disregard of the desire of non-western peoples to order their own future.[29]

It is not, however, only by implication and analogy that missionaries can be associated with imperialism. In some cases, admittedly on a small scale, they became temporal rulers themselves when they established governmental jurisdiction over freed slaves or over the discontented from contiguous tribes. They were also usually keen on any extension of consular services to the areas where they were established and often requested the granting of consular or vice-consular status to one of their members—requests which were in no case granted.[30] By the late eighties British missionaries consistently expressed favourable responses to the prospect of imperial control by the British government. This response was more than a simple acceptance of the inevitable. Firstly, there was a striking absence of missionary objections to the prospect of British imperial control in the decade of the eighties. Secondly, and more indicative, a sentiment in favour of imperialism had been in existence, if discontinuously, from the very inception of missionary contact. In the sixties Livingstone, James Stewart, and Horace Waller had all entertained imperialist ideas.[31] An East Coast Sierra Leone had been favourably discussed by Krapf and New, two of the earliest missionaries in the Mombasa region.[32] Towards the end of the seventies one L.M.S. missionary in Matabeleland, rejoicing at the rumours of the British defeat of Cetewayo ('which I sincerely trust is true'), wrote that many things inclined him to the belief that the British either by diplomacy or by war, intended to take over the 'whole country to the Zambezi'.

> Everything confirms the report that the whole of Mashonaland is exceedingly fertile and rich in gold and other ores, whilst the subjugation of the country would be comparatively an easy task. British occupation could stop the bloody marauding expeditions both of Lobengula and of Umzila, a brother Zulu chieftain due East from here, and also stop the Portuguese slave traffic which is carried on wholesale between here and the Zambezi.[33]

The conditions in which the missionary in Central Africa found himself exerted an irresistible impulse towards imperialism.[34] The pre-imperialist period was marked by few significant missionary successes. Missionaries could doctor chiefs, run mission villages, discover

THE BEGINNING OF A NEW ERA

new geographical features, and in extreme cases lead war parties over the hills to maintain their prestige or protect the helpless. In converting the African, however, they achieved only minimal results. While the time span of this early contact was short, it does seem that the missionary faced a task verging on the impossible. The incentive for Africans in any large numbers to change their moral and spiritual beliefs was highly limited. The environmental pressures working against Christianity were most clearly illustrated by the widespread missionary fear that his own standards might be eroded by too prolonged and intimate contact with African culture. In such a situation the likely direction of social change was by no means clear.

The problem facing the missionary was astutely noted by J. S. Moffat:

> It is where the political organization is most perfect, and the social system still in its aboriginal vigour, that the missionary has the least success in making an impression. Where things have undergone a change and the old feudal usages have lost their power, where there is a measure of disorganization, the new ideas which the gospel brings with it do not come into collision with any powerful political prejudice. The habits and modes of thinking have been broken up, and so there is a preparation for the seed of the word. I am not sanguine on this point in regard to the Matabele.[35]

The missionary soon realized that although a certain individualism was inherent in proselytization—the seeking of conversions implied conscious choice by individual Africans—the individuals whom his message confronted belonged to cultures expressing values antagonistic to the acceptance of his ethical and spiritual system. Although most Africans were eager for calico, and although oppressed tribes might welcome the advent of a mission station for political or security reasons, and individuals with a sense of grievance might flee to the sanctuary of a mission station, there was, in this period, no widespread pressure for change from below. Africans were not faced with the disintegration of their own way of life, or by a clear indication of the future advantages of various aspects of westernization, either of which would have served as a stimulus to a widespread acceptance of new values. The missionary was left with the problem that there was no pressing reason for the African to desert tribalism for a new way of life. The position was complicated by the fact that in many areas where religious change was occurring, it manifested itself in the acceptance of a nominal Islam. In this latter case missionaries assumed that imperialism, by increasing the prestige of their religion and diminishing that of Islam, would tilt the scales in the struggle for the spiritual control of Central Africa to the side of Christianity.

THE BEGINNING OF A NEW ERA

The realization that religious change was closely related to conditions of social breakdown, in the words of Krapf when 'a nation . . . is on the brink of destruction',[36] or in 'heathenism become unbelieving'[37] in the phrase of Warneck, the German missionary historian, led missionaries to look for those external factors capable of creating situations in which the gospel would find more receptive hearers.[38] The most obviously disruptive influence was imperialism. The acceptance of this can be seen most clearly in Matabeleland where L.M.S. missionaries experienced deep despondency as the decades slipped by and the Matabele remained immune to their ministrations. As early as 1878 T. M. Thomas, then an independent missionary, had written to François Coillard that things were not improving in Matabeleland:

> Indeed I may remark that my own impression is that ere even South Africa can be Christianized the European power must be extended to the River Zambesi and all these heathenish customs (such as polygamy, slave holding, rain making, plundering &c.) must be crushed. There may be a few instances in which success may be realized as it is now; but under the present state of things no solid and extensive prosperity can be reasonably looked for.[39]

By the late eighties, as the portents of European control became more apparent, the missionaries began to write favourably of the impending break-up of the Matabele hegemony—seeing in such an event the destruction of the tyranny which prevented positive approaches to the Christian message.[40]

In these circumstances the L.M.S. missionaries had no sympathy for British critics who questioned the desirability of a Chartered Company replacing Matabele rule, and who seemed ignorant of years of Matabele plundering and savage treatment of the Mashona. The missionaries were prone, as Elliott did, to 'hail the Charter with joy as a God-sent deliverer. Indeed it is not difficult to see the hand of God in this whole business, and we are devoutly thankful for the turn events are taking.'[41] A colleague saw the 'wrath of God' being brought down on the Matabele, 'that stiff-necked tribe', after their 'constant and persistent refusal' of the gospel for a whole generation. God, he remarked with satisfaction, was about to 'speak in a very different manner' to the Matabele than his L.M.S. emissaries had been constrained to adopt.[42]

The willingness of the L.M.S. missionaries in Matabeleland to see the Matabele given a sharp military lesson by the agents of the Chartered Company was part of what seems to have been a general tendency for missionaries in Central Africa to replace the loving God of the New Testament with Old Testament conceptions of God as a harsh if just ruler of the universe. In a sermon to his co-workers in

THE BEGINNING OF A NEW ERA

1883 Robert Laws noted that his contemporaries in Britain were distressed at God's commands to the Israelites to utterly destroy other tribes. He attributed the widespread acceptance of the conception of a benevolent God to 'the political condition of our native land', and the long absence of foreign invasion making many people ignorant of the horrors of war. The result was a 'higher and better conception of the attributes of God' which led people to think of him as almost exclusively a God of love, and to forget that he was also a 'God of justice and of inflexible rectitude in all his dealings with man'. The God of the Old Testament was old-fashioned in Britain, but in Africa where so much cruelty and oppression existed, such a God became once again meaningful to Europeans.[43] The significance of such views with respect to race relations and imperialism is obviously that they tended to sanction many of the repressive measures which accompanied the arrival and evolution of imperial control. This view of the nature of God made it possible to explain, to justify, and to interpret some past or anticipated crushing disaster to an African tribe as divine chastening or retribution for their cruelties to neighbouring tribes, or for their refusal to accept the gospel which missionaries presented to them.[44]

The specific factors which led missionaries to look favourably on the arrival of British imperial power varied from region to region. In Matabeleland it was total missionary failure which led to the vision of the Chartered Company as an instrument of God to crush the Matabele and provide missionary access to a haughty warrior nation. In the region of Lake Nyasa the main factors were fear of possible extensions of Portuguese or Arab authority, and the special insecurity of conditions south of the Lake which led to missionary satisfaction at the arrival of Johnston and the establishment of a British protectorate.[45] The Church of Scotland mission at Blantyre, shortly to become an articulate critic of the administration, displayed its enthusiasm and patriotism by turning the manse dining room into 'a factory with half-a-dozen sewing machines, for the manufacture of Union Jacks' for presentation to the chiefs.[46] In Buganda a surfeit of religious success in response to competition between French Roman Catholics, British Anglicans, and Arab and Swahili Moslems in a highly developed pagan kingdom resulted in bloody civil war and the martyring of individual Christians by burning at the stake. Here imperialism was required to keep newly established religious passions in check and to preserve the Baganda from fruitless internecine destruction.[47]

In more general terms the missionary tended to see Christianity and imperialism as complementary, with the latter acting as a vehicle for the spread of the former. As Mackay of Uganda stated: 'Is it not for this very end that the Protestant powers have been given the supremacy among nations, that they may use their power and influence in spreading abroad the knowledge of the truth?'[48] Within this general context there was a natural predisposition for British missionaries to favour the assumption of imperial control by their own government rather than by some other European nation. Indeed, violent objections were often made at the prospect of being placed under Portuguese, and, to a lesser extent, German rule. These were accompanied by highly emotional arguments that the priority of British exploratory and missionary activity rendered the rule of any other European power illegitimate. The graves of martyrs held not only the seeds of the new church, but also provided justification for British as opposed to non-British imperialism.[49]

3

The arrival of imperial power in Central Africa terminated the period of race and culture contact with which previous chapters have been concerned. The partition of Central Africa among Germany, Portugal, and Britain drastically changed the context in which Europeans and Africans confronted each other. Imperialism brought the peace and stability required by commerce. The tribulations of the African Lakes Corporation—a war with half-caste Arabs at the north end of Lake Nyasa, disputes with tribesmen on the Shire and Zambesi which resulted in the sinking of the Company's steamers, and widespread robbing and pilfering of goods in transit—indicated the uncongenial atmosphere for commerce in the pre-imperial period. The missionary need for peace was only slightly less urgent. As long as Central Africa remained Balkanized among hostile tribes the missionary was constantly being drawn into intertribal disputes to the detriment of his proper work. Mission stations often became centres of refuge, and by implication threats to the political power of nearby chiefs. Missionaries did not have the forbearance to desist from participation in tribal conflicts, nor the capacity to enforce their will on recalcitrant Africans. The U.M.C.A. mission station at Masasi was sacked; the Frere Town freed slave mission was the scene of constant threats and interruptions from the Arabs and Swahili of the Mombasa vicinity, and the Church of Scotland mission at Blantyre, like its U.M.C.A. predecessor at Magomero, was frequently involved in tribal war with the Yao. Imperialism not only solved these problems, but helped to overcome other practical difficulties. By breaking down isolation it reduced the time and money spent on transportation and the provision of western goods. By providing law and order it relieved the missions of the burdens which the exercise of civil jurisdiction imposed, and which had resulted in a scandalous misuse of power on several occasions.

The change in race relations brought about by imperialism was more complex than a cumulative increase in European influence and power until finally the scales were tipped on behalf of the whites. There was a change in the quality of their power as well as in the quantity. Some of the early pioneers had had much influence with particular African chiefs, but such influence depended very largely on their personal characteristics and the particular set of circumstances which prevailed. The new governmental administrations possessed a continuity of influence independent of their personnel at any given time. In addition, they possessed the coercive powers of the state to back up their dictates.

For the African, imperialism altered the whole framework by which he interpreted and evaluated the desirability of social change in a western direction. Prior to the arrival of European governments the selectivity of the African as to the facets of civilization which he wished to incorporate into his social fabric was conditioned by the dominance of tribal values. In the imperial era, by contrast, the ineffectiveness of tribalism in terms of power was made increasingly obvious to Africans by the fact that they were kept in subordination by a minority of whites whose cultural values were in the ascendant. This necessitated a radical psychological adjustment as Africans were abruptly faced with their own technological and military inferiority. The recognition of this was not only the most important sanction of European control, but it also constituted a basic stimulus to social change. More specifically, the range of African choice was widened by the possibility of access to the lower rungs of the new colonial society in governmental and church hierarchies, and in an incipient market and wage economy. In the old tribal society mission schooling was of little relevance, and Africans frequently demanded pay for school attendance. In the new mixed society of tribalism and western civilization the education dispensed by the mission schools was an important aid to social mobility. Imperialism also facilitated religious change by shedding an aura of prestige and authority over the religion of the conquerors. Further, as conversions increased, the converted African was no longer an outcast faced with the well nigh impossible task of living a Christian life in an environment predominantly heathen. Finally, a certain degree of change was imposed on the African by legislation and taxation.

The establishment of colonial governments elevated whites into a ruling caste. Race relations increasingly took place within the framework of a clearly defined white-ruled racial hierarchy. The indignity of finding oneself shabbily treated by Africans—'worse than being in prison' as Frank Johnson described it—no longer had to be tolerated. In the new imperial situation indignities increased, but the recipients were African. Although the norms of racial contact under imperial governments were dictated by white interests, and thus bore most onerously on the subject African group, they also served to restrict certain types of white conduct. Much of the easy equality which had existed in relations between hunter and African chief, trader and his African mistress, or missionary and his potential convert came to be increasingly frowned upon by status and race conscious whites who conceived such intimacies as incompatible with the whole structure of racial authority which was fundamentally beneficial to them.

The way of life of these early pioneers, no less than that of the African, was coming to an end—a factor which helps explain some of the difficulties, particularly in British Central Africa, between the new administration and the small white community which antedated its arrival. The opposition of the Church of Scotland mission to the administration of Harry Johnston was not unrelated, as Johnston shrewdly noted, to an unwillingness on the part of the missionaries to see the unofficial political power they had enjoyed removed from their hands and taken over by the government.[50] Hunters were hostile to administration attempts to tax them for the privilege of shooting elephants,[51] while land grabbers were irritated at the government's attempt to see that there was at least a plausible relationship between the amounts they had paid to chiefs and the oftentimes vast tracts of land they had received in exchange.[52]

In a sense, all of these difficulties, which seem to have been most pronounced in British Central Africa, constituted the inevitable teething troubles of a new administration. But at a deeper level they represented a resistance to the new way of life which imperialism brought in its wake. After all, a fundamental attraction of Africa had been that it provided an opportunity for an escape from civilization, and now in this, the last continent to be opened up by the white man, civilization and European governments were arriving. As early as the mid-eighties Joseph Thomson, sensing the coming change, had regretfully observed that the 'iron heel of commerce'had knocked romance out of African travel. The attitude of looking at palm trees for their producing capacity, rather than for their beauty, prompted him to indicate a preference for the North Pole should such an attitude prevail.[53] Even among the most convinced advocates of imperialism there was an ambivalence about the whole process they helped to set in motion. Knight-Bruce, a vigorous supporter of the desirability of imperial control to protect the Mashona, expressed an emotional preference for the 'good old days' a few years after its

THE BEGINNING OF A NEW ERA

introduction.[54] A. J. Swann, perhaps the most ardent exponent of imperialism among the early missionaries, at the very time when he was engaged on a treaty-signing expedition for H. H. Johnston, had private doubts as to whether it might not have been better to leave the African alone in his simple uncivilized condition.[55] Such thoughts, whatever their basis, represented an unrealistic sentimental nostalgia for an age of cultural diversity that was dying.[56]

4

The final resting place of imperialism as an historical event will doubtless be found somewhere between the exultant enthusiasm of those who rhapsodized over its birth, and the indifference and hostility of those who now watch and hasten its demise with no pangs of regret.

In the mid-twentieth century the wheel has come full circle, and imperialism has become a term of abuse. Yet imperialism in Central Africa was a necessary and a valuable phenomenon. Its most obvious justification rests on the basic fact that the social disruption of tribal life was so grievous that the establishment of peace and law was the over-riding requirement for any amelioration of conditions in the interior. Here, indeed, was the fundamental justification of empire, for the creation of law and order is the prime requisite for the utilization of foresight, without which planned change or orderly development is impossible. In more general terms, the historical contribution of imperialism is to be found in the broader sense that it helped to regulate an inevitable process of social change. Even if the slave trade and tribal war had not existed, tribal man was an anachronism in a world being shaped by the inexorable demands of technology, the revolutions in communications, and the demands of developed economies for markets and resources. Since isolation from the world which these forces were in process of creating was impossible, imperialism must be judged in the light of available alternatives which might have given the African some control over the new type of environment to which he was to be compelled to adapt.

It is readily seen that no satisfactory alternative existed. It is fanciful to suggest that the forces of social change would have by-passed Central Africa had imperial control not intervened, and thus left the African in the enjoyment of his traditional culture. Imported religions had already caused civil war in Buganda. The slave trade, which so appalled western observers, was partly a reflection of the demands of western civilization for ivory to grace the piano keyboards and dressing tables of middle-class homes. The guns and powder which Africans employed the more efficiently to kill each other were produced by European workmen. Even, however, had the existing economic intercourse of Central Africa with the outside world been less socially harmful, it was on too small a scale to make any noticeable contribution to overcoming the marked material poverty of tribalism with its attendant harvest of disease, ill health, hunger and short life span. Voluntary acceptance of hardship as a spur to spiritual growth may be deliberately chosen by the saintly, but inescapable hardship and involuntary suffering for millions constitute remediable evils whose solution was to be found in economic techniques beyond the range of tribal practice.

The African was incapable of intelligently controlling the inrush of new forces he was inevitably destined to encounter, or mastering the skills and techniques of the west without the massive impulse to social change given by imperialism, and the framework of law with which it surrounded that change. The necessity for imperialism is essentially to be found in the failure of existing forms of contact between Africa and the outside world to lead to a successful adaptation of Africans to the penetrating universalism of that world in technology, economics, and religion.

In the long run the coexistence of civilized and primitive man was impossible. It was not a question of the inferiority of the African in any racial sense, or even of his cultural poverty. Both tribalism and western civilization represented differing evolutions, and differing attempts to cope with the problems of human existence. In the abstract, both were capable of global application, given the pliability of human nature and man's consequent capacity for cultural experimentation. The superiority of civilization simply reflected its capacity to create conditions making tribalism obsolete. Western technological superiority and the aggressive nature of the white race created conditions in which tribal man was culturally inadequate to face a future for which his past experience had little relevance.

Within their tribal cultures African men and women experienced all the usual range of human emotions from love to hate, from happiness to despair. They worked and played, became proud parents, educated their children in tribal values, and shared their meagre material possessions with the less fortunate in their own social group. From this viewpoint, as Conrad stated: 'The conquest of the earth, which mostly means the taking it away from those who have a different complexion or slightly flatter noses than ourselves, is not a pretty thing when you look into it too much.'[57]

Yet, sordid as some of its motives may have been, and brutal as some of its manifestations undoubtedly were, imperialism took from the African the control of his future at a time when he was incapable of exercising it. The reassertion of African control has occurred at a time when imperialism is no longer capable of further constructive contributions to societies whose transformation into nation states it helped to bring about. One of the saving paradoxes of imperialism has been that although its inception and operation were deeply imbued with racialism, the social changes which it helped to bring about have created a westernized African élite whose rise to power signals not only the end of the imperial era, but a step in the direction of a future in which increasing cultural similarities among all men may serve to diminish the significance of race.

It is readily admitted that the civilizing process of imperialism was often half-hearted, without a sense of direction, and accompanied by much human indignity to those who were on its receiving end. It is no less true that the racial hierarchies which imperialism established, even if only of administrators over 'savages', and the racist thinking of its purveyors, presented major barriers to the type of social contact among peoples by which culture is most easily spread. Further, racist thought at times militated against acceptance even of the possibility that 'primitive' peoples could be civilized. Imperialism, in fact, often helped to diffuse civilization in spite of itself. Yet, if the means were imperfect, the results remain. In general, formerly technologically backward peoples who have experienced imperial rule are more capable of meeting the demands of the mid-twentieth century than the peoples of Nepal, Ethiopia, and Liberia, who have not.

NOTES

PREFACE

[1] 'Our concern is with race as a social rather than a biological fact. In a biological sense race is irrelevant to racial attitudes and thinking. It is the social creation of race, the tendency to categorize individuals as representatives of a given biological or supposed biological group, which is significant for the investigator.' K. Little, *Race and Society*, Paris, 1952, 6-7.

[2] Cited in L. E. Elliott-Binns, *English Thought 1860-1900, The Theological Aspect*, London, 1956, 4.

[3] See L. H. Gann, 'Liberal Interpretations of South African History: a review article', *Rhodes-Livingstone Journal*, XXV, March, 1959, especially 44-5.

[4] See the excellent discussion of bias in J. Dollard, *Caste and Class in a Southern Town*, New York, 1957, chap. iii.

[5] Foreword to L. H. Gann, *The Birth of a Plural Society*, Manchester, 1958, ix, x.

[6] *East Africa and its Invaders*, Oxford, 1956; *The Exploitation of East Africa 1856-1890*, London, 1939.

[7] A. J. Hanna, *The Beginnings of Nyasaland and North-Eastern Rhodesia 1859-95*, Oxford, 1956.

[8] Gann, *Birth of a Plural Society*.

[9] R. Oliver, *The Missionary Factor in East Africa*, London, 1952.

[10] M. Perham, *Lugard—The Years of Adventure, 1858-1898*, London, 1956.

[11] R. Oliver, *Sir Harry Johnston and the Scramble for Africa*, London, 1957.

[12] R. Benedict, *The Chrysanthemum and the Sword*, Boston, 1946, 16.

I: THE CENTRAL AFRICAN FRONTIER

[1] E. Stock, *The History of the Church Missionary Society*, 3 vols., London, 1899, II, 133; I, 461-2.

[2] *Proc. R.G.S.*, I, No. 4 (June 23, 1856).

[3] 'The Results of European Intercourse with the African', *Contemporary Review*, March, 1890, 339.

[4] I. Burton, *The Life of Captain Sir Richard F. Burton*, 2 vols., London, 1893, I, 330.

[5] 'Bamang-wato', *To Ophir Direct: Or, the South African Gold Fields*, London, 1868, 14. E. C. Tabler attributes this pamphlet to Albert Broderick, 'hotel keeper, landowner, and merchant of Pretoria who became a director of goldmining companies in the Transvaal'. *The Far Interior*, Cape Town and Amsterdam, 1955, 288.

[6] *Through Masai Land*, 2nd ed., London, 1885.

[7] *To the Central African Lakes and Back*, 2 vols., London, 1881, I, 291-2.

[8] H. H. Johnston, *The Nile Quest*, London, 1906, 141.

[9] *To Lake Tanganyika in a Bath Chair*, London, 1889, 158.

[10] Foot to Granville, March 19, 1884, F.O. 84/1662; Goodrich to Granville, Dec. 20, 1884, F.O. 84/1662.

NOTES: CHAPTER I

[11] Tabler, *Far Interior*, 142–3.
[12] *Private Journal of Guy C. Dawnay*, London, by author, n.d., VII, 63–4.
[13] Burton, *Life of Burton*, I, 271.
[14] R. Price to J. S. Moffat, Feb. 9, cont., Feb. 19, 1876, J. S. Moffat Papers.
[15] The price of a waggon varied depending on quality, local labour costs, and time of purchase. On the average it fluctuated around £100 in the period 1840–1880. A span of oxen, usually fourteen, cost about £100 in the 1870's. Tabler, *Far Interior*, 124, 132–3.
[16] In Mashonaland and Matabeleland the horse, although subject to 'horse sickness', was a partial supplement to oxen. It was especially useful to the hunter, but was useless for purposes of heavy transport over long distances.
[17] Three of the mission societies, the L.M.S., U.M.C.A., and the United Free Church of Scotland, had placed approximately 300 missionaries and their wives in Central Africa up to 1890. The Church of Scotland, the Methodists at Ribe, and the C.M.S. would probably add another 100 to the total. The addition of secular whites produces a figure somewhat under 800.
[18] In general I have tried to avoid the use of value loaded words such as progressive. Where they appear without quotation marks, unless the context clearly indicates a particular meaning, they are descriptive not of my own attitudes but of the assumptions of the British in this period of culture contact.
[19] In the long run, contact with the diversity of human custom, coupled with a decline in European self-confidence after World War I, led to an increased cultural relativism and eclecticism manifested by the growth and popularity of such academic disciplines as anthropology and comparative religion, an aesthetic appreciation of 'primitive' art, and an intellectual escapism which led to an exaltation of the apparent lack of inhibitions of tribal man. By the thirties this had produced the curious situation in which 'progressive' whites sought to preserve tribalism from the intruding forces of civilization at a time when 'progressive' Africans were increasingly attempting to emerge into western freedom.
[20] Stock, *History of C.M.S.*, III, 73, asserted that directly or indirectly Livingstone's death in the heart of Africa 'led to most of the great missionary advances that date from the years following 1873'. His influence on the C.M.S. is noted in Stock, III, 79. The Free Church of Scotland mission was designed as a memorial to Livingstone and was named Livingstonia. The Church of Scotland mission site was named Blantyre after Livingstone's birthplace. The choice of Ujiji by the L.M.S. was partly dictated by its sentimental associations with the famous Livingstone-Stanley meeting.
[21] This study of the British excludes consideration of Roman Catholic missions which, in this period, came exclusively from continental Europe. The evolution of Catholic mission work can be traced in Oliver, *Missionary Factor*, and C. W. Mackintosh, *Some Pioneer Missions in Northern Rhodesia and Nyasaland*, Occasional Papers of the Rhodes-Livingstone Museum, No. 8, Lusaka, 1950. See also J. Bouniol, ed., *The White Fathers and their Missions*, London, 1929. For details of a few other Protestant mission attempts not treated here see C. P. Groves, *The Planting of Christianity in Africa*, London, 1948, 1954, 1955, 1958, 4 vols., II, 94–95, 114–16, and K. S. Latourette, *The Great Century in the Americas, Australasia and Africa A.D. 1800–A.D. 1914*, Vol. V of *A History of the Expansion of Christianity*, London, 1943, 402.
[22] J. Stewart, *Dawn in the Dark Continent*, Edinburgh and London, 1903, 236.
[23] A. E. M. Anderson-Morshead, *The History of the Universities' Mission to Central Africa, 1859–1909*, new rev. ed., London, 1909, 431–4. The statistics are not completely reliable due to the absence, in many cases, of a specific date for

NOTES: CHAPTER I

death. The withdrawal figures probably represent a considerable underestimate as no date is given for forty-four withdrawals.

[24] H. Drummond, *Tropical Africa*, 13th ed., London, 1908, 42–5.
[25] Tabler, *Far Interior*, 247.
[26] *Far Interior*, 248.
[27] Moffat to Tidman, Nov. 12, 1860, quoted in *L.M.S. Chronicle*, Feb., 1861.
[28] H. Goodwin, *Memoir of Bishop Mackenzie*, 2nd ed., Cambridge, 1865, 273–4.
[29] From the *Liverpool Daily Courier*, Nov. 3, 1868, reporting on the U.M.C.A. Annual Meeting in Liverpool. Vol. 14859, S.P.G. offices.
[30] Anderson-Morshead, *History of U.M.C.A.*, 44–5.
[31] Livingstone to Tozer, Dec. 19, 1863, copy enclosed in Livingstone to Maclear, March 22, 1864. D. Livingstone Papers.
[32] 'What would Gregory the Great have said if St. Augustine had landed in the Channel Islands?' D. & C. Livingstone, *Narrative of an Expedition to the Zambesi and its Tributaries*, London, 1865, 571.
[33] Livingstone to Maclear, Oct. 28, 1865, D. Livingstone Papers.
[34] *Mackenzie's Grave*, London, 1959, 234.
[35] Price to J. S. Moffat, Feb. 9, cont. Feb. 19, 1876, J. S. Moffat Papers.
[36] Mullens to J. S. Moffat, Oct. 19, 1876, J. S. Moffat Papers.
[37] Price Diary, Oct. 31, 1877, Price Papers. The Directors were already well informed of the missionaries' dissatisfaction with proposals to locate stations deep in the interior with the consequent problems of communication when there were thousands of unevangelized heathen near the coast. Hore to Mullens, Oct. 13, 1877; Price, Thomson, Clarke, and Hore to Mullens, Oct. 29, 1877; Price to Mullens, Sept. 5, 1877; Price to Mullens, Oct. 1, 1877; Clarke to Mullens, Oct. 14, 1877; L.M.S.T.
[38] Price to J. S. Moffat, Jan. 8, 1878, J. S. Moffat Papers. See also Price Diary, Jan. 5, 1878, Price Papers, for a report of a meeting of the Southern Committee where he was, in his own words, 'hotly cross questioned and great disappointment was manifested at the failure of the scheme of the Directors'.
[39] Price to J. S. Moffat, April 23, cont. April 29, 1878, enclosing copies of correspondence with the Board. J. S. Moffat Papers.
[40] D. P. Jones, 'Decennial Report of the Central Africa Missions of the L.M.S.' (1880–1890), L.M.S.T.
[41] R. Lovett, *The History of the London Missionary Society*, London, 1899, 2 vols., I, 669–70, 649–51.
[42] J. P. R. Wallis, ed., *The Southern African Diaries of Thomas Leask, 1865–1870*, Oppenheimer Series No. 8, London, 1954, 224–5.
[43] Kirk to Granville, June 28, 1881, Vol. Q 25, Z.A.
[44] Kirk to Granville, July 26, 1881, Vol. Q 25, Z.A.
[45] 'On the Twelve Tribes of Tanganyika', *J.R.A.I.*, 1882, 4.
[46] R. U. Moffat, *John Smith Moffat, C.M.G. Missionary, a Memoir*, London, 1921, 45.
[47] J. S. Moffat to Mullens, July 6, 1876, J. S. Moffat Papers.
[48] A. M. Mackay, *Pioneer Missionary of the Church Missionary Society to Uganda*, by his Sister, 8th ed., London, 1898, 445. He felt that a strong coastal base and occasional way stations were required to support mission centres deep in the interior. From bitter experience this was the plan adopted by Bishop Steere of the U.M.C.A. who informed Roger Price that mission stations should be placed about a week's journey apart on healthy sites 'irrespective of the population to be found at such places at a particular time'. Price Diary, May 26, 1876, Price Papers. See also T. M. Thomas, *Eleven Years in Central South Africa*,

NOTES: CHAPTER I

London, 1873, 307, and E. W. Smith, *Great Lion of Bechuanaland, The Life and Times of Roger Price, Missionary*, London, 1957, 30, for missionary criticism of the Matabele and Makololo ventures for the reasons advanced by Mackay and Steere.

[49] R. M. Heanley, *A Memoir of Edward Steere*, 2nd ed. rev., London, 1890, 326. See also *Centenary of the London Missionary Society, Proceedings of the Founders' Week Convention . . . 1895*, London, n.d., 7–8.

[50] Elliott to Whitehouse, Dec. 12, 1879, L.M.S.M.

[51] Jones to Thompson, May 21, 1885, L.M.S.T.

[52] Hore to Thompson, April 24, 1885; Hore to Thompson, June 22, 1885; Swann to Thompson, June 20, 1885; Shaw to Thompson, Jan. 8, 1886, L.M.S.T. Shaw's aspersions were clearly unjustified. See Jones to Thompson, June 20, 1885, L.M.S.T.

[53] *Narrative of Zambesi Expedition*, 573.

[54] Stock, *History of C.M.S.*, I, chap. xiv, 'The Finished Course', a discussion of missionary deaths in West Africa, reveals this martyr aspect of missionary psychology very clearly. One missionary biographer found 'it difficult to escape from feeling a kind of religious envy' of those fortunate enough to become saints and martyrs in Africa while he had 'only been called to plod on in a humdrum way at home. . . .' B. W. Randolph, *Arthur Douglas, Missionary on Lake Nyasa*, Westminster, 1912, 284.

[55] Sykes to Whitehouse, Sept. 16, 1880, L.M.S.M.

[56] Bouniol, *White Fathers*, 172–83.

[57] *Proceedings of the Conference on Foreign Missions . . . 1886*, London, 1886, 147. H. Waller, *Trafficking in Liquor with the Natives of Africa*, London, 1887, 29–30.

[58] The C.M.S. was compelled to rely on German agents for its Rabai Mpia mission until the seventies, a situation regarded as 'deplorable' by Livingstone. Wm. Monk, ed., *Dr. Livingstone's Cambridge Lectures*, 2nd ed., Cambridge, 1860, 166. It took the Church of Scotland almost a year to recruit a clergyman to take charge of their Blantyre mission. Hanna, *Beginnings of Nyasaland*, 24–5.

[59] Waddell Diary, Jan. 21, 1883, Waddell Papers.

[60] Romans 12: 1 quoted in Waddell Diary, May 4, 1883, Waddell Papers. He arrived in Barotseland in 1885. Nine years later he found that he had contracted an incurable disease. By 1901 he was blind, and in 1909 after years of pain and suffering he died at the age of fifty-one. See Chadwick, *Mackenzie's Grave*, 111–12, for the case of Edward Hawkins whose acceptance of a dangerous missionary career with the U.M.C.A. finally satisfied his desire of many years standing 'that I have the power of self-sacrifice'. After a short experience of African conditions Hawkins returned to Britain shattered in health and died shortly afterwards. A. F. Sim stated of his decision to become a missionary that 'one is always preaching about self-sacrifice, and this seems a call to put one's theories into practice'. 'One has to leap in the dark when He bids us,' he wrote elsewhere. A. F. Sim, *Life and Letters of Arthur Fraser Sim*, Westminster, 1896, 39, 61. Sim joined the U.M.C.A. in 1894 and died a year and a half later.

[61] W. P. Johnson, *My African Reminiscences 1875–1895*, Westminster, n.d., 11–13. B. H. Barnes, *Johnson of Nyasaland*, Westminster, 1933, 22.

[62] J. Mackenzie, L.M.S. Missionary Application, Aug. 15, 1854; *L.M.S. Chronicle*, June, 1870, 128.

[63] I. Schapera, ed., *David Livingstone: Family Letters, 1841–1856*, 2 vols., London, 1959, I, 17–18.

[64] H. Waller, *The Last Journals of David Livingstone in Central Africa*, 2 vols., London, 1874, I, 13–14.

NOTES: CHAPTER I

⁶⁵ Waller to Stewart, Oct. 18, 1864; Waller to Stewart, Oct. 28, 1864, J. Stewart Papers.
⁶⁶ Waller to Stewart, Nov. 13, 1864, Stewart Papers.
⁶⁷ Waller to Stewart, April 11, 1865, Stewart Papers.
⁶⁸ Chadwick, *Mackenzie's Grave*, 134. In Fiji, comments J. D. Legge, missionaries 'were often able to wield considerable authority, and to exercise, albeit on the limited stage of native politics, powers which might perhaps have been denied to them in a wider field. At home, one suspects, many of them would have been undistinguished ministers. In the Pacific they were statesmen and men of consequence.' *Britain in Fiji: 1858–1880*, London, 1958, 24.
⁶⁹ His rise to fame was favourably chronicled in Samuel Smiles, *Self-Help*, London, 1921, 210–13.
⁷⁰ Poole to his Mother, June 14, 1895, Poole Papers. 'Perhaps this however is peculiar to the Scotch,' he added, 'the only ones I have met as yet.' Harry Johnston noted 'an undoubted tendency on the part of missionaries to hold and set forth the opinion that no one ever did any good in Africa but themselves.... It is their belief that they hold an always privileged position, that they are never to fit into their proper places in an organized European community, which causes so much friction between them and other European settlers or lay officials....' *British Central Africa*, 3rd ed., London, 1906, 192.
⁷¹ Variations of this phenomenon were widespread. China, comments P. A. Varg, 'was to many a missionary something of a monastery where he could attain more fully his religious aspiration to be Christ-like. Denial to oneself of the material advantages of the West, an escape from the absorbing and demanding competition of making a living in order to be free to live a religious life, an opportunity to live ascetically, these were the advantages offered to a missionary in China.' *Missionaries, Chinese, and Diplomats*, Princeton, 1958, 323.
⁷² 'British East Africa', *Proc. R.C.I.*, 1890–1, 12 n. A much higher cost, £250 to £300 per ton, for a slightly greater distance, Mombasa to Uganda, is given in Perham, *Lugard—Years of Adventure*, 195.
⁷³ *Proc. R.G.S.*, 1876–7, 16.
⁷⁴ 'England's Work in Central Africa', *Proc. R.C.I.*, 1896–7, 51.
⁷⁵ C. F. Harford-Battersby, *Pilkington of Uganda*, London, n.d., 76–7.
⁷⁶ Thomson to Mullens, March 25, 1873, L.M.S.M.
⁷⁷ Tabler, *Far Interior*, 20, 51–52. W. M. Kerr, 'The Upper Zambesi Zone', *S.G.M.*, July, 1886, 394–95, comments on the 'slaughter of elephants' by the Portuguese in the upper Zambesi regions. G. Casati, *Ten Years in Equatoria and the Return with Emin Pasha*, 2 vols., trans. Mrs. J. R. Clay, London and New York, 1891, I, 290, gives figures for ivory export from Equatoria between 1853–79. For the beginning of a counter-reaction, a sportsman's lament over the destruction of great game animals, see H. A. Bryden, *Nature and Sport in South Africa*, London, 1897, chap. xxiii, especially 284.
⁷⁸ Selous to his Mother, July 20, 1878, Selous Papers. Tabler, *Far Interior*, 5.
⁷⁹ Tabler, *Far Interior*, gives an exhaustive account of these early pioneers up to 1879.
⁸⁰ W. P. Livingstone, *Laws of Livingstonia*, London, 1921, 242. Harry Johnston estimated that there were fifty-seven Europeans in the British Central Africa Protectorate and the adjoining sphere of the B.S.A. Co., in 1891, all but three of whom were British. *British Central Africa*, 146–7.
⁸¹ *Zanzibar: City, Island, and Coast*, 2 vols., London, 1872, I, 16–17.
⁸² A. J. Swann, *Fighting the Slave-Hunters in Central Africa*, London, 1910, 45.
⁸³ *How I Found Livingstone*, London, n.d., 63.

NOTES: CHAPTER I

[84] D. Stanley, ed., *The Autobiography of Sir Henry Morton Stanley*, 3rd ed., London, n.d., vi–vii.
[85] *How I Found Livingstone*, 262.
[86] *Through the Dark Continent*, new ed., London, 1890, 446 n.
[87] F. Hird, *H. M. Stanley: the Authorized Life*, London, 1935, 131, 229.
[88] T. H. Parke, *My Personal Experiences in Equatorial Africa as Medical Officer of the Emin Pasha Relief Expedition*, 2nd ed., London, n.d., 7.
[89] Perham, *Lugard—Years of Adventure*, 59–73.
[90] Perham, *Lugard—Years of Adventure*, 34.
[91] *The Rise of Our East African Empire*, 2 vols., Edinburgh and London, 1893.
[92] W. D. M. Bell, *The Wanderings of an Elephant Hunter*, London, 1958, 15. See also Baker's description of the 'indescribable feeling of supremacy' of the hunter, cited in D. Middleton, *Baker of the Nile*, London, 1949, 51–2. For the curious and ambivalent attitude of the hunter—an intense appreciation of the beauty of wild animals, a lust to kill them, and pity at their death—see S. Baker, *The Nile Tributaries of Abyssinia*, new ed., London, 1883, 131.
[93] W. C. Harris, *The Wild Sports of Southern Africa*, 4th ed., London, 1844, 284.
[94] Bryden, *Nature and Sport*, 290.
[95] Bryden, *Nature and Sport*, 292.
[96] Harris, *Wild Sports*, 197.
[97] Wilson Diary, Dec. 21, 1888, Wilson Papers.
[98] *Five Years with the Congo Cannibals*, 3rd ed., London, 1891, 21.
[99] T. D. Murray and A. S. White, *Sir Samuel Baker: A Memoir*, London, 1895, 41.
[100] Lugard, *East African Empire*, I, 243. See also Perham, *Lugard—Years of Adventure*, 101, 199.
[101] J. B. Thomson, *Joseph Thomson—African Explorer*, 2nd ed., London, 1897, 199. In the novel *Ulu: an African Romance*, 2 vols., London, 1888, by Thomson and Miss E. Harris-Smith, the Scottish hero, Gilmour, went to Africa for 'excitement, perhaps forgetfulness', after the woman he loved married a 'bantling millionaire whom she made no pretense of loving'. Gilmour was distressed with the values of a society where 'money, position, and pleasure were the goals of universal ambition and universal effort'. Civilized society was described as the 'most monstrous fraud and imposture in the world'. II, 217, 216, 212; I, 148.
[102] W. M. Kerr, *The Far Interior*, 2 vols., London, 1886, I, 2.
[103] Parke, *Personal Experiences*, 2.
[104] F. C. Selous, *A Hunter's Wanderings in Africa*, 5th ed., London, 1907, 1.
[105] J. P. R. Wallis, ed., *The Northern Goldfields Diaries of Thomas Baines*, 3 vols., London, 1946, I, 103.
[106] Parke, *Personal Experiences*, 483–7.
[107] Sykes to Tidman, March 3, 1862, L.M.S.M.
[108] Thomas Diary, April 18, 1879, Thomas Papers.
[109] J. S. Moffat Diary, Aug. 20, 1864, J. S. Moffat Papers.
[110] Tabler, *Far Interior*, 146.
[111] Mackay to Kirk, June 8, 1885, E 87, Z.A.
[112] Emily Moffat to J. S. Unwin, Dec. 1, 1861, and same to same Nov. 18, 1860, J. P. R. Wallis, ed. *The Matabele Mission*, Oppenheimer Series No. 2, London, 1945, 156, 118.
[113] Bouniol, *White Fathers*, 74.
[114] E. W. Smith, *The Blessed Missionaries*, Cape Town, 1950, 6. See in this connection Harford-Battersby, *Pilkington of Uganda*, 257–60; R. S. Watt, *In the Heart of Savagedom*, 4th ed., London, n.d., 206; J. Mackenzie, 'Bechuanaland,

NOTES: CHAPTER II

with some Remarks on Mashonaland and Matabeleland', *S.G.M.*, June, 1887, 301 n. D. P. Jones, 'After Livingstone', 79–80, t/s, L.M.S.T.

[115] O. Mannoni, *Prospero and Caliban, the Psychology of Colonization*, London, 1956. The criticism is from L. H. Gann and P. Duignan, *White Settlers in Tropical Africa*, Penguin Books, 1962, 18.

II: WHITE MEETS BLACK

[1] J. P. R. Wallis, ed., *The Zambesi Expedition of David Livingstone 1858–1863*, 2 vols., Oppenheimer Series No. 9, London, 1956, II, 420–5.

[2] Baines, *Goldfields Diaries*, II, 568; E. D. Young, *Nyassa: A Journal of Adventure*, London, 1877, 53–4, 86; Leask, *Diaries*, 83. Significantly, all three were practising Christians.

[3] Tabler, *Far Interior*, 158. See also Bryden, *Nature and Sport*, 301–2, on the generally high character of the hunters.

[4] In one of his infrequent moments of doubt and uncertainty Livingstone was reassured by the fact that Jesus was a 'gentleman of the most sacred and strictest honour', who, having said 'I am with you alway even unto the end of the world', would unfailingly respect his word. W. G. Blaikie, *The Personal Life of David Livingstone*, 8th ed., London, 1897, 151.

See also F. D. Lugard, 'A Glimpse of Lake Nyassa', *Blackwood's Magazine*, Jan., 1890, 20, and V. L. Cameron, 'Colonisation of Central Africa', *Proc. R.C.I.*, 1875–6, 281–2, for the gentleman concept. Lugard's attitude is discussed in Perham, *Lugard—Years of Adventure*, 197–8.

[5] It also had a commercial basis—the necessity for trust in business—but this is not its essential meaning here.

[6] See R. Maunier's discussion of the relation between the ideal of the gentleman and imperialism—'in the interest of the whole world, domination should be in the hands of *gentlemen*'. *The Sociology of Colonies*, 2 vols., ed. and trans. E. O. Lorimer, London, 1949, I, 30, 34; and also A. Zimmern, *The Third British Empire*, London, 1926, 75, on the gentleman as the 'unrivalled primary teacher of peoples'.

[7] *The Story of the Universities' Mission to Central Africa*, 2nd ed., London, 1867, 360.

[8] *To the Central African Lakes*, I, 253. See also Baker's emphasis on willpower and duty as a basis for success. *The Albert N'yanza*, new ed., London, 1898, xxvii, 1.

[9] Middleton, *Baker*, 156; F. C. Selous, *Travel and Adventure in South-East Africa*, London, 1893, 383–4, 394; and Selous, *A Hunter's Wanderings*, 255–56, indicate this relationship. Livingstone argued that field sports hardened the character, and thus proved 'serviceable to the whole nation by preventing the growth of effeminacy'. I. Schapera, ed., *Livingstone's Private Journals*, London, 1960, 174.

[10] J. P. R. Wallis, ed., *The Zambesi Journal of James Stewart, 1862–1863*, Oppenheimer Series No. 6, London, 1952, 5. For energy as a British character trait see Maunier, *Sociology of Colonies*, I, 34.

[11] *Travel and Adventure*, 285–6.

[12] *Travel and Adventure*, 300. For a similar incident see Thomson, *Through Masai Land*, 255. A classic example of the necessity for members of a dominant race to display courage in order to retain respect is found in George Orwell's 'Shooting an Elephant', in *Shooting an Elephant and Other Essays*, London, 1950.

[13] *How I Found Livingstone*, 330.

[14] *How I Found Livingstone*, 236.

[15] *How I Found Livingstone*, 351.

NOTES: CHAPTER II

[16] Harford-Battersby, *Pilkington of Uganda*, 68–9.

[17] See the remarks of Sir Roderick Murchison on Livingstone's 'noble and courageous conduct' in returning the Makololo, thus 'proving to the people of Africa what an English Christian is'. *Proc. R.G.S.*, 1857–8, 123–4.

[18] J. F. Elton, *Travels and Researches among the Lakes and Mountains of Eastern and Central Africa*, London, 1879 (ed. and completed by H. B. Cotterill), 363, 396.

[19] H. H. Johnston, *The Kilima-Njaro Expedition*, London, 1886, 49.

[20] Barnes, *Johnson of Nyasaland*, 31, reveals the shock of one missionary at the discovery that flogging was the accepted practice on mission caravans.

[21] R. N. Cust, *Notes on Missionary Subjects*, London, 1889, Part III, 29–30. Although Cust did not name Hannington the identification is obvious. See E. C. Dawson, ed., *The Last Journals of Bishop Hannington*, London, 1888, 144, 173, 178–9.

[22] For a discussion see Perham, *Lugard—Years of Adventure*, 195–8; Watt, *Heart of Savagedom*, 83–7.

[23] *Personal Experiences*, 39.

[24] *To the Central African Lakes*, I, 220–5; II, 104–5, 115–19; *Through Masai Land*, 104–5.

[25] Maunier, in discussing the tendency to despotism among white colonists, stated: 'This attitude is encouraged by the colonists' vision of the tyrannies to which the native was accustomed passively to submit.' *Sociology of Colonies*, I, 110.

[26] *Nyassa*, 46–7.

[27] F. D. Lugard, 'The Fight Against Slave-Traders on Nyassa', *Contemporary Review*, Sept., 1889, 343. This war is described in Hanna, *Beginnings of Nyasaland*, 79–105. Lugard's role in the war is discussed in Perham, *Lugard—The Years of Adventure*, 106–42.

[28] H. Faulkner, *Elephant Haunts*, London, 1868, 73–4, 82, 40.

[29] R. F. Burton, *The Lake Regions of Central Africa*, 2 vols., London, 1860, II, 327, 340. See also J. Cooper-Chadwick, *Three Years with Lobengula*, London, 1894, 21; C. Chaille-Long, *Central Africa: Naked Truths of Naked People*, London, 1876, 325.

[30] *Memories of Mashonaland*, London, 1895, 167, 176; *Journals of the Mashonaland Mission 1888 to 1892*, London, 1892, 45–6.

[31] Such self-restraint was not always easily attained. Dodgshun, L.M.S., furious at the insolence and tribute demands of the Wagogo, described them as 'bloodthirsty wild beasts and if I shoot it will be as against wolves'. Dodgshun to Mullens, Nov. 25, 1878, L.M.S.T. Someone, he wrote in his journal, 'ought to come and scour Ugogo from end to end with bullets. The insolence and extortion of the whole lot need punishment.' Dodgshun Journal, Nov. 25, 1878, L.M.S.T. 'Such wretches cannot claim the rights of men. They are wild beasts, only to be kept in their place by superior force.' Dodgshun to Mullens, Dec. 28 [or 29?], 1878, L.M.S.T. This last statement was made after he had heard that the Wagogo had killed Penrose, a missionary of the C.M.S.

[32] *How I Found Livingstone*, 223.

[33] *Mr. Henry M. Stanley and the Royal Geographical Society, 1878*, cited in C. Tsuzuki, *H. M. Hyndman and British Socialism*, London, 1961, 18.

[34] *How I Found Livingstone*, 118.

[35] *The Arab and the African*, London, 1891, 185–6.

[36] *How I Found Livingstone*, 404–7.

[37] The problems of civil jurisdiction are discussed in Oliver, *Missionary Factor*, 50–65; and Gann, *Birth of a Plural Society*, 26–9. A useful description of the

NOTES: CHAPTER II

U.M.C.A. settlement at Masasi is given by C. Maples, 'A Village Community in East Africa', *Mission Life*, March, 1882, and April, 1882. Curiously, while Maples was ruling Masasi, his superior, Bishop Steere, was arguing that such powers should not be assumed by missionaries because of the potential abuse in their employment. 'Missions and the Civil Power', *Mission Life*, May, 1881.

[38] *The Times*, July 8, 1880, Letter to editor.

[39] The situation was exposed in Andrew Chirnside's pamphlet *The Blantyre Missionaries—Discreditable Disclosures*, London, 1880. See also Rev. J. C. Herdman, *The Blantyre Mission Case—Report of the Committee for the Propagation of the Gospel in Foreign Parts . . . To the Commission of the General Assembly of the Church of Scotland, March, 1881*. A detailed analysis of the Blantyre episode is found in Hanna, *Beginnings of Nyasaland*, 25-34.

[40] D. Macdonald, *Africana: or, the Heart of Heathen Africa*, 2 vols., London, 1882, II, 84.

[41] Kirk to Granville, July 21, 1881, with enclosures Holmwood to Kirk, July 7, 1881, and Commander Byles to Captain Brownrigg, July 12, 1881, a 'Report on the Treatment of Natives living on the Church Mission Station at Mombaza'. Q 25, Z.A.

[42] Thomson, *To the Central African Lakes*, II, 130.

[43] J. Petherick, *Egypt, the Soudan and Central Africa*, Edinburgh and London, 1861, 458-62.

[44] *Africana*, II, 171-2.

[45] *Albert Nyanza*, 202.

[46] *Ismailia*, 2nd ed., London, 1879, 7, 51, 279, 285, 334-5, 358, 468.

[47] Petherick, *Egypt, the Soudan and Central Africa*, 466-7.

[48] Stanley, *How I Found Livingstone*, 259.

[49] *Central Africa*, 101-2, 91.

[50] Sharpe to Johnston, Sept. 8, 1890, to Jan. 27, 1891, encl. in Johnston to Salisbury, May 6, 1891, F.O. 84/2114.

[51] Johnson Diary, Aug. 21, 1887, Johnson Papers.

[52] Johnson Diary, Aug. 31, 1887, Johnson Papers. The restraining hand of Selous did not indicate equanimity over Matabele obstructiveness. In a letter of protest he called Lobengula 'Chief of the thrice accursed tribe of the Amandabele', and accused him of believing any lies his 'accursed, God forgotten, Hell begotten, slaves' chose to tell him. Selous to Lobengula, Aug. 31, 1887, Selous Papers. One of the whites in the area, Jameson, offered £5,000 to help equip any expedition to wipe out the Matabele. Johnson Diary, Aug. 31, 1887, Johnson Papers.

[53] *East African Empire*, I, 73-4. H. L. Duff, *Nyasaland under the Foreign Office*, London, 1903, 381-3, placed great stress on the necessity for Africans regarding Europeans with awe as being 'mysteriously apart from them, infinitely wiser, and, above all, infinitely more powerful. . . .'

[54] Lugard, *East African Empire*, I, 19-20. Richard Burton had, like Lugard, a background of Indian experience, and felt equally strongly about the necessity for maintaining prestige. *Lake Regions*, I, 142; Burton, *Life of Burton*, I, 352, 354-55; II, 88, indicate his attitude.

[55] The Foreign Office thought the action 'well merited', while Acting Consul Prideaux regarded it as salutary even though taken in direct opposition to the advice of the Governor of Lamoo who had proposed a prior reference to the Sultan. The Sultan was furious, and wrote to Prideaux: 'And perhaps you do not know that when the boats came to Kuinga they destroyed the town and cut down the cocoanut trees, and killed a woman, and burnt the village with fire, and destroyed the mosque, the house of God, and there was in it a great deal of property

NOTES: CHAPTER II

belonging to people which was lost.' Derby to Prideaux, Aug. 8, 1874, Q13, Z.A.; Prideaux to Derby, April 4, 1874, enclosing Barghash to Prideaux, 7th Safar, A. H., 1291, E 64, Z.A.

[56] Kirk to Derby, Dec. 9, 1875, E72, Z.A.
[57] Coupland, *Exploitation*, 263-4.
[58] R. P. Ashe, *Two Kings of Uganda*, London, 1889, 134-9.
[59] Ashe, *Two Kings*, 171.
[60] *Two Kings*, 239-40.
[61] Swann, *Fighting Slave Hunters*, 186-7.
[62] Jones to Thompson, Nov. 18, 1889, L.M.S.T. See also Jones to Thompson, Dec. 2, 1884, and Hore to Whitehouse, Sept. 25, 1883, L.M.S.T., for discussions of the security problems attendant on a decline of awe.
[63] Jones to Thompson, Dec. 2, 1884, L.M.S.T.
[64] E. Maples, ed., *Journals and Papers of Chauncy Maples*, London, 1899, 185-6.
[65] G. Warneck, *Modern Missions and Culture, Their Mutual Relations*, new ed., trans. T. Smith, Edinburgh, n.d., 314-15; R. N. Cust, *Essay on the Prevailing Methods of the Evangelization of the Non-Christian World*, London, 1894, 251.
[66] Bouniol, *White Fathers*, 40, 31.
[67] G. Ward and E. F. Russell, Eds., *The Life of Charles Alan Smythies*, 2nd ed., London, 1899, 203-4.
[68] Heanley, *Memoir of Steere*, 412.
[69] J. E. Hine, *Days Gone By*, London, 1924, 86.
[70] Livingstone, *Laws*, 250.
[71] He distrusted the growth in influence of Likoma Island with its well established station and large cathedral. He preferred small mission centres less disruptive of tribal life. Barnes, *Johnson of Nyasaland*, 138, 144, 146; *African Reminiscences*, 183.
[72] Barnes, *Johnson of Nyasaland*, 102-4, 107, 132.
[73] Livingstone, *Private Journals*, 272.
[74] Numerous writers noted how quickly they forgot the 'blackness' of Africans. Sim, *Life and Letters*, 138, 156; Ward and Russell, *Life of Smythies*, 45. In fact, on occasion, whites seem to have become ashamed of their own pallid skin colour. Thomson, *To the Central African Lakes*, I, 271.
[75] Watt, *Heart of Savagedom*, 224-25; Livingstone, *Last Journals*, I, 259; H. H. Johnston, *The Uganda Protectorate*, 2 vols., London, 1902, II, 473-4; H. Rowley, *Africa Unveiled*, London, 1876, 35-7.
[76] Baines, *Goldfields Diaries*, I, 76, also II, 290.
[77] F. Mandy, *Matabeleland: The Future Gold Fields of the World*, Cape Town, 1889, 24.
[78] For offers of women on a temporary or permanent basis see Faulkner, *Elephant Haunts*, 256-7; Chaille-Long, *Central Africa*, 150-1, 154; Stewart, *Zambesi Journal*, 153.
[79] For offers of wives to missionaries and their rejection see E. Baker, *The Life and Explorations of Frederick Stanley Arnot*, London, 1921, 84, 225-6; C. T. Wilson and R. W. Felkin, *Uganda and the Egyptian Soudan*, 2 vols., London, 1882, I, 330-31; II, 16-17. Watt, *Heart of Savagedom*, 37, gives an example of an offer to exchange wives made by an African chief.
[80] *Zanzibar*, I, 379.
[81] Baker correlates tropical climates with sensuality, polygamy and sexual passion in *Albert Nyanza*, xxiii, 48.
[82] 'Sexual Education and Nakedness', chap. iii of Havelock Ellis, *Sex in Relation to Society*, Vol. IV of *Studies in the Psychology of Sex*, New York, 1936. 'The simple child of Nature sees in nakedness nothing at all; the clothed man

NOTES: CHAPTER II

sees in the uncovered body only a sensual irritation.' 103. Peter Nielson asserts that the deep brown skin colour of African women and the texture of the skin, 'usually finer and more pleasant to the touch than that of the European', are factors in cross-racial sexual attraction from the European viewpoint. *The Colour Bar*, Cape Town and Johannesburg, n.d., 18–19.

[83] B. Farwell, *The Man Who Presumed. A Biography of Henry M. Stanley*, London, 1958, 67–8, notes the promiscuity of Shaw on Stanley's Livingstone expedition.

[84] In the diary of E. G. Alston there is a cryptic comment about a white at Fort Mangoche in British Central Africa, 'an ex-corporal in R. E. who drinks gin and whiskey all day and has 8 native wives'. Alston Diary, Feb. 13, 1896, Alston Papers.

[85] Casati, *Ten Years in Equatoria*, II, 300, noted that Stokes, a trader and caravan leader, gained great influence from his marriage to a chief's daughter. H. Rangeley, 'The Memoirs of Henry Rangeley', t/s, 34, mentions a mixed marriage in which the African wife brought trade to the store of her husband.

[86] I. Fry, 'Reminiscences', t/s, 53.

[87] Examples are given in Wilson, Supplementary Diary Notes, 27–9, Wilson Papers.

[88] Fry, 'Reminiscences', 52.

[89] Knight-Bruce claimed, doubtless with some exaggeration, that nine-tenths of the deaths among the non-missionary group were 'directly or indirectly from the effects of drink'. E. Fripp and V. W. Hiller, eds., *Gold and the Gospel in Mashonaland, 1888*, London, 1949, 18.

[90] Moffat, *J. S. Moffat*, 235. Knight-Bruce stated that 'it apparently will never be forgotten . . . how an Englishman who came here to hunt, fell, when drunk, into the Chief's dish of meat'. Fripp and Hiller, eds., *Gold and the Gospel*, 109.

[91] R. N. Acutt, 'The Reminiscences of Robert Noble Acutt: Sidelights on South African Life', reprinted from *South Africa*, Jan., 1926, 30–1.

[92] Moffat to Gifford, Oct. 1, 1890, J. S. Moffat Papers.

[93] Fry, 'Reminiscences', 44.

[94] W. Finaughty stated 'that the Matabele women bore a splendid reputation for virtue so far as the white visitors to the country were concerned'. *The Recollections of William Finaughty, Elephant Hunter, 1864–1875*, Philadelphia, 1916, 22. This was, however, only true of the early stages of contact when 'voluntary prostitution to a white man was . . . almost unknown. [By 1870 it was] . . . of common occurrence.' Baines attributed the early unwillingness to enter into promiscuous intercourse with whites not to any respect for chastity, but simply to the fact that the women were not accustomed to sexual advances from members of a different race. Baines, *Goldfields Diaries*, II, 488.

[95] Baines, *Goldfields Diaries*, II, 488.

[96] *A Visit to Lobengula in 1889*, Pietermaritzburg, 1947, 86–7, 97, 107–9, 100. Fry, 'Reminiscences', 46, 51, also mentions the easy availability of the Matabele women.

[97] Edwards to Dawson, July 14, 1890, Dawson Papers in Hole Collection.

[98] Moffat to Loch, Sept. 24, 1890; Moffat to Thompson, Feb. 11, 1888; Moffat to Loch, Sept. 24, 1890. See also Moffat to Shippard, Aug. 1, 1889; Moffat to Miss E. Unwin, Sept. 1, 1889; Moffat to Miss E. Unwin, Oct. 6, 1889, all from J. S. Moffat Papers. Also Moffat, *J. S. Moffat*, 235.

[99] Marshal Hole asserted that sexual relationships 'between white men and black women were the rule rather than the exception'. Memo by Hole in Dawson Papers in Hole Collection. Fry, 'Reminiscences', 43–7, 51, and P. D. Crewe. 'Reminiscences of Life in Natal, the Transvaal and Rhodesia', 34, confirm Hole's

NOTES: CHAPTER II

assertion. See also Tabler, *Far Interior*, 171–2, and N. Rouillard, ed., *Matabele Thompson, an Autobiography*, London, 1936, 114–15.

[100] The family of Robert Moffat, with three daughters married to missionaries, Livingstone, Price, and Fredoux, provides an extreme example of missionary endogamy. The second marriage of T. M. Thomas is also instructive. The father of his bride refused to let his daughters marry outside of the missionary circle. Two daughters, unable to wed their choices, remained single, while three others, including Mrs. Thomas, married missionaries and received paternal blessings. C. C. Thomas, 'Thomas Morgan Thomas—Pioneer Missionary—1828–1884', Duplo-Type, n.d., 33.

Livingstone's unromantic, almost cold-blooded notification of his impending marriage with Mary Moffat illustrates the practical missionary attitude to the selection of a wife. D. Chamberlin, ed., *Some Letters from Livingstone, 1840–1872*, London, 1940, 76.

[101] 'British Missions and Missionaries in Africa', *Nineteenth Century*, Nov., 1887, 717. Johnston repeated this argument in *British Central Africa*, 198–99.

[102] Southon to Thompson, June 12, 1882; Griffiths to Whitehouse, June 15, 1883; Swann to Thompson, Jan. 25, 1886; Tomory to Thompson, Nov. 24, 1888, all from L.M.S.T. See also Baker, *Life of Arnot*, 134–5.

[103] Carson to Thompson, Sept. 6, 1890, L.M.S.T.

[104] B. Frere, *Eastern Africa as a Field for Missionary Labour*, London, 1874, 97.

[105] Mary Moffat to Mrs. Helmore, July 22, 1850, Helmore Papers.

[106] Moffat to Mullens, July 6, 1876, J. S. Moffat Papers. For his wife's similar view see Wallis, ed., *The Matabele Mission*, 164.

[107] *Tanganyika: Eleven Years in Central Africa*, London, 1892, 251.

[108] W. A. Elliott, *Gold from the Quartz*, London, 1919, 61. See also J. Johnston, *Reality versus Romance in South Central Africa*, London, 1893, 333; Emily Moffat to J. S. Unwin, Dec. 20, 1865, J. S. Moffat Papers; Livingstone, *Family Letters*, II, 122, 144.

[109] *Fighting Slave Hunters*, 152–3.

[110] *Albert Nyanza*, xxiii, 2.

[111] *Narrative of Zambesi Expedition*, 416.

[112] Westbeech Diary, t/s, 55–6, Westbeech Papers. R. N. Cust strongly deprecated the use of force, but admitted that it might be necessary to protect 'life and female honour'. *Notes on Missionary Subjects*, Part I, 11; Part IV, 28. The murder of white women and children was a main factor in the strong vengeance feelings which motivated Rhodesian whites at the time of the Matabele Rebellion. P. Mason, *The Birth of a Dilemma—The Conquest and Settlement of Rhodesia*, London and New York, 1958, 197–8. To verify Mason's assertion see W. H. Brown, *On the South African Frontier*, New York, 1899, 340–1; R. S. S. Baden-Powell, *The Matabele Campaign*, London, 1897, 64, 131–2; F. C. Selous, *Sunshine and Storm in Rhodesia*, 2nd ed., London, 1896, 30, 36–7, 65, 199–200, 209; R. B. Taylor Diary, May 23, May 25, June 6, 1896, Taylor Papers.

[113] *Fighting Slave Hunters*, 137. The British attitude is remarkably parallel to the idealization of white women in the American South and the contrasting image of the Negro woman as 'a seducing accessible person dominated by sexual feeling. . . .' Dollard, *Caste and Class*, 136–7.

[114] 'British Missions and Missionaries in Africa', *Nineteenth Century*, Nov., 1887, 718. See also Johnston, *British Central Africa*, 200.

[115] Wallis, ed., *Livingstone's Zambesi Expedition*, I, 126–7.

[116] Wallis, ed., *The Matabele Mission*, 75, 97.

[117] *To Lake Tanganyika*, 192.

[118] W. C. Devereux, *A Cruise in the Gorgon*, London, 1869, 412, 357.

NOTES: CHAPTER II

[119] Devereux, *Cruise*, 129. See also 192, 239, for more of Devereux's strictures on the conduct of British sailors.

[120] Stewart, *Zambesi Journal*, 190.

[121] Select Committee on the East African Slave Trade in 1871; *Report* (no. 420 of 1871), Questions 1071 to 1075. Former Consul Rigby denied Steere's allegations. Question 1194. C. Lloyd, however, believes that Steere's charges were probably substantially correct. *The Navy and the Slave Trade*, London, 1949, 257. Devereux's account supports Lloyd's interpretation. See Devereux, *Cruise*, 348, for a humorous example.

[122] H. H. Johnston, 'The Development of Tropical Africa Under British Auspices', *Fortnightly Review*, Nov., 1890, 692.

[123] Johnston to Sir P. Anderson, Oct. 10, 1893 (Private), F.O. 2/55. Johnston to Anderson, Jan. 21, 1893 (Private) F.O. 2/54, entertainingly discusses the case of a 'wild Irishman' on Mount Mlanje, and his energetic attempts to get a nearby chief to send over one of his wives. In 1895 A. J. Wookey, L.M.S., indicated that mistresses were widespread among the Bechuanaland Border Police at Lake Ngami. One lieutenant had purchased a slave girl, while one of the police had stated that orders had been given to have 'a sufficient number of women in the camp to ensure the health of the men'. Wookey to J. S. Moffat, Jan. 29, 1895, J. S. Moffat Papers.

[124] E. Ruete, *Memoirs of an Arabian Princess*, trans. L. Strachey, New York, 1907, 170. The conduct of one French Consul who purchased a Negress and then gave the resultant 'excessively black little daughter' to the French mission also offended the Arab 'sense of propriety', 170-1. Burton stated that most of the white residents of Zanzibar kept Abyssinian or Galla concubines. *Zanzibar*, I, 380. Galla women had a reputation for beauty among Europeans, Baker, *Nile Tributaries*, 349-50.

[125] Joseph Conrad, 'Heart of Darkness', in *A Conrad Argosy*, New York, 1942, contains numerous illuminating insights relevant to this section.

[126] And one must note its frequency. Surgeon Parke, medical officer of the Emin Pasha expedition, stated: 'I think each of the Europeans on Mr. Stanley's staff, seven in number, who crossed Africa, had fever probably 150 or 200 times.' In discussion on G. S. Mackenzie, 'British East Africa', *Proc. R.C.I.*, 1890-1, 23.

[127] Livingstone, *Laws*, 84.

[128] *African Reminiscences*, 25.

[129] J. S. Moffat, an independent missionary financed by Livingstone from 1859-64, and then a member of the L.M.S., sided with Sykes against Thomas, both of the L.M.S.

[130] A full account of this sorry and tragic dispute is contained in *London Missionary Society Papers Respecting the Matabele Mission, South Africa*, Printed for the Directors only, London, 1873. Ultimately, one of the missionaries, T. M. Thomas, was dismissed.

[131] A. Schulz and A. Hammar, *The New Africa*, London, 1897, 29-30.

[132] Stewart, *Zambesi Journal*, 49.

[133] Stewart, *Zambesi Journal*, 28, 136, 135, 109, 190.

[134] *Life, Wanderings, and Labours in Eastern Africa*, London, 1873, 132-3, 149-50.

[135] Waddell Diary, May 21, 1884, Waddell Papers.

[136] Emily Moffat to J. S. Unwin, June 24, 1860, in Wallis ed., *The Matabele Mission*, 98.

[137] E. Maples, *Chauncy Maples, Pioneer Missionary in East Central Africa*, London, 1897, 122-3.

[138] H. Waller, quoted in *U.M.C.A. Annual Report, 1861*, 48.

NOTES: CHAPTER II

¹³⁹ See C. Northcott, *Robert Moffat: Pioneer in Africa 1817–1870*, London, 1961, Appendix I, for an analysis of this friendship.
¹⁴⁰ Barnes, *Johnson of Nyasaland*, 174.
¹⁴¹ Tabler, *Far Interior*, 158.
¹⁴² Stanley, *How I Found Livingstone*, 348; Farwell, *H. M. Stanley*, 317.
¹⁴³ R. C. Maugham, *Nyasaland in the Nineties*, London, 1935, 25.
¹⁴⁴ Macdonald, *Africana*, II, 116.
¹⁴⁵ Livingstone, *Laws*, 73.
¹⁴⁶ Wallis, ed., *The Matabele Mission*, 21.
¹⁴⁷ Burton, *Life of Burton*, I, 286.
¹⁴⁸ See Pruen, *Arab and African*, 254–7, for a general discussion of British-Arab relationships on the social level.
¹⁴⁹ H. Arendt, *The Origins of Totalitarianism*, 2nd ed., New York, 1960, 190.
¹⁵⁰ Elliott, *Gold from the Quartz*, 124.
¹⁵¹ Elliott to Thompson, Dec. 11, 1882, L.M.S.M.
¹⁵² *Gold from the Quartz*, 201–2.
¹⁵³ Elliott, *Gold from the Quartz*, 57.
¹⁵⁴ Moffat, *J. S. Moffat*, 219. See also Moffat to Thompson, Feb. 11, 1888, and Moffat to Thompson, Sept. 11, 1888, J. S. Moffat Papers. Wardlaw Thompson, the Foreign Secretary of the L.M.S., stated that the mobility of the Matabele meant that missionaries were not permanently connected with any one section of the tribe. 'There are, however, always towns within easy reach of both stations; and, from the habits and character of the Matabele, it is better that the Missionaries should not reside in immediate contact with them.' *London Missionary Society. Deputation to South Africa.... 1883–1884. Report of the Rev. R. Wardlaw Thompson, Foreign Secretary*, Printed for the use of the Directors, 34.
¹⁵⁵ Note, for example, the white tendency to believe in witchcraft and other aspects of tribal belief. J. G. Wood, *Through Matabeleland*, Grahamstown, 1893, 120–2; E. Mohr, *To the Victoria Falls of the Zambesi*, trans. N. D'Anvers, London, 1876, 207.
¹⁵⁶ *Arab and African*, 106.
¹⁵⁷ One U.M.C.A. bishop in the early imperial period told a colleague that on long tours through heathen districts 'he felt the evil spirits all about him. They pestered him with horrible thoughts which he in no way liked; and this went on till he got down to the Lake again into the midst of Mission life, when his life resumed its normal condition. He told me that he always noticed the same thing—the extraordinary power of the spirits of evil—whenever he was walking through heathen parts.' Randolph, *Arthur Douglas*, 230.
¹⁵⁸ *L.M.S. Chronicle*, Oct., 1865, 287, quoting T. M. Thomas.
¹⁵⁹ G. Seaver, *David Livingstone: His Life and Letters*, London, 1957, 186.
¹⁶⁰ Seaver, *Livingstone*, 192.
¹⁶¹ Stanley, *How I Found Livingstone*, 350–1.
¹⁶² J. I. Macnair, *Livingstone the Liberator*, London and Glasgow, n.d., 328–9; Macdonald, *Africana*, II, 143–4; Elliott, *Gold from the Quartz*, 64.
¹⁶³ See Coillard's very revealing comments about the missionary difficulty in retaining ethical standards and religious faith. *On the Threshold of Central Africa*, 2nd ed., London, 1902 (trans. and ed., by C. W. Mackintosh), 150, 289, and 504, 289–90, for the missionary sense of failure. 'Have I laboured in vain? Have I spent my strength for nought, and in vain?'
¹⁶⁴ Griffiths to Whitehouse, June 16, 1881, L.M.S.T.
¹⁶⁵ Hore, *Tanganyika*, 177.
¹⁶⁶ *To Lake Tanganyika*, 189.
¹⁶⁷ *Missionary Travels and Researches in South Africa*, London, 1857, 228.

NOTES: CHAPTER III

This would appear to be the proper interpretation of a remark in Livingstone's lecture at Cambridge. 'I might,' he stated, 'have gone on instructing the natives [the Makololo] in religion, but as civilization and Christianity must go on together, I was obliged to find a path to the sea, in order that I should not sink to the level of the natives.' *Cambridge Lectures*, 151. The realization that many civilized values rested on an assured and steady supply of western goods and services was also noted by Stanley, *Autobiography*, 358, and Kerr, *Far Interior*, II, 202.

[168] Oliver, *Missionary Factor*, 200.
[169] *Modern Missions and Culture*, 223.
[170] This problem, the fear of 'going native', was also present for later generations of Europeans on isolated outposts in the imperial era. It is revealed with exceptional clarity in the diary of a young subaltern in Kenya at the turn of the century who wrote *inter alia* of 'the dread of eventually being overcome by savage Africa, the horror of losing one's veneer of western civilization'. R. Meinertzhagen, *Kenya Diary—1902-1906*, Edinburgh and London, 1957, 217-19, 293.
[171] D. Carnegie, *Among the Matabele*, 2nd ed., London, 1894, 100.
[172] Baines, *Goldfields Diaries*, II, 551, also 558.
[173] *Through Masai Land*, 193-5, 248.
[174] *East African Empire*, I, 73-5, 84.

III: CONTEMPORARY ANCESTORS

[1] *Sunshine and Storm*, 31.
[2] See Basil Davidson, *The Lost Cities of Africa*, Boston, 1959, for an exemplification of this approach.
[3] The statement of Melvin J. Lasky is apposite. 'I would much prefer equal treatment and political rights to be argued from "the brotherhood of man" than from devious theses of ancient cultural achievement, for I am appalled at the implication that if Africans had no glorious past behind them they would somehow be ineligible for freedom and fraternity.' 'Africa for Beginners', *Encounter*, Feb., 1962, 26 n.
[4] For some of the complex factors involved in the possibility of establishing a hierarchy of cultures see M. Leiris, *Race and Culture*, Paris, 1952, 35-9.
[5] *Primitive Culture*, 2 vols., London, 1920, I, 26.
[6] *The Expansion of England*, London, 1925, 291.
[7] *Narrative of Zambesi Expedition*, 533-4.
[8] For the Portuguese see G. Freyre, *Brazil—an Interpretation*, New York, 1951, 19-22.
[9] And in official propaganda. The motto on the first postage stamps in the British Central Africa Protectorate was 'Light in Darkness'. Johnston, *British Central Africa*, 129.
[10] See the comments of J. Bryce in *Impressions of South Africa*, 3rd ed., rev., London, 1899, 351-2.
[11] 'Notes on Certain Matters Connected with the Dahoman', *Memoirs Read Before the Anthropological Society of London, 1863-4*, Vol. I, London, 1865, 321.
[12] For contemporary observation on the growing military discrepancy and its attendant dangers for race relations see H. Merivale, *Lectures on Colonization and Colonies*, London, 1928, 561; John Mackenzie in *L.M.S. Chronicle*, June, 1870, 130.
[13] Bryce, *Impressions of South Africa*, 56-7.
[14] See Wilson and Felkin, *Uganda and Egyptian Soudan*, I, 135, for the Wanyamwesi town of Uyui; Southon to Directors, Sept. 8, 1879, L.M.S.T., for the

NOTES: CHAPTER III

Wanyamwesi town of Urambo with a population of about 10,000 living inside the walls of the town; Goodrich to Granville, March 19, 1885, F.O. 84/1702, for a very favourable description of the Arab-influenced Yao town of chief Makanjira. Alston commented that 'Makanjira's place is simply enormous. I have never seen such a large town and such large fine houses, with proper doors and chairs, etc!!' Alston Diary, Nov. 18, 1895, Alston Papers.

[15] Gann, *Birth of a Plural Society*, foreword by Gluckman, xii.
[16] *Story of U.M.C.A.*, 22.
[17] *Zanzibar*, II, 101.
[18] *Tropical Africa*, 36.
[19] *Nyasaland*, 291–93.
[20] *How I Found Livingstone*, 69.
[21] *How I Found Livingstone*, 108.
[22] *Missionary Travels*, 213–14, 506.
[23] *Narrative of Zambesi Expedition*, 599.
[24] *Proc. R.G.S.*, 1863-4, 249 n. Murchison's argument was extensively and favourably quoted by Baker, in *Albert Nyanza*, 448–52.
[25] A. Carson, 'Journey from Quillimane to Niamkolo, March 28–July 4, 1886', 58, L.M.S.T.
[26] *A Journey from Matope on the Upper Shire to Newala on the Rovuma by the Right Rev. the Bishop in 1885*, Corrected ed., Zanzibar, 1885, 4. To Harry Johnston, the banana plantain around the Lake Victoria basin which supplied food, drink, and building materials, was, in the words of his biographer, 'the most corrupting asset' of the whole area. Oliver, *Johnston*, 317–18. See also J. H. Speke, *What Led to the Discovery of the Source of the Nile*, Edinburgh and London, 1864, 344, for the relationship between the 'excessive bounty' of nature and the 'dreadful sloth' of man.
[27] Shaw to Thompson, July 10, 1890, L.M.S.T.
[28] *Tanganyika*, 164–5.
[29] G. Myrdal, *Value in Social Theory, A Selection of Essays on Methodology*, ed. P. Streeter, London, 1958, 60.
[30] *Life*, 95–9, 129.
[31] *Tropical Africa*, 56, 59, 63–5.
[32] *Nyassa*, 59.
[33] *Albert Nyanza*, xxiii.
[34] Young, *Nyassa*, 48–9 for an example.
[35] Gann, *Birth of a Plural Society*, foreword by Gluckman, ix.
[36] See chap. vii, 'Mind', by M. Fortes in E. E. Evans-Pritchard *et al.*, *The Institutions of Primitive Society*, Oxford, 1954, esp. 85–6. See also E. E. Evans-Pritchard, *The Nuer*, Oxford, 1940, chap. iii, for a fascinating discussion of Nuer attitudes to time and space, and A. I. Hallowell, 'Temporal Orientation in Western Civilization and in a Pre-Literate Society', *American Anthropologist*, 1937.
[37] *The Shire Highlands (East Central Africa) as Colony and Mission*, Edinburgh and London, 1885, 171–2.
[38] A minor but revealing difficulty faced by the trader reflected the absence of a clock-conscious approach to the passing of time in African cultures. Time, pointed out Macdonald, 'is of no value to the native, and he demands for his goods the same price in the interior that he would get at the coast'. *Africana*, II, 144. For an illustration see Young, *Nyassa*, 156–7. Livingstone found it difficult to explain the cost implications of distance to the Makololo who were convinced that the cheapness of prices on the coast meant that they had been cheated in the interior. *Missionary Travels*, 373.
[39] The Earl of Cromer, *Modern Egypt*, 2 vols., London, 1908, II, 146–8. This

NOTES: CHAPTER III

whole passage, too long to quote here, is an excellent example of a sophisticated British attitude to the difference in mental processes between the British and the Egyptians.

[40] Pruen, *Arab and African*, 103.

[41] For an exception see Thomson's comments on the accurate knowledge of geography acquired by the Masai as a result of their nomadic habits, knowledge which they freely imparted. *Through Masai Land*, 337.

[42] J. MacConnachie, *An Artisan Missionary on the Zambesi—Being the Life Story of William Thomson Waddell*, Edinburgh and London, n.d., 88.

[43] *Travel and Adventure*, 411.

[44] *The Gospel and the African*, Edinburgh, 1932, 35.

[45] *Narrative of Zambesi Expedition*, 309.

[46] New, *Life*, 162. He added that 'by dint of questioning and cross questioning, however, you may, in the end, get at the truth'.

[47] E. R. Leach, 'Aesthetics', chap. iii of Evans-Pritchard *et al.*, *Institutions of Primitive Society*, 29. See also G. Lienhardt, 'Modes of Thought', chap. viii, 104-6. W. P. Johnson noted that much cultural misunderstanding sprang from the African tendency to use parables and allegories which Europeans took seriously. It was also difficult to get Africans to believe things literally, 'for allegory with them is not strictly divided from reality'. *Nyasa, The Great Water*, London, 1922, 132-3. This is probably the explanation for an incident in which Charles New, after giving a sermon which had been listened to with rapt attention, was complimented by being called a liar. 'He does not mean to call you a liar offensively; at any rate, the expression has not the same force in Kinika that it has in English: nevertheless it is most humiliating, and not a little disheartening, to an anxious missionary to meet with such a response at the close of an earnest address.' *Life*, 148. Similar instances were cited by Macdonald in *Africana*, I, 185, 263.

[48] Sultan Seyyid Said of Zanzibar, commented Burton, did not want the tides to be measured, refused to allow a census to be taken, and knew neither the population of Zanzibar nor of his own household. *Zanzibar*, I, 306, 312.

[49] Stewart, *Zambesi Journal*, 102, 112, 251.

[50] Wells, *Stewart of Lovedale: The Life of James Stewart*, 3rd ed., London, 1909, 211.

[51] Stewart, 'City of Mozambique', *Cape and Its People*, ed. P. Noble, Cape Town, 1869, 114.

[52] Stewart, *Zambesi Journal*, 189.

[53] Wells, *Stewart of Lovedale*, 207, 209; Stewart, *Dawn in the Dark Continent*, 52.

[54] Stewart, *Zambesi Journal*, 113, 258, 104. In later years Stewart wrote: 'The gospel of work does not save souls, but it saves peoples. It is not a Christian maxim only, that they who do not work should not eat; it is also in the end a law of nature and of nations. Lazy races die or decay. Races that work prosper on the earth. The British race, in all its greatest branches, is noted for its restless activity. Its life motto is WORK! WORK! WORK! And its deepest contempt is reserved for those who will not thus exert themselves.' Wells, *Stewart of Lovedale*, 216-17.

[55] J. H. Speke, *Journal of the Discovery of the Source of the Nile*, London, n.d., 18.

[56] *The Times*, Jan. 20, 1874, the account of a banquet given by the Mayor and Town Council of Brighton in Baker's honour.

[57] *Central Africa Mission, Report of Anniversary Service Meeting, 1882*, Westminster, n.d., 20. Bishop Steere painted an equally gloomy picture for an Oxford

NOTES: CHAPTER III

audience. E. Steere, *The Universities' Mission to Central Africa, A Speech Delivered at Oxford*, London, 1875.

⁵⁸ *Narrative of Zambesi Expedition*, 199. See also *Missionary Travels*, 553–4.

⁵⁹ Fraser, *Winning a Primitive People*, London, 1914, 28; R. Laws, *Reminiscences of Livingstonia*, Edinburgh, 1934, 82–3; Thomson, *To the Central African Lakes*, I, 188, 231–4, 317–19.

⁶⁰ *Government and Politics in Tribal Societies*, London, 1956, 202. He points out that the personal rather than bureaucratic nature of tribal leadership facilitated breakaway movements. 209. Gluckman argues that political instability was partially due to a lack of economic differentiation in internal economic relations which, by rendering minimal explicit relations of interdependence between various sections of the tribe, minimized ties of tangible interest holding the tribe together. 'Social Anthropology in Central Africa', *Rhodes-Livingstone Journal*, XX, 1956.

⁶¹ Evans-Pritchard has pointed out that among the Nuer it is probable that the 'distance between the beginning of the world and the present day remains unalterable'. The tree under which mankind came into being was still standing in Nuer land a few years before his visit. *The Nuer*, 108. See also G. and M. Wilson, *The Analysis of Social Change*, Cambridge, 1945, 27–8, 32–41, for the shallowness of African historical time.

⁶² After their return from Luanda, Livingstone's Makololo stated 'we are the true ancients who can tell wonderful things'. *Missionary Travels*, 408.

⁶³ *Birth of Dilemma*, 65–6. For an illustration see Rev. F. H. Surridge, 'Matabeleland and Mashonaland', *Proc. R.C.I.*, 1890–1, 305, 314.

⁶⁴ *Medieval Rhodesia*, London, 1906, vii. He found not a 'particle of evidence' to support the theories of those who tried to limit the African contribution to these impressive constructions to a servile role under the guidance of a foreign race. 85. N. Jones, *The Guide to the Zimbabwe Ruins*, 2nd ed., rewritten by R. Summers, Bulawayo, 1959, 5, states that all of the early research workers 'accepted as an axiom that one or other of the great civilizations of the Near East was responsible for the erection of Zimbabwe'. J. T. Bent, for example, felt it 'obvious' that Zimbabwe and other ruins were not 'in any way connected with any known African race'. Mining shafts in the Hartley Hills and elsewhere, and 'the acres of alluvial turned over, point to vast enterprise incompatible with the character of the African native, and I have no hesitation in assigning this enterprise to Arabian origin'. 'The Ruins of Mashonaland and Explorations in the Country', *Proc. R.G.S.*, 1892, 288–9.

⁶⁵ *The Religion of the Africans*, London, n.d., 10, 12–13. See also Rowley, *Africa Unveiled*, 32, 42–3, and Rowley, *Story of U.M.C.A.*, 230–1.

⁶⁶ References to it are found in Mackay, *Pioneer Missionary*, 83; J. L. Krapf, *Travels, Researches, and Missionary Labours*, London, 1860, 393, and New, *Life*, 94–5, but their mention of it is exceptional rather than typical.

⁶⁷ *Evolution and Ethics and Other Essays*, New York, 1898, 83.

⁶⁸ Thomson, *To the Central African Lakes*, I, 109.

⁶⁹ D. P. Jones, 'After Livingstone', 45.

⁷⁰ *Lake Regions*, II, 324. 'The Wanyika,' he declared, 'affords a curious study of rudimental mind. A nation of semi-naturals as regards moral and intellectual matters, their ideas are all in confusion. To the incapacity of childhood they unite the hard-headedness of age, and with the germs of thought that make a Bacon or a Shakespeare they combine an utter incapability of developing them.' *Zanzibar*, II, 84.

⁷¹ *Christianity, Islam and the Negro Race*, London, 1887, 316.

⁷² *The Lowell Lectures on the Ascent of Man*, London, 1894, 178. This con-

NOTES: CHAPTER III

temporary ancestor approach to the African was further developed on pages 179–80.

[73] *Tropical Africa*, 4.

[74] *Race and History*, Paris, 1952, 13.

[75] Drummond, *Tropical Africa*, 60. See also Hore, *Tanganyika*, 163–4.

[76] R. H. Lowie, *The History of Ethnological Theory*, London, 1937, 23–4. See chap. iii, 'Biology, Pre-History, and Evolution', for a summary of the evolutionary school. For a nineteenth-century example of this 'fatal fallacy', see Tylor, *Primitive Culture*, I, 21.

[77] The tendency to place cultures on a scale of ascending achievement is effectively criticized by Levi-Strauss. He points out that all peoples are in their adulthood; that the idea of a stationary society is dangerous, for it is usually ethnocentric and depends on the observer's criteria of meaningful events; that the thesis that 'primitive' men are our contemporary ancestors is false. *Race and History*, 16–19, 24–7.

[78] 'The Development of Tropical Africa under British Auspices', *Fortnightly Review*, Nov., 1890, 705. J. E. Hine stated that when 'you get to know [Africans] they are strangely similar to us English people, and you feel there is a kinship which you do not feel with the people of the East. The character of the "inscrutable Chinese" is quite alien from the African tribes. You never feel you understand the Hindu or the Banyan in Zanzibar in the same way that you do the Swahili or the boy from the interior of the continent.' *Days Gone By*, 303.

[79] *Primitive Culture*, I, 21, 32–69; *Researches into the Early History of Mankind*, 2nd ed., London, 1870, 152–93.

[80] *Narrative of Zambesi Expedition*, 507–10; J. R. Campbell, *Livingstone*, London, 1929, 52–3.

[81] Livingstone, *Private Journals*, 156.

[82] Jones, 'After Livingstone', 55–6. John Mackenzie claimed that Bechuana customs 'carry the astonished European back through many centuries, to the time when the patriarchs lived and tended their flocks'. 'Bechuanaland, with Some Remarks on Mashonaland and Matabeleland', *S.G.M.*, June, 1887, 301.

[83] See Dollard, *Caste and Class*, 435–41, for a discussion of the child analogy as applied to the American Negro.

[84] Note the tendency to go from slum work in Britain to mission work in Africa. Heanley, *Memoir of Steere*, 31–5; Livingstone, *Laws*, 30, 34; Pruen, *Arab and African*, 158; Harford-Battersby, *Pilkington of Uganda*, 38–9. For the similarity between 'the work to be done in the darkest regions of heathendom, and the neglected districts of our own country', see Frere, *Eastern Africa*, 96.

[85] *Missionary Travels*, 298; Seaver, *Livingstone*, 297 n; Livingstone, *Narrative of Zambesi Expedition*, 180.

[86] Heanley, *Memoir of Steere*, 51.

[87] *Lake Regions*, II, 337.

[88] Macdonald, *Africana*, I, 266.

[89] *Lake Regions*, I, 147.

[90] *Kilima-Njaro Expedition*, 55–6.

[91] *Fighting Slave Hunters*, 105.

[92] *Tropical Africa*, 55.

[93] J. P. R. Wallis, ed., *The Matabele Journals of Robert Moffat, 1829–1860*, 2 vols., London, 1945, I, 29–30.

[94] *Nyasa*, 92. See chap. vi.

[95] Tylor, *Primitive Culture*, I, 31.

[96] And in the imperial period served to justify that control. See J. C. Smuts, *Africa and Some World Problems*, Oxford, 1930, 74–6.

NOTES: CHAPTER III

[97] J. Johnston, ed., *Report of the Centenary Conference on the Protestant Missions of the World . . . London, 1888*, 2 vols., London, 1889, I, 290. See also W. H. Rankine, *A Hero of the Dark Continent, Memoir of Rev. Wm. Affleck Scott*, Edinburgh and London, 1896, 233.

[98] Lugard, *East African Empire*, I, 74. For a similar comment by another soldier see G. Wolseley, 'The Negro as a Soldier', *Fortnightly Review*, Dec. 1888, 702.

[99] Hore, *To Lake Tanganyika*, 167-68. See also Wilson and Felkin, *Uganda and Egyptian Soudan*, II, 104-5, 189.

[100] *Autobiography*, 376-7.

[101] See E. E. Evans-Pritchard, 'Levy-Bruhl's Theory of Primitive Mentality', *Bulletin of the Faculty of Arts of the Egyptian University*, Vol. II, Part I, 1934 (Copy, Anthropological Library, Oxford University), for a valuable discussion of the social determination of thought patterns, and the similarity of logic involved in thought processes deriving from different cultural traditions. He gives an interesting instance of the mutual inability of Africans and missionaries to believe in the invisible beings of the other party, for 'both missionaries and Negroes alike were dominated by the collective representations of their cultures', 8. For an illustration see Baker's discussion of the after-life with an African chief. *Albert Nyanza*, 155-8.

[102] It took Rowley a long time to get used to the 'faces of women thus outraged, by this the most hideous fashion the perverted fancy of woman has ever devised'. He wrote of a 'feminine ugliness almost overpowering' as the women 'disfigured themselves so vilely'. *Story of U.M.C.A.*, 20-1, 72.

[103] Faulkner, *Elephant Haunts*, 202-3.

[104] In the racist lecture 'On the Negro's Place in Nature', *Memoirs Read Before the Anthropological Society of London, 1863-4*, 31, James Hunt, after a vehement attack on Negro capacity, stated that 'the European, for ever restless, has migrated to all parts of the world, and traces of him are to be found in every quarter of the globe. Everywhere we see the European as the conqueror and the dominant race, and no amount of education will ever alter the decrees of Nature's laws.'

[105] *What Led to the Discovery of the Source of the Nile*, 349-50.

[106] See Fripp and Hiller, eds., *Gold and the Gospel*, 84, for an example.

[107] Condemnation was global, and did not stop at 'primitive' religions. At the *Centenary Conference on Protestant Missions, 1888*, Hinduism, Buddhism, and Islam were attacked in a polemical fashion, critically discussed, and then dismissed to await their inevitable overthrow. Hinduism was labelled the 'masterpiece of human error . . . [which] illustrates in the very highest degree the exhaustive effort of human philosophy to find out God, and at the same time the most successful of all Satan's devices to obscure the knowledge of God with innumerable lies'. Islam and its founder were treated in contemptuous fashion with special attention directed to treatment of women, the immoral and cruel life of Mohammed, and its tendency to depopulation. Buddhism was treated in a more scholarly manner by Sir Monier Monier-Williams of Oxford University, but even to ask 'rational and thoughtful men in the nineteenth century' whether Christ or Buddha should be followed seemed a 'mere mockery'. I, 50, 17-20, 33-40.

[108] *Conference on Missions Held in 1860 at Liverpool*, rev., London, 1860 (ed. by the Secretaries), 54-5.

[109] See, for example, the statements of H. Grattan Guinness, quoted in *Proceedings of the Conference on Foreign Missions . . . 1886*, London, 1886, 136, and the comments in the *L.M.S. Chronicle*, June, 1876, 138, 142, on the inauguration of the Lake Tanganyika mission project.

NOTES: CHAPTER III

[110] E. C. Dewick, *The Christian Attitude to Other Religions*, New York, 1953, 183.

[111] *Prevailing Methods of Evangelization*, 146. F. C. C. Egerton, *Angola in Perspective*, London, 1957, 12-13, describes C.M.S. meetings in his youth when 'hideous little idols' were displayed to attract funds to the mission cause. Stock, *History of C.M.S.*, I, 132, mentions the practice. Cust remarked that some mission reports led the home Christian to believe that 'the non-Christian world is living in the practice of shameless and abominable sins'. He bitterly satirized the folly of the 'raving' of young men or women 'ignorant of the sins of Christian Europe' who publicized non-Christian sins in a fashion 'shocking to read'. The reports from Africa led him to believe that some of the missionaries 'loathe and hate the Natives'. He claimed if one wanted to know what was really happening it would never be gained 'from the one-sided Reports, and Publications, of different Societies, and the authors of some of the volumes on the general subject are so sanguine, so full of worship of their particular Missionary-hero, they burn so much incense to their own Society, they are so unwilling, or fearful, to state the failures, the difficulties, the gross errors, that they are like the prophets who deceived the Kings of Israel and Judah.' *Prevailing Methods of Evangelization*, 100, 103, 233, 2, 7.

[112] A comparison of Wells, *Stewart of Lovedale*, chaps, vii, viii, ix, with Stewart's *Zambesi Journal* makes it difficult to believe that both deal with the same man. Unfavourable facets of Stewart's character, in marked evidence in his journals to which Wells clearly had access, are completely ignored in this eulogistic biography. In addition to hero worshipping, Wells refers in an exceptionally derogatory fashion to Africans throughout the book. See 158-60, 162, 212, 217, 218, 363.

[113] Wallis, ed., *The Matabele Mission*, 151.

[114] See Heanley, *Memoir of Steere*, 206, 384, for relevant comments.

[115] The use of military metaphors in missionary writing is indicative of this attitude. S. Wright, 'Boring In, or, Pioneering on Lake Tanganyika,' t/s, 3, L.M.S.T., provides several examples. Dewick discusses the militant missionary attitude to other religions, and some of the main alternatives. He reminds us that a militant attitude is present in many missionary hymns. *The Christian Attitude to Other Religions*, 40-55.

[116] F. S. Arnot, *Garenganze*, London, n.d., 5; MacConnachie, *Life of Waddell*, 77.

[117] Dewick, *The Christian Attitude to Other Religions*, 186-7.

[118] Bishop Steere of the U.M.C.A., a man of rare gifts and ability, spent nearly two decades of his life in mission work. Yet he never had any natural liking for Africans as he found their weakness and 'shiftiness' galling to his strong and inflexible will. Heanley, *Memoir of Steere*, 291. Mackay, the strongest personality in the early C.M.S. mission to Buganda, forced himself to overcome an 'almost uncontrollable aversion to black people . . . [by a] childlike sense of duty'. Mackay, *Pioneer Missionary*, 315. Compare Orwell's illuminating comments on the attitude of the middle class socialist intellectual to the proletariat. *The Road to Wigan Pier*, London 1937, 168, 193, 194, 197.

[119] Whatever Europeans have done in Africa, remarked Joseph Thomson, 'has been at the dictates of civilization and for the good of the negro, while, as if not content with that, more than one leader of African enterprise, on looking back over his blood and ruin marked path, has seen the evidence of a guidance and support more than human'. 'Results of European Intercourse with the African', *Contemporary Review*, March, 1890, 340.

NOTES: CHAPTER IV

IV: THE NOBLE SAVAGE

1 *Albert Nyanza*, 158.
2 H. H. Johnston, *The Uganda Protectorate*, 2 vols., London, 1902, II, 675.
3 Johnston, *Reality versus Romance*, 210-11.
4 Johnston, *Uganda*, II, 697. Livingstone commented that among the Bechuana 'the human mind has remained as stagnant to the present day, in reference to the physical operations of the universe, as it once did in England. No science has been developed, and few questions are ever discussed except those which have an intimate connection with the wants of the stomach.' *Missionary Travels*, 123-4.
5 M. A. Pringle, *A Journey in East Africa towards the Mountains of the Moon*, new ed., Edinburgh and London, 1886, 287.
6 *Africana*, I, 39.
7 *Africana*, I, 41-2.
8 *Far Interior*, I, 249-53.
9 'East Africa as it Was and Is', *Contemporary Review*, Jan., 1889; 'The Results of European Intercourse with the African', *Contemporary Review*, March, 1890; 'Note on the African Tribes of the British Empire', *J.R.A.I.*, 1886.
10 *To the Central African Lakes*, I, 226-75.
11 *Adventures in Nyassaland*, London, 1891, 32.
12 *A Lady's Letters from Central Africa*, Glasgow, 1891, 77, 85.
13 Mathews to Smith, May 25, 1885, encl. in Smith to Granville, June 10, 1885, E 84, Z.A.
14 *Through Masai Land*, 113-18.
15 *Kilima-Njaro Expedition*, 74, 432. Also H. H. Johnston, 'The People of Eastern Equatorial Africa', *J.R.A.I.*, 1885, 8-10.
16 *Scouting for Stanley in East Africa*, London, n.d., 52. See the favourable description of both country and people in *C.M.I.*, July, 1885, with the qualification that 'the good qualities of this pleasing people are, however, darkened by gross superstition and terrible conjugal laxity, the lassitude of the climate inducing the corruption of their morals', 513. For additional favourable attitudes see Willoughby, *Big Game*, 81, 86; Harford-Battersby, *Pilkington of Uganda*, 74, 76.
17 Stevens, *Scouting for Stanley*, 51-2, stated: 'with all due respect and reverence for the aims and objects of these reverend gentlemen [the missionaries] in carrying the good tidings of peace and good will to the savages of Africa, one cannot help thinking that to "enlighten" the Wa-Taveta would spoil them.'
18 'The End of the Slave Trade in British Central Africa: 1889-1912', *Rhodes-Livingstone Journal*, XVI, 1954.
19 *Through Masai Land*, 160, 272, 301, 338.
20 'Uganda', *Proc. R.C.I.*, 1893-4, 110.
21 Livingstone, *Laws*, 121. Anthropologists have been similarly attracted by the Ngoni. See J. A. Barnes' review of M. Read, *The Ngoni of Nyasaland*, London, 1956, in *Rhodes-Livingstone Journal*, XXIII, June, 1958, 68-70.
22 *Story of U.M.C.A.*, 60. See also Rowley, *Africa Unveiled*, 50-1.
23 *Zambesi Journal*, 39, 38.
24 Pringle, *Journey in East Africa*, 76.
25 Krapf, *Travels*, 74.
26 Wallis, ed., *Livingstone's Zambesi Expedition*, II, 353.
27 E. S. Wakefield, *Thomas Wakefield, Missionary and Geographical Pioneer in East Equatorial Africa*, London, 1904, 165-9.
28 *Story of U.M.C.A.*, 170, 201, 318.
29 Mason, *Birth of Dilemma*, 148.
30 Fripp and Hiller, eds., *Gold and the Gospel*, 137-8, 66 n.

NOTES: CHAPTER IV

[31] Mandy, *Matabeleland*, 35.
[32] Selous, *A Hunter's Wanderings*, 66.
[33] *Memories of Mashonaland*, 70.
[34] *The Making of Rhodesia*, London, 1926, 281–2, and *Old Rhodesian Days*, London, 1928, 32, 49–50, 106–7. G. E. Finlason, *A Nobody in Mashonaland*, London, 1894, 104, 110–12, 189, 191, displays a contemptuous attitude to the Mashona. Leask, *Diaries*, 82, indicates that many of the early hunters had a similar attitude to this most 'lazy useless set of Kaffirs ever they saw. . . .'
[35] Hole, *Old Rhodesian Days*, 17. See also C. W. H. Donovan, *With the Victoria Column in Matabeleland*, Aldershot, 1894, 5.
[36] F. R. de Bertodano, Marques del Moral, Diary, June 21, 1896, Marques del Moral Papers. On June 18, 1896, when he first heard of the Mashona rising, he wrote: 'no one has much use for Mashonas who are a dirty crowd.' The Brazilian tendency to consider the Amerindian superior to the Negro provides an interesting parallel. It is based, according to G. Freyre, on the legend of Amerindian 'independence', 'bravery', and 'nobility', due to the vigour of their struggle against the Portuguese and to the fact that they made bad slaves for the first sugar-cane plantations. *Brazil—an Interpretation*, 117.
[37] Major A. St. H. Gibbons, who visited Barotseland in the mid-nineties, before the Chartered Company had effectively established itself, was especially impressed. 'Few tribes in Africa have had less intercourse with white men than the inhabitants of Marotseland, and yet they possess an unwritten constitution, a system of government, and a society with its classes and masses—a king, royal family, and various popular grades.' Significantly, he advocated a system of indirect rule which would take account of the sensitivities of the people and utilize their governmental framework, for 'if the king co-operates with the Company's administrator, the native population is in absolute control'. 'Marotseland and the Tribes of the Upper Zambesi', *Proc. R.C.I.*, 1897–8, 268–9. See also A. St. H. Gibbons, *Exploration and Hunting in Central Africa*, London, 1898, 95.
Praise of the Barotse was offset by the fact that the country was in a state of insecurity for almost a quarter of a century after the overthrow of the Makololo in 1864. Sepopo, who ruled for over a decade before he was assassinated, appears to have been a particularly cruel and vindictive tyrant. E. Holub, *Seven Years in South Africa*, trans. E. E. Frower, 2 vols., London, 1881, II, 226–7, 240–1.
The internecine fighting which raged during the civil wars before the successful seizure of power by Lewanika, was waged with a ferocity shocking even to whites reasonably acquainted with African conditions. Partly for this reason, and partly because the chief informant on Barotse life was an unbending French Protestant, François Coillard, the general picture of the Barotse in this period is not flattering.
[38] Their handicrafts received particularly high praise. Gibbons, *Exploration and Hunting*, 134; MacConnachie, *Life of Waddell*, 94; Johnston, *Reality versus Romance*, 142.
[39] Wilson and Felkin, *Uganda and Egyptian Soudan*, I, 198; II, 4.
[40] Wilson and Felkin, *Uganda and Egyptian Soudan*, II, 7.
[41] Mackay, *Pioneer Missionary*, 106.
[42] Wilson and Felkin, *Uganda and Egyptian Soudan*, I, 146–7.
[43] Johnston, *Uganda*, II, 646.
[44] *Two Kings*, 57.
[45] Felkin, 'Uganda', *S.G.M.*, April, 1886, 214.
[46] Livingstone portrayed him as a wise, kind, and powerful martial leader who led his men into battle and dealt summarily with cowardice. The story of his life and conquests reminded Livingstone of the Commentaries of Caesar, and of

NOTES: CHAPTER IV

the history of the British in India. When he died Livingstone wrote: 'I never felt so much grieved by the loss of a black man before.' *Missionary Travels*, 86, 90.

⁴⁷ Myth, inasmuch as many other whites were far less enamoured of the Makololo than Livingstone. Sekeletu, cheered in London at a farewell R.G.S. meeting for Livingstone (*Proc. R.G.S.*, 1857–8, 125), cheated traders mercilessly in Africa and used threats to extort more goods from them. After 1853 few whites visited the Makololo, and those that did went away in disgust and never returned. See Tabler, *Far Interior*, 176, for Sekeletu's unfriendliness to whites. Note also the especially brutal Makolo treatment, under Sekeletu, of the L.M.S. mission party, described in R. Moffat to J. S. Moffat, Jan. 8, 1861, cont. Jan. 26, 1861, and Price to J. S. Moffat, April 22, 1861, in Wallis, ed., *The Matabele Mission*, 125–27, 142–46. See also Price to Tidman, Feb. 20, 1861, Helmore Papers. It has been suggestively argued by Gluckman that the special Makololo treatment of Livingstone was related to their foreign policy. 'As Men are Everywhere Else', *Rhodes-Livingstone Journal*, XX, 1956, 69–70.

⁴⁸ A. Hetherwick, *The Romance of Blantyre*, London, 1931, 70–1.

⁴⁹ *Amongst the Wild Ngoni*, Edinburgh and London, 1899, 106–7, 118. The reference to Burton is from *The Lands of Cazembe, Lacerda's Journey to Cazembe in 1798*, trans. R. F. Burton, London, 1873, 5, where he states that 'the subjects of the African despot are a distinct improvement upon the lawless republican neighbours of civilization, and one chief after another proves himself something very like a friend'. For other favourable comments on the relation of despotism to civil order see Arnot, *Garenganze*, 193, 229, and Hawes to Rosebery, July 7, 1886, F.O. 84/1751. Johnston, *Uganda*, II, 685, asserted that 'the cruelty of despots always seems to engender politeness. The freest nations are generally the rudest in manners.'

⁵⁰ *Travels*, 370, 385, 275, 376.

⁵¹ *C.M.I.*, Jan., 1850, 203. 'What a difference there is,' he added, 'between the social order and kingly power of Usambara, and the confusion of the Wanika and their mightless chiefs.'

⁵² Price to J. S. Moffat, Oct. 4, 1876, J. S. Moffat Papers.

⁵³ *C.M.I.*, July 1885, 515. See also Thomas to Mullens, Aug. 26, 1867, *L.M.S. —Papers Respecting the Matabele Mission, South Africa*, London, 1873 (Printed for the Directors only), 179.

⁵⁴ *Life and Letters*, 190.

⁵⁵ This preference for independent martial races crops up again and again. *Conference on Missions, 1860*, 185–6, for the tribes around Peshawar in British India; *Conference on Missions, 1886*, 150, for the New Zealand Maori; Earl of Cromer, *Modern Egypt*, II, 173, for the 'Turco-Egyptian . . . a race which but yesterday was imperial'; Zimmern, *Third British Empire*, 83, for ' "the Turk . . . a gentleman" . . . [whose] indifference to the prestige of "British character" . . . [appealed] to the English preference for upstanding impassivity over subservient admiration.'

⁵⁶ G. Shepperson and T. Price, *Independent African*, Edinburgh, 1958.

⁵⁷ *Notes on South African Hunting and Notes on a Ride to the Victoria Falls of the Zambesi*, London, 1887, 24–6.

⁵⁸ *Notes on South African Hunting*, 27.

⁵⁹ Mirambo was a 'brave and liberal man without any of the superstitions of the African'. Rev. J. P. Farler in *The Times*, Aug. 9, 1878. Mtesa was 'too shrewd and intelligent to believe in many of the grosser superstitions which find credit among his people'. Wilson and Felkin, *Uganda and Egyptian Soudan*, I, 199. In like fashion Lobengula was reported to have only a politic rather than a personal belief in Matabele 'superstitions'. Cockin to Mullens, May, 1879, L.M.S.M. In

NOTES: CHAPTER V

each case intelligence is equated with a capacity to regard important aspects of tribal belief and customs in the manner of the European, namely as superstitions supported only by ignorance.

[60] While in this section attention will be directed to chiefs who favourably impressed Britons, other chiefs, such as Sekeletu, Sepopo, Mwanga, and Chikusi (Makololo chief on the lower Shire), were almost unanimously detested.

[61] One missionary told the chief that whenever he did wrong he must tell Christ about it, and 'put everything on him that he would bear our sins for us'. Lobengula replied: 'it was a good religion of the white man's' and indicated what he had often noticed, 'that whenever they did anything wrong, they always wanted to throw the blame on to others'. Wilson Supplementary Diary Notes, 28, Wilson Papers.

[62] Elliott, *Gold from the Quartz*, 116.

[63] Wilson Diary, Nov. 4, 1893, Wilson Papers.

[64] Wilson, Supplementary Diary Notes, 11, Wilson Papers. Fry, 'Reminiscences', 72; P. D. Crewe, 'Reminiscences of Life in Natal, the Transvaal and Rhodesia', 12; and M. Wilson, 'Lobengula as I Knew Him', 4–5, Wilson Papers, refute the allegation that Lobengula was cruel.

[65] *The Times*, Aug. 9, 1878.

[66] *Through the Dark Continent*, 314. Ashe, *Two Kings*, 25–6, believed that Mirambo was superior to Mtesa of Buganda.

[67] Southon to Whitehouse, Dec. 2, 1879, L.M.S.T.

[68] Manuscript History of Unyamwesi, enclosed in Southon to Whitehouse, March 28, 1880, L.M.S.T.

[69] Hutley to Thompson, Dec. 23, 1881, L.M.S.T. Williams to Whitehouse, Dec. 27, 1880, L.M.S.T.

[70] *To the Central African Lakes*, I, 168.

[71] *Narrative of Zambesi Expedition*, 558.

V: THE IMPOSSIBILITY OF CULTURAL RELATIVISM

[1] Macdonald, *Africana*, II, 24.

[2] Chadwick, *Mackenzie's Grave*, gives an excellent account of the impact of war and the slave trade south of Lake Nyasa in the early sixties.

[3] *African Reminiscences*, 163.

[4] *Wild Ngoni*, 79.

[5] A. Carson, 'Journey from Quillimane to Niamkolo, Mar. 28–July 4, 1886', 70, L.M.S.T. H. Von Wissman, *My Second Journey Through Equatorial Africa*, trans. M. J. A. Bergmann, London, 1891, 272, noted that among the Bemba 'there exists a perfectly developed rank, determined by the number of heads of the enemies they have killed . . . we often saw human skeletons, but never skulls'.

[6] Kirk to F.O., Dec. 22, 1884, E 83, Z.A.

[7] Kirk to F.O., Jan. 16, 1885, E 89, Z.A.

[8] 'This is only one of the many such tales they told me.' Wilson Diary, May 1, 1889, Wilson Papers.

[9] Wilson Diary, entry date unclear, between Nov. 17 and Nov. 26, 1889, Wilson Papers.

[10] Coillard, *On the Threshold*, 527.

[11] Waddell Diary, Aug. 26, 1888, Waddell Papers, and Coillard, *On the Threshold*, 471–2, for the Barotse. Pearson of the C.M.S. has left a description of captive women from a war with Busoga arriving for Mtesa. 'I saw the remains of the King's share of women going to the palace—over three hundred wretched creatures in a half dying state. . . . It is stated that one thousand captives died

NOTES: CHAPTER V

on the way here. I never saw such a sight in my life as these women for the king.... All the best of the women were taken by the chiefs; the number must have been very great. The Arabs are in full feather and great slave buying is going on.' Pearson to Mackay, July 29, 1880, encl. in Mackay to Kirk, Nov. 1, 1880, Q 25, Z.A. See also Ashe, *Two Kings*, 91–2, 122–4, for a description of Mtesa's raids.

[12] Westbeech to Fairbairn, May 9, 1886, Hole Papers.
[13] Chadwick, *Mackenzie's Grave*, 48, 88.
[14] Mackay, *Pioneer Missionary*, 198–9.
[15] Baker, *Life of Arnot*, 66–7.
[16] *Religion of the Africans*, 144.
[17] *Journals and Papers*, 111–20. Rowley, who witnessed witchfinders in action, 'found it difficult to get over the impression that the rod-holders were for the time being under supernatural influence'. *Religion of the Africans*, 133–5. A graphic description of female witchdoctors and their ecstatic visions and activities is given in Macdonald, *Africana*, I, 207–11.
[18] Gann, *Birth of a Plural Society*, 97–8; G. and M. Wilson, *Analysis of Social Change*, 144; M. Wilson, *Good Company*, London, 1951, 100. *Africa*, Oct., 1935, contains an excellent series of articles on witchcraft. M. Gluckman, *Custom and Conflict in Africa*, Oxford, 1955, chap. vi, 'The Logic in Witchcraft', is a valuable recent discussion.
[19] Marques del Moral Diary, May 27, 1896, with note [c. 1949], Marques del Moral Papers.
[20] 'After Livingstone', 20.
[21] Chadwick, *Mackenzie's Grave*, 178. See also Rowley, *Story of U.M.C.A.*, 380–81. 'Even Englishmen' became accustomed to the slave trade and slavery, sadly reflected the missionary Charles New. *Life*, 40.
[22] Colenbrander to Harris, Mar. 24, 1890, Colenbrander Papers.
[23] Fry, 'Reminiscences', 72–3.
[24] Wilson Diary, Nov. 27, 1890, Wilson Papers.
[25] Kerr, *Far Interior*, I, 119.
[26] *Congo Cannibals*, 262.
[27] Fripp and Hiller, eds., *Gold and the Gospel*, 124.
[28] 'Commonly identified as the OviMbundu of Central Angola, though Dr. J. Tucker says that correctly the name refers to "individuals, either slaves or descendants of slaves, who acted as agents for white traders" (*Africa*, Vol. 26, 1956, 187),' cited by Schapera in Livingstone, *Private Journals*, 37 n.
[29] Livingstone, *Missionary Travels*, 91–92; Livingstone, *Private Journals*, 39, 42–3, 126, 178–9, 205, 232–3, 277. This trade had been regularly carried on since the late thirties. E. Colson and M. Gluckman, eds., *Seven Tribes of British Central Africa*, London, 1951, 5.
[30] *Eastern Africa*, 120–1.
[31] The opinion of Coupland, *East Africa and its Invaders*, 70.
[32] *Narrative of Zambesi Expedition*, 448–9.
[33] L. McLeod, *Travels in Eastern Africa*, 2 vols., London, 1860, I, 301. McLeod arrived early in 1857 and left in May 1858 after arousing Portuguese hostility by his overt hatred of the slave trade. For a brief description of his career see Hanna, *Beginnings of Nyasaland*, 51–2. Rowley, *Story of U.M.C.A.*, 49, also noted the connection between low pay and slave trade activities.
[34] M. V. Jackson, *European Powers and South-East Africa*, London, 1942, 35.
[35] Devereux, *Cruise*, 66, 74, 162.
[36] *Narrative of Zambesi Expedition*, 48, 50. See also Rowley, *Story of U.M.C.A.*, 51; W. M. Kerr, 'The Upper Zambesi Zone', *S.G.M.*, July 1886, 396. Instances

NOTES: CHAPTER V

of Portuguese brutality are cited in Rowley, *Africa Unveiled*, 186-8. For an excellent description of the Portuguese *prazo* system see J. Duffy, *Portuguese Africa*, Cambridge, Mass., 1959, 82-8.

[37] For his favourable impression of mixed marriages on the west coast see *Missionary Travels*, 371-2, and Chamberlin, *Letters from Livingstone*, 234. For his comments on the east coast see *Missionary Travels*, 663.

[38] Wallis, ed., *Livingstone's Zambesi Expedition*, I, 146; also Livingstone to Stewart, Jan. 26, 1860, in Stewart, *Zambesi Journal*, 207.

[39] For reference to syphilis see C. Livingstone to Fitch, Nov. 4, 1862, cont. Nov. 19, 1862, C. Livingstone Papers; R. Coupland, *Kirk on the Zambesi*, Oxford, 1928, 162. After noting that the Governor of Quilimane gave syphilis to his English wife, which blinded her, and then married again, Livingstone commented: 'This case shews one of the benefits English girls derive from foreign marriages.' Wallis, ed., *Livingstone's Zambesi Expedition*, I, 140. Rowley stated: 'The most loathsome forms of vice are common, and perpetrated almost without concealment.' *Africa Unveiled*, 186.

[40] *The Search after Livingstone*, London, 1868 (rev. H. Waller), 251.

[41] The Portuguese, stated R. C. F. Maugham, 'have always known how to deal with the negro, and want of respect on the part of the latter is scarcely ever seen ... one will never see the insolent demeanour of the black man toward the white which is such a constant and lamentable spectacle of everyday occurrence in our Colonies and Protectorates in almost all parts of Africa'. *Portuguese East Africa*, London, 1906, 302-3, quoted in Duffy, *Portuguese Africa*, 355-6 n.

[42] Livingstone, *Cambridge Lectures*, 45.

[43] Frere to Granville, May 29, 1873, F.O. 84/1391.

[44] Frere to Granville, March 12, 1873, F.O. 84/1389.

[45] For a description of two of these men, Lobo and Kanyemba, the latter with at least 10,000 armed men at his disposal, see Kerr, *Far Interior*, II, 46. Kanyemba is also described by Selous, *A Hunter's Wanderings*, 315-16. Matakenya and Kanyemba are described in Johnston to Anderson, March 23, 1893, F.O. 2/54. Kankune (or Sakakaka), a bloodthirsty half-caste monster who lived on the banks of the Revuqwe, is described by W. M. Kerr in 'The Upper Zambesi Zone', *S.G.M.*, July, 1886, 388-9.

[46] For the career of Mariano, the son of a Portuguese from Goa, and the havoc and devastation he caused with his armed slave soldiers in the neighbourhood of Sena and Mount Morumbala in the sixties, see Rowley, 'Life among the Portuguese in Eastern Africa', *Mission Life*, March 1, 1868.

[47] Thomson to Bolton, April 17, 1891, Hole Papers. See also Harry Johnston's comments on Portuguese half-caste traders south-west of Lake Nyasa, 'utterly heartless Portuguese bastards [who] burn, kill, waste, and retire with their ivory and slaves to the neighbourhood of Tete and Zumbo'. Johnston to Salisbury, July 7, 1891, F.O. 84/2114.

[48] Kerr, *Far Interior*, II, 46. See also Duffy, *Portuguese Africa*, 88-9, for the significance of this half-caste power on the Zambesi.

[49] *Missionary Travels*, 659. See also Stewart's comment on Mozambique in 'City of Mozambique', *Cape and Its People*. ed., Noble, 106; the comments of Lyons McLeod on Sofala, Mozambique, and Lourenco Marques, in *Travels*, I, 155, 222-4, 296; and Livingstone's comments on Sena and Zumbo in *Missionary Travels*, 584-7, 658, 663, and in *Narrative of Zambesi Expedition*, 204.

[50] *Narrative of Zambesi Expedition*, viii-x, 607.

[51] Coupland, *Kirk on the Zambesi*, 234.

[52] 'Zambesi Journal', t/s, Aug. 31, 1861, Stewart Papers.

[53] In 1882 Selous described the five Portuguese at Zumbo as 'mere wrecks of

NOTES: CHAPTER V

men—frail, yellow, and fever-stricken' in striking contrast to the 'robust and powerful figure of the natives'. *Travel and Adventure*, 62. Lacerda, writing of the rotting humidity of Quilimane, stated: 'In such a place everything conspires to produce in the population fevers, malaria, bilious attacks, infections, dysentery ... every sort of chronic disease coming from rottenness. ... All this contributes to another worse misfortune: the population does not increase; this year fifteen people died and three were born.' Quoted in Duffy, *Portuguese Africa*, 94.

[54] For an unusual recognition of the difficulties faced by the Portuguese see Kerr, 'Upper Zambesi Zone', *S.G.M.*, July, 1886, 401-2.

[55] *Narrative of Voyages to Explore the Shores of Africa, Arabia, and Madagascar*, 2 vols., London, 1833.

[56] See for example F. D. Lugard, 'A Glimpse of Lake Nyassa', *Blackwood's Magazine*, Jan., 1890. Poole to his brother, March 23, 1895, Poole Papers, and Alston Diary, Jan. 26, 1895, and Feb. 6, 1895, Alston Papers, contain typically sarcastic comments of two early officials in British Central Africa for the Portuguese administration and the Portuguese record.

[57] Quoted in Duffy, *Portuguese Africa*, 363 n.

[58] Frere to Granville, May 29, 1873, F.O. 84/1391. Ten years earlier Horace Waller had asserted that Portuguese claims to the interior were 'frivolous and vexatious in the extreme, as well might we claim all the interior of Africa that lies between the latitudes of Cape Town and Sierra Leone'. Waller to Bishop Gray, July 1 and 5, 1863, U.M.C.A. Papers.

[59] Hore to Whitehouse, Sept. 18, 1879, L.M.S.T.

[60] Burton, *Lake Regions*, II, 348. Livingstone also commented on Arab indifference to converting the African. *Narrative of Zambesi Expedition*, 513-15, 602-3.

[61] *Travels*, 125.

[62] Ruete, *Memoirs*, 99.

[63] Krapf, *Travels*, 428, 183.

[64] Pruen, *Arab and African*, 257-8.

[65] Kirk to Derby, Dec. 25, 1875, E 72, Z.A. This toleration did not extend to a willingness to see Moslems converted to Christianity. Steere reported that there were many people in Zanzibar who would consider it a duty to cut the throat of any converts to Christianity. One Arab who showed an interest in Christianity was imprisoned for four years by the Sultan. Heanley, *Memoir of Steere*, 310-11.

[66] Many Africans had flocked to them for protection, and 'all their power and influence must be attributed to the possession of guns and gunpowder'. *Narrative of Zambesi Expedition*, 512. By 1885 the population of Kota Kota and vicinity had reached 6,000. Goodrich to Granville, Feb. 19, 1885, F.O. 84/1702.

[67] *Lake Regions*, I, 328.

[68] S. L. Hinde, *The Fall of the Congo Arabs*, London, 1897, 184-5, 187-8, 200-1.

[69] Hutley to Directors, August, 1881, article titled 'Mohammedanism in Central Africa', L.M.S.T.

[70] V. L. Cameron, *Across Africa*, new ed., London, 1885, 285.

[71] Ruete, *Memoirs*, 7.

[72] Hamerton to Secretary to Bombay Government, July 13, 1841, Z.M.

[73] Hamerton to Secretary to Bombay Government, Jan. 2, 1842, Z.M.

[74] Frere to Granville, May 7, 1873, 'Memo Regarding Banians or Natives of India in East Africa', F.O. 84/1391. British demands that the Arabs should give up the slave trade, he asserted, must appear to the Arab in much the same light as an argument against hunting or shooting, on grounds of inhumanity, would to the average Englishman. Frere to Granville, May 7, 1873, 'Memo on the Position and Authority of the Sultan of Zanzibar', F.O. 84/1391.

NOTES: CHAPTER V

[75] See E. Glyn-Jones, 'Britain and the End of Slavery in East Africa', Thesis submitted for the degree of B.Litt. at the University of Oxford, Dec., 1956, for clear indications of the exaggerated tales of Arab cruelty and atrocities circulated by anti-slavery propagandists.

[76] *Tanganyika*, 74.

[77] J. A. Grant, *A Walk Across Africa*, Edinburgh and London, 1864, 97. W. P. Johnson stated that 'hardly a single native of Central Africa believes that we act disinterestedly in freeing men from their masters'. *Central Africa*, April 1, 1884. For offers to sell slaves to Europeans see Wood, *Through Matabeleland*, 105, 111; Stewart, 'To the Murchison Cataracts', Stewart Papers.

[78] In his widely read book *Tropical Africa* Henry Drummond claimed that it was impossible for people in England to 'understand how literally savage man is a chattel, and how much his life is spent in the mere safeguarding of his main asset, *i.e.* himself. There are actually districts in Africa where *three* natives cannot be sent on a message in case two should combine and sell the third before they return', 37. Versions of this story were widespread. See Lugard, *East African Empire*, I, 28; C. S. Gissing in discussion on G. Mackenzie, 'British East Africa', *Proc. R.C.I.*, 1890–1, 25. See A. Ambali, *Thirty Years in Nyasaland*, 2nd ed., Westminster, n.d., 16–17, for an African's description of the casualness with which he was bought and sold several times before being released by the British anti-slavery patrol and handed over to the U.M.C.A. mission.

[79] So Hore wrote to Kirk, April 15, 1879, cont. April 14 (?), 1879, Q 22, Z.A., concerning the chiefs around Ujiji.

[80] P. Broyon, 'Description of Unyamwesi, the Territory of King Mirambo, and the Best Route Thither from the East Coast', *Proc. R.G.S.*, 1877–8, 35. These same Manyuema, stimulated by the Arab example, embarked on their own career of devastation, enslaving weaker villages, and levying tribute in ivory. Perham, *Lugard—Years of Adventure*, 266–7.

[81] Rowley, *Africa Unveiled*, 184.

[82] Von Wissman, *Second Journey through Equatorial Africa*, 145.

[83] Carson to Thompson, Feb. 6, 1889, L.M.S.T.; Boustead Ridley & Co. to Thompson, Feb. 14, 1890, L.M.S.T.

[84] Kirk to F. O., May 8, 1884, E. 83, Z.A., a report on a runaway slave colony west of Lamu. 'Their history has always been the same on this coast. So far from helping the cause of freedom they invariably become kidnappers and holders of slaves themselves.' Elton reported that at Kilwa the one fixed business and idea was slave dealing. 'You free a slave and find his ambition is to join a slave caravan! You ask a free born man of the Mrima why he does not cultivate his land—his answer with a laugh is "Why should I take the trouble—I can buy [*sic*] slaves when I want money".' Elton to Prideaux, March 2, 1874, E 64, Z.A.

[85] In 1884 a famine resulted in the inhabitants of the Giriama country selling their own slaves and children for grain. The following year Kirk reported a famine in the Wazaramo country with a resultant growth in kidnapping and slave selling. In 1886 it was reported that 'in the Wazaramo country the people of one village kidnap their neighbours and fathers exchange their children for food while the population are subsisting as best they can on wild grass, seeds and roots'. Kirk to Granville, Sept. 23, 1884, E. 83, Z.A.; Kirk to F. O., April 13, 1885, E 89, Z.A.; Kirk to Granville, Oct. 24, 1886, E 83, Z.A. See also Speke, *What Led to the Discovery of the Source of the Nile*, 164, for a similar situation at Rabai thirty years earlier.

[86] Rowley, *Africa Unveiled*, 175–6.

[87] Harford-Battersby, *Pilkington of Uganda*, 134. When J. C. Willoughby proposed to purchase the freedom of his favourite gun-bearer, 'he told me he would

NOTES: CHAPTER V

prefer to remain a slave, as he would then have a home to go to when out of employment'. *East Africa and its Big Game*, London, 1889, 259. For a somewhat similar case see Stevens, *Scouting for Stanley*, 184-5.

[88] C. Livingstone to Mrs. Fitch, April 14, 1859, C. Livingstone Papers. Macdonald pointed out that a man often entered slavery voluntarily to get a wife from a master possessed of many females. *Africana*, I, 166.

[89] Glyn-Jones, 'Britain and the end of Slavery in East Africa', 80.

[90] *Last Journals*, II, 132-9.

[91] Fotheringham, *Adventures in Nyassaland*, 80-2. For a recent account see Hanna, *Beginnings of Nyasaland*, 80-2.

[92] This defence was offered to Thomas Stevens by 'an old half-caste Arab, who had passed most of his life in the interior of Africa, buying and hunting slaves'. *Scouting for Stanley*, 201.

[93] There was also the constant problem of replacement. Von Wissman reported that the life expectancy of a working slave at Ujiji was less than a year. *Second Journey Through Equatorial Africa*, 246.

[94] Kirk to F. O., Dec. 11, 1880, Q 24, Z.A. See also Kirk to Derby, Dec. 4, 1877, Q 18, Z.A., for the exchange of slaves for ivory in the interior by the Yao. C. Livingstone to Fitch, Feb. 4, 1862, C. Livingstone Papers, reported the sale of slaves for ivory in the interior by the Portuguese.

[95] Sharpe to Johnston, Dec. 17, 1892, enclosed in Johnston to Rosebery, Jan. 2, 1893, F.O. 2/54. Elsewhere Sharpe stated: 'I do not think we can ever hope, so long as Africans exist in Africa, to do away with slavery among themselves. It seems to be one of the instincts born in them: a boy's first desire is to own a slave.' 'Central African Trade and the Nyasaland Water-Way', *Blackwood's Magazine*, Feb., 1892, 323.

[96] Oliver, *Johnston*, 166-7.

[97] Hore, *Tanganyika*, 233-8.

[98] H. A. Fraser, Bishop Tozer and J. Christie, *The East African Slave Trade and the Measures proposed for its Extinction as viewed by Residents in Zanzibar*, London, 1871, *passim*. In discussing the preceding pamphlet Tozer pointed out that Arabs had a much more kindly feeling towards their slaves than Englishmen did to a free African, and sarcastically stated: 'Hence all the twaddle and jargon about "inhuman traffic" with which every official paper is bespattered, is like doctored beer, manufactured to suit the taste of the British public.' G. Ward, ed., *Letters of Bishop Tozer and His Sister*, London, 1902, 226. See also *Report from the Select Committee on Slave Trade . . . 1871*, answers to questions 158, 325, 326, 327, 569, by Vivian, Churchill, and Rigby; L. W. Hollingsworth, *Zanzibar under the Foreign Office 1890-1913*, London, 1953, 158.

[99] C. E. B. Russell, *General Rigby, Zanzibar and the Slave Trade*, London, 1935, 334; Devereux, *Cruise*, 99.

[100] Enclosure No. 4, Jan. 16, 1873, in Frere to Granville, March 26, 1873, F.O. 84/1390.

[101] Pelly to Bombay Government, Jan. 1, 1862, Z.M. Consul Playfair asserted that 'no class of the community is so happy, so free from care, and so well treated as the Mohammedan slave'. Quoted in Russell, *Rigby*, 203. See also Hamerton to Secretary to Bombay Government, Jan. 2, 1842, Z.M.

[102] *Last Journals*, I, 7.

[103] Palmerston's phrase, which General Rigby translated into Arabic and distributed among the principal Zanzibar Arabs. *Report from the Select Committee on Slave Trade . . . 1871*. Rigby's answer to question 574.

[104] *Life*, 34.

[105] Frere to Granville, May 7, 1873, 'Memorandum on the Position and

NOTES: CHAPTER VI

Authority of the Sultan of Zanzibar', F.O. 84/1391. Burton, a sympathetic observer, claimed that wealth had done much 'to degenerate the breed, climate more, and slavery most'. By the second generation, he stated, Arab indolence was endemic with all work being performed by Swahili and Africans. *Zanzibar*, I, 376.

[106] Russell, *Rigby*, 331-2, quoting Rigby's 'Report on the Zanzibar Dominions, July 1, 1860'.

[107] Pelly to Bombay Government, April 5, 1862, Z.M. See also Hamerton to Secretary to Bombay Government, July 13, 1841, Z.M.

[108] For missionary comparisons of Zanzibar with Sodom see W. S. Price, *My Third Campaign in East Africa*, London, 1890, 44; New, *Life*, 43.

[109] 'Perhaps there is no remark one has heard more often about Mohammedanism than that it was so successful because it was so sensual; but there is none more destitute of truth, as if any religion could owe its permanent success to its bad morality!' R. B. Smith, *Mohammed and Mohammedanism*, 3rd ed., rev., London, 1889, 196.

[110] Heanley, *Memoir of Steere*, 316-18.

[111] *Central Africa*, Dec., 1887.

[112] G. P. Badger, *Christianity in its Relations to Islam, a Paper Read at the Missionary Conference, Oxford, 3rd May, 1877*, London, 1877, 10.

[113] Tozer, *Letters* 86.

[114] *Cruise*, 98.

[115] Pelly to Bombay Government, Nov. 27, 1861, Z.M.

[116] Frere to Granville, May 7, 1873, 'Memorandum on the Position and Authority of the Sultan of Zanzibar', F.O. 84/1391. He went on to discuss this 'nominal sovereignty, so devoid of any fixed rule of succession, of such very recent creation, possessing so narrow a basis of territorial authority, such a hollow semblance of real power, and such limited financial resources'. See also Frere to Granville, March 10, 1873, F.O. 84/1389.

[117] Kirk to Derby, April 9, 1875, E 71, Z.A.

[118] Hollingsworth, *Zanzibar*, 60.

[119] 'The "State",' wrote a daughter of Seyyid Said, 'as it is understood by Europeans, means nothing in Zanzibar. National income and national revenue being unknown there, everything levied by way of imposts was my father's own personal property. . . . [At his death his] whole private property, then, was divided up, even the warships going to Tueni and Majid between them.' Ruete, *Memoirs*, 109.

VI: BRITISH, CHRISTIAN AND WHITE

[1] Quoted in Stanley, *How I Found Livingstone*, xvii.

[2] 'It was taken for granted that the world was marked out by Providence for exploitation by the European white man and that the principle of every man for himself and the devil take the hindmost was natural law.' W. L. Langer, *The Diplomacy of Imperialism 1890-1902*, 2 vols., New York and London, 1935, II, 797. It was in this context that the first great victory by the Japanese over the Russians in the Russo-Japanese war was described by Alfred Zimmern as 'the most important historical event which has happened, or is likely to happen, in our lifetime, the victory of a non-white people over a white people'. *Third British Empire*, 82.

[3] Cameron's *Across Africa* and Baker's *Albert Nyanza* were dedicated to Queen Victoria. Baker dedicated *Nile Tributaries* to the Prince of Wales.

[4] When he reached the lake Baker wrote: 'It is impossible to describe the triumph of that moment;—here was the reward for all our labour—for the years

NOTES: CHAPTER VI

of tenacity with which we had toiled through Africa. England had won the sources of the Nile! ... As an imperishable memorial of one loved and mourned by our gracious Queen ... I called this great lake "the Albert N'yanza".' *Albert Nyanza*, 308. Speke was more prosaic. *What Led to the Discovery of the Source of the Nile*, 307 n.

The littering of Africa with the names of British royalty did not meet with unanimous public approval. James Macqueen, fellow of the Royal Geographical Society, was disgusted 'to find the first names in Europe prostituted, and especially the name of our great and gracious Sovereign insulted and degraded, in giving names to places in this most barbarous and degraded country'. Quoted by K. Ingham in 'John Hanning Speke: A Victorian and his Inspiration', *Tanganyika Notes and Records*, Dec., 1957, 307.

[5] *To the Central African Lakes*, I, 150.

[6] Russell, *Rigby*, 224, 229.

[7] Livingstone, *Cambridge Lectures*, 166.

[8] Hird, *Stanley*, 105-6. The best account of Stanley's discovery of Livingstone and the resultant furore is given in I. Anstruther, *I Presume: Stanley's Triumph and Disaster*, London, 1956.

[9] Baker, *Albert Nyanza*, 110.

[10] Which led R. N. Cust to comment that missionaries of smaller powers could not use 'Consuls or Ships to bully' the local people, and that St. Paul had not been 'protected by the United States Man-of-War "Essex", or by Consul O'Neill in the "Ilala" '. *Notes on Missionary Subjects*, Part III, 62, 67.

[11] Livingstone, *Private Journals*, 167-8.

[12] Livingstone, *Private Journals*, 168.

[13] *Narrative of Zambesi Expedition*, 8.

[14] *Proc. R.G.S.*, 1857-8, 126.

[15] *Missionary Travels*, 679.

[16] Wallis, ed., *Livingstone's Zambesi Expedition*, II, 416, instructions to John Kirk.

[17] T. M. Thomas, L.M.S. Application form, March 18, 1858, L.M.S.M.

[18] See *Conference on Missions 1878*, 16-17, 93, 103; *Centenary of L.M.S. ... 1895*, 11; *Centenary Conference on Protestant Missions, 1888*, I, 91-110; *World Missionary Conference, 1910, Report of Commission VI, The Home Base of Missions*, Edinburgh and London, n.d., chap. xvii.

[19] Macdonald, *Africana*, II, 20.

[20] 337-8 (Wm. Monk).

[21] Seaver, *Livingstone*, 345, 364.

[22] See the speech by E. Baines, M.P., chairman of the sixty-seventh anniversary meeting of the L.M.S. *L.M.S. Chronicle*, June, 1861, 151-2.

[23] W. R. Hogg, *Ecumenical Foundations*, New York, 1952, 49. He adds that at American and British missionary conferences there was 'almost complete failure to regard Continental missions as of any consequence ... one is astonished by the provincialism which assumed that everything happening in missions was British or American in origin'.

[24] Speech by the Rev. R. Roberts, *L.M.S. Chronicle*, June, 1865, 183.

[25] Livingstone, *Cambridge Lectures*, 300. See also Rev. S. Minton in *L.M.S. Chronicle*, June, 1865, 185-6.

[26] Badger, *Christianity in its Relations to Islam*, 6. James Stewart attributed Portuguese decadence and lack of political control on the mainland to the slave trade, not for sociological, economic, or political reasons, but simply because there was 'a certain moral law ... Thou shalt not export slaves and prosper.' 'City of Mozambique', *Cape and Its People*, ed. Noble, 122-3.

NOTES: CHAPTER VI

²⁷ For the correlation of Islam with backwardness see Frere, *Eastern Africa*, 18–20, and Heanley, *Memoir of Steere*, 309–10.

²⁸ *Story of U.M.C.A.*, 379.

²⁹ Extract from the *Liverpool Daily Courier*, Nov. 3, 1868, S.P.G. Archives Vol. 14859.

³⁰ Goodwin, *Memoir of Bishop Mackenzie*, 241. See the comments of Professor Sedgwick in Livingstone, *Cambridge Lectures*, 129, 136.

³¹ *C.M.I.*, July 1849, 52. See also Stock, *History of C.M.S.*, I, 94,104, 116–17, for the relation between faith, good works, and divinely granted blessings.

³² See *C.M.I.*, Nov., 1857, 'National Sins the Sources of National Calamities', and *C.M.I.*, Dec., 1857, 'Governmental Principles Considered, More Especially with Reference to India'. See also *Conference on Missions, 1860*, 323, 337–8, 347–53, and Stock, *History of C.M.S.*, II, 228, 232–3.

³³ *Centenary Conference on Protestant Missions, 1888*, I, xvi.

³⁴ Chamberlin, *Letters from Livingstone*, 122.

³⁵ D. Williams, 'Zanzibar to Urambo, Jan. 4, 1881', t/s, 3, L.M.S.T.

³⁶ *Conference of Missions, 1878*, 27, 387.

³⁷ Mackay, *Pioneer Missionary*, iv. See also Elmslie, *Wild Ngoni*, 164. For Livingstone's similar attitude see *Cambridge Lectures*, 167, and *Private Journals*, 97–8, 132–3.

³⁸ Laws, Sermon Book, Sermon preached on Feb. 25, 1883.

³⁹ *Private Journals*, 47, 29, 166–8.

⁴⁰ Schapera points out that Livingstone was most impatient for results in his early mission work among the Bechuana, highly frustrated at their non-appearance, and unwilling to stay with a tribe which did not respond with alacrity to the gospel. Livingstone, *Family Letters*, I, 13–15.

⁴¹ Laws, Sermon Book, Sermons preached on April 29 and June 3, 1883.

⁴² Brooks to Thompson, Aug. 15, 1887, L.M.S.T.

⁴³ Harris to Thompson, March 15, 1885, L.M.S.T.

⁴⁴ *African Reminiscences*, 168.

⁴⁵ J. R. Mott, *The Evangelization of the World in this Generation*, New York, 1900, 196–97. This motto did not mean the conversion of the world.

⁴⁶ Baker, *Life of Arnot*, 169–70.

⁴⁷ Livingstone, *Last Journals*, I, 178.

⁴⁸ Seaver, *Livingstone*, 79.

⁴⁹ Livingstone, *Private Journals*, 120–1.

⁵⁰ *Private Journals*, 244. See also *Missionary Travels*, 377, where a discussion of the 'epochs of geology' which exemplified the 'mighty power of God', led to the conclusion that 'the exhibition of mercy we have in the gift of his Son, may possibly not be the only manifestation of grace which has taken place in the countless ages, during which, works of creation have been going on'. Livingstone's concept of nature as an interdependent system of beneficial interaction between all living forms and their environment was very closely related to his beliefs in the beneficial effects of trade and commerce. In both cases an invisible hand worked to maximize the common good.

⁵¹ *Reminiscences*, 5. For analogous views see D. Fraser, *The Future of Africa*, London, 1911, 4, 62; Hetherwick, *Gospel and the African*, 175.

⁵² 'African Slave Trade and Slavery', *Mission Life*, Oct. 1, 1867, 94–5.

⁵³ *Travels*, 423, 73, 523.

⁵⁴ Krapf, *Travels*, 289; New, *Life*, 197, 224–5; Blaikie, *Personal Life of Livingstone*, 112; Livingstone, *Private Journals*, 85; Livingstone, *Family Letters*, II, 186. New asserted that he was motivated to go to Africa by the providential saving of

NOTES: CHAPTER VI

his life in a terrible train crash when he was going to the Annual Assembly of the United Methodist Free Churches. *Life*, 18-19.

[55] Arnot, *Garenganze*, 84-5.

[56] *Garenganze*, 132.

[57] See also Watt, *Heart of Savagedom*, 65, 214-15, 220-1, 289, 310, for the case of another independent missionary who was delivered in wondrous fashion by a watching God from numerous perilous situations.

[58] *How I Found Livingstone*, 344-5, for an example. See also Stanley, *In Darkest Africa*, new ed., London, 1898, 1-6, for Stanley's extensive citing of divine aid on the Emin Pasha expedition.

[59] The thesis of the Rev. Monk, editor of Livingstone's *Cambridge Lectures*, 14.

[60] Cust, *Prevailing Methods of Evangelization*, 162.

[61] Livingstone, *Cambridge Lectures*, 167.

[62] This was especially true of Livingstone. He justified his actions by a variety of providential happenings indicative of divine approval. *Private Journals*, 71-2, 111, 146-7; *Missionary Travels*, 677-8.

[63] *Tropical Africa*, 105.

[64] *Tropical Africa*, 96-7, 93. Thesis and antithesis were blithely presented by Drummond in the same diary entry of Oct. 1, 1883.

[65] Sir Garnet Wolseley was reported to have told his troops before going into battle with the Ashanti that they should never forget 'that Providence has implanted in the heart of every native of Africa a superstitious awe and dread of the white man that prevents the Negro from daring to meet us face to face in combat'. Quoted in Blyden, *Christianity, Islam and Negro Race*, 21.

[66] Burton, *Life of Burton*, I, 357 n.

[67] *Through the Dark Continent*, 52. See also Speke, *What Led to the Discovery of the Source of the Nile*, 366.

[68] *Ismailia*, 261.

[69] *Search*, 167-8.

[70] *Nyassa*, 127-8, 205-6.

[71] *Search*, 195.

[72] *Across Africa*, 537-8.

[73] See, for example, the astonishment of Sykes of the L.M.S. at the loyalty of the Matabele during the interregnum between the death of Moselekatse and the accession of Lobengula. 'The loyalty of these unenlightened heathens was something more than ordinary; nay, it was nothing less than infatuation. I have never heard of such devotion to a royal family and to the will of a sovereign as the Amantebele were showing. . . .' Sykes to Mullens, Dec. 25, 1868, in Wallis, ed., *The Matabele Mission*, 248.

[74] On the other hand the Old Testament provided a certain insight into tribal conditions. Biblical comparisons were frequent and some missionaries claimed that their experience of Africa helped their understanding of conditions described in the Old Testament. Jones, 'After Livingstone', 55-6; Macdonald, *Africana*, II, 142; Livingstone, *Family Letters*, I, 42-3. This point is also made in Gann and Duignan, *White Settlers in Tropical Africa*, 12.

[75] *Eastern Africa*, 102-7.

[76] *Dawn in the Dark Continent*, 335. The lack of special missionary training in the social sciences was a recurring theme of the 1910 Edinburgh Conference. *World Missionary Conference, 1910, Report of Commission V, The Training of Teachers*, Edinburgh and London, n.d., 37, 59, 165-72.

[77] *L.M.S. Chronicle*, June, 1882, 178-9.

[78] *Wild Ngoni*, 69-70.

[79] Frere, *Eastern Africa*, 69-70, 14-16.

NOTES: CHAPTER VII

⁸⁰ Letter from C. P. Rigby in *Mission Life*, April 1, 1866.
⁸¹ *Story of U.M.C.A.*, 229.
⁸² *Nyasaland*, 224.
⁸³ Buchanan, *Shire Highlands*, 146.
⁸⁴ Smith, *Price*, 6.
⁸⁵ At the *Centenary Conference on Protestant Missions, 1888*, in the discussions dealing with missionary training there was a conspicuous lack of enthusiasm for a broad and varied academic background. The emphasis was almost entirely on biblical knowledge and spiritual zeal. Two speakers, indeed, argued that a 'prolonged course of merely literary and intellectual culture is in most cases fatal to a thoroughly spiritual and evangelistic career', II, 14, 17. Varg, *Missionaries, Chinese, and Diplomats*, 18–19, mentions an antipathy to comparative religion among American Protestant missionaries in China.
⁸⁶ For a balanced discussion see Smith, *Blessed Missionaries*, 7–10, in which, while admitting that some missionaries have been guilty of unjustly condemning African society in a wholesale fashion, he also instances a number of basic missionary contributions to anthropology.
⁸⁷ *Days Gone By*, 133.

VII: REVOLUTIONARIES BEFORE THE REVOLUTION

¹ *Narrative of Zambesi Expedition*, 181–2.
² *Far Interior*, II, 127.
³ Burton, *Lake Regions*, I, 262. For other instances of African fears, often Arab inspired, see Krapf, *Travels*, 231–2, 273, 420; G. A. Spottiswoode, ed., *The Official Report of the Missionary Conference of the Anglican Communion . . . 1894*, London, 1894, 240, speech by H. Waller; Hutley to Whitehouse, Oct. 19, 1879, L.M.S.T.; Southon to Whitehouse, May 4, 1880, L.M.S.T.; Young, *Nyassa*, 161; Livingstone, *Narrative of Zambesi Expedition*, 519. Shepperson and Price, *Independent African*, 9–11, discuss the African belief that whites were cannibals.
⁴ A classic case of cultural misunderstanding involving the throne of the Asantahene is related in E. Smith, *The Golden Stool*, London, 1926, chap. i. See also L. Levy-Bruhl, *How Natives Think*, trans. L. A. Clare, London, 1926, 71–3, for examples of some European attribute being held responsible for disaster or good fortune.
⁵ Elmslie, *Wild Ngoni*, 199–200; Livingstone, *Laws*, 200–1.
⁶ Ashe, *Two Kings*, 108–9, with illustrations. To the African, the strangeness of many European actions often seemed to have a particularly close causal relationship with the weather. Ludwig Krapf, a specialist in bizarre adventures, related how in the interior he was once nearly sacrificed when a drought was attributed to him, then 'with no less haste . . . was all but deified' when a sudden fall of rain was credited to his presence. *Travels*, 70.
⁷ Johnson, *African Reminiscences*, 169, 69–72, 152–6, 197–200.
⁸ Lewanika, the Barotse chief, would not let Arnot proceed up the Zambesi to the tribes living to the north on the grounds that they 'were the dogs of the Barotse, and missionaries would not be allowed to visit them'. Baker, *Life of Arnot*, 104. See also Coillard, *On the Threshold*, 448. For Matabele refusal to allow missionaries into Mashonaland or even to increase their numbers among the Matabele see *On the Threshold*, 36; Fripp and Hiller, eds., *Gold and the Gospel*, 17; Wallis, ed., *The Matabele Mission*, 179–81.
⁹ Laws, *Reminiscences*, 90; Livingstone, *Laws*, 230–7; Elmslie, *Wild Ngoni*, 97–8.
¹⁰ Maples, *Pioneer Missionary*, 21–2, 182–96.

NOTES: CHAPTER VII

[11] Missionaries, for example, wrote of the 'natural impulse of an Englishman' to free slaves, and declared that it was 'naturally repugnant to the heart of a Britisher's love of freedom to hand back to masters or owners who might maltreat or sell any who sought his protection'. Swann, *Fighting Slave Hunters*, 50, and Hetherwick, *Romance of Blantyre*, 27.

[12] In a letter to *The Times*, July 8, 1880, Waller emphasized the anti-slave-trade background to the first U.M.C.A. mission and to the Free Church of Scotland mission at Livingstonia. See also Waller, cited in Groves, *Planting of Christianity*, II, 195. The importance of the slave trade in attracting the L.M.S. to Lake Tanganyika is noted in Mullens to J. S. Moffat, Oct. 19, 1876, J. S. Moffat Papers. See Swann, *Fighting Slave Hunters*, 21, for this motivation in an individual missionary of the L.M.S.

[13] *Narrative of Zambesi Expedition*, 416-17.

[14] Hutchinson to Granville, Jan. 14, 1881, copy enclosed in Lister to Kirk, Feb. 8, 1881, N 24, Z.A. The missionary quoted was Menzies.

[15] *Conference on Missions, 1886*, 146.

[16] *Search*, 12.

[17] Livingstone, *Laws*, 41.

[18] Livingstone, *Laws*, 96.

[19] Young, *Nyassa*, 71; Laws, *Reminiscences*, 14; Livingstone, *Laws*, 44, 70-1, 174-5. See also Mackay's active interference with slave caravans, including the exchange of gunfire. *Pioneer Missionary*, 51-2. See also Watt, *Heart of Savagedom*, 62.

[20] *Africana*, II, 198.

[21] *Nyasa*, 130.

[22] Interview between Frere and Barghash, Jan. 27, 1873, enclosure 18 in Frere to Granville, March 26, 1873, F.O. 84/1390.

[23] Meeting between Kirk and the Sultan, enclosure 23 in Frere to Granville, March 26, 1873, F.O. 84/1390.

[24] Interview with Badger, Jan. 16, 1873, enclosure 4 in Frere to Granville, March 26, 1873, F.O. 84/1390.

[25] Frere's comments on enclosure 4, enclosure 5 in Frere to Granville, March 26, 1873, F.O. 84/1390.

[26] Goodrich to Granville, April 14, 1885, F.O. 84/1702, gives Mombera's attitude. An analogous statement from Lobengula is recorded in Fry, 'Reminiscences', 61. When the traveller W. M. Kerr asked Lobengula what he thought of the mission teaching, he replied: 'I suppose it is right, because they say so; but then they are paid for saying so.' *Far Interior*, I, 66. For Lobengula's conservative attitude to the possibilities of religious change see also Baines, *Goldfields Diaries*, II, 546-7, and Thomson to Mullens, Dec. 2, 1870, L.M.S.M.

[27] C. Maples, 'The Magwangwara Raid Upon Masasi', *Central Africa*, Feb. 1, 1883.

[28] Carnegie stated that on one occasion Lobengula almost became a Christian until he realized the conflict between the message of peace and the war oriented tribe which he ruled. *Among the Matabele*, 103-4.

[29] *Ten Years North of the Orange River*, Edinburgh, 1871, 332.

[30] Thomson to Mullens, March 25, 1873, L.M.S.M.

[31] Wallis, ed., *The Matabele Mission*, 101-2; Moffat, *J. S. Moffat*, 100-1; Arnot, *Garenganze*, 73. See also Baker, *Life of Arnot*, 102, for Lewanika's fury when Arnot told the story of Nebuchadnezzar and his downfall, and compared him to Lewanika.

[32] When T. M. Thomas stated that 'God ... made the Sun' in a sermon before Moselekatse, an excited and indignant induna shouted, 'You lie, Thomas. . . .

NOTES: CHAPTER VII

Moselekatse made the Sun!' The chief was then carried away from the mission service. Finaughty, *Recollections*, 53-4.

[33] Sykes to Tidman, Aug. 3, 1863, L.M.S.M.

[34] Christian 'converts are conscious of being members of world organizations. They contrast the range of their obligations with those of pagans, laying special emphasis on hospitality to strangers.' G. and M. Wilson, *Analysis of Social Change*, 12.

[35] *Life*, 119. Perhaps the classic denunciation was given by a missionary in Northern Rhodesia in the early imperial period. The Bantu 'are a people whose national business is polygamy, their national pastime beer-drinking, and their national sport fornication'. *World Missionary Conference, 1910, Report of Commission IV, The Missionary Message in relation to Non-Christian Religions*, Edinburgh, n.d., 15.

[36] Gann, *Birth of a Plural Society*, xi.

[37] A. R. Radcliffe-Brown and D. Forde, eds., *African Systems of Kinship and Marriage*, London, 1956, 43-6.

[38] G. and M. Wilson, *Analysis of Social Change*, 126, discuss the difficulty of combining monogamy with hospitality.

[39] Wilson and Felkin, *Uganda and Egyptian Soudan*, I, 186.

[40] *Knowing the African*, London, 1946, 93.

[41] One missionary to the Bechuana advised his church members to take by force a woman who had run away to the local initiation ceremonies. In the resultant mob riot several homes were burnt, and the incident was only quelled with difficulty by the local administrator. Moffat, *J. S. Moffat*, 211.

[42] Elmslie, *Wild Ngoni*, 43.

[43] Wilson and Felkin, *Uganda and Egyptian Soudan*, I, 187.

[44] Burton, *Lake Regions*, II, 332.

[45] See the discussion in Smith, *Price*, 276-8, of the attempt of the L.M.S. missionaries in Bechuanaland to outlaw this custom.

[46] See Rowley, *Africa Unveiled*, 166-7; Thomas, *Central South Africa*, 261; Livingstone, *Narrative of Zambesi Expedition*, 285.

[47] Radcliffe-Brown and Forde, eds., *African Systems of Kinship and Marriage*, 53.

[48] W. V. Lucas and E. O. James, *Christianity and Native Rites*, 2nd ed., London, 1950, 31. See also Smith, *Knowing the African*, 86-90.

[49] Interview with Mr. Chisykhata Mkandawiri, Sept. 23, 1959.

[50] Lucas and James, *Christianity and Native Rites*, 13.

[51] This paragraph is, unavoidably, an oversimplification of the differences between Christianity and African religious concepts. Ideally, each tribe should be studied separately.

[52] Rowley, *Religion of the Africans*, 190-1. See also Rowley, *Africa Unveiled*, 116, 143, 231.

[53] *Story of U.M.C.A.*, 225-6.

[54] *U.M.C.A. Annual Report, 1879-80*, 19.

[55] *Days Gone By*, 172-3.

[56] *Africana*, I, 272.

[57] Mackay, *Pioneer Missionary*, 220-221. A statement of Archbishop Trench is apposite: 'To have taught them to pour contempt on all, with which hitherto they have linked feelings of sacredness and awe, may prove but a questionable preparation for making them humble and reverent scholars of Christ.' Cited in Cust, *Prevailing Methods of Evangelization*, 265-6.

[58] Thomas to Directors, Oct. 10, 1860, L.M.S.M.

[59] Thomas to Directors, Oct. 10, 1860, L.M.S.M.

NOTES: CHAPTER VII

⁶⁰ See Gann, *Birth of a Plural Society*, 38, on the conflict between the individualistic concept of sin and tribal collectivism. See also Northcott, *Robert Moffat*, 241.

⁶¹ *Travels*, 158, 163, 190.

⁶² Swinny Diary, Oct. 4, 1885.

⁶³ *Wild Ngoni*, 148–9.

⁶⁴ *Wild Ngoni*, 138–40. See R. Firth, *Elements of Social Organization*, 2nd ed., London, 1956, 190-2, for the irritation of an anthropologist with the Tikopia who based friendship on material reciprocity. 'In theory,' he commented, 'I was perfectly well equipped to understand all this from the start. . . . But it is only by living through an experience personally that one comes to appreciate the issues involved. I discovered on Tikopia the reality of the cultural differences in moral standards and moral judgements on matters such as friendship and making gifts . . . it takes one some time to realize that one's own judgement is culturally dictated, not simply a free objective view.'

⁶⁵ Macdonald, *Africana*, II, 83.

⁶⁶ For Felkin and Mtesa see Wilson and Felkin, *Uganda and Egyptian Soudan*, I, 269, 271; II, 8–11. Southon, L.M.S., was accorded high status by the Wanyamwesi. He performed several operations to remove tumours from the arm of the chief, and in one year treated 1,600 patients. Southon to Directors, Sept. 8, 1879, L.M.S.T.; Southon to Whitehouse, Dec. 31, 1880, L.M.S.T.

⁶⁷ M. Gelfand, *Tropical Victory—An Account of the Influence of Medicine on the History of Southern Rhodesia, 1890-1923*, Cape Town and Johannesburg, 1953, 7. For examples of Moffat's medical work see R. Moffat, *Journals*, II, 213, 226.

⁶⁸ Young, *Nyassa*, 147. See, for example, Baker, *Albert Nyanza*, 152, 290, 350–351, 354, 367.

⁶⁹ J. C. Yarborough, ed., *The Diary of a Working Man (William Bellingham) in Central Africa, December, 1884, to October, 1887*, London, n.d., 93.

⁷⁰ Mackay, *Pioneer Missionary*, 164–5.

⁷¹ E. W. Smith, *The Life and Times of Daniel Lindley*, London, 1949, 77, cites Matebele interest in guns while they still resided in the Transvaal. By 1870 Baines could write, perhaps with some exaggeration, that 'the Matabele have elected by acclamation the musket to the dignity of the king of weapons'. *Goldfields Diaries*, II, 451.

⁷² R. Moffat to Helmore, Feb. 22, 1860, Helmore Papers.

⁷³ Sykes to Directors, Oct. 28, 1859, L.M.S.M.; Sykes to Directors, Sept. 20, 1861, cont. Dec. 11, 1861, L.M.S.M.

⁷⁴ Sykes of the L.M.S. also refused. Sykes to Tidman, July 29, 1862, L.M.S.M. The artisan missionary Waddell turned a deaf ear to a plague of Barotse requests that he mend guns. Waddell Diary, Aug. 11, 1890, Waddell Papers.

⁷⁵ Moffat to Unwin, Jan. 14, 1862, and Dec. 20, 1863, Wallis, ed., *The Matabele Mission*, 161, 228. It is doubtful if missionary gun-mending made much difference, for traders were willing to undertake the task. Mohr, *To Victoria Falls*, 245.

⁷⁶ Elton, *Travels and Researches*, 394.

⁷⁷ Rowley, *Religion of the Africans*, 170-1, 176, 180; Rowley, *Story of U.M.C.A.*, 148–50.

⁷⁸ *Through Masai Land*, 123.

⁷⁹ Waddell Diary, Oct. 2, 1892, and Nov. 14, 1892, Waddell Papers.

⁸⁰ Sykes to Tidman, Aug. 3, 1863, L.M.S.M.

⁸¹ Thomas to Tidman, July 2, 1866, *L.M.S.—Papers Respecting the Matabele Mission*, 57.

⁸² Thomas to Tidman, July 2, 1866, *L.M.S.—Papers Respecting the Matabele Mission*, 57–63.

NOTES: CHAPTER VIII

⁸³ Thomas Diary, Sept. 14, 1880, Thomas Papers.
⁸⁴ Johnson, *African Reminiscences*, 126.
⁸⁵ *Africana*, II, 82.
⁸⁶ See Mandara's attempts to get Charles New to supply him with mechanics, artisans, and European manufactures. New, *Life*, 433. He also attempted to persuade H. H. Johnston to train his soldiers and teach his workmen to 'make cannon'. *Kilima-Njaro Expedition*, 105-6. Lewanika, the Barotse chief, had similar ideas for the missionaries of the Paris Evangelical Mission. Johnston, *Reality versus Romance*, 142.
⁸⁷ Southon Diary, *passim*, L.M.S.T.
⁸⁸ D. Williams, 'Zanzibar to Urambo, June 14–Sept. 11, 1880', 3, L.M.S.T.
⁸⁹ Shaw to Thompson, July 10, 1890, L.M.S.T.
⁹⁰ Shaw to Thompson, March 9, 1885, L.M.S.T.
⁹¹ To cite only one further example, Professor M. Gluckman has elaborated a most convincing hypothesis that the special Makololo treatment of Livingstone was related to their hopes that he could be used as an agent of their foreign policy with respect to their most dangerous enemies, the Matabele. 'As Men are Everywhere Else', *The Listener*, Sept. 22, 1955.
⁹² *Dawn in the Dark Continent*, 282, 60.
⁹³ Mackay, *Pioneer Missionary*, 218.
⁹⁴ R. Moffat, *Journals*, II, 64.
⁹⁵ J. V. Taylor, *The Growth of the Church in Buganda*, London, 1958; D. A. Low, *Religion and Society in Buganda, 1875–1900*, Kampala, [1958?].
⁹⁶ See the recent book by D. E. Apter, *The Political Kingdom in Uganda*, Princeton, 1961.
⁹⁷ Arnot, *Garenganze*, 235.
⁹⁸ Casati, *Ten Years in Equatoria*, II, 62-6; Gann, *Birth of a Plural Society*, 151.
⁹⁹ F. S. Arnot, *Bihe and Garenganze*, London, n.d., 60-1.
¹⁰⁰ The number of guns in African hands is impossible to assess. The estimates of various writers, however, help to indicate the magnitude of the trade. Perham, *Lugard—Years of Adventure*, 224, indicates from 6,000 to 9,000 guns in Buganda in 1890; a somewhat smaller figure is given in Harford-Battersby, *Pilkington of Uganda*, 122; Parke, *Personal Experiences*, 226, mentions 2,000 rifles possessed by Kabba Rega, King of Bunyoro, in 1888; Tabler, *Far Interior*, 172, states that by 1875 about 2,300 guns had been distributed among the Barotse since the commencement of the trade.

VIII: HOW CAN SAVAGES BE CIVILIZED?

¹ Burton, *Life of Burton*, I, 401.
² The impact of Burton's *Lake Regions* on the formation of an exceptionally unfavourable stereotype of the African can be seen in the speech by Earl de Grey and Ripon, President of the R.G.S., *Proc. R.G.S.*, 1859-60, 176. Burton's *Wanderings in West Africa*, 2 vols., London, 1863, provided part of the ammunition used by James Hunt in his racist paper 'On the Negro's Place in Nature', *Memoirs Read before Anthropological Society of London, 1863–4*, 57-9. See Joseph Thomson's criticism of Burton and other travellers who generalized about the African's capacity after seeing him 'degraded from ages of exposure to the curse of slavery, every man fighting like a wild beast for his very existence, his hand against every man, and every man's hand against him'. *To the Central African Lakes*, I, 139–40, and 135-6, 159–60, 238.
³ *Life*, 283.

NOTES: CHAPTER VIII

[4] 'The Development of Tropical Africa under British Auspices', *Fortnightly Review*, Nov., 1890, 705.

[5] *Uganda and Egyptian Soudan*, I, 227.

[6] *Across Africa*, 207.

[7] *Missionary Travels*, 115. Compare the case of Fiji where it was 'freely assumed by planters that the Fijian people was inevitably doomed to extinction'. Legge, *Britain in Fiji: 1858–1880*, 62. See also J. Miller, *Early Victorian New Zealand, A Study of Racial Tension and Social Attitudes, 1839–1852*, London, 1958, 104, for similar beliefs about the Maori.

[8] *Proc. R.G.S.*, 1877-8, 21-2.

[9] 'The Results of European Intercourse with the African', *Contemporary Review*, March, 1890.

[10] *Missionary Travels*, 5.

[11] *Missionary Travels*, 673–4.

[12] *Missionary Travels*, 28; Blaikie, *Personal Life of Livingstone*, 184.

[13] *Missionary Travels*, 28.

[14] Coupland, *Kirk on the Zambesi*, 106–7.

[15] Livingstone, *Private Journals*, 142–3, 160.

[16] When he first noted the slave trade among the Makololo, the idea was suggested by his colleague Oswell that 'if the slave-market were supplied with articles of European manufacture by legitimate commerce, the trade in slaves would become impossible'. *Missionary Travels*, 92.

For the background to this 'positive policy' for undercutting the slave trade— 'the deliverance of Africa by calling forth her own resources' (T. F. Buxton)— see Groves, *Planting of Christianity*, II, 4–12. For a general discussion of British anti-slave-trade policies see R. Coupland, *The British Anti-Slavery Movement*, London, 1933.

[17] Chamberlin, *Letters from Livingstone*, 151–2, 155–6. Commerce was to be accompanied by 'Commissioners appointed by Government in the different sections [of] the slave producing territory'. Livingstone, *Private Journals*, 132, 44. The functions of these Commissioners were never clearly spelled out.

[18] *Narrative of Zambesi Expedition*, 128–9.

[19] Wallis, *Livingstone's Zambesi Expedition*, I, xviii.

[20] Livingstone to Mr. and Mrs. N. Livingston, July 28, 1850, *Family Letters*, II, 93.

[21] *Family Letters*, II, 114–15, 152–3, 158, in letters to his parents and his sister.

[22] *Narrative of Zambesi Expedition*, 264.

[23] Blaikie, *Personal Life of Livingstone*, 216, 221.

[24] Livingstone, *Cambridge Lectures*, 378.

[25] Blaikie, *Personal Life of Livingstone*, 221. For his praise of the civilizing effect of medieval monasteries see *Missionary Travels*, 117.

[26] Wallis, ed., *Livingstone's Zambesi Expedition*, I, 52–3.

[27] Blaikie, *Personal Life of Livingstone*, 228. See also *Narrative of Zambesi Expedition*, 199.

[28] Seaver, *Livingstone*, 444.

[29] *Cambridge Lectures*, 353, 378.

[30] Wallis, ed., *Livingstone's Zambesi Expedition*, I, 53.

[31] Wallis, ed., *Livingstone's Zambesi Expedition*, I, 136–7.

[32] *Missionary Travels*, 678.

[33] *Missionary Travels*, 108.

[34] This is especially noticeable in his economic descriptions. He claimed that the area in the Shire Valley and on the shores of Lake Nyasa was 'one of the finest cotton-fields in the world', and stated that the lands stretching from the

NOTES: CHAPTER VIII

Kongone Canal to beyond Mazaro were capable of supplying 'all Europe with sugar'. *Narrative of Zambesi Expedition*, 21, 588.

[35] J. I. Macnair, ed., *Livingstone's Travels*, London, 1954, 39.

[36] Wallis, ed., *Livingstone's Zambesi Expedition*, I, xviii.

[37] See Smith, *Knowing the African*, 14 17, for a discussion.

[38] Carson to Thompson, Jan. 12, 1888, L.M.S.T.

[39] See *L.M.S. Chronicle*, June, 1877, 142, for the comments of H. H. Fowler, Director of Wesleyan Missionary Society.

[40] See Frere's argument that there was a greater necessity for the missionary to play a civilizing role in Africa than in India, China or Japan. *Eastern Africa*, 73-4.

[41] *Life*, 90-1. For similar views by Erhardt and Rebmann, German missionaries of the C.M.S., see Krapf, *Travels*, 498, 224.

[42] *Arab and African*, 310-11.

[43] Mackay, *Pioneer Missionary*, 72.

[44] An exhaustive presentation of this aspect of the Protestant missionary thesis was given by the Rev. James S. Dennis, an American with missionary experience in Syria. In three massive volumes he argued the incapacity of any but the Christian religion to supply a sufficient motive power to elevate society in almost every conceivable aspect of social life. *Christian Missions and Social Progress, a Sociological Study of Foreign Missions*, 3 vols., New York, 1897, 1899, 1906.

[45] Significantly, a powerful indictment of this aspect of missionary belief occurred in the thirties. See H. Kraemer, *The Christian Message in a Non-Christian World*, London, 1938, especially chap. iv. 'Recommending Christianity as the bringer of enlightenment and freedom, as a capital national and social tonic to make powerful nations, as the infallible guide to progress, has come to naught. It has even proved a great danger, because it . . . offers promises which often will not be fulfilled, and therefore necessarily entails disillusionment. . . . The spell of the erroneous identification of Christianity and the progressive West is broken, and still deadlier, the prestige of Western culture has decreased enormously. To promise that Christianity will dispel economic misery and social disturbance is to invite inevitable disillusionment, because economic misery and social disturbance are caused and cured by many factors entirely outside the control of Church or missions. . . . The real motive and ultimate purpose [of missionary endeavour] are not founded in anything that men or civilizations or societies call for', 59-60.

His argument is opposed by E. C. Dewick who is unable to admit that there can be no objective verification of the superiority of Christianity. *The Christian Attitude to Other Religions*, 164, 179.

[46] Sermon Book, Sermon Preached on April 8, 1883. See H. G. Wood, *Belief and Unbelief since 1850*, Cambridge, 1955, 28-36, for the decline in the belief in eternal punishment in Britain.

[47] R. Moffat, *Journals*, I, 110-11, 119, 170.

[48] Livingstone, Moffat's son-in-law, gradually outgrew the belief that souls were actually perishing because the gospel had not reached them. Seaver, *Livingstone*, 49, 65-6, 138-9, 242, and *Missionary Travels*, 90. Maples of the U.M.C.A., although he claimed that the heathen would certainly be judged, was convinced that it would be by a different standard 'from that by which we enlightened Christians will have to take our judgement'. Maples, *Pioneer Missionary*, 136. The range of Christian theologies and divergent individual attitudes complicate general discussion on the 'hell fire' thesis. An important factor in the relative insignificance of the 'eternal damnation' approach was the absence of fundamentalist Protestant groups among the early missionaries.

[49] Speech by the Rev. G. S. Barrett, *L.M.S. Chronicle*, June, 1876, 130-1. Five

NOTES: CHAPTER VIII

years later, at another annual conference, the Rev. R. W. Dale asserted that 'It was believed by many of our fathers that these millions were drifting generation after generation, without a solitary exception to "adamantine chains and penal fires".' It must be recognized, he continued, that to large numbers of Christian people the future destiny of the heathen world was surrounded by 'grave uncertainty', and that the theory of eternal damnation had been 'by very many altogether abandoned'. *L.M.S. Chronicle*, June, 1881, 132-3. See also *Centenary of L.M.S. . . . 1895*, 201-3.

⁵⁰ See R. Rouse, 'A Study of Missionary Vocation', *The International Review of Missions*, April, 1917, for valuable material on the changed conceptual framework surrounding missionary activity.

⁵¹ *Modern Missions and Culture*, 35-6.

⁵² Middleton, *Baker*, 161, 22.

⁵³ Middleton, *Baker*, 46.

⁵⁴ Baker to Major Wingate, Aug. 20, 1892, cited in Murray and White, *Baker*, 375.

⁵⁵ *Albert Nyanza*, 41-2, 47.

⁵⁶ *Ismailia*, 479.

⁵⁷ *Albert Nyanza*, 153.

⁵⁸ *Albert Nyanza*, xxiv, xxiii.

⁵⁹ *Albert Nyanza*, 183.

⁶⁰ *Nile Tributaries*, ix-x.

⁶¹ *The Times*, Jan. 20, 1874.

⁶² *The Times*, Jan. 20, 1874. Still, he felt that civilized people might not understand his actual conduct during his gubernatorial tenure of office in Equatoria. He entreated the European members of his expedition 'not to write to our friends about the harsh measures he had used towards the natives, as he said they would possibly not understand them'. Two members of the expedition contracted not to write anything connected with the expedition to the press during their service, nor to publish any book till two years after the completion of the expedition. J. McWilliams, chief engineer on the Ismailia expedition, however, somewhat dubious about the civilizing propensity of 'superior force', professed himself willing to give testimony 'as to the barbarous manner in which the expedition was conducted, the wholesale murders, pillage, and ruin of the country'. *The Times*, Aug. 1, 1874. He amplified his views in *The Times*, Aug. 11, 1874. Middleton, *Baker*, 191-2, contains a brief discussion.

⁶³ *Albert Nyanza*, 181. Baker inclined to the belief that Africans were vestiges of what existed in a 'pre-Adamite creation', a conjecture based on the argument that 'the tribes of Central Africa know no God'. This placed them outside the main stream of humanity which 'from the creation of Adam' has everywhere believed in a deity. *Albert Nyanza*, 446-7.

⁶⁴ Murray and White, *Baker*, 150-3.

⁶⁵ *Albert Nyanza*, xxiii. His eulogy of commerce far surpassed philanthropy at 5 per cent. In a lecture at Liverpool on the economic prospects of Egypt and the Sudan, he stated: 'Legitimate trade has been introduced, and the inhabitants exchange ivory . . . for Manchester goods, hardware, beads, brass, etc. . . . leaving a *minimum* profit of 150 per cent to the Government. The foundations are laid for a great future. . . . Thus [by trade] will Central Africa receive the first seeds of civilization.' *The Times*, March 23, 1874. See also *Ismailia*, 340-1, where Baker mentions some ivory purchases at '2,000 per cent profit. . . . This was the perfection of business.'

⁶⁶ *Albert Nyanza*, xxii.

⁶⁷ *The Times*, Jan. 20, 1874.

NOTES: CHAPTER VIII

⁶⁸ *Zanzibar*, II, 101-3.

⁶⁹ *Report by Commissioner Johnston of the First Three Years' Administration of the Eastern Portion of British Central Africa*, Africa No. 6 (1894), C-7504, 31.

⁷⁰ For Johnston's views see H. H. Johnston, 'England's Work in Central Africa', *Proc. R.C.I.*, 1896-97, 57; H. H. Johnston, 'The Commercial Development of Central Africa, and Its Beneficent Results on the Slave Traffic', *Journal of the Tyneside Geographical Society*, Dec., 1894, *passim*; H. H. Johnston, 'British Central Africa', *New Review*, July, 1894, *passim*. See also Oliver, *Johnston*, 253-4, and Hanna, *Beginnings of Nyasaland*, 226-8.

Initially Johnston thought that the Arabs might perform this middleman role, but he rapidly became disillusioned and finally reached the conclusion that they were a barrier to white civilization and should be removed, to which end he bribed some of them to leave British Central Africa. H. H. Johnston, 'The Development of Tropical Africa under British Auspices', *Fortnightly Review*, Nov., 1890, 703-4; 'British Central Africa', *New Review*, July, 1894, 22; Johnston to Salisbury, Feb. 20, 1892, F.O. 84/2197; Johnston to Rosebery, Sept. 1, 1893, F.O. 2/55; *Report by Commissioner Johnston of the First Three Years' Administration of the Eastern Portion of British Central Africa*, C-7504, 25, 30.

For another advocate of selective breeding to raise the African see C. Eliot, *The East Africa Protectorate*, London, 1905, 102, 107, 304-5.

⁷¹ Johnston 'believed in Evolution as in a God, and in himself as its devoted, and perhaps its only intelligent, servant'. Oliver, *Johnston*, 5.

⁷² *Last Journals*, I, 278-9.

⁷³ See J. M. Gray, 'Ahmed bin Ibrahim—The First Arab to reach Buganda', *Uganda Journal*, Sept., 1947.

⁷⁴ *Travels*, 84, 20, 65, 138-9, 391.

⁷⁵ Jones to Thompson, Feb. 10, 1885, L.M.S.T.

⁷⁶ Harris to Thompson, March 15, 1885, L.M.S.T.

⁷⁷ Jones to Thompson, Jan, 23, 1889, L.M.S.T.

⁷⁸ Oliver, *Missionary Factor*, 106-16.

⁷⁹ See Frere, *Eastern Africa*, 19-20, for a discussion of the appeal of Islam.

⁸⁰ *Tropical Africa*, 5.

⁸¹ *Travels and Researches*, 47.

⁸² *African Reminiscences*, 15.

⁸³ *Mohammed and Mohammedanism*, 46-8, 238-9, 249-50, 258-9, 30, 32, 209-211, 239. In 'Mohammedanism in Africa', *Nineteenth Century*, Dec., 1887, Smith seemed much less enamoured of Islam and his tone is distinctly critical compared with his book.

⁸⁴ For a short sketch of Blyden's career see G. A. Gollock, *Sons of Africa*, London, 1928, 159-64.

⁸⁵ *Christianity, Islam and Negro Race*, 297, 18, 152-3, 215-16, iii-iv, 7, 28-9, 277.

⁸⁶ *The Times*, Oct. 8, 1887. Taylor later exempted East Central Africa south of the Equator from his analysis. The Arabs in this area, he claimed, were Moslems only in name. Further, the 'great Bantu-family . . . the higher Bantu tribes south of the Congo' were superior to the west coast Africans. *The Times*, Oct. 31, 1887. Taylor expanded on his views in *The Times*, Oct. 26, 1887; Oct. 31, 1887; Nov. 7, 1887; Nov. 17, 1887; Jan. 24, 1888. A comparison of *The Times*, Oct. 8, 1887, with Smith, *Mohammed and Mohammedanism*, 36, makes clear Taylor's indebtedness to the latter writer. See Stock, *History of C.M.S.*, III, 345-8, for a short discussion of the controversy aroused by Taylor's statements.

⁸⁷ *The Times*, Oct. 31, 1887.

⁸⁸ *The Times*, Nov. 17, 1887.

NOTES: CHAPTER VIII

[89] *The Times*, Nov. 14, 1887. For additional material bearing on Thomson's views see 'Note on the African Tribes of the British Empire', *J.R.A.I.*, 1886, 184-6; 'The Results of European Intercourse with the African', *Contemporary Review*, March, 1890, 349; Thomson and Harris-Smith, *Ulu: An African Romance*, I, 125-6, and II, 19-22. His attitude was very close to that of Mary Kingsley. See M. H. Kingsley, 'The Development of Dodos', *National Review*, March, 1896.

[90] *The Times*, Nov. 14, 1887; 'The Results of European Intercourse with the African', *Contemporary Review*, March, 1890, 350. His doubts as to the ultimate results of Islam seem to have been caused by a trip to Morocco. Thomson, *Thomson—African Explorer*, 226-7.

[91] *To the Central African Lakes*, I, 48-9; *Through Masai Land*, 15-16.

[92] *To the Central African Lakes*, II, 86-8. See also 'The Results of European Intercourse with the African', *Contemporary Review*, March, 1890, 351-52, for his praise of the industrial work of the Scottish missions.

[93] Pruen, *Arab and African*, 264, 301.

[94] *Across Africa*, 540-1. See also his irrational attack on the calibre of missionaries in 'Colonisation of Central Africa', *Proc. R.C.I.*, 1875-6, 281-2.

[95] *Big Game*, 23, 25-6. It might be mentioned here that the non-missionary element tended to accord praise to the 'hard' missionary, the man who minimized the doctrinal content of his task, and placed much emphasis on inculcating the virtue of work and the mechanical arts. This approach, with its thinly veiled bias in favour of keeping the African in his place, constituted an attempt to transform the missionary into an agent for transmitting the useful subordinate virtues, thus rendering the dissemination of Christianity innocuous by neutralizing its egalitarian assumptions. For various aspects of this attitude see Lugard, *East African Empire*, I, 69-74; J. R. Rodd, *Social and Diplomatic Memories, 1884-1893*, London, 1922, 294-5; Eliot, *East Africa Protectorate*, 241; L. P. Bowler, *Facts about the Matabele, Mashonas, and the Middle Zambesi*, Pretoria, 1889, 9; Speke, *What Led to the Discovery of the Source of the Nile*, 366. See the comments of Fraser, *Future of Africa*, 153, on this non-mission attitude, and compare Dollard, *Caste and Class*, 191, for similar attitudes to the American Negro.

[96] See 'The Anthropological Society and Christian Missions', *C.M.I.*, July, 1865, for an attack on Burton and Reade.

[97] See the refutation of Burton's advocacy of Islam for the African by the Rev. R. Roberts. 'The great question is, is Mahometanism true? or is it false? If it be true, then, certainly, not only the Kaffirs, but ourselves, ought to embrace it. If it be false, we ought to reject it, and they ought to reject it.' *L.M.S. Chronicle*, June, 1865, 180. See also *Centenary of L.M.S. . . . 1895*, 39-40, 58-9, 79, 204, 206-7, for a refutation of the ethnic religion concept.

[98] Smith, *Mohammed and Mohammedanism*, 148. For an illustration see the polemical attack by G. Knox on Islam and Canon Taylor, 'A Rejoinder', *C.M.I.*, Dec., 1887.

[99] *L.M.S. Chronicle*, June, 1863, 193.

[100] *Arab and African*, 298-9.

[101] *C.M.I.*, Aug., 1874, 225.

[102] *C.M.I.*, Nov., 1887, 649-54.

[103] Swann to Thompson, June 19, 1890, L.M.S.T. See also Swann to Thompson, Jan. 30, 1889, L.M.S.T., and Swann to Thompson, Aug. 14, 1889, L.M.S.T.

[104] Mackay, *Pioneer Missionary*, 259.

[105] This theological problem falls outside the purview of this analysis and the competence of the writer. It was, nevertheless, an important question to the missionary and one which he found impossible to answer to his satisfaction.

NOTES: CHAPTER VIII

James Stewart commented that no theory fully explained how Islam, as an event permitted by God, could be fitted into 'the progress of the world, or into what may be called the evolution of its spiritual history'. *Dawn in the Dark Continent*, 57. For representative views of Islam as divine chastisement see Rowley, *Africa Unveiled*, 222–4; Badger, *Christianity and its Relations to Islam*, 5–6; *C.M.I.*, May, 1852, 99–100; *C.M.I.*, Aug., 1874, 227; *C.M.I.*, Oct., 1887, 586–7.

[106] Maples, *Journals and Papers*, 177. The argument was often confused. The *C.M.I.* attributed the success of Islam to sensualism, formalism, and its incitement of war-like passions, and stated that the greatest danger posed by Islam was its similarity to Christianity, Satan's 'policy of opposing God by imitation'. Aug., 1874, 236, 238.

[107] Preface by Steere to Fraser, Tozer, Christie, *East African Slave Trade*, 5. Tozer stated that Steere's statement was 'painfully true'. Tozer, *Letters*, 226.

[108] Three sons of Seyyid Said who eventually became Sultans, Barghash, Khalifa and Ali, had concubine mothers. Hollingsworth, *Zanzibar*, 137.

[109] See the comments of H. H. Johnston, *The Story of My Life*, London, 1923, 101.

[110] L. P. Harries, *Islam in East Africa*, London, 1954, 33.

[111] Harries, *Islam in East Africa*, 19, points out that the spread of Islam was not due to missionary work, but to the 'influence of the Muslim community' and the process of overcoming social distinctions. See J. S. Trimingham, *The Christian Church and Islam in West Africa*, I.M.C. Research Pamphlets No. 3, London, 1955, 30–3, for analogous comments on Islam in West Africa.

[112] Heanley, *Memoir of Steere*, 318–19.

[113] Heanley, *Memoir of Steere*, 335–6.

[114] Pruen, *Arab and African*, 287. See also Maples, *Pioneer Missionary*, 58.

[115] Tozer, *Letters*, 98, 187–9, 196, is the most striking illustration. The unhealthiness of the climate to Europeans was also an important factor in giving urgency to the creation of an indigenous ministry. Ward and Russell, *Life of Smythies*, 168; Frere, *Eastern Africa*, 45.

[116] Tozer, *Letters*, 189–91.

[117] *Letters*, 186, 182, 221–2.

[118] *Letters*, 104, 103.

[119] 'The Universities' Mission to Central Africa—Twenty-first Anniversary', Abridged Account, U.M.C.A. London offices.

[120] The comment of Bishop Hine who joined the U.M.C.A. in 1889 and became the eighth bishop was typical of the U.M.C.A. attitude. 'Why waste time and money in teaching a few handicrafts which have to do with the things that are seen, when we are sent out to be witnesses of the things that are not seen and teachers of that which is eternal?' *Days Gone By*, 118.

[121] Heanley, *Memoir of Steere*, 385.

[122] On the argument of E. B. Reuter that 'Dominant races have a vested interest in the perpetuity of the cultures of weaker races'. E. B. Reuter, ed., *Race and Culture Contacts*, New York and London, 1934, 43.

[123] Oliver, *Missionary Factor*, 180–1.

[124] Jones to Thompson, Jan. 23, 1889, L.M.S.T.

[125] J. E. Hine, *Introductory Words Spoken at a Conference of Clergy and Laity, held at Likoma, April 24, 1899*, Likoma, n.d. In 1896 at a Diocesan Synod of Zanzibar a suggestion was put forward that 'we should encourage simplicity of life in our native clergy . . . but after a long discussion [it] was dropped, at the evident wish of the native Clergy'. *An Account of the Sacred Synod of the Diocese of Zanzibar, 1896*, [Zanzibar?, 1896].

[126] *Britain in Fiji: 1858–1880*, 147–8.

NOTES: CHAPTER VIII

[127] *Emin Pasha and the Rebellion at the Equator*, London, 1890, 299-300.

[128] Selous, *A Hunter's Wanderings*, 34-5; Baines, *Goldfields Diaries*, 669-70.

[129] Ward and Russell, *Life of Smythies*, 100; Tozer, *Letters*, 44, 50, 102-3.

[130] *Africana*, II, 248. For a strong exposition of this viewpoint from a prolific writer on missionary subjects see Cust, *Prevailing Methods of Evangelization*, 16, 36, 96, 150.

[131] Sykes to Mullens, July 12, 1870, L.M.S.M.; Thomson to Mullens, March 25, 1873, L.M.S.M.

[132] Thomson to Mullens, Dec. 20, 1877, L.M.S.T. See also Thomson to Mullens, Oct. 18, cont. Oct. 26, 1877, L.M.S.T.

[133] See above, Chapter 8, Section 2.

[134] F. D. Lugard, 'The Extension of British Influence (and Trade) in Africa', *Proc. R.C.I.*, 1895-6; F. D. Lugard, 'A Glimpse of Lake Nyassa', *Blackwood's Magazine*, Jan. 1890, 28; Lugard, *East African Empire*, I, 380-3; H. M. Stanley, 'Central Africa and the Congo Basin', *S.G.M.*, January-March, 1885; H. H. Johnston, *Kilima-Njaro Expedition*, chap. xxi; H. H. Johnston, 'The Development of Tropical Africa under British Auspices', *Fortnightly Review*, Nov., 1890, 688; H. H. Johnston, 'The Value of Africa: A Reply to Sir John Pope Hennessy', *Nineteenth Century*, Aug., 1890, a reply to 'The African Bubble', by Hennessy in *Nineteenth Century*, July, 1890. For the counter reply see Hennessy and E. Dicey, 'Is Central Africa Worth Having?' *Nineteenth Century*, Sept., 1890.

[135] 'The Trade of Central Africa, Present and Future', *Journal of the Society of Arts*, Jan. 26, 1877, 169. H. H. Johnston stated: 'Great as our Indian Empire is it can only employ a half of the intelligent, well-educated British youth who are anxious to enter Government service. Africa, well-developed, can easily find employment for the remainder. . . .' 'The Development of Tropical Africa under British Auspices', *Fortnightly Review*, Nov., 1890, 688.

[136] For Thomson's views see 'East Africa as it Was and Is', *Contemporary Review*, Jan., 1889, 45-6; *To the Central African Lakes*, II, 280-1, 284-6; 'East Central Africa, and its Commercial Outlook', *S.G.M.*, Feb., 1886. Nevertheless, Thomson did regard trade as an important civilizing agency. *To the Central African Lakes*, I, 161-2.

[137] 'Journey Across Africa, From Bagomoyo to Benguela', *Proc. R.G.S.*, 1875-1876, 323; *Across Africa*, 530-4.

[138] Mandy, *Matabeleland*, 30.

[139] *Old Rhodesian Days*, 36.

[140] See, for example, Faulkner, *Elephant Haunts*, 259; Devereux, *Cruise*, 213; McLeod, *Travels*, see the dedication.

[141] Hore to Kirk, Sept. 15, 1880, Q 22, Z.A.

[142] Mackay, *Pioneer Missionary*, 369-70. See also Wilson and Felkin, *Uganda and Egyptian Soudan*, I, 344, for advocacy of missionaries promoting trade.

[143] *L.M.S. Chronicle*, June, 1880, 131; *Centenary Conference on Protestant Missions, 1888*, I, 112-13; II, 577.

[144] In.1888 when it appeared possible that either Portuguese or Arab hegemony might be established in the Lake Nyasa region, the Church of Scotland and the Free Church of Scotland petitioned members of parliament to obtain a declaration that Nyasaland north of the Ruo River was a British sphere of influence. To support their case they emphasized their investment in the area, £35,000 by the Church of Scotland and £49,000 by the Free Church since their arrival, and a joint annual expenditure of over £8,000. *East Central Africa Mission—Statement on behalf of the Foreign Mission Committee of the Church of Scotland and of the Free Church of Scotland* (For members of both Houses of Parliament), Edinburgh, 1888. As R. N. Cust pointed out, 'this smacks more of Com-

NOTES: CHAPTER VIII

merce than of Gospel-preaching'. He appealed to all churches to resist this insidious approach which 'destroys the character of the Missionary [when he states] that his Society had invested so much capital in this Region, or that, as if he had taken shares in a Joint-Stock Company, and call[s] upon his Government to get him compensation'. *Notes on Missionary Subjects*, Part III, 61, 67.

[145] H. B. Cotterill, 'On the Nyassa and a Journey from the North End to Zanzibar', *Proc. R.G.S.*, 1877-8, 235.

[146] W. K. Hancock, *Survey of British Commonwealth Affairs*, II, *Problems of Economic Policy, 1918-1939*, Part 2, London, 1942, 160-1.

[147] Glyn-Jones, 'Britain and the End of Slavery in East Africa', 19.

[148] *Central South Africa*, 408, 398-405.

[149] Thomson to Mullens, Jan. 14, 1870, L.M.S.M.

[150] Thomson to Mullens, July 24, 1876, L.M.S.M.

[151] Thomas, *Central South Africa*, 406-7. Lobengula asked Thomas what use the missionary teaching would be, for all the white men in the country could read and write, 'but their knowledge does not make them good'. This remark, admitted Thomas, was true, 'and the truth of it is perhaps the most formidable obstacle in the way of the Gospel in this country'. Thomas Diary, May 23, 1878, Thomas Papers.

[152] Elliott to Thompson, Dec. 11, 1882, L.M.S.M.

[153] Thomas, *Central South Africa*, 330-1.

[154] See Hanna, *Beginnings of Nyasaland*, 65-7, for the case of the trader Fenwick.

[155] For a good indication of the missionary definition of, and attitude to, commerce, see the speech by the Rev. Professor Cairns, Principal of the United Presbyterian College, Edinburgh, in *Centenary Conference on Protestant Missions*, 1888, I, 114-18.

[156] The unreality of the ideal colony desired by the missionary is well illustrated by Rebmann's comments in Krapf, *Travels*, 246-7.

[157] Elliott to Thompson, Sept. 5, 1890, L.M.S.M.

[158] *Impressions of South Africa*, 228.

[159] *The Bulawayo Sketch*, Aug. 11, 1894; May 4, 1895; July 20, 1895.

[160] July 20, 1895.

[161] Reed to Thompson, April 10, 1896, L.M.S.M. In an earlier letter he claimed that 'a fair equivalent for rent from a native [squatter] is the whole year's service gratis, or any such part of this as may seem good' to the white farmers. Reed to Thompson, Oct. 20, 1895, L.M.S.M. For the widespread resort to forced labour see C-8547, *Report by Sir R. E. R. Martin, On the Native Administration of the British South Africa Company*, London, 1897, 5-8.

[162] Rees to Thompson, April 27, 1894, L.M.S.M.

[163] Rees to Thompson, Aug. 26, 1895, L.M.S.M.

[164] Oliver, *Johnston*, 67-68.

[165] *British Central Africa*, 183.

[166] Livingstone, *Laws*, 258.

[167] See Hanna, *Beginnings of Nyasaland*, 205-6, for a discussion. G. Shepperson has modified Dr. Hanna's vendetta account in 'The Literature of British Central Africa', *Rhodes-Livingstone Journal*, XXIII, June, 1958, 22.

[168] Oliver, *Johnston*, 202.

[169] Maugham, *Nyasaland in the Nineties*, 22-3.

[170] Goodrich to Granville, Dec. 20, 1884, F.O. 84/1622. Comments on the poor quality of A.L.C. employees were widespread. Hawes to Salisbury, Dec. 1, 1885, F.O. 84/1702. Johnston to Anderson, Jan. 21, 1893, F.O. 2/54; Poole to his Mother, July 25, 1895, Poole Papers. On the other hand some of the employees

NOTES: CHAPTER IX

engaged in active mission work in their free time. Lugard, *East African Empire*, I, 98; Fotheringham, *Adventures in Nyassaland*, 26; H. Von Wissman, *Second Journey through Equatorial Africa*, 279.

[171] Hore to Thompson, Aug. 1, 1884, L.M.S.T.

[172] See above, 45-6.

[173] Hancock, *Survey of British Commonwealth Affairs*, II, *Problems of Economic Policy 1918-1939*, Part 2, 120.

IX: THE BEGINNING OF A NEW ERA

[1] *Journal of Discovery of the Source of the Nile*, 8, 45. For Speke's ideas on opening up Africa and destroying the slave trade see 'Considerations for Opening Africa', and 'Scheme for Opening Africa', Z.M.

[2] Livingstone to F.O., Feb. 22, 1862; F.O. to Livingstone, Aug. 3, 1862, both from D. Livingstone Papers.

[3] Stewart, *Zambesi Journal*, 167.

[4] Waller to Gray, July 1, cont. July 5, 1863, U.M.C.A. Papers.

[5] Frere to Granville, 'Memorandum on the Position and Authority of the Sultan of Zanzibar', May 7, 1873, F.O. 84/1391. Six months earlier he left a memorandum with the Italian Minister of Commerce and Finance advocating an increase in Italian trade with East Africa for the sake of Italy and because of the impact it would make on the slave trade. Frere to Granville, Dec. 4, 1872, F.O. 84/1385.

[6] Frere to Granville, May 29, 1873, F.O. 84/1391.

[7] Oliver, *Johnston*, 84 n.

[8] Cotterill to Kirk, March 13, 1877, Q 18, Z.A.

[9] 'Colonisation of Central Africa', *Proc. R.C.I.*, 1875-6, 282, 274, 277, 280.

[10] *Across Africa*, 544; 'Slavery in Africa—The Disease and the Remedy', *National Review*, Oct., 1888, 268. Cameron's actions are summarized in S. E. Crowe, *The Berlin West African Conference 1884-1885*, London, 1942, 202-3.

[11] *Modern Egypt*, II, 124.

[12] *British Central Africa*, 182-3.

[13] *The Bulawayo Sketch*, Sept. 8, 1894.

[14] *Cruise*, 345-6.

[15] Fripp and Hiller, eds., *Gold and the Gospel*, 137-8. Mandy, *Matabeleland*, 38, and Wilson Diary, March 22, 1889, Wilson Papers, also advocated imperialism on humanitarian grounds in this area. For more general employment of the humanitarian argument see Cameron, *Across Africa*, 155; Lugard, *East African Empire*, I, 87; Lugard, 'A Glimpse of Lake Nyassa', *Blackwood's Magazine*, Jan. 1890, 26-9.

[16] *Two Kings*, 122-4.

[17] 'Great days: the autobiography of an Empire Pioneer', 91-2, Proof Copy, Johnson Papers.

[18] 'Memorandum of a confidential agreement made and entered into on this 7th day of December 1889 between the Hon. Cecil John Rhodes . . . and Frank William Frederick Johnson and Maurice Heany', Clause 3, Johnson Papers.

[19] 'Great days', 90, Proof Copy, Johnson Papers. Rhodes was to pay all expenses of the operation. Had it succeeded Heany and Johnson were to receive £150,000, plus at least 50,000 morgen of land, plus all cattle, horses, and other livestock captured by the invading party. Clause 2, 9, 10, 4, of agreement cited in previous note.

[20] Harris to Colenbrander, Feb. 9, 1892, Colenbrander Papers. Harris did not say justification for what, but in the same letter he stated: 'when the bell really

NOTES: CHAPTER IX

rang for their [Matabele] disappearance from the stage, that I would be there to help them leave—but that day is still 2 years at least distant—possibly it will never come as they may accommodate themselves to their white environment as the Swazies have.'

[21] Poole to his Mother, April 6, 1896, Poole Papers. See also Poole to his Father, Nov. 13, 1895, where he states: 'It is a considerable farce this slave freeing business. In the first place I've no doubt that a great many of the so-called slaves are not slaves at all. But like the mission converts, freed slaves pay well at home. People get K.C.M.G.'s and C.M.G.'s and so on for freeing slaves.' Poole Papers.

[22] Poole to his Mother, Oct. 15, 1895, Poole Papers. In yet another letter he pointed out that there was more than a verbal difference between reporting 'we were surprised by a party of the enemy, instead of we surprised a party of the enemy'. He added that 'reports too are hatched in order to get more land from the Portuguese'. Poole to his Mother, Oct. 9, 1895, Poole Papers.

[23] Surprising in view of the part these theories are held to have played in stimulating and supporting late nineteenth-century European imperialistic ideas. See Langer, *Diplomacy of Imperialism*, I, 85–90, 95–6; C. J. H. Hayes, *A Generation of Materialism 1871–1900*, New York, 1941, 9–13.

[24] 'A lot of fellows seriously are wishing to kill *everything* with a black skin, friends and enemies alike.' D. R. Pelly to his parents, June 12, cont. June 29, 1896, Pelly Papers.

[25] See Selous, *Sunshine and Storm*, xix, 65–7, for a harsh application of the 'survival of the fittest' philosophy to European African relations, written under the strain of the Matabele rebellion. See also Brown, *On the South African Frontier*, 349–50, 390–2, 397, 399–401, 420, for similar views.

[26] See, for example, *Centenary Conference on Protestant Missions, 1888*, I, xv–xvi, and *L.M.S. Chronicle*, June, 1882, 199, 211.

[27] 'Expansion as a permanent and supreme aim of politics is the central political idea of imperialism.' Arendt, *Origins of Totalitarianism*, 125.

[28] Latourette stated that nineteenth-century Christian missions were 'largely a paternalistic enterprise, a kind of spiritual imperialism'. *The Great Century in Europe and the United States of America A.D. 1800—A.D. 1914*, 3rd ed., Vol. IV of *A History of the Expansion of Christianity*, New York and London, 1941, 52. See also Hogg, *Ecumenical Foundations*, 49.

[29] It is perhaps not without significance that Lugard, the son of missionary parents in India, prayed for the 'poor heathen' as a child, desired to be a clergyman, and eventually became a great imperial proconsul and ruler of millions. Perham, *Lugard—Years of Adventure*, 19.

[30] For the Free Church of Scotland see Livingstone, *Laws*, 43; for C.M.S. at Freretown see Price to Euan Smith, July 16, 1875, E 72, Z.A.; for L.M.S. on Lake Tanganyika see Hore to Kirk, Dec. 26, 1879, Q 24, Z.A.

[31] Waller to Stewart, Oct. 18, 1864; Stewart, *Zambesi Journal*, 233–4, reveal Waller's attitude. For Stewart and Livingstone see above, 231–2.

[32] Krapf, *Travels*, 134; New, *Life*, 506. See also Stock, *History of C.M.S.*, III, 74–5, 77.

[33] Cockin to Mullens, May, 1879, L.M.S.M.

[34] Oliver, *Missionary Factor*, 86, has noted that there was little pressure on the British government for imperial take-overs from 1875 to 1885. Perham has also written of the missionary reluctance to openly advocate direct imperial control in Nyasaland, *Lugard—Years of Adventure*, 111–12, 127–8. Yet the sentiment in favour of imperialism had a history going back to Livingstone.

[35] Wallis, ed., *The Matabele Mission*, 70–1.

[36] *Travels*, 402.

NOTES: CHAPTER IX

[37] Warneck, *Modern Missions and Culture*, 222-3.

[38] This explains the statement of A. F. Sim, U.M.C.A. missionary at Kota Kota: 'if it [i.e. smallpox] comes it may be a God-sent opportunity for making the spirit of Christianity known among these people'. *Life and Letters*, 171.

[39] Thomas to Coillard, April 23, 1878, Coillard Papers.

[40] Carnegie to Thompson, March 26, 1889, L.M.S.M.; Carnegie to Thompson, Sept. 6, 1889, L.M.S.M. J. S. Moffat, onetime missionary, reluctantly agreed, stating that 'there is very little hope for the Matabele until the plough-share of war has broken up the present state of things'. J. S. Moffat to Miss E. Unwin, April 28, 1889. See also J. S. Moffat to Knight-Bruce, April 28, 1889, and J. S. Moffat to Miss E. Unwin, Sept. 1, 1889, all from J. S. Moffat Papers.

[41] Elliott to Thompson, Feb. 19, 1890, L.M.S.M. For his later interpretation of the defeat of the Matabele as the judgement of God see *Gold from the Quartz*, 81, 154-5. For hostility to misguided humanitarians in Britain who defended the Matabele see Carnegie to Thompson, Feb. 14, 1890, L.M.S.M.; Carnegie to Thompson, April 16, 1890, L.M.S.M.; J. S. Moffat to Fisher, Sept. 4, 1889, J. S. Moffat Papers.

[42] Carnegie to Thompson, June 27, 1890, L.M.S.M.

[43] Sermon Book, Sermon Preached on April 8, 1883.

[44] See, for example, Livingstone, *Private Journals*, 90-1; Watt, *Heart of Savagedom*, 169; Fripp and Hiller, eds., *Gold and the Gospel*, 97; *London Missionary Society, Deputation to South Africa . . . 1883-1884. Report of the Rev. R. Wardlaw Thompson, Foreign Secretary* (Printed for the use of the Directors), 35; Smith, *Price*, 134-5.

The attitude was not confined to missionaries. In 1888 Sidney Shippard, resident commissioner of Bechuanaland, wrote to Francis James Newton that: 'I am [not] naturally of a cruel or bloodthirsty disposition but I must confess that it would afford me sincere and lasting satisfaction if I could see the Matabele Matjaha cut down by our rifles and machine guns like a cornfield by a reaping machine, and I would not spare a single one if I had my way. The cup of their iniquities must surely be full or nearly full now. Never till I saw these wretches did I understand the true mercy and love of humanity contained in the injunction given to the Israelites to destroy the Canaanites. I understand it perfectly now.' Shippard to Newton, Oct. 29, 1888, Newton Papers.

[45] Hanna, *Beginnings of Nyasaland*, 145.

[46] Hetherwick, *Romance of Blantyre*, 69.

[47] Bishop Tucker of the C.M.S. raised over £16,000 to finance the administration of the I.B.E.A. Co. in Uganda when its withdrawal was imminent. Subsequently the C.M.S. played an important part in the organizing of public sentiment on behalf of the retention of Uganda. See the excellent analysis by A. Low, 'British Public Opinion and the Uganda Question: October-December 1892', *Uganda Journal*, Sept., 1954.

[48] Mackay, *Pioneer Missionary*, 325. The U.M.C.A., probably the least political of all the British missions in Central Africa, saw, in the words of its annual report, evidence that the 'Providence of God is moulding events for the more effectual spread of His Gospel' in the British assumption of power in the Lake Nyasa area. *U.M.C.A. Annual Report, 1889-90*, 3. See also Swann to Thompson, June 19, 1890, L.M.S.T., for a coupling of the L.M.S. missionaries as 'Pioneers of the Gospel, and of the Union Jack'. Shortly after writing the above Swann undertook a treaty signing expedition for H. H. Johnston. He realized the dubious nature of his position, but he felt that 'to refuse the open door would be to soil the hitherto unstained banner of our great Society—a crime with which I refused to allow my name to be associated'. Swann to Thompson, Aug. 2, 1890,

NOTES: CHAPTER IX

L.M.S.T. His colleagues sympathized with Swann's preference for British rule, but were divided in their attitude to his political proclivities. In general they felt it necessary to 'abide by our instructions and leave the consequences in the hands of God'. Carson to Thompson, Aug. 2, 1890, with enclosures; L.M.S.T.

[49] For the special British claims to the Lake Nyasa area coupled with hostility and, frequently, contempt for their competitors see H. Waller, *Title Deeds to Nyassa-Land*, London, 1887; F. L. M. Moir, 'Englishmen and Arabs in East Africa', *Murray's Magazine*, Nov., 1888; Buchanan, *Shire Highlands*, 52-3, 72; Drummond, *Tropical Africa*, 209-11, 220-1; Lugard, 'A Glimpse of Lake Nyassa', *Blackwood's Magazine*, Jan., 1890, 21-2, 27-9. Maples, *Pioneer Missionary*, 306, 308, 317, instances the action of Chauncy Maples in having Chitesi, a chief on the east shore of Lake Nyasa opposite Likoma Island, take down the Portuguese flag. Maples hoped that 'all of the east side of the Lake [would be] under British protection'. See also the U.M.C.A. periodical *Central Africa* in 1889 and 1890 for the aggressive campaign waged by the London headquarters of the mission against the Germans and the Portuguese. In Feb., 1888, *Central Africa* reproduced an essay by an African boy at Kiungani Theological College giving a positive answer to the question 'Are African Races Profited by Foreign Rule?' including comparisons with the Roman empire. J. P. Farler, 'England and Germany in East Africa', *Fortnightly Review*, Feb., 1889, is a bitter attack on the betrayal of British interests involved in the creation of German East Africa. See Livingstone, *Laws*, 252, for attempts by the Livingstonia mission to ensure that their missions at the north end of Lake Nyasa did not fall into German hands. Wakefield (Methodist) to Kirk, July 6, 1885, E 84, Z.A., is a very bitter letter on the possibility that the Germans might acquire control of the Galla country and perhaps expel the Methodist missions established there.

[50] Oliver, *Johnston*, 209-13; Johnston, *British Central Africa*, 77, 107-8.
[51] Johnston to Anderson, Jan. 21, 1893, F.O. 2/54.
[52] Johnston, *British Central Africa*, 107-8.
[53] Thomson, *Thomson—African Explorer*, 132.
[54] *Memories of Mashonaland*, 2-3.
[55] *Fighting Slave Hunters*, 234.
[56] One of the most surprising examples occurs in *The Bulawayo Sketch*, Aug. 4, 1894. 'It was a glorious scheme to open up such a vast country to Europeans, glorious for us, but the pathos is there all the same disguise it as we may. Natives selling their beautiful Ostrich Feather Head Gear for a mere song which they offer with a sad smile of deprecating air, saying, "Our Glory is done, our Fighting Days over".'
[57] 'Heart of Darkness', *A Conrad Argosy*, 30.

BIBLIOGRAPHY

I. ARCHIVAL SOURCES AND GOVERNMENT DOCUMENTS
  (a) *Government Documents*
  (b) *Archival Sources*
II. PERIODICALS AND NEWSPAPERS
III. BACKGROUND MATERIAL
IV. THE MISSIONARY MOVEMENT
  (a) *History of Missions*
  (b) *Missionary Movement: Analytical Accounts*
  (c) *Missionary Conferences and Meetings*
  (d) *David Livingstone*
  (e) *Accounts of and by Missionaries about Their Work, Travel, and African Conditions*
V. ACCOUNTS OF AND BY NON-MISSIONARIES ABOUT THEIR WORK, TRAVEL, AND AFRICAN CONDITIONS
VI. SOCIOLOGICAL, ANTHROPOLOGICAL AND COMPARATIVE MATERIAL
VII. NOVELS

I. ARCHIVAL SOURCES AND GOVERNMENT DOCUMENTS

(a) *Government Documents*

  Report by Commissioner Johnston of the First Three Years' Administration of the Eastern Portion of British Central Africa, C-7504, London, H.M.S.O.
  Report by Commissioner Sir Harry Johnston, K.C.B., on the Trade and General Condition of the British Central Africa Protectorate, April 1, 1895, to March 31, 1896, C-8254, London, H.M.S.O.
  Report by Consul and Acting Commissioner Sharpe on the Trade and General Condition of the British Central Africa Protectorate from April 1, 1896, to March 31, 1897, C-8438, London, H.M.S.O.
  Report by Sir R. E. R. Martin, K.C.M.G., on the Native Administration of the British South Africa Company, C-8547, London, H.M.S.O., 1897.
  Report from the Select Committee on Slave Trade (East Coast of Africa), No. 420, 1871.

(b) *Archival Sources*

  Livingstonia Archives, Livingstonia Mission, Malawi.
  Laws, R., Sermon Book.

BIBLIOGRAPHY

L.M.S. Archives, London, England.
> Missionary Correspondence, 1876–90, dealing with the Lake Tanganyika Mission of the L.M.S.
> Missionary Correspondence, 1860–96, dealing with the Matabele Mission of the L.M.S.
> Jones, D. P., 'After Livingstone', t/s.

National Archives of Southern Rhodesia, Salisbury, Southern Rhodesia.
> I have made much use of the valuable and growing collection of diaries, reminiscences, letters, etc., of the early pioneers, including some from the early years of Charter Co. rule. The quantity varies from, in some instances, a few letters, to the wealth of material in the papers of J. S. Moffat and 'Matabele' Wilson. I have used the following:
> Alston, F. G.; Boggie, A.; Boggie, W. J.; Carnegie, D.; Coillard, F.; Colenbrander, J. W.; Crewe, P. D.; Cross, A.; Dawnay, Guy C.; Dawson, J. F.; Fairbairn, J.; Fry, I.; Fry, W. E.; Hole, H. M.; Helmore, H.; Johnson, F. W. F.; Livingstone, C.; Livingstone, D.; Milton, W. H.; Moffat, J. S.; Moral, F. R. de Bertodano, Marques del; Newton, F. J.; Pelly, D. R.; Poole, W.; Posselt, H. E.; Price, R.; Rangeley, H.; Stewart, J.; Selous, F. C.; Taylor, R. B.; Thomas, C. C.; Thomas, T. M.; Waddell, W.; Westbeech, G.; Wilson, 'Matabele'; U.M.C.A. Papers.; Usher, W. F.

Public Record Office, London, England.
> F.O. 84 and F.O. 2 series, 1883–93, dealing with the Nyasa Consulate and later with the British Central Africa administration.
> F.O. 84/1385—F.O. 84/1393, dealing with the Frere Mission to Zanzibar 1872–73. Very valuable for information on Zanzibar, the coastal settlements, and the slave trade.

U.M.C.A. Archives, London, England.
> Swinny, G. H., Diaries.

U.M.C.A. Archives, Zanzibar.
> U.M.C.A. Zanzibar Diary, 1864–88.
> Numerous other miscellaneous items found in the records in the Bishop's residence are not listed here.

Zanzibar Archives, Secretariat Building.
> A huge quantity of comparatively unclassified correspondence, including drafts of outgoing letters to the Foreign Office, and numerous letters from missionaries and travellers on the mainland. I have only been able to skim the surface for the period 1870 to 1890.

Zanzibar Museum.
> Typed copies of some of the most important material in the Zanzibar Archives have been deposited in the Museum by Sir John Gray.

II. PERIODICALS AND NEWSPAPERS

Note: Abbrevations used in the text have been placed in brackets.

Central Africa, A Monthly Record of the Work of the Universities' Mission, 1883–90.

BIBLIOGRAPHY

The Church Missionary Intelligencer (C.M.I.), 1849–90.
The Journal of the (Royal) Anthropological Institute of Great Britain and Ireland (J.R.A.I.), 1871–90.
The Journal of the Royal Geographical Society (J.R.G.S.), 1856–80.
The Missionary Magazine and Chronicle: Chiefly Relating to the Missions of the London Missionary Society (L.M.S. Chronicle), 1859–90.
The Nyasaland Journal (N.J.), 1948–60.
Proceedings of the Royal Colonial Institute (Proc. R.C.I), 1869–1901.
Proceedings of the Royal Geographical Society (Proc. R.G.S.), 1856–90.
The Rhodes-Livingstone Journal (R.L.J.), 1944–60.
The Scottish Geographical Magazine (S.G.M.), 1885–90.
Tanganyika Notes and Records (T.N.R.), 1936–60.
The Times, London, 1860–90.
The Uganda Journal (U.J.), 1934–60.
Universities Mission to Central Africa, *Occasional Papers*, I–XIX.

III. BACKGROUND MATERIAL

AXELSON, E. *South-East Africa 1488–1530*, London, Longmans, 1940.
BOGGIE, A. *From Ox-Waggon to Railway, Being a Brief History of Rhodesia and the Matabele Nation*, Bulawayo, Times Printing Works, 1897.
BRADY, C. T., Jr. *Commerce and Conquest in East Africa*, Salem, The Essex Institute, 1950.
BRODE, H. *Tippoo Tib, the Story of His Career in Central Africa*, London, Edward Arnold, 1907 (trans. H. Havelock).
BRYCE, J. *Impressions of South Africa*, 3rd ed., rev., London, Macmillan, 1899.
CLARK, J. D. *The Prehistory of Southern Africa*, Penguin Books, 1959.
COLE, S. *The Prehistory of East Africa*, Penguin Books, 1954.
COUPLAND, R. *The British Anti-Slavery Movement*, London, Butterworth, 1933.
—— *East Africa and its Invaders*, Oxford, Clarendon Press, 1956.
—— *The Exploitation of East Africa 1856–90*, London, Faber, 1939.
CROFTON, R. H. *The Old Consulate at Zanzibar*, London, O.U.P., 1935.
CROWE, S. E. *The Berlin West African Conference 1884–85*, London, Longmans, 1942.
DAVIDSON, B. *The Lost Cities of Africa*, Boston, Little, Brown, 1959.
DEBENHAM, F. *Nyasaland—The Land of the Lake*, London, H.M.S.O., 1955.
DUFF, H. L. *Nyasaland Under the Foreign Office*, London, George Bell, 1903.
DUFFY, J. *Portuguese Africa*, Cambridge, Mass., Harvard University Press, 1959.
ELIOT, C. *The East Africa Protectorate*, London, Edward Arnold, 1905.
FOSBROOKE, H. A. 'Tanganyika's Population Problem: an historical explanation', *R.L.J.*, (XXIII), June, 1958.
FRASER, H. A., TOZER, BISHOP, and CHRISTIE, J. *The East African Slave*

BIBLIOGRAPHY

Trade and the Measures Proposed for its Extinction as viewed by Residents in Zanzibar, London, Harrison, 1871.

GANN, L. H. *The Birth of a Plural Society*, Manchester, Manchester University Press, 1958.

—— 'The End of the Slave Trade in British Central Africa: 1889–1912', *R.L.J.* (XVI), 1954.

—— 'Liberal Interpretations of South African History: a review article', *R.L.J.* (XXV), March, 1959.

—— and Duignan, P. *White Settlers in Tropical Africa*, Penguin Books, 1962.

GELFAND, M. *Tropical Victory—An Account of the Influence of Medicine on the History of Southern Rhodesia, 1890–1923*, Cape Town and Johannesburg, Juta, 1953.

GLYN-JONES, E. 'Britain and the End of Slavery in East Africa', Thesis submitted for the degree of B.Litt. at the University of Oxford, Dec., 1956.

GRAY, J. M. 'Ahmed bin Ibrahim, the First Arab to reach Buganda', *U.J.*, Sept., 1947.

—— 'Albrecht Roscher', *T.N.R.*, June, 1958.

—— *The British in Mombasa 1824–1826*, London, Macmillan, 1957.

—— 'The British Vice-Consulate at Kilwa Kivinji, 1884–1885', *T.N.R.*, Dec., 1958.

—— 'Correspondence Relating to the Death of Bishop Hannington', *U.J.*, March, 1949.

—— 'Mutesa of Buganda', *U.J.*, Jan., 1934.

—— 'A Precursor to Krapf and Rebmann', *U.J.*, Jan., 1934.

HANCOCK, W. K. *Problems of Economic Policy 1918–1939*, Part 2 of Vol. II, *Survey of British Commonwealth Affairs*, London, O.U.P., 1942.

HANNA, A. J. *The Beginnings of Nyasaland and North-Eastern Rhodesia 1859–95*, Oxford, Clarendon Press, 1956.

HARVEY, R. J. 'Mirambo', *T.N.R.*, Jan., 1950.

HAYES, C. J. H. *A Generation of Materialism 1871–1900*, New York, Harper, 1941.

HENNESSY, J. POPE. 'The African Bubble', *Nineteenth Century*, July, 1890.

—— and DICEY E. 'Is Central Africa Worth Having?' *Nineteenth Century*, Sept., 1890.

HOLE, H. M. *Lobengula*, London, Philip Allen, 1929.

—— *The Making of Rhodesia*, London, Macmillan, 1926.

—— *Old Rhodesian Days*, London, Macmillan, 1928.

HOLLINGSWORTH, L. W. *Zanzibar Under the Foreign Office, 1890–1913*, London, Macmillan, 1953.

HUTCHINSON, E. *The Slave Trade of East Africa*, London, Sampson Low, 1874.

INGHAM, K. *The Making of Modern Uganda*, London, Allen and Unwin, 1958.

JACKSON, M. V. *European Powers and South-East Africa*, London, Longmans, 1942.

BIBLIOGRAPHY

JOHNSTON, H. H. *British Central Africa*, 3rd ed., London, Methuen, 1906.
—— *The History of a Slave*, London, Kegan Paul, 1889.
—— *The Nile Quest*, London, Alston Rivers, 1906.
—— *The Uganda Protectorate*, London, Hutchinson, 1902, 2 vols.
JONES, N. *Guide to the Zimbabwe Ruins*, 2nd ed., Bulawayo, Belmont Printers, 1959 (rewritten by R. Summers).
LANGER, W. L. *The Diplomacy of Imperialism 1890–1902*, New York and London, Knopf, 1935, 2 vols.
LEYS, N. *Kenya*, 3rd ed., London, Hogarth Press, 1926.
LLOYD, C. *The Navy and the Slave Trade*, London, Longmans, 1949.
LOFTUS, E. A. *Elton and the East African Coast Slave Trade*, London, Macmillan, 1958.
LOW, A. 'British Public Opinion and the Uganda Question: October–December 1892', *U.J.*, Sept., 1954.
MASON, P. *The Birth of a Dilemma—The Conquest and Settlement of Rhodesia*, London and New York, O.U.P., 1958.
MAUGHAM, R. C. F. *Africa as I Have Known It*, London, John Murray, 1929.
—— *Nyasaland in the Nineties*, London, Lincoln Williams, 1935.
NEWMAN, H. S. *Banani: The Transition from Slavery to Freedom in Zanzibar and Pemba*, 2nd ed., London, Headley Brothers, n.d.
RANDALL-MACIVER, D. *Medieval Rhodesia*, London, Macmillan, 1906.
RANGELEY, W. H. 'Early Blantyre', *N.J.*, Jan., 1954.
ROBINSON, R., GALLAGHER, J., and DENNY, A. *Africa and the Victorians, the Official Mind of Imperialism*, London, Macmillan, 1961.
RUETE, E. *Memoirs of an Arabian Princess*, New York, Doubleday, 1907 (trans. L. Strachey).
SEELEY, J. R. *The Expansion of England*, London, Macmillan, 1925.
SHEPPERSON, G. 'The Literature of British Central Africa: a review article', *R.L.J.* (XXIII), June, 1958.
—— and PRICE, T. *Independent African*, Edinburgh, Edinburgh University Press, 1958.
SILLERY, A. *Sechele*, Oxford, George Ronald, 1954.
SLADE, R. *King Leopold's Congo*, London, O.U.P., 1962.
SMUTS, J. C. *Africa and Some World Problems*, Oxford, Clarendon Press, 1930.
STEWART, J. 'The City of Mozambique', *The Cape and Its People*, ed. P. Noble, Cape Town, Juta, 1869.
TABLER, E. C. *The Far Interior*, Cape Town and Amsterdam, Balkema, 1955.
THOMAS, H. B. and SCOTT, R. *Uganda*, London, O.U.P., 1935.
THORNTON, A. P. *The Imperial Idea and its Enemies*, London, Macmillan, 1959.
TIP, TIPPU. *Maisha ya Hamed bin Muhammed el Murjebi yaani Tippu Tip, Kwa maneno yake mwenyewe*, Supplement to the East African Swahili Committee Journals No. 28/2, July, 1958, and No. 29/1, January, 1959 (trans. W. H. Whiteley).

BIBLIOGRAPHY

WALLER, H. *Title-Deeds to Nyassa-Land*, London, Clowes, 1887.
—— *Trafficking in Liquor with the Natives of Africa*, London, Clowes, 1887.
WORTHINGTON, E. B. *Science in Africa*, London, O.U.P., 1938.
ZIMMERN, A. *The Third British Empire*, London, O.U.P., 1926.

IV. THE MISSIONARY MOVEMENT

(a) *History of Missions*

AMBALI, A. *Thirty Years in Nyasaland*, 2nd ed., Westminster, U.M.C.A., n.d.
ANDERSON-MORSHEAD, A. E. M. *The History of the Universities' Mission to Central Africa, 1859–1909*, new rev. ed., London, U.M.C.A., 1909.
BOUNIOL, J., ed. *The White Fathers and Their Missions*, London, Sands, 1929.
CHADWICK, O. *Mackenzie's Grave*, London, Hodder and Stoughton, 1959.
CHIRNSIDE, A. *The Blantyre Missionaries: Discreditable Disclosures*, London, Ridgway, 1880.
East Central Africa Mission—Statement on behalf of the Foreign Missions Committee of the Church of Scotland and of the Free Church of Scotland, Edinburgh, Frank Murray, 1888. (For members of both Houses of Parliament.)
FRERE, B. *Eastern Africa as a Field for Missionary Labour*, London, John Murray, 1874.
GRAY, J. M. *Early Portuguese Missionaries in East Africa*, London, Macmillan, 1958.
GREEN, S. 'The Blantyre Mission', *N.J.*, July, 1957.
GROVES, C. P. *The Planting of Christianity in Africa*, London, Lutterworth, 1948, 1954, 1955, 1958, 4 vols.
HANNA, A. J. 'The Role of the London Missionary Society in the Opening up of East Central Africa', *Transactions of the Royal Historical Society*, 5th series, Vol. 5, 1955.
HERDMAN, J. C. *The Blantyre Mission Case—Report of the Committee for the Propagation of the Gospel in Foreign Parts . . . To the Commission of the General Assembly of the Church of Scotland, March, 1881.*
JACK, J. W. *Daybreak at Livingstonia*, Edinburgh and London, Oliphant, Anderson and Ferrier, 1901.
LATOURETTE, K. S. *The Great Century in the Americas, Australasia, and Africa A.D. 1800–A.D. 1914*, Vol. V of *A History of the Expansion of Christianity*, 2nd ed., New York and London, Harper, 1943.
—— *The Great Century in Europe and the United States of America A.D. 1800–A.D. 1914*, Vol. IV of *A History of the Expansion of Christianity*, 3rd ed., New York and London, Harper, 1941.
London Missionary Society. Deputation to South Africa . . . 1883–1884.

BIBLIOGRAPHY

Report of the Rev. R. Wardlaw Thompson, Foreign Secretary. (Printed for the use of the Directors.)

London Missionary Society—Papers Respecting the Matabele Mission, South Africa, London, L.M.S., 1873. (Printed for the Directors only.)

LOVETT, R. *The History of the London Missionary Society,* London, Frowde, 1899, 2 vols.

MACKINTOSH, C. W. *Some Pioneer Missions of Northern Rhodesia and Nyasaland,* Lusaka, 1950. (Occasional Papers of the Rhodes-Livingstone Museum No. 8.)

OLIVER, R. *The Missionary Factor in East Africa,* London, Longmans, 1952.

PRETORIOUS, J. H. 'The Story of the Dutch Reformed Church Mission in Nyasaland', *N.J.,* Jan., 1957.

ROWLEY, H. *The Story of the Universities' Mission to Central Africa,* 2nd ed., London, Saunders, Otley, 1867.

SLADE, R. M. 'English-Speaking Missions in the Congo Independent State, 1878–1908', Thesis submitted for the degree of Doctor of Philosophy in the University of London, May, 1957.

STEWART, J. *Dawn in the Dark Continent,* Edinburgh and London, Oliphant, Anderson and Ferrier, 1903.

STOCK, E. *The History of the Church Missionary Society,* London, C.M.S., 1899, 3 vols.

U.M.C.A. Annual Reports, 1860–1891.

WALLIS, J. P. R., ed. *The Matabele Mission,* London, Chatto and Windus, 1945. (Oppenheimer Series No. 2.)

(b) *Missionary Movement: Analytical Accounts*

ANDERSON, W. *Towards a Theology of Mission: A Study of the Encounter between the Missionary Enterprise and the Church and its Theology,* London, S.C.M., 1955. (I.M.C. Research Pamphlet No. 2.)

CUST, R. N. *Essay on the Prevailing Methods of the Evangelization of the Non-Christian World,* London, Luzac, 1894.

—— *Notes on Missionary Subjects,* London, Elliot Stock, 1889.

DENNIS, J. S. *Christian Missions and Social Progress,* New York, F. H. Revell, 1897–1906, 3 vols.

DEWICK, E. C. *The Christian Attitude to Other Religions,* New York, Cambridge University Press, 1953.

GOODLOE, R. W. 'Missionaries as Transmitters of Western Civilization in Nineteenth Century Africa', Thesis submitted for the degree of Ph.D. to the University of St. Andrews, Sept., 1955.

HARRIES, L. P. *Islam in East Africa,* London, U.M.C.A., 1954.

HOGG, W. R. *Ecumenical Foundations,* New York, Harper, 1952.

JOHNSTON, H. H., 'British Missions and Missionaries in Africa', *Nineteenth Century,* Nov., 1887.

KRAEMER, H. *The Christian Message in a Non-Christian World,* London, Edinburgh House Press, 1938.

BIBLIOGRAPHY

LUCAS, W. V. and JAMES, E. O. *Christianity and Native Rites*, 2nd ed., London, Central Africa House Press, 1950.
MOTT, J. R. *The Evangelization of the World in this Generation*, New York, Student Volunteer Movement for Foreign Missions, 1900.
PRICE, M. T. *Christian Missions and Oriental Civilizations*, Shanghai, Privately Printed, 1924.
ROUSE, R. 'A Study of Missionary Vocation', *International Review of Missions*, April, 1917.
SMITH, E. W. *The Blessed Missionaries*, Cape Town, O.U.P., 1950.
SUNDKLER, B. G. M. *Bantu Prophets in South Africa*, London, Lutterworth, 1948.
TAYLOR, J. V. *The Growth of the Church in Buganda*, London, S.C.M., 1958.
—— *Processes of Growth in an African Church*, London, S.C.M., 1958. (I.M.C. Research Pamphlet No. 6.)
TRIMINGHAM, J. S. *The Christian Church and Islam in West Africa*, London, S.C.M., 1955. (I.M.C. Research Pamphlet No. 3.)
WARNECK, G. *Modern Missions and Culture, Their Mutual Relations*, new ed., Edinburgh, Ballantyne, Hanson, n.d. (trans. T. Smith).

(c) *Missionary Conferences and Meetings*

BADGER, G. P. *Christianity in its Relations to Islam, a Paper Read at the Missionary Conference, Oxford, 3rd May, 1877*, London, William Wells Gardner, 1877.
Centenary of the London Missionary Society, Proceedings of the Founders' Week Convention . . . 1895, London, L.M.S., n.d.
Central Africa Mission, Report of Anniversary Services and Meeting, 1882, Westminster, U.M.C.A., n.d.
Conference on Missions Held in 1860 at Liverpool, rev., London, James Nisbet, 1860 (ed. by the Secretaries).
JOHNSTON, J., ed. *Report of the Centenary Conference on the Protestant Missions of the World . . . London, 1888*, London, James Nisbet, 1889, 2 vols.
Proceedings of the Conference on Foreign Missions . . . 1886, London, Shaw, 1886.
Proceedings of the General Conference on Foreign Missions . . . 1878, London, Shaw, 1879 (ed. by the Secretaries).
Report of the Proceedings at a Meeting Held in the Law Association Rooms, Liverpool, in connection with the Universities' Mission to Central Africa: Including an Address delivered by the Right Rev. Bishop Steere, Liverpool, Thomas Brakell, 1882.
SPOTTISWOODE, G. A., ed. *The Official Report of the Missionary Conference of the Anglican Communion . . . 1894*, London, S.P.C.K., 1894.
'Universities Mission to Central Africa, Annual Meeting in Liverpool', from the *Liverpool Daily Courier*, Nov. 3, 1868, in S.P.G. London offices, Vol. 14859.

BIBLIOGRAPHY

(d) *David Livingstone*

BLAIKIE, W. G. *The Personal Life of David Livingstone*, 8th ed., London, John Murray, 1897.
CAMPBELL, J. R. *Livingstone*, London, Benn, 1929.
CHAMBERLIN, D., ed. *Some Letters from Livingstone 1840-1872*, London, O.U.P., 1940.
COUPLAND, R. *Livingstone's Last Journey*, London, Collins, 1945.
DEBENHAM, F. *The Way to Ilala: David Livingstone's Pilgrimage*, London, Longmans, 1955.
FRAZER, A. Z. *Livingstone and Newstead*, London, John Murray, 1913.
GELFAND, M. *Livingstone the Doctor*, Oxford, Blackwell, 1957.
LIVINGSTONE, D. *Missionary Travels and Researches in South Africa*, London, John Murray, 1857.
LIVINGSTONE, D. and C. *Narrative of an Expedition to the Zambesi and its Tributaries*, London, John Murray, 1865.
MACNAIR, J. I. *Livingstone the Liberator*, London and Glasgow, Collins, n.d.
—— *Livingstone's Travels*, London, Dent, 1954.
MONK, W., ed. *Dr. Livingstone's Cambridge Lectures*, 2nd ed., Cambridge, Deighton, Bell, 1860.
SCHAPERA, I., ed. *David Livingstone: Family Letters, 1841-1856*, London, Chatto and Windus, 1959, 2 vols.
—— ed. *Livingstone's Private Journals 1851-53*, London, Chatto and Windus, 1960.
SEAVER, G. *David Livingstone: His Life and Letters*, London, Lutterworth, 1957.
WALLER, H., ed. *The Last Journals of David Livingstone in Central Africa*, London, John Murray, 1874, 2 vols.
WALLIS, J. P. R., ed. *The Zambesi Expedition of David Livingstone 1858-1863*, London, Chatto and Windus, 1956, 2 vols. (Oppenheimer Series No. 9.)

(e) *Accounts of and by Missionaries about their work, travel and African conditions*

ARNOT, F. S. *Bihe and Garenganze*, London, Hawkins, n.d.
—— *Garenganze*, London, Hawkins, n.d.
ASHE, R. P. *Chronicles of Uganda*, London, Hodder and Stoughton, 1894.
—— *Two Kings of Uganda*, London, Sampson Low, 1889.
AWDRY, F. *An Elder Sister, A Short Sketch of Anne Mackenzie, and her Brother, the Missionary Bishop*, 3rd ed., London, Bemrose, 1904.
BAKER, E. *The Life and Explorations of Frederick Stanley Arnot*, London, Seeley, Service & Co., 1921.
BARNES, B. H. *Johnson of Nyasaland*, Westminster, U.M.C.A., 1933.
CARNEGIE, D. *Among the Matabele*, 2nd ed., London, Religious Tract Society, 1894.

BIBLIOGRAPHY

COILLARD, F. *On the Threshold of Central Africa*, 2nd ed., London, Hodder and Stoughton, 1902 (trans. and ed. by C. W. Mackintosh).

CROSS, D. KERR. 'Dawn in Nyasaland', *Blackwood's Magazine*, Nov., 1891.

—— 'Geographical Notes on the Country between Lakes Nyassa, Rukwa, and Tanganyika', *S.G.M.*, June, 1890.

DAWSON, E. C. *James Hannington, First Bishop of Eastern Equatorial Africa*, London, Seeley & Co., 1890.

—— ed. *The Last Journals of Bishop Hannington*, London, Seeley & Co., 1888.

DU PLESSIS, J. *A Thousand Miles in the Heart of Africa*, Edinburgh and London, Oliphant, Anderson and Ferrier, 1905.

ELLIOTT, W. A. *Gold from the Quartz*, London, L.M.S., 1910.

ELMSLIE, W. A. *Among the Wild Ngoni*, Edinburgh and London, Oliphant, Anderson and Ferrier, 1899.

FARLER, J. P. 'England and Germany in East Africa', *Fortnightly Review*, Feb., 1889.

—— *The Work of Christ in Central Africa*, London, Rivingtons, 1878.

FELKIN, R. W. 'Can Europeans become Acclimatised in Tropical Africa?' *S.G.M.*, Nov., 1886.

—— 'Uganda', *S.G.M.*, April, 1886.

FRASER, A. R. *Donald Fraser of Livingstonia*, London, Hodder and Stoughton, 1934.

FRASER, D. *African Idylls*, London, Seeley, Service & Co., 1923.

—— *The Future of Africa*, London, C.M.S., 1911.

—— *Winning a Primitive People*, London, Seeley, Service & Co., 1914.

FRIPP, E. and HILLER, V. W., eds. *Gold and the Gospel in Mashonaland, 1888*, London, Chatto and Windus, 1949. (Oppenheimer Series No. 4.)

GOODWIN, H. *Memoir of Bishop Mackenzie*, 2nd ed., Cambridge, Deighton, Bell, 1865.

HARFORD-BATTERSBY, C. F. *Pilkington of Uganda*, London, Marshall Bros., n.d.

HEANLEY, R. M. *A Memoir of Edward Steere*, 2nd ed. rev., London, George Bell, 1890.

HETHERWICK, A. *The Gospel and the African*, Edinburgh, Clark, 1932.

—— *The Romance of Blantyre*, London, Clarke, 1931.

HINE, J. E. *Days Gone By*, London, John Murray, 1924.

HINE, J. E. *Introductory Words Spoken at a Conference of Clergy and Laity, held at Likoma, April 24, 1899*, Likoma, U.M.C.A., n.d. (for private circulation only).

HORE, A. B. *To Lake Tanganyika in a Bath Chair*, London, Sampson Low, 1889.

HORE, E. C. 'Lake Tanganyika', *Proc. R.G.S.*, Jan., 1882.

—— *Tanganyika: Eleven Years in Central Africa*, London, Edward Stanford, 1892.

—— 'On the Twelve Tribes of Tanganyika', *J.R.A.I.*, 1882.

JOHNSON, W. P. *My African Reminiscences 1875–1895*, Westminster, U.M.C.A., n.d.

BIBLIOGRAPHY

JOHNSON, W. P. *Nyasa the Great Water*, London, O.U.P., 1922.
KNIGHT-BRUCE, G. H. W. *Journals of the Mashonaland Mission. 1888 to 1892*, London, S.P.G., 1892.
—— *Memories of Mashonaland*, London, Edward Arnold, 1895.
KRAPF, J. L. *Travels, Researches, and Missionary Labours*, London, Trubner, 1860.
LAWS, R. *Reminiscences of Livingstonia*, Edinburgh, Oliver and Boyd, 1934.
LIVINGSTONE, W. P. *Laws of Livingstonia*, London, Hodder and Stoughton, 1921.
—— *A Prince of Missionaries: The Rev. Alexander Hetherwick*, London, Clarke, n.d.
MACCONNACHIE, J. *An Artisan Missionary on the Zambesi—Being the Life Story of William Thomson Waddell*, Edinburgh and London, Oliphant, Anderson and Ferrier, n.d.
MACDONALD, D. *Africana: or, the Heart of Heathen Africa*, London, Simpkin Marshall, 1882, 2 vols.
A. M. Mackay—Pioneer Missionary of the Church Missionary Society to Uganda, by his Sister, 8th ed., London, Hodder and Stoughton, 1898.
MACKENZIE, J. 'Bechuanaland, with some Remarks on Mashonaland and Matabeleland', *S.G.M.*, June, 1887.
—— *Ten Years North of the Orange River*, Edinburgh, Edmonston and Douglas, 1871.
MAPLES, C. 'A Village Community in East Africa', *Mission Life*, March, 1882; April, 1882.
MAPLES, E. *Chauncy Maples, Pioneer Missionary in East Central Africa*, London, Longmans, 1897.
MOFFAT, R. *Missionary Labours and Scenes in Southern Africa*, London, John Snow, 1842.
MOFFAT, R. U. *John Smith Moffat, C.M.G. Missionary, A Memoir*, London, John Murray, 1921.
MULLENS, J. 'A New Route and New Mode of Travelling into Central Africa, adopted by the Rev. Roger Price in 1876, described by the Rev. Joseph Mullens, D.D.', *Proc R.G.S.*, 1876–7.
NEW, C. *Life, Wanderings, and Labours in Eastern Africa*, London, Hodder and Stoughton, 1873.
NORTHCOTT, C. *Robert Moffat: Pioneer in Africa 1817–1870*, London, Lutterworth, 1961.
PRICE, W. S. *My Third Campaign in East Africa*, London, Hunt, 1890.
PROCTER, L. T. 'Life among the Manganja', *Mission Life*, Aug., 1867; Sept., 1867; Oct., 1867; Dec., 1867.
PRUEN, S. T. *The Arab and the African*, London, Seeley, 1891.
RANDOLPH, B. W. *Arthur Douglas, Missionary on Lake Nyasa*, Westminster, U.M.C.A., 1912.
RANKINE, W. H. *A Hero of the Dark Continent, Memoir of Rev. Wm. Affleck Scott*, Edinburgh and London, Blackwood, 1896.
ROWLEY, H. *Africa Unveiled*, London, S.P.C.K., 1876.

BIBLIOGRAPHY

ROWLEY, H. 'African Slave Trade and Slavery', *Mission Life*, Oct., 1867; Dec., 1867.

—— 'Life among the Portuguese in Eastern Africa', *Mission Life*, March, 1868.

—— *The Religion of the Africans*, London, William Wells Gardner, n.d.

SHAW, M. *God's Candlelights*, New York, Friendship Press, 1943.

SIM, A. F. *Life and Letters of Arthur Fraser Sim*, Westminster, U.M.C.A., 1896.

SMITH, E. W. *Great Lion of Bechuanaland. The Life and Times of Roger Price, Missionary*, London, Independent Press, 1957.

—— *The Life and Times of Daniel Lindley (1801–80)*, London, Epworth Press, 1949.

Smythies, Bishop. *Address delivered by the Right Rev. the Bishop of the Universities' Mission to Central Africa to the Clergy and Members of the Mission, assembled in Synod in Christ Church, Zanzibar, in the third week after Easter, 1884*, 2nd ed., Zanzibar, U.M.C.A., 1886.

—— *A Journey from Matope on the Upper Shire to Newala on the Rovuma by the Right Rev. the Bishop in 1885*, Corrected ed., Zanzibar, U.M.C.A., 1885.

—— *Pastoral Letter addressed to the Clergy and Members of the Universities' Mission to Central Africa, by the Right Rev. the Bishop*, Zanzibar, U.M.C.A., 1885.

—— *Pastoral Letter by the Bishop of the Universities' Mission to Central Africa*, Zanzibar, U.M.C.A., 1888.

STEERE, E. *Central African Mission—Its Present State and Prospects*, London, Rivingtons, 1873.

—— *Letter of Bishop Steere to the Late Secretary of the Universities' Mission Prayer Union*, 3rd ed., Exmouth (no publisher), 1877.

—— 'Missions and the Civil Power', *Mission Life*, May, 1881.

—— *The Universities' Mission to Central Africa, A Speech Delivered at Oxford*, London, Harrison, 1875.

—— *A Walk to the Nyassa Country*, London, R. Clay, 1876.

SWANN, A. J. *Fighting the Slave-Hunters in Central Africa*, London, Seeley, 1910.

THOMAS, H. B. 'The Last Days of Bishop Hannington', *U.J.*, Sept., 1940.

THOMAS, T. M. *Eleven Years in Central South Africa*, London, John Snow, 1873.

TOZER, BISHOP, *Pastoral Letter from Bishop Tozer*, Zanzibar, U.M.C.A., 1870.

WAKEFIELD, E. S. *Thomas Wakefield, Missionary and Geographical Pioneer in East Equatorial Africa*, London, Religious Tract Society, 1904.

WALLIS, J. P. R., ed. *The Matabele Journals of Robert Moffat, 1829–1860*, London, Chatto and Windus, 1945, 2 vols. (Oppenheimer Series No. 1.)

—— ed. *The Zambesi Journal of James Stewart, 1862–1863*, London, Chatto and Windus, 1952. (Oppenheimer Series No. 6.)

BIBLIOGRAPHY

WARD, G., ed. *Letters of Bishop Tozer and his Sister*, London, U.M.C.A., 1902.
—— and RUSSELL, E. F., eds. *The Life of Charles Alan Smythies*, 2nd ed., London, U.M.C.A., 1899.
WATT, R. S. *In the Heart of Savagedom*, 4th ed., London, Pickering and Inglis, n.d.
WELLS, J. *Stewart of Lovedale: The Life of James Stewart*, 3rd ed., London, Hodder and Stoughton, 1909.
WILSON, C. T. and FELKIN, R. W. *Uganda and the Egyptian Soudan*, London, Sampson Low, 1882, 2 vols.
YARBOROUGH, J. C. ed. *The Diary of a Working Man (William Bellingham) in Central Africa, December 1884, to October, 1887*, London, S.P.C.K., n.d.

V. ACCOUNTS OF AND BY NON-MISSIONARIES ABOUT THEIR WORK, TRAVEL, AND AFRICAN CONDITIONS

ACUTT, R. N. 'The Reminiscences of Robert Noble Acutt: Sidelights on South African Life', reprinted from *South Africa*, January, 1926.
ANSTRUTHER, I. *I Presume: Stanley's Triumph and Disaster*, London, Geoffrey Bles, 1956.
BADEN-POWELL, R. S. S. *The Matabele Campaign 1896*, London, Methuen, 1897.
BAKER, J. N. L. 'Sir Richard Burton and the Nile Sources', *U.J.*, March, 1948.
BAKER, S. *The Albert N'yanza*, new ed., London, Macmillan, 1898.
—— *Ismailia*, 2nd ed., London, Macmillan, 1879.
—— *The Nile Tributaries of Abyssinia*, new ed., London, Macmillan, 1883.
BALDWIN, W. C. *African Hunting and Adventure from Natal to the Zambesi*, 2nd ed., London, Bentley, 1863.
BALFOUR, A. B. *Twelve Hundred Miles in a Waggon*, London, Edward Arnold, 1895.
'BAMANG-WATO.' *To Ophir Direct: Or, the South African Gold Fields*, London, Edward Stanford, 1868. (Attributed by Tabler, *Far Interior*, 1955, 288, to A. Broderick.)
BELL, W. D. M. *The Wanderings of an Elephant Hunter*, London, Neville Spearman and the Holland Press, 1958.
BENT, J. T. 'The Ruins of Mashonaland and Explorations in the Country', *Proc. R.G.S.*, May, 1892.
BERTRAND, A. *The Kingdom of the Barotsi*, London, Fisher Unwin, 1899 (trans. A. B. Miall).
BETHELL, A. J., *Notes on South African Hunting and Notes on a Ride to the Victoria Falls of the Zambesi*, London, Whittaker, 1887.
BLAKE, J. Y. F. 'Golden Rhodesia—a Revelation', *National Review*, Aug., 1897.
—— 'Native Rhodesia', *National Review*, Oct., 1897.
—— 'Second Thoughts on Rhodesia', *National Review*, March, 1898.

BIBLIOGRAPHY

BLENNERHASSETT, R. and SLEEMAN, L. *Adventures in Mashonaland by Two Hospital Nurses*, London, Macmillan, 1893.

BOWLER, L. P. *Facts about the Matabele, Mashonas, and the Middle Zambesi*, Pretoria, B. Gluckstein, 1889.

BROWN, W. H. *On the South African Frontier*, New York, Scribner's, 1899.

BROYON, P. 'Description of Unyamwesi, the Territory of King Mirambo, and the Best Route Thither from the East Coast', *Proc. R.G.S.*, 1877-8.

BRYDEN, H. A. *Nature and Sport in South Africa*, London, Chapman and Hall, 1897.

BUCHANAN, J. *The Shire Highlands (East Central Africa) as Colony and Mission*, Edinburgh and London, Blackwoods, 1885.

BURNHAM, F. R. *Scouting on Two Continents*, London, Heinemann, 1927.

BURTON, I. *The Life of Captain Sir Richard F. Burton*, London, Chapman and Hall, 1893, 2 vols.

BURTON, R. F. *The Lake Regions of Central Africa*, London, Longmans, 1860, 2 vols.

—— *The Lands of Cazembe, Lacerda's Journey to Cazembe in 1798*, London, John Murray, 1873.

—— *Zanzibar: City, Island and Coast*, London, Tinsley, 1872, 2 vols.

CADDICK, H. *A White Woman in Central Africa*, London, Fisher Unwin, 1900.

CAMERON, V. L. *Across Africa*, new ed., London, Philip, 1885.

—— 'On the Anthropology of Africa', *J.R.A.I.*, 1877.

—— 'Colonization of Central Africa', *Proc. R.C.I.*, 1875-6.

—— 'Journey Across Africa, From Bagomoyo to Benguela', *Proc. R.G.S.*, 1875-6.

—— 'Slavery in Africa—The Disease and the Remedy', *National Review*, Oct., 1888.

—— 'Slavery in its Relation to Trade in Tropical Africa', *Journal of the Society of Arts*, March 1, 1889.

—— 'The Trade of Central Africa, Present and Future', *Journal of the Society of Arts*, Jan. 26, 1877.

—— 'Zanzibar. Its Past, Present and Future', *Revue Coloniale Internationale*, Tome I, 1885.

CARDEW, C. A. 'Nyasaland in the Nineties', *N.J.*, Jan., 1955.

CASATI, G. *Ten Years in Equatoria and the Return with Emin Pasha*, London and New York, Warne, 1891, 2 vols. (trans. Mrs. J. R. Clay).

CHAILLE-LONG, C. *Central Africa: Naked Truths of Naked People*, London, Sampson Low, 1876.

CHALMERS, J. *Fighting the Matabele*, London, Blackie, 1898.

CHURCHILL, LORD RANDOLPH S. *Men, Mines and Animals in South Africa*, new ed., London, Sampson Low, 1895.

CLARK, P. M. *The Autobiography of an Old Drifter*, London, Harrap, 1936.

COLQUHOUN, A. R. 'Matabeleland', *Proc. R.C.I.*, 1893-4.

COTTERILL, H. B. 'On the Nyassa and a Journey from the North End to Zanzibar', *Proc. R.G.S.*, 1877-8.

BIBLIOGRAPHY

COOPER-CHADWICK, J. *Three Years with Lobengula*, London, Cassell, 1894.

COUPLAND, R. *Kirk on the Zambesi*, Oxford, Clarendon Press, 1928.

DAWNAY, G. C. *Private Journal of Guy C. Dawnay*, London, Privately Printed, n.d. (Vol. vii?)

DEARDEN, S. *The Arabian Knight: A Study of Sir Richard Burton*, rev. ed., London, Barker, 1953.

DEVEREUX, W. C. *A Cruise in the Gorgon*, London, Bell and Daldy, 1869.

DONOVAN, C. W. H. *With the Victoria Column in Matabeleland*, Aldershot, Gale and Polden, 1894.

DRUMMOND, H. *Tropical Africa*, 13th ed., London, Hodder and Stoughton, 1908.

ELTON, J. F. *Travels and Researches among the Lakes and Mountains of Eastern and Central Africa*, London, John Murray, 1879 (ed. and completed by H. B. Cotterill).

ELTON, LORD. *General Gordon*, London, Collins, 1954.

FARWELL, B. *The Man Who Presumed. A Biography of Henry M. Stanley*, London, Longmans, 1958.

FAULKNER, H. *Elephant Haunts*, London, Hurst and Blackett, 1868.

FINAUGHTY, W. *The Recollections of William Finaughty, Elephant Hunter, 1864–1875*, Philadelphia, Privately Printed, 1916.

FINLASON, G. E. *A Nobody in Mashonaland*, London, Vickers, 1894.

FORAN, W. R. *African Odyssey—The Life of Verney Lovett Cameron*, London, Hutchinson, 1937.

FOTHERINGHAM, L. M. *Adventures in Nyassaland*, London, Sampson Low, 1891.

GIBBONS, A. ST. H. *Exploration and Hunting in Central Africa*, London, Methuen, 1898.

—— 'Marotseland and the Tribes of the Upper Zambesi', *Proc. R.C.I.*, 1897–8.

GLAVE, E. J. 'Glave in Nyasaland', *Century Illustrated Magazine*, August, 1896.

GRANT, J. A. 'Summary of Observations on the Geography, Climate, and Natural History of the Lake Region of Equatorial Africa, made by the Speke and Grant Expedition, 1860–63', *J.R.G.S.*, 1872.

—— *A Walk Across Africa*, Edinburgh and London, Blackwood, 1864.

GRAY, J. M. 'Speke and Grant', *U.J.*, Sept., 1953.

GREEN, E. G. *Raiders and Rebels in South Africa*, London, Newnes, 1896.

HARRIS, W. C. *The Wild Sports of Southern Africa*, 4th ed., London, Pelham, Richardson, Cornhill, 1844.

HINDE, S. L. *The Fall of the Congo Arabs*, London, Methuen, 1897.

HIRD, F. *H. M. Stanley: The Authorized Life*, London, Stanley Paul, 1935.

HOLUB, E. 'On the Central South African Tribes from the South Coast to the Zambesi', *J.R.A.I.*, 1880.

—— 'The Past, Present and Future Trade of the Cape Colonies with Central Africa', *Proc. R.C.I.*, 1879–80.

—— *Seven Years in South Africa*, London, Sampson Low, 1881, 2 vols. (trans. E. E. Frewer).

BIBLIOGRAPHY

INGHAM, K. 'John Hanning Speke: A Victorian and his Inspiration', *T.N.R.*, Dec., 1957.

JOHNSON, F. *Great Days: The Autobiography of an Empire Pioneer*, London, Bell, 1940.

JOHNSTON, A. *The Life and Letters of Sir Harry Johnston*, London, Jonathan Cape, 1929.

JOHNSTON, H. H. 'British Central Africa', *New Review*, July, 1894.

—— 'The Commercial Development of Central Africa, and Its Beneficent Results on the Slave Traffic', *Journal of the Tyneside Geographical Society*, Dec., 1894.

—— 'The Development of Tropical Africa under British Auspices', *Fortnightly Review*, Nov., 1890.

—— 'England's Work in Central Africa', *Proc. R.C.I.*, 1896–7.

—— *The Kilima-Njaro Expedition*, London, Kegan Paul, 1886.

—— 'The People of Eastern Equatorial Africa', *J.R.A.I.*, 1885.

—— *The Story of my Life*, London, Chatto and Windus, 1923.

—— 'The Value of Africa: A Reply to Sir John Pope Hennessy', *Nineteenth Century*, Aug., 1890.

JOHNSTON, J. *Reality versus Romance in South Central Africa*, London, Hodder and Stoughton, 1893.

KERR, W. M. *The Far Interior*, London, Sampson Low, 1886, 2 vols.

—— 'The Upper Zambesi Zone', *S.G.M.*, July, 1886.

KINGSLEY, M. H. 'The Development of Dodos', *National Review*, March, 1896.

LAING, D. T. *The Matabele Rebellion, 1896: With the Belingwe Field Force*, London, Dean and Son, n.d.

LUGARD, F. D. 'The Extension of British Influence (and Trade) in Africa', *Proc. R.C.I.*, 1895–6.

—— 'The Fight Against Slave-Traders on Nyassa', *Contemporary Review*, Sept., 1889.

—— 'A Glimpse of Lake Nyassa', *Blackwood's Magazine*, Jan., 1890.

—— *The Rise of Our East African Empire*, Edinburgh and London, Blackwood, 1893, 2 vols.

MACKENZIE, G. S. 'British East Africa', *Proc. R.C.I.*, 1890–1.

MANDY, F. *Matabeleland: The Future Gold Fields of the World*, Cape Town, Argus, 1889.

MANN, R. J. 'Account of Mr. Baines's Exploration of the Gold Bearing Region between the Limpopo and Zambesi Rivers', *J.R.G.S.*, 1871.

MAUND, E. A. 'Mashonaland and its Development', *Proc. R.C.I.*, 1891–2.

MCLEOD, J. *Travels in Eastern Africa*, London, Hurst and Blackett, 1860, 2 vols.

MEINERTZHAGEN, R. *Kenya Diary—1902–1906*, Edinburgh and London, Oliver and Boyd, 1957.

MIDDLETON, D. *Baker of the Nile*, London, Falcon Press, 1949.

MILLAIS, J. G. *Life of Frederick Courtenay Selous*, London, Longmans, 1919.

MOHR, E. *To the Victoria Falls of the Zambesi*, London, Sampson Low, 1876 (trans. N. D'Anvers).

BIBLIOGRAPHY

MOIR, F. L. M. *After Livingstone: An African Trade Romance*, 3rd ed., London, Hodder and Stoughton, 1924.
—— 'Eastern Route to Central Africa', *S.G.M.*, April, 1885.
—— 'Englishmen and Arabs in East Africa', *Murray's Magazine*, Nov., 1888.
MOIR, J. F. *A Lady's Letters from Central Africa*, Glasgow, Maclehose, 1891.
MOUNTENEY-JEPHSON, A. J. *Emin Pasha and the Rebellion at the Equator* London, Sampson Low, 1890.
MURRAY, T. D. and WHITE, A. S. *Sir Samuel Baker: A Memoir*, London, Macmillan, 1895.
OATES, C. G., ed. *Matabele Land and the Victoria Falls*, 2nd ed., London, Kegan Paul, 1889.
OLIVER, R. *Sir Harry Johnston and the Scramble for Africa*, London, Chatto and Windus, 1957.
O'NEILL, H. E. 'East Africa, Between the Zambesi and Rovuma Rivers: Its People, Riches, and Development', *S.G.M.*, Aug., 1885.
—— 'Eastern Africa between the Zambesi and Rovuma Rivers', *Proc. R.G.S.*, July, 1885.
OSWELL, W. E. *William Cotton Oswell, Hunter and Explorer*, London, Heinemann, 1900, 2 vols.
OWEN, W. F. W. *Narrative of Voyages to Explore the Shores of Africa, Arabia, and Madagascar*, London, Bentley, 1833, 2 vols.
PARKE, T. H. *My Personal Experiences in Equatorial Africa as Medical Officer of the Emin Pasha Relief Expedition*, 2nd ed., London, Sampson Low, n.d.
PATTERSON, J. H. *The Man-Eaters of Tsavo*, London, Macmillan, 1952.
PAULET, C. J. 'Early Days in Rhodesia', *New Review*, June, 1896.
PERHAM, M. *Lugard—The Years of Adventure, 1858-1898*, London, Collins, 1956.
PETHERICK, J. *Egypt, the Soudan and Central Africa*, Edinburgh and London, Blackwood, 1861.
PRINGLE M. A. *A Journey in East Africa towards the Mountains of the Moon*, new ed., Edinburgh and London, Blackwood, 1886.
RANKIN, D. J. 'The Discovery of the Chinde Entrance to the Zambesi River', *Fortnightly Review*, Dec., 1892.
RISLEY, R. C. H. 'Burton: An Appreciation', *T.N.R.*, Dec., 1957.
RODD, J. R. *Social and Diplomatic Memories*, London, Edward Arnold, 1922.
RORKE, M. *Melina Rorke: Her Amazing Experiences in the Stormy Nineties of South Africa's Story*, London, Harrap, 1939.
ROUILLARD, N., ed. *Matabele Thompson, an Autobiography*, London, Faber, 1936.
RUKAVINA, K. *Jungle Pathfinder*, Arrow Books, 1957.
RUSSELL, C. E. B., ed. *General Rigby, Zanzibar and the Slave Trade*, London, Allen and Unwin, 1935.
SCHULZ, A., and HAMMAR, A. *The New Africa*, London, Heinemann, 1897.

BIBLIOGRAPHY

SCOTT, E. D. *Some Letters from South Africa, 1894–1902*, Manchester and London, Sherratt and Hughes, 1903.

SELOUS, F. C. 'Incidents of a Hunter's Life in South Africa', *Proc. R.C.I.*, 1892–3.

—— 'The History of the Matabele, and the Cause and Effect of the Matabele War', *Proc. R.C.I.*, 1893–4.

—— *A Hunter's Wanderings in Africa*, 5th ed., London, Macmillan, 1907.

—— *Sunshine and Storm in Rhodesia*, 2nd ed., London, Rowland Ward, 1896.

—— *Travel and Adventure in South-East Africa*, London, Rowland Ward, 1893.

SHARPE, A. 'Central African Trade, and the Nyasaland Water-Way', *Blackwood's Magazine*, Feb., 1892.

SPEKE, J. H. *Journal of the Discovery of the Source of the Nile*, London, Dent, n.d. (Everyman Edition).

—— *What Led to the Discovery of the Source of the Nile*, Blackwood, Edinburgh and London, 1864.

STANLEY, D., ed. *The Autobiography of Sir Henry Morton Stanley*, 3rd ed., London, Sampson Low, n.d.

STANLEY, H. M. 'Central Africa and the Congo Basin', *S.G.M.*, Jan.–March, 1885.

—— 'The Emin Pasha Relief Expeditions', *S.G.M.*, July, 1890.

—— *How I Found Livingstone*, London, Sampson Low, n.d.

—— *In Darkest Africa*, new ed., London, Sampson Low, 1893.

—— *Through the Dark Continent*, new ed., London, Sampson Low, 1890.

STARKIE, E. *Arthur Rimbaud in Abyssinia*, Oxford, Clarendon Press, 1937.

STEPHENSON, J. E. *Chirupula's Tale*, London, Geoffrey Bles, 1937.

STEVENS, T. *Scouting for Stanley in East Africa*, London, Cassell, n.d.

SURRIDGE, F. H. 'Matabeleland and Mashonaland', *Proc. R.C.I.*, 1890–1.

THOMSON, J. *Africa and the Liquor Traffic. A Lecture delivered at Manchester on May 18th, 1887*, London, Native Races and the Liquor Traffic United Committee, n.d.

—— 'East Africa as It was and Is', *Contemporary Review*, Jan., 1889.

—— 'East Central Africa and Its Commercial Outlook', *S.G.M.*, Feb., 1886.

—— 'Note on the African Tribes of the British Empire', *J.R.A.I.*, 1886.

—— 'The Results of European Intercourse with the African', *Contemporary Review*, March, 1890.

—— *Through Masai Land*, 2nd ed., London, Sampson Low, 1885.

—— *To the Central African Lakes and Back*, London, Sampson Low, 1881, 2 vols.

THOMSON, J. B. *Joseph Thomson—African Explorer*, 2nd ed., London, Sampson Low, 1897.

VAUGHAN-WILLIAMS, H. *A Visit to Lobengula in 1889*, Pietermaritzburg, Shuter and Shooter, 1947.

VON HOHNEL, L. *Discovery of Lakes Rudolf and Stefanie*, London, Longmans, 1894, 2 vols. (trans. N. Bell).

BIBLIOGRAPHY

VON WISSMAN, H. *My Second Journey through Equatorial Africa*, London, Chatto and Windus, 1891 (trans. M. J. A. Bergmann).
WALLIS, J. P. R. ed. *The Northern Goldfields Diaries of Thomas Baines*, London, Chatto and Windus, 1946, 3 vols. (Oppenheimer Series No. 3.)
—— ed. *The Southern African Diaries of Thomas Leask, 1865–1870*, London, Chatto and Windus, 1954. (Oppenheimer Series No. 8.)
—— *Thomas Baines of King's Lynn*, London, Jonathan Cape, 1941.
WARD, H. *Five Years with the Congo Cannibals*, 3rd ed., London, Chatto and Windus, 1891.
WILLIAMS, W. H. 'Uganda', *Proc. R.C.I.*, 1893–4.
WILLOUGHBY, J. C. *East Africa and its Big Game*, London, Longmans, 1889.
—— *A Narrative of Further Excavation at Zimbabye (Mashonaland)*, London, Philip, 1893.
WILLS, W. A. and COLLINGRIDGE, L. T. *The Downfall of Lobengula: The Causes, History, and Effect of the Matabele War*, London, Simpkin, Marshall, n.d.
WOLSELEY, G. 'The Negro as a Soldier', *Fortnightly Review*, Dec., 1888.
WOOD, J. G. *Through Matabeleland*, Grahamstown, Grocott and Sherry, 1893.
YOUNG, E. D. *Nyassa: A Journal of Adventures*, London, John Murray, 1877 (rev. H. Waller).
—— *The Search after Livingstone*, London, Simpkin, Marshall, 1868 (rev. H. Waller).

VI. SOCIOLOGICAL, ANTHROPOLOGICAL AND COMPARATIVE MATERIAL

Africa, October, 1935. (Special witchcraft issue.)
ARENDT, H. *The Origins of Totalitarianism*, 2nd ed., New York, Meridian Books, 1960.
BANTON, M. *White and Coloured*, London, Jonathan Cape, 1959.
BARNES, J. A. 'History in a Changing Society', *R.L.J.* (XI), 1951.
BENEDICT, R. *The Chrysanthemum and the Sword*, Boston, Houghton Mifflin, 1946.
BLYDEN, E. W. 'The African Problem', *North American Review*, Sept., 1895.
—— *Christianity, Islam and the Negro Race*, London, Whittingham, 1887.
BOWIE, D. F. 'The Lip Plug or "Ndonya" among the Tribes of the Southern Province', *T.N.R.*, June, 1949.
BURTON, R. F. 'Notes on Certain Matters Connected with the Dahoman', *Memoirs Read before the Anthropological Society of London*, 1863–4.
COLSON, E. and GLUCKMAN, M. eds. *Seven Tribes of British Central Africa*, London, O.U.P., 1951.
COMAS, J. *Racial Myths*, Paris, U.N.E.S.C.O., 1953.
CROMER, EARL OF. *Modern Egypt*, London, Macmillan, 1908, 2 vols.

BIBLIOGRAPHY

DOLLARD, J. *Caste and Class in a Southern Town*, 3rd ed., New York, Doubleday, 1957.

DRUMMOND, H. *The Lowell Lectures on the Ascent of Man*, London, Hodder and Stoughton, 1894.

DUNN, L. C. *Race and Biology*, Paris, U.N.E.S.C.O., 1952.

EVANS-PRITCHARD, E. E. et al. *The Institutions of Primitive Society*, Oxford, Blackwell, 1954.

—— 'Levy-Bruhl's Theory of Primitive Mentality', Extract from the *Bulletin of the Faculty of Arts* of the Egyptian University, Vol. II, Part I, 1934.

—— *The Nuer*, Oxford, Clarendon Press, 1940.

FIRTH, R. *Elements of Social Organization*, 2nd ed., London, Watts, 1956.

FORDE, D., ed. *African Worlds*, London, O.U.P., 1954.

FREYRE, G. *Brazil an Interpretation*, New York, Knopf, 1951.

—— *The Masters and the Slaves*, New York, Knopf, 1946.

GLUCKMAN, M. 'As Men are Everywhere Else', *The Listener*, Sept. 22, 1955.

—— 'As Men are Everywhere Else', *R.L.J.* (XX), 1956.

—— *Custom and Conflict in Africa*, Oxford, Blackwell, 1955.

—— 'The Origins of Social Organization', *R.L.J.* (XII), 1951.

—— 'Social Anthropology in Central Africa', *R.L.J.* (XX), 1956.

—— MITCHELL, C., and BARNES, J. A. 'The Village Headman in British Central Africa', *Africa*, April, 1949.

GOWER, R. H. 'Two Views on the Masai', *T.N.R.*, Dec., 1948.

HALLOWELL, A. I., 'Temporal Orientation in Western Civilization and in a Pre-Literate Society', *American Anthropologist*, 1937.

HANDLIN, O. *Race and Nationality in American Life*, New York, Doubleday, 1957.

HOCKLY, H. E. *The Story of the British Settlers of 1820 in South Africa*, 2nd ed. rev., Cape Town and Johannesburg, Juta, 1957.

HOFSTADTER, R. *Social Darwinism in American Thought*, rev. ed., Boston, Beacon Press, 1955.

HUNT, J. 'On the Negro's Place in Nature', *Memoirs Read Before the Anthropological Society of London*, 1863-4.

HUXLEY, T. *Evolution and Ethics and Other Essays*, New York, Macmillan, 1898.

KLINEBERG, O. *Race and Psychology*, Paris, U.N.E.S.C.O., 1953.

KLUCKHOHN, C. and MURRAY, H. A., eds. *Personality in Nature, Society, and Culture*, London, Jonathan Cape, 1949.

KUPER, H. *The Uniform of Colour*, Johannesburg, Witwatersrand University Press, 1947.

LEGGE, J. D. *Britain in Fiji: 1858–1880*, London, Macmillan, 1958.

LEIRIS, M. *Race and Culture*, Paris, U.N.E.S.C.O., 1952.

LEVY-BRUHL, L. *How Natives Think*, London, Allen and Unwin, 1926 (trans. L. A. Clare).

LEVI-STRAUSS, C. *Race and History*, Paris, U.N.E.S.C.O., 1952.

LIND, A. W., ed. *Race Relations in World Perspective*, Honolulu, University of Hawaii Press, 1955.

BIBLIOGRAPHY

LINTON, R. *The Cultural Background of Personality*, London, Kegan Paul, 1947.
LITTLE, K. L. *Race and Society*, Paris, U.N.E.S.C.O., 1953.
LOW, D. A. *Religion and Society in Buganda 1875–1900*, Kampala, East African Institute of Social Research (1958?) (East African Studies No. 8).
LOWIE, R. H., *The History of Ethnological Theory*, London, Harrap, 1937.
MANNONI, O. *Prospero and Caliban, The Psychology of Colonization*, London, Methuen, 1956 (trans. P. Powesland).
MASON, P. *An Essay on Racial Tension*, London and New York, Royal Institute of International Affairs, 1954.
MAUNIER, R. *The Sociology of Colonies*, London, Kegan Paul, 1949, 2 vols. (ed. and trans. by E. O. Lorimer).
Memoirs Read Before the Anthropological Society of London, 1863–69, London, Trubner, 1865, 1866, Longmans, 1870, 3 vols.
MERIVALE, H. *Lectures on Colonization and Colonies*, London, O.U.P., 1928.
MILLER, J. *Early Victorian New Zealand, A Study of Racial Tension and Social Attitudes, 1839–1852*, London, O.U.P., 1958.
MITCHELL, J. C. *The Yao Village*, Manchester, Manchester University Press, 1956.
MYRDAL, G. *Value in Social Theory, a Selection of Essays on Methodology*, London, Kegan Paul, 1958 (ed. P. Streeter).
NIELSON, P. *The Colour Bar*, Cape Town and Johannesburg, Juta, n.d.
ORWELL, G. *The Road to Wigan Pier*, London, Gollancz, 1937.
PENNIMAN, T. K. *A Hundred Years of Anthropology*, 2nd ed. rev., London, Duckworth, 1952.
PRICE, A. G. *White Settlers and Native Peoples*, Melbourne, Georgian House, 1950.
RADCLIFFE-BROWN, A. R. and FORDE, D., eds. *African Systems of Kinship and Marriage*, London, O.U.P., 1956.
REUTER, E. B., ed. *Race and Culture Contacts*, New York and London, MCGRAW-HILL, 1934.
ROSE, A. M. *The Roots of Prejudice*, Paris, U.N.E.S.C.O., 1952.
SCHAPERA, I. *Government and Politics in Tribal Societies*, London, Watts, 1956.
SHAPIRO, H. L. *Race Mixture*, Paris, U.N.E.S.C.O., 1953.
SMITH, E. W. *The Golden Stool*, London, Holborn, 1926.
—— *Knowing the African*, London, Lutterworth Press, 1946.
SMITH, R. B. *Mohammed and Mohammedanism*, 3rd ed. rev., London, John Murray, 1889.
—— 'Mohammedanism in Africa', *Nineteenth Century*, Dec., 1887.
TOYNBEE, A. *The World and the West*, London, O.U.P., 1953.
TYLOR, E. B. *Primitive Culture*, London, John Murray, 1920, 2 vols.
—— *Researches into the Early History of Mankind*, 2nd ed., London, John Murray, 1870.
VARG, P. A. *Missionaries, Chinese, and Diplomats*, Princeton, Princeton University Press, 1958.

BIBLIOGRAPHY

WILSON, G. and M. *The Analysis of Social Change*, Cambridge, Cambridge University Press, 1945.
WILSON, M. *Good Company: A Study of Nyakyusa Age-Villages*, London, O.U.P., 1951.
WOOD, H. G. *Belief and Unbelief Since 1850*, Cambridge, Cambridge University Press, 1955.

VII. NOVELS

CONRAD, J. 'HEART OF DARKNESS'. *A Conrad Argosy*, New York, 1942.
SCHREINER, O. *Trooper Peter Halket of Mashonaland*, Boston, Roberts, 1897.
STANLEY, H. M. *My Kalulu*, new ed., London, Sampson Low, 1893.
THOMSON, J. and HARRIS-SMITH, E. *Ulu: An African Romance*, London, Sampson Low, 1888, 2 vols.

INDEX

African Lakes Corporation, 25, 70, 223–4, 229, 244; employees of, 297–8n.[170]
African languages, admiration for, 33; study of, 33
Alcock, R., 191
Arabs, British attitudes to, 140–2, 144–6, 281n.[105]; British policy to, 234; economic activity of, 133–140; interior, influence in, 133–4, 143–4; political system of, 142–4, 281n.[116, 119]; Portuguese, conflict with, 127; religion of, 278n.[65], 293n.[86] (*see also* Islam); settlement of, 134; sexual morals of, 63, 141–2. See also Islam, Swahili
Arnot, F. S., 157, 159
Ashe, R. P., 111, 236

Baganda, 110–11, 112, 187
Baines, T., 261n.[94, 95]
Baker, S., 3, 60, 79, 81, 86, 102, 161, 203, 234, 281–2n.[4], 292n.[54, 62, 63, 65]; racism of, 203–6
Barotse, 110, 273n.[37]
Bell, W. D. M., 256n.[92]
Blaikie, W. G., 257n.[4]
Blyden, E. W., 210–11, 214
'bride price'. See Lobola
British, character traits, 36–9, 257n.[4, 6, 8, 9, 10], 258n.[17, 31]; chauvinism of, 160–1; foreign policy of, 1–3, 143–4, 234; humanitarian objectives of, 233, 238; moral superiority of, 238; national pride of, 148; self-assurance, 148; self-evaluation, 147–50, 160–2; trustees, 35

British South Africa Company, The, 228, 237, 242, 255n.[80]
Bryce, James, Lord, 77, 228
Bryden, H. A., 255n.[77]
Buganda. *See* Baganda
Bulawayo Sketch, The, 228
Burton, R., 3, 25–6, 54, 66, 76, 78, 93, 113, 160, 169, 189, 206, 289n.[2]

Cameron, V. L., 3, 161–2, 212–13, 223, 232–3
Chadwick, O., 254n.[60], 255n.[68], 275n.[2]
Christianity, civilization, relation to, 199–203, 205, 218–22; economic progress and, 200, 202; evolutionary theories and, 206–207; heathenism and, 217–18; imperialism, relation to, 243–4; Islam as preparation for, 210–11, 213–15; Islam, conflict with, 208–218, 294n.[97, 98, 105], 295n.[106]; nineteenth century and, 200; prosperity and, 200
Civilization, British concept of, 222; commerce, relation to, 222, 292n.[65]; superiority of, 35, 76–82
Coillard, F., 264n.[163]
Colonists, 228–30; missionary hostility to, 230
Colonization, 226–30; ideals and reality, 226–30
Communications and transportation, 5–7, 253n.[37, 48]; horse, use of, 252n.[16]; waggon, price of, 252n.[15]
Conrad, J., 248, 263n.[125]
Cotterill, H. B., 232

325

INDEX

Coupland, R., 143
Cultural imperialism, 200, 235
Cultural isolation, 63–70; 'going native', fear of, 52, 65–6, 264n.[154, 157], 265n.[170]; missionaries, 66–70; psychological hardships of, 63–70
Cultural relativism, xiv, 118, 252n.[19]; barriers to, 105; religion and, 209–210

Dennis, J. S., 291n.[44]
Derby, Lord, 189
Devereux, W. C., 142, 235
Drummond, H., 89, 160
Duff, H., 164–5

Ethnocentrism, 73–4, 96–101, 190–1, 269n.[77], 270n.[101]; hierarchical comparisons, 74–6, 265n.[3, 4], 269n.[77] *See also* Social Darwinism, Stereotypes
Evans-Pritchard, E. E., 266n.[36], 268n.[61], 270n.[101]
Exploration, financing of, 22
Explorers. *See* Secular Whites

Firth, R., 288n.[64]
Frere, B., 86, 129, 131, 135, 140, 164, 172, 232, 278n.[58, 74], 281n.[116], 283n.[27]
Frontier life, accommodation, 31; African cooperation, lack of, 31; difficulties of, 30–2; food, 31

Game animals, slaughter of, 255n.[77]
Gibbons, A. St. H., 273n.[37]
Gluckman, M., 77, 81, 268n.[60], 276n.[18], 289n.[91]
Gordon, C., 234
Grant, J. A., 3

Hamerton, A., 135
Hancock, W. K., 230
Hannington, Bishop, 41, 50
Harris, W. C., 237
Heany, M., 236
Hine, Bishop, 167, 220

History, climatic theory of, 204
Hole, M., 223, 261n.[99]
Hore, A., 4–5, 70
Hore, E. C., 132, 135, 212, 229–30
Hunters. *See* Secular whites
Huxley, T., 88

Imperialism, 231–49, 299n.[23, 27, 28, 34]; Central Africa, arrival in, 244–7; Christianity, relation to, 243–4; early pioneers and, 231–3; humanitarian arguments for, 235–7, 298n.[15]; justification for, 118–26, 223, 232–6, 247–9; peace and stability and, 244–5; religious change and, 241–2, 245
Islam, 132–3, 208–18 *passim*, 281n.[109], 283n.[27], 293n.[83]; Africans, suitability for, 145, 209–18 *passim*, 294n.[97]. *See also* Christianity, Arabs, Swahili

Johnson, F., 48, 236
Johnson, W. P., 63, 156, 172–3
Johnston, H. H., 41, 62–3, 90, 93–4, 190, 207, 229, 234–5, 246, 255n.[80], 272n.[2, 3, 4, 15], 277n.[45, 47], 293n.[70, 71]
Jones, D. P., 125, 208

Kerr, W. M., 104, 125, 169
Kirk, J., 16, 27, 50, 121, 130, 133, 143, 172–3, 279n.[79, 84, 85]
Knight-Bruce, Bishop, 109, 236, 246–7, 261n.[89, 90]
Krapf, J. L., 2, 113, 133, 158, 181, 208, 242, 285n.[6]

Langer, W. L., 281n.[2]
Lasky, M. J., 265n.[3]
Laws, R., 155, 158, 171, 229, 243
Leach, E. R., 267n.[47]
Legge, J. D., 220–1
Leiris, M., 265n.[4]
Levi-Strauss, C., 89, 269n.[77]
Lewanika, Barotse chief, 175
Little, K., 251n.[1]

INDEX

Livingstone, C., 137
Livingstone, D., 3, 8–10, 20, 40, 60–1, 68–9, 70, 75, 78–9, 83, 86–8, 91, 126–8, 130, 137, 139, 147, 149–51, 155, 157–9, 168, 171, 222, 252n.[20], 257n.[1, 4, 9], 258n.[17], 265n.[167], 277n.[37, 38, 49], 283n.[37, 40, 50], 291n.[48]; social philosophy of, 192–9 *passim*
Livingstonia Mission, 229
Lobengula, Matabele chief, 56, 70–71, 109, 116, 118, 236, 259n.[52], 274n.[59], 275n.[61], 284n.[73], 286n.[26, 28], 297n.[151]
Lobola, 176–8
Lowie, R. H., 89–90
Lugard, F. D., 27, 49, 294n.[95], 299n.[29]

Macdonald, D., 103–4, 120, 172, 184
Mackay, A. M., 111, 154, 179–80, 223, 243–4, 271n.[118], 276n.[11, 14]
Mackenzie, Bishop, 12, 174–5
Mackintosh, C. W., 252n.[21]
McLeod, L., 128, 276n.[33]
Makololo, 70, 108, 112, 126, 273n.[37], 274n.[47]
Marriage, monogamy and polygamy, 176–7, 287n.[35, 38]
Masai, 107–8, 121
Mashona, 109–10, 125, 236, 238, 242, 273n.[34, 36]
Matabele, 31, 48, 109–10, 112, 116, 121–2, 125–6, 236, 238, 242–3, 264n.[154]
Maugham, R. C. F., 277n.[41]
Maunier, R., 257n.[6]
Mirambo, Wanyamwesi chief, 116–118, 154, 185
Missionaries, Anthropology, contributions to, 285n.[86]; asceticism of, 255n.[77]; calling of, 19–20; cultural ignorance of, 163; European settlers and, 255n.[70]; force, use of, 45–6, 258n.[20, 31], 262n.[112]; 'hard' missionary, 294n.[95]; hardships, 10–22, 66–70; humanitarian psychology of, 20–2; imperialism, attitudes to, 243–4, 299n.[34], 300n.[48], 301n.[49]; martyrdom, 17–18, 159, 254n.[54]; mentality of, 18–19, 154–9, 178; moral conduct of, 36; propaganda of, 99–100, 270n.[107], 271n.[111, 115]; racial superiority of, 154, 239; religious imperialism of, 239–40; self-image, 150–9, 202–3; sexual gratification, barriers to, 54, 67; social change, agents of, 160, 165–7, 203, 239 (*see also* Social Change); teleological explanations, 158–9; U.M.C.A., philosophy of, 218–221; wives and, 57–62, 252n.[17], 262n.[100]; zeal of, 10–22, 32–3, 155–6, 254n.[54, 60], 285n[85]. *See also* Race relations, Roman Catholic Missionaries
Missionary activity, 285n.; crusading movement, 154–5, 162–5; expansion of, 7–10, 150–1, 238–9; rationale of, 150–4; success, lack of, 181–8, 240–1
Moffat, J. S., 14, 17, 56–8, 68, 183, 241, 253n.[27, 35, 36, 38, 39, 47]
Moffat, R., 14, 182–3, 202
Monk, W., 152
Moselekatse, Matabele chief, 4, 56, 109, 175, 180, 182, 184, 284n.[73], 286n.[32]
Mtesa, King of Buganda, 110, 187, 236, 274n.[59]

New, C., 64–5, 80, 276n.[21], 283n.[54], 289n.[86]

Oliver, R., 252n.[21]
Orwell, G., 257n.[12]

Perham, M., 279n.[80], 299n.[29]
Pioneers. *See* Missionaries, Secular whites
Poole, W., 237, 299n.[21, 22]
Portuguese, Arabs, conflict with, 127; British attitudes to, 129–32,

INDEX

Portuguese (*cont.*)
144–6, 278n.[56, 58]; colonial policy of, 130–1, 278n.[58]; decadence of, 127–9, 277–8n.[53], 282n.[26]; military capacity of, 129, 277n.[46]; 'natives', ability to handle, 129, 277n.[41]; sexual relations with Africans, 128
Price, R., 14, 166, 253n.[35, 37, 38, 39, 48]
Progress, Christianity and, 201; cultural concepts of, 85–92
Pruen, S. T., 201, 214

Race, defined, 251n.[1]
Race relations, class relations, analogy with, 92–3; flexibility of, 72; force, use of by British, 41–6; hierarchical framework of, 39; ignorance and misunderstanding in, 168–70, 267n.[47], 285n.[4]; imperialism and, 245–7; imperial period, xi, 119, 245–7; master–servant relationship, 39–40; missionary superiority, 154; missionary wives and, 57–9; moral influence of British, 187; parent–child analogy, 43, 88–9, 92–6, 235 (*see also* Stereotypes); power, equality of, 70–2; pre-imperial period, xi, xiii, 72; technology and, 4–5, 76–82, 248; tensions in, 168–81 *passim*; white healing and, 182–6, 288n.[66]; white leadership in, 162; white settlers and, 230; white skills in weaponry and, 182–3, 185–6, 288n.[74, 75], 289n.[86]; whites, African awe of, 46–51, 259n.[53], 284n.[65] *See also* Sexual relations
Randolph, B. W., 254n.[54]
Rebmann, J., 2–3
Rhodes, C., 236, 298n.[18, 19]
Roman Catholic Missionaries, 252n.[21]
Rowley, H., 108, 276n.[36]
Ruete, E., 281n.[119]
Russell, John, Lord, 231

Schapera, I., 87, 283n.[40]
Secular whites, 25–30; achievement, desire for, 26; drunkenness, 55–7, 261n.[89, 90]; ethnocentrism of, 30; freedom and adventure, desire for, 28; industrial society, antipathy to, 29, 103, 256n.[101]; integration into tribal society, 188 (*see also* Tribalism, Race Relations); romance of, 27–8; sexual gratification, 54–6, 261n.[94, 96, 99]
Sekeletu, Makololo chief, 194
Selous, F. C., 37, 259n.[52], 278–9n.[53]
Sexual relations, 53–7, 62–3, 261n.[94, 96, 99], 262n.[113], 263n.[123, 124], 277n.[39]; fear of African violation of white women, 59–62, 262n.[112]
Sim, A. F., 114, 254n.[60]
Slave trade, 118–19, 134, 171, 175, 275n.[2]; Arabs and, 136, 172, 275–6n.[11], 278n.[74]; commerce and, 223–6 *passim*, 290n.[16], 293n.[70], 298n.[5]; morality and, 225, 286; Portuguese participation in, 128, 276n.[33]; suffering caused by, 138–9; ubiquity of, 137–8
Slavery, 279n.[75, 77, 78, 84, 85], 280n.[88, 93, 94, 95, 98, 101], 299n.[21]; anti-slavery societies, 35; Arabs and, 135, 139–40, 279n., 280n.[80]; British attitudes to, 139–40, 171, 276n.[21, 33], 279n.[75, 78, 84], 286n.[11, 19]; economic growth and, 140; legitimate trade and, 223–4; morality and, 225, 280n.[98]; Portuguese and, 128; suffering caused by, 138–9; tribal, 136–7, 175; United States and, 225
Smith, E. W., 285n.[4]
Smith, R. B., 209–10, 214, 281n.[109], 293n.[83, 86]
Smythies, Bishop, 52, 79–80
Social change, 165, 189–92, 203; African resistance to, 162, 165–7, 170–81, 186–8, 241; Anthropology and, 165; British simplification of, 160–1, 192, 199; evolu-

328

INDEX

tionary theories of, 206–8 (*see also* Social Darwinism); force, use in, 204–5; imperialism and, 245, 249; Livingstone's theories of, 192–9; religion and, 209–13, 291n.[44, 45]; revolutionary scope of, 174, 178–9

Social Darwinism, 88–92, 114, 125, 191, 238, 299n.[23]. *See also* Ethnocentrism, Stereotypes

Southon, Dr., 117, 185–6

Speke, J. H., 3, 85–6, 98, 169, 231, 298n.[1]

Stanley, H. M., 3–4, 26–7, 44, 69, 78, 117, 185, 284n.[58]

Steere, Bishop, 33, 52, 62, 141, 215–219 *passim*, 253n.[48], 271n.[118], 278n.[65]

Stereotypes of Africans, 289n.[2]; as barbarians, 97; as faithful porters, 40; as happy children, 94–6, 98; as individuals, 114–18, 274–275n.[59]; as liars, 83; as objects of humour, 98, 115; indolence of, 76, 80–1, 85, 273n.[34]; sensuality of women, 54, 262n.[113]. *See also* Ethnocentrism, Race relations, Social Darwinism

Stewart, J., 37, 63–4, 84–5, 130, 163, 186, 231–2, 267n.[49, 50, 51, 52, 53, 54], 271n.[112], 282n.[26]

Stock, E., 252n.[20], 254n.[54]

Swahili, Arabs and, 132–3; coastal civilization of, 132

Swann, A. J., 26, 59, 94, 138, 214, 247, 300n.[48]

Tabler, E. C., 251n.[5], 252n.[11]

Taylor, I., Canon, 211, 214, 293n.[86]

Thomas, T. M., 150, 180, 184, 226–7, 242

Thompson, W., 163

Thomson, J. B., 226

Thomson, Joseph, 3, 42, 104–5, 129–30, 148, 183, 211–12, 246, 256n.[101], 271n.[119], 289n.[2]

Time and space, cultural concepts of, 82–5, 266n.[36]

Tozer, Bishop, 12–13, 142, 218–19, 280n.[98]

Trade and commerce, Arabs and, 133–40; civilization, agency of, 222–7; ivory and, 24; Livingstone and, 192–4; pre-imperial period, 22–5

Traders. *See* Secular whites

Tribalism, xiv–xv; admiration for, 103–6, 220–2, 273n.[37]; anarchy aided by Arabs and Portuguese, 126–44 *passim*; British acceptance of, 125; Christianity and, 178–81; civilized tribes, admiration for, 110–12, 273n.[37]; cruelty of, 122–6; economic performance, 77–8; imperialism, effect on, 245; instability of, 86–7, 268n.[60]; inter-tribal conflict, 120–123, 173, 273n.[37], 275–6n.[11]; Islam and, 216–17; martial tribes, respect for, 106–10, 112–14, 274n.[55]; social organization, 5, 7, 107, 111–12; vulnerability to civilization, 76, 118–19, 191, 221–2; white ignorance of, 162–5, 199, 267n.[47]; white intervention, 125–126, 190–1. *See also* Social change

Truth, differing attitudes to, 82–4; technology and, 84. *See also* Stereotypes

Tylor, E. B., 74, 91, 269n.[76, 95]

Varg, P. A., 255n.[71]

Waller, H., 232, 278n.[58]

Warneck, G., 203, 242

Weber, M., 79

Wells, J., 271n.[112]

Willoughby, J., 213

Wilson, C. T., 190

Wilson, G. and M., 268n.[61]

Witchcraft, 123–4, 172; British attitudes to, 123–4, 276n.[17, 18]. *See also* Tribalism

Work, contrasting attitudes to, 79–82, 85, 266n.[76], 267n.[54]. *See also* Stereotypes

Yao, 108
Young, E. D., 43, 129, 161, 171

Zimmern, A., 281n.[2]
Zulu, 108